ROUTLEDGE LIBRARY EDITIONS:
INTERNATIONAL BUSINESS

MULTINATIONALS, TECHNOLOGY AND COMPETITIVENESS

MULTINATIONALS, TECHNOLOGY AND COMPETITIVENESS

JOHN H. DUNNING

Volume 13

LONDON AND NEW YORK

First published in 1988

This edition first published in 2013
by Routledge
2 Park Square, Milton Park, Abingdon, Oxfordshire OX14 4RN

Simultaneously published in the USA and Canada
by Routledge
711 Third Avenue, New York, NY 10017

First issued in paperback 2014

Routledge is an imprint of the Taylor and Francis Group, an informa company

© 1988 John H. Dunning

All rights reserved. No part of this book may be reprinted or reproduced or utilised in any form or by any electronic, mechanical, or other means, now known or hereafter invented, including photocopying and recording, or in any information storage or retrieval system, without permission in writing from the publishers.

Trademark notice: Product or corporate names may be trademarks or registered trademarks, and are used only for identification and explanation without intent to infringe.

British Library Cataloguing in Publication Data
A catalogue record for this book is available from the British Library

ISBN: 978-0-415-65814-0 (Volume 13)
ISBN: 978-0-415-75199-5 (pbk)

Publisher's Note
The publisher has gone to great lengths to ensure the quality of this reprint but points out that some imperfections in the original copies may be apparent.

Disclaimer
The publisher has made every effort to trace copyright holders and would welcome correspondence from those they have been unable to trace.

Multinationals, Technology and Competitiveness

John H. Dunning

London
UNWIN HYMAN
Boston   Sydney   Wellington

© John H. Dunning, 1988
This book is copyright under the Berne Convention. No
reproduction without permission. All rights reserved.

Published by the Academic Division of
Unwin Hyman Ltd.
15/17 Broadwick Street, London W1V 1FP

Unwin Hyman, Inc.
8 Winchester Place, Winchester, Mass. 01890, USA

Allen & Unwin (Australia) Ltd.,
8 Napier Street, North Sydney, NSW 2060, Australia

Allen & Unwin (New Zealand) Ltd
in association with the Port Nicholson Press Ltd,
60 Cambridge Terrace, Wellington, New Zealand

First published in 1988

British Library Cataloguing in Publication Data

Dunning, John H. (John Harry), 1927–
Multinationals, technology and competitiveness.
1. Multinational companies.
I. Title.
338.8'8
ISBN 0–04–445175–X

Library of Congress Cataloging-in-Publication Data

Dunning, John H.
Multinationals, technology, and competitiveness.
Bibliography: p.
Includes index.
1. International business enterprises. 2 Technology transfer—Economic
aspects. 3. Competition, International.
I. Title.
HD2755.5.D869   1988   388.8'8   88–10667
ISBN 0–04–445175–X (alk. paper)

Typeset by Computape (Pickering) Ltd, North Yorkshire
and printed in Great Britain by Biddles of Guildford

For Judith

Contents

Acknowledgements	xiii
List of Figures	xv
List of Tables	xvii

1 *Introduction* — 1
Some Themes of This Monograph — 1
The Plan of the Book — 5

2 *International Business in a Changing World Environment* — 9
Introduction — 9
Antecedents of the MNE — 9
Multinational Enterprises and Host Country Interaction:
   The Last Thirty Years — 16
Towards a New Understanding Between MNEs
   and Governments — 21
Some Observations on the Future of MNEs:
   Government Relationships — 25
Conclusions — 27

**3 *Market Power of the Firm and International Transfer
   of Technology*** — 29
Introduction — 29
Phase 1: The Industrial Revolution – To Around 1870 — 31
Phase 2: 1870–1914 — 33
Phase 3: 1919–1939 — 35
Phase 4: 1945–1965 — 37
Phase 5: 1965–1985 — 40

**4 *Multinational Enterprises, Technology Transfer and
   National Competitiveness*** — 47
Introduction — 47
Some Theoretical Issues — 47
Technology Traded Through the Market — 50
Technology Transfers Within the MNE — 54
The Influence of MNEs on National Competitiveness — 57
Measuring and Interpreting National Competitiveness — 59
Some Evidence Concerning the Impact of the Transfer of
   Technology Through MNEs on European Competitiveness — 61
Summary and Conclusions — 63

5	*Inward Direct Investment from the USA and Europe's Technological Competitiveness*	69
	Introduction	69
	The Changing Competitive Position of European Industry	74
	The Growth of the Leading US and European Firms	78
	The Contribution of US Manufacturing Subsidiaries to European Exports	80
	The Changing Pattern of the US/European Direct Investment in Manufacturing	90
	The Technological Balance of Payments: The USA Compared with Europe	91
	Conclusions	95
	Appendix	102

6	*The Changing Role of MNEs in the Creation and Diffusion of Technology*	103
	Introduction	103
	The Historical Trend Towards Technological Systems	104
	The Dependence of International Technology Transfer and Diffusion on the Structure of Industries	106
	The Dependence of International Technology Creation and Dissemination on the Global Investment Strategy of MNEs	111
	The Policy Implications of the Closer Relationship Between the International Creation, Transfer and Diffusion of Technology	115

7	*International Direct Investment in Innovation: The Pharmaceutical Industry*	123
	Introduction	123
	The Scale in International Investment in Pharmaceutical R & D	123
	Motives for International Investment in Research	128
	The Choice of Host Country	130
	Gains and Losses: A General Review	133
	The UK Pharmaceutical Industry	136
	Conclusions	141

8	*The Consequences of the International Transfer of Technology by MNEs: A Home Country Perspective*	144
	Introduction	144
	The Problem Stated	145
	The Conditions of Technology Transfer	147
	Multinational Enterprises and Technology Transfer to Developing Countries	151
	Implications for Industrialized Countries	159
	Conclusions: Some Policy Implications	167

9	*Multinational Enterprises, Industrial Restructuring and Competitiveness: A UK Perspective*	172
	Introduction	172
	Historical Background	173
	A New International Division of Labour	176
	The Impact of New Technology	177

Contents   xi

The Structural Impact of MNEs in the 1960s and 1970s:
   Some Theoretical Considerations   178
Measuring the Impact of MNEs on UK Industrial Structure   180
The Statistical Testing   183
Policy Implications   195
Conclusions   199
Appendix   201

10 *The UK's International Direct Investment Position*
    in the Mid-1980s   203
Introduction   203
Some Theoretical Issues   203
Foreign Direct Investment and Economic Welfare   204
UK Inward and Outward Investment: The Statistical Picture   208
An Explanation of the Data   218
Some Structural Considerations   223
International Direct Investment and the Efficiency of
   Resource Allocation   224
Conclusions   230
Appendix   232

11 *The Anglo–American Connection and Global*
    Competition   233
Introduction   233
An Historical Perspective   234
Anglo–American Investment Flows Since 1970   236
The Japanese Challenge and New Technological Advances   239
Some Effects of Globalization   240
The Concept of 'Engineered' Comparative Advantage   244
Summary and Conclusions   247

12 *Multinational Enterprises and the Organization of*
    Economic Interdependence   251
Introduction: Some Taxonomic Issues   251
The Organization of Economic Interdependence   252
The Nature of Transactions   253
An Historical Review   254
The Situation Prior to the First World War   256
The Retreat into Protectionism   257
The Movement Towards Regional Integration   258
The Schizophrenic Nature of International Economic Relations 260
Conclusions   262

References   264

Index   275

Acknowledgements

I am grateful to several journals and the publishers of books in which earlier versions of some of the chapters first appeared for permission to make use of the material. Three of these studies were originally co-authored – two with John Cantwell of the University of Reading and one with Michael Burstall of the University of Surrey. I much appreciate the willingness of these colleagues to be associated with this volume.

I would also like to thank Bob Pearce and Paul Campayne of the University of Reading for helping me to update some of the statistics in Chapters 5, 8 and 10, and Udo Zander of the Stockholm School of Economics for his research assistance in the preparation of Chapter 5. Senta Butzel of the Graduate School of Management, Rutgers University, Jill Turner, Sandra Winter and Pat Elgar of the University of Reading, and Anne Irving of Berkeley, California, all assisted in the typing of this volume; to them, I extend my warmest thanks.

Much of the final writing was undertaken at the Graduate School of Management, Rutgers University, and the University of California at Berkeley, where I was on leave during the year of 1987. I much appreciated the hospitality of both universities as well as the financial assistance they provided towards the preparation of this volume.

Rutgers University   *John H. Dunning*
March 1988

Acknowledgement is also due to the copyright holders for their kind permission to reprint the following: Chapter 2 is a revised version of an article of the same title which first appeared in the *Banco Nationale del Lavoro Quarterly Review*, no. 143, December 1982, pp. 351–74; Chapter 3 is a revised version of an article of the same title which first appeared in the *International Journal of Industrial Organisation*, vol. 1, 1983, pp. 333–51; Chapter 5 is a substantially revised and updated version of an article, jointly authored with John Cantwell, which first appeared as 'Investissements Americains Directs et Compétitivité Technologique Européene' in *Actualité Economique*, July–September, 1982, pp. 341–79; Chapter 6 is a revised version of a chapter, jointly authored with John Cantwell and of the same name, which appeared in F. Arcangeli, P. A. David and G. Dosi (eds) *The Diffusion of New Technologies* (Oxford: Oxford University Press, 1988); Chapter 7 is a substantially revised and extended version of a chapter, jointly authored with M. Burstall, in N. Wells (ed.) *Pharmaceuticals Among the Sunrise Industries* (London and Sydney: Croom Helm, 1985); an earlier version

xiv *Acknowledgements*

of Chapter 8 was published as Chapter 12 in J. H. Dunning, *International Production and the Multinational Enterprise* (London: Allen & Unwin, 1981); Chapter 9 is based upon a chapter of the same title first published in J. H. Dunning (ed.) *Multinational Enterprises, Economic Structure and International Competitiveness* (Chichester and New York: Wiley, 1985) and an article 'Multinational enterprises and industrial restructuring in the UK', first published in *Lloyds Bank Review*, October 1985, pp. 1–18; Chapter 10 is a completely revised and updated version of Chapter 6 in J. H. Dunning, *International Production and the Multinational Enterprise* (London: Allen & Unwin, 1981); and Chapter 12 is a revised version of a chapter of the same title in J. H. Dunning and M. Usui (eds) *Structural Change, Economic Interdependence and World Development*, vol. 4, *Economic Interdependence* (Basingstoke and London: Macmillan).

Chapters 1, 4 and 11 contain completely new material.

List of Figures

		Page
2.1	The ESP Paradigm	14
6.1	Cumulative Causation in International Trade, Production and Technology Dissemination	116
7.1	Possible Gains and Losses Resulting from Change in Location of Innovatory Activities by MNEs	139
11.1	The Three Stages of the Anglo-American Business Partnership	234
11.2	1970–1985: Three Events Affecting the Anglo-American Business Partnership	237
11.3	Some Characteristics and Implications of Global Competition	245

List of Tables

		Page
5.1	Changing Share of EEC, European and US Exports According to Degree of Research Intensity 1955–85	75
5.2	Growth in Exports of Selected Products: USA, Europe and the EEC 1955–85	76
5.3	Growth in Exports of European Countries and the USA by Broad Industrial Groups 1955–85	77
5.4	Rate of Growth of Sales, 1962–7, 1967–72, 1972–7, 1977–82, For Constant Sample of Firms, by Industry and Country	79
5.5	Ratio of Sales of US Manufacturing Affiliates to Exports from USA 1957–82	81
5.6	The Contribution of US Affiliates in Europe to Total European and US Exports of Selected Manufactured Products 1957–82	84
5.7	Share of Majority-Owned Affiliates of US Firms in Total Exports of European Countries 1957–82	86
5.8	US Direct Investment in European Manufacturing Industry and European Direct Investment in US Manufacturing Industry 1962–85	90
5.9	The Euro–US Investment Stake Position	92
5.10	Growth of Royalties and Fees of the USA and Selected European Countries 1977–85.	94
5.11	Growth in Patents Taken Out in the USA Classified by Country of Origin 1965–83	96
7.1	Location of R & D Facilities of the Leading Thirty Pharmaceutical Companies in 1985	124
7.2	Estimated R & D Expenditure by Pharmaceutical Companies in Various Countries in 1982	125
7.3	International Biotechnology Agreements 1981–First Quarter of 1986	127
7.4	Opportunities of R & D: Host Country Characteristics 1985	131
7.5	Some Possible Gains and Losses from the Internationalization of R & D	134
8.1	Participation Rates of MNE Affiliates in Manufacturing Sectors of Selected Developing Countries and Manufacturing Exports 1965–85	153

8.2	Ranking of Countries in Selected Developing Countries According to Degree of MNE Penetration in Manufacturing Industry and Export Performance	154
8.3	Breakdown of Foreign Direct Investments in Developing Regions by Broad Type 1970	157
8.4	US Related-Party Imports as a Percentage of Total Imports of Selected Manufactured Products from Selected Newly Industrializing Countries 1977	158
9.1	The Industrial Structure of UK Inward and Outward Direct Investment in the 1960s	175
9.2	Comparisons Between Industrial Distribution of Sales of UK and MNE-Related Companies and Selected Structural Characteristics 1979 and 1971–79	182
10.1	The UK's Direct Investment Stake Position (1974–85)	207
10.2	The Significance of Outward and Inward Investment for the UK Economy: Selected Indicators 1975/85	208
10.3	Distribution of UK Outward and Inward Direct Capital Stake by Broad Geographical Area 1962–84	210
10.4	Geographical Distribution of Outward and Inward Direct Capital Stake 1974/1984	211
10.5	Distribution of Outward and Inward Direct Capital Stake by Economic Sector 1965/1984	213
10.6	Distribution of Annual Outward and Inward Investment by Geographical Area and Sector of Economic Activity 1960–83	214
10.7	Distribution Within Manufacturing Industry of UK Net Assets Abroad and Foreign Net Assets in the UK 1971 and 1981	216
10.8	Ratio Between Net Assets Owned by UK Firms Abroad (K_o) and Foreign Firms in UK (K_i) 1971 and 1981	217
10.9	UK–Foreign Investment Ratios in Manufacturing Industry, Ownership and Location-Specific Advantages 1961–84	220
10.10	Some Determinants of Foreign Capital Ratios Classified by Industry 1971–3 and 1979–81.	223
10.11	Profitability of UK and Foreign Firms in UK Manufacturing Industry and of UK Firms in Foreign Manufacturing Industry 1962–84	225
10.12	Profitability of UK Overseas Direct Investment, Foreign Investment in UK, and UK Domestic Firms 1972–81	226
10.13	Estimated Gains and Losses to the UK as a Result of Outward and Inward Direct Investment in Manufacturing Industry	228
11.1	The Anglo–American Direct Investment Stake 1914–85	235
11.2	(a) US Direct Investment Stake in the UK as a Percentage of All US Investment in Europe 1950–85 (b) UK Direct Investment Stake in the USA as a Percentage of All European Investment in the USA	238

11.3	Total UK and European Direct Investment Assets in the USA by Manufacturing Industry 1974–85	241
11.4	UK and European Direct Investment Assets in the USA by Industry 1985	242

Chapter One

Introduction

SOME THEMES OF THIS MONOGRAPH

This monograph explores some aspects of the interface between technology, competitiveness and the role of multinational enterprises (MNEs) in the modern world economy. In so doing it makes use of a number of paradigms and theories, but its starting point is the eclectic paradigm of international production set out in Dunning (1988). This paradigm suggests that existence and growth of firms and the location of their production will depend upon their ability, first, to generate and sustain some income-generating advantage or set of advantages over and above that of their competitors or potential competitors; second, to make the best use of these advantages, either by extending their own activities or by selling their right of use to other firms; and, third, to choose the most effective locations to create these advantages and to produce value-added activity and co-ordinate inter- and intra-firm transactions arising from them. The paradigm draws upon two main streams of economic thought; they are the theory of the distribution of factor endowments and the theory of economic organization, and particularly that part of each concerned with the relative efficiencies of markets and hierarchies in allocating resources both between and within sectors.

Although the paradigm has been mainly used to explain international production, it can also be helpful in evaluating the competitiveness of firms, and particularly those in an international economy. From a firm's viewpoint, its ability to compete rests on its ability to produce the kind of products which consumers wish to buy (or can be persuaded to buy), and to organize the activities required to do so in such a way which minimizes production and transaction costs. Both these tasks have a locational dimension and all three – the choice of 'what and how to produce', of 'how to organize production' and 'where to locate value adding activities' – reflect the ability of firms to make the best use of factor endowments, including the creation of new endowments, and the organizational routes for their management such as the spot market, various contractual relations including strategic alliances, joint ventures, etc. and internal hierarchies. At any rate, competitiveness is usually defined in terms either of the firm's performance as a whole in relation to what it perceives to be its main competitors, or its ability to produce and sell a particular range of products or capture specific markets. Measures include profitability, growth of asset value, market share or change in market share, export performance, productivity, and so on.

This monograph contends that the internationalization of production not only affects the competitiveness of the firms undertaking the production but that of other firms which are part of its sphere of influence or network of activities. Foremost among these are suppliers and competitors in both the home countries of MNEs and the host countries in which their affiliates operate, but, through such avenues as managerial and labour turnover, the overall repercussions are often much wider than this. Both within industries and between industries, MNEs affect the way economic activity is organized, the pattern of that activity and its outcome; in short, the competitiveness of countries.

The competitiveness of countries is an even more elusive concept to define than the competitiveness of firms. Interpretations and definitions abound. At a macro level, national competitiveness might mean the ability of a country to sustain a comparable rate of growth of its gross national product (GNP) to that of other countries with a similar structure of resources and stage of development.[1] However, most definitions tend to get behind the reasons for this and concentrate on the efficiency of resource usage within sectors using some measure of productivity, and on the efficiency of resource allocation between sectors using some method of revealed comparative advantage, including export-import ratios, for particular sectors. Chapters 4, 5 and 9 in this book examine the role of MNEs in promoting this kind of competitiveness.

The interesting aspect of the internationalization of business is that it highlights the difference between the competitiveness of firms and that of countries. Multinational enterprises judge their success by how successful they perform relative to other firms independently of *where* they produce their output;[2] indeed, many MNEs produce the majority of the value-added outside their national boundaries (Stopford and Dunning 1982; UNCTC 1983, 1988). In the language of the eclectic paradigm the competitiveness of firms will be ownership-specific but will depend on the ability of firms to make the best use of both endogenous and exogenous resources to attain their objectives, wherever the value-adding activities might be located. Countires, however, judge success by the efficiency at which their own resources, or those which their firms may use abroad, can create value-added activities for their own citizens. Although this depends partly on the ownership of firms, essentially it rests on the extent, use and pattern made of location specific or immobile resources.

The difference was not always so. Indeed, 100 years ago the assumption of the classical theory of trade that resources were immobile across boundaries, and that the only advantage which firms of one nationality possessed over those of another was their access to the natural endowments of the country in which they located was basically true in practice. Neither does the neo-classical model of trade allow for any ownership-specific advantages of firms, and international resource allocation is assumed to be based purely on the distribution of factor endowments.

Introduction 3

Two interrelated factors have changed this situation, and they both have done so by introducing the economics of market failure into the equation.

The first is what might be called the *knowledge of asset creation and usage*. This essentially refers to the ability of firms and countries to innovate new products, processes and materials or to make better use of existing products, processes and materials, and to co-ordinate the production and marketing of these in the most efficient way. Such knowledge not only embraces product or process technology, but also that relating to complementary activities such as purchasing, finance, marketing and so on.

The second is what might be called the *knowledge of organizing economic activity*; this is the capacity of firms, either internally or by establishing a contractual but ongoing relationship with other firms, to engage in, and/or co-ordinate activities which might otherwise have been undertaken by independent firms. Such value-adding activities may be integrated (that is, internalized) by firms of a given value-added chain (for example, vertical integration) or across value-added chains (for instance, horizontal integration). These activities may take place within or across national boundaries. But the net result of both forms of knowledge of co-ordination has been the extension of the boundaries of firms; the first through the economies of variable proportions or scale of the plant and the latter through the economies of scope and synergy.

The point to notice about both forms of knowledge is that:

(1) they cannot be thought of as natural factor endowments; they have to be created;[3]
(2) their creation need not rest on the presence of location-specific resources in the country of creation;
(3) since often (and particularly the technology of asset creation) takes on the characteristics of a public good, this means that in order to ensure their production, the firms have to be given some protection against the value of the output of this production being dissipated before a normal profit is earned (they can only exist in imperfect markets);
(4) whatever the ability of firms to co-ordinate separate economic activities, the fact that they choose to do so rather than use alternate routes, notably the market, suggests there is some kind of market failure causing extended transaction costs to be higher than hierarchical transaction costs.

Moreover, as has been described in great detail elsewhere – Rugman (1981, 1986), Teece (1986), Buckley and Casson (1985), Casson (1987), Hennart (1986), Dunning (1988) – markets as an organizational route for many kinds (but not all) of goods and services have become increasingly imperfect over the past century. This is due to three main reasons:

(1) the increasing element of uncertainty (this particularly applies to some cross-border transaction) of the market to guarantee the

buyer or the seller the terms of the agreement (for example, with respect to quality, price, delivery dates, protection of property rights); and the increasing costs of redressing the failures of the market.[4]

(2) the increasing extent to which the economic consequences of the exchange are not captured in the terms agreed by the buyer and seller, that is, there are external costs or benefits to a transaction which a buyer or seller may wish to capture for himself. These economies might include those arising from the co-ordination of the use of the assets which are necessary to supply the products separately.[5] Economies of scope are another externality.

(3) the increasing extent to which economies of large-scale production can only be fully reaped if only one or a few firms competing under the oligopolistic conditions make up the market. This conflict, between the gains of lower costs and the losses arising from imperfect competition, has led to the concept of workable competition and contestable markets being developed by industrial economists.

There are a whole set of exogenous circumstances which have led to an increase in market failure in recent years. Interacting with the technology and the volatility of the environment, (Kogut, 1985) has been the role of governments. Governments may and do affect a nation's competitiveness and that of its firms in a myriad of ways. They do so by affecting the ability of economic agents within their governance (1) to create and sustain and efficiently utilize innovatory and productive capacity, and (2) to co-ordinate their domestic and international activities at least as well as their foreign competitors. As the factors influencing the location of industries are increasingly having more to do with technology and less with natural factors endowments, governments as the custodians of the educational system, the providers of the modern equivalent of nineteenth-century public utilities, notably road, rail and airport facilities, and a telecommunications infrastructure, play a crucial role not only in determining their own trade and foreign investment policies but how these may impact on those of other countries at the international negotiating table.[6]

At the same time, governments may influence competitiveness in more indirect ways. Some of these are described in Chapter 4. These include not only their responsibility for defence and space-related activities (for exchange rate monetary and fiscal policies, for anti-trust and consumer protection legislation, and a gamut of other mandatory and persuasive measures); but also by promoting a particular economic ethos and consensus among their constituents about a nation's economic goals and strategy and how these might best be implemented.

It is the way in which governments have dealt with some of these less intangible issues that have distinguished the successful industrial nations of the world from some of their less successful counterparts in the last twenty years (Lodge and Vogel 1987; McGraw 1986). This is not a

Introduction 5

subject which we will explore in any detail in this volume – in any case the jury is still out! But we would emphasize that it is incorrect to think of government intervention always as a market distortion. Like private hierarchies, governments may, and often do, add to economic welfare by helping to overcome the failure of markets. Indeed, in some cases we would argue that only governments have the resources and power to do so, and this particularly applies to the inability of other instruments of capitalism to adjust speedily enough to changes in demand and supply conditions, brought about either by technological change or the emergence of new competitors which themselves have often been assisted by their own governments. In this respect, governments may stimulate efficient markets, by helping to ease the restructuring constraints and rigidities which markets seem unable to remove. It is this kind of positive interventionism by government which we see as a fundamental feature of modern-day industrial societies, and it arises both because a country's competitive advantage is increasingly resting on its technological capabilities and because of the way in which it organizes its activities in imperfect market conditions. Also, because of the operation of MNEs, the economic activities in the sectors in which such countries are likely to have a comparative advantage are becoming more footloose, and more influenced by government-related locational variables.[7]

THE PLAN OF THE BOOK

The book takes up the themes identified in the previous paragraphs and discusses them primarily, but not exclusively, from the perspective of the advanced industrialized countries. Chapter 2 presents an overview of the main factors influencing the growth of international business over the past century; it pays especial attention to the role of technology and that of government policy in fashioning the extent and pattern of foreign direct investment (FDI) and MNE-related activity. Chapter 3 also takes a historical look at the changing form of international technology transfer undertaken by MNEs. More particularly, it distinguishes between the role of MNEs as creators and disseminators of specific technological assets, and their role as controllers of the modalities in which a network of activities, using interrelated technologies, are organized.

Chapter 4 deals with the interface between technology, competitiveness and FDI. It starts with a simple closed economy model in which the competitiveness of firms and countries rests on the location-bound resource endowments of the economy, and then examines the ways in which the character of the two kinds of competitiveness are changed when one first introduces technology and, second, the cross-border mobility of resources into the picture. Chapter 5 continues the discussion by focusing on the changing competitive position of Europe vis-à-vis the US over the period 1955–82; and especially the part played by US direct investment in Europe in bringing this about. Again, technology is seen to act as the means of improving competitiveness, but FDI is the main institutional mechanism for achieving this. However, we shall also argue that the extent and geographical pattern of US direct investment in Europe during this period was greatly influenced by the economic policies and systems pursued by individual European governments.

Chapter 6 looks at the interaction between technology transfer and competitiveness in a different way. It introduces the notion of technological cumulation and the related concepts of 'virtuous' and 'vicious' technology-induced circles. It argues that in international industries MNEs may play a crucial role in either improving the competitiveness of the countries in which they operate, for example, by helping to upgrade the ownership-specific (O) advantages of indigenous firms and the location-specific (L) advantages of countries, or by bringing about the reverse phenomenon. The chapter illustrates its argument from the viewpoint of two MNE-dominated industries in the UK, one which has performed well, that is, pharmaceuticals, and the other which is generally uncompetitive by world standards – motor vehicles.

Chapter 7 looks in more detail into the location of technology-creating activities by MNEs in the pharmaceutical industry, and makes some reasonably informed guesstimates of how selected industrialized countries have fared in their attempts to build up indigenous technological capacity in this sector.

Chapter 8 turns its attention to the way in which the technology transfer by MNEs to the newly industrializing countries (NICs) has affected the technological competitiveness of the investing countries. This is a subject of increasing concern among US and European legislators, particularly with respect to those sectors in which there are serious domestic unemployment or structural adjustment problems. The chapter explores some of the arguments for controlling the outflow of technology to developing countries, but concludes that this is neither a viable nor a sensible course of action. Excepting where the development of its NICs is distorted by government subsidies, aid and import controls, the chapter argues that governments should confine their intervention to reducing the domestic transactional costs of structural change.

Chapters 9 and 10 focus on the structural adjustment problems of the UK and examine the way in which outward and inward direct investment has aided or inhibited such adjustment. Chapter 9 looks in some detail into the UK's international direct investment position, and attempts to identify whether changes in the amount and pattern of inward and outward investment and the balance between them reflects changes in the competitive advantages of UK firms and that of the UK as a location for value-adding activity. The chapter concludes by making a crude assessment of the benefits of MNE activity to the GNP of the UK. Chapter 10 takes up this issue in more detail, and tests a number of hypotheses about the possible impact of inward and outward foreign direct investment on the competitiveness of the UK. While the chapter argues that, on balance, both the foreign activities of UK MNEs and those of foreign affiliates in the UK have generally aided sectoral productivity, resource allocation, growth and performance in inter-

Introduction 7

national markets, it concludes with a caveat about the new challenges offered to the UK government by the increasing integration of the UK activities of MNEs into their global strategy. The chapter asserts that domestic policies which do not fully appreciate the demands of a global economy on their own MNEs, or of the growing mobility of both foreign and domestic MNEs in their value-adding activities, do so at their peril.

Chapter 11 focuses on the role of government in influencing the location of the pattern of economic activity by MNEs. It takes as its starting point the interaction between US direct investment in the UK and UK direct investment in the US over the past century, and goes on to argue that the bilateral economic relationship which dominated these flows up to around 1970 has been almost completely replaced by each being part of a network of multilateral relationships since that time. The chapter then gives attention to the challenges to both US and UK competitiveness being posed by the industrial renaissance of Japan, the emergence of some of the NICs as major industrial powers and the growing role of government as a shaper of resource allocation. It concludes by arguing that, just as companies need to adopt a global stance to remain competitive, governments, too, need to recognize that, on behalf of their constituents, they are in competition with other governments in their policies and actions designed to attract the location of footloose activities by MNEs.

The final chapter explains the interaction between some of the issues analysed in the previous chapters and the movement towards regional economic integration. It focuses particularly on the way in which MNEs can help fashion the integration of national economies, and the impact which such integration may have on the growth of MNEs by the removal of some of the obstacles to the common governance of cross-border activities. The chapter also discusses the conditions under which a reallocation of economic activity in response to regional integration may lead to a genuine economic interdependence between the participating nations, and to conditions in which it leads to one country dominating the pattern of economic activity of another country.

NOTES

1 This is a variation of a definition which has been coined by Peter Jones at the Centre for Research in Management Studies at the University of California at Berkeley.
2 Although this latter decision may also affect their competitiveness. An example is where a host government gives investment incentives to foreign firms to produce in its country which it does not give to domestic firms.
3 Admittedly from natural endowments, including imported resources, for example, some kinds of labour; however, the value-added by the 'knowledge' inputs can be so large that they can be thought of as factor endowments in their own right.
4 There are two kinds of market relationships. The first is between an independent buyer and seller who have completely separate interests, and

whose relationship ceases once the transaction is made. The second is where the relationship is between firms in which at least one of the parties to the exchange perceives that it may be affected by what the other party does subsequent to the exchange. For example, it is in the interests of a manufacturer to buy raw materials at the lowest price and highest quality, or for a seller or licensor to ensure the quality of the good produced by the buyer, which may bear his name, is protected. Such transactions then fulfil some of the criteria of a principal/agent relationship. The uncertainty of the principal as to whether the agent is fully acting on his behalf is one of the reasons for the internalization of this kind of market.

5 Obvious examples includes two identical distribution networks, both of which are operating at surplus capacity to supply two (or more) products. If the two products were distributed by one firm there would be this saving, but this externality may not be captured in the selling price.

6 Again, traditional trade models ignore the role of governments. But with most governments in the Western world allocating, or reallocating, 30 to 40 per cent of the value-adding activities of their countries it is difficult to see how one can justify this stance.

7 In a neo-classical world, the role of governments is simply to ensure that the economy is managed in such a way that the allocation of economic activity accords with the principle of comparative advantage. In a world in which resources are mobile across national boundaries, the assumption that there will always be some activity in which each country has a comparative advantage is no longer true. In this situation, the concept of absolute advantage, as espoused by Adam Smith, seems to be much more relevant in explaining the location of economic activity.

Chapter Two

International Business in a Changing World Environment

INTRODUCTION

In this chapter, we consider some aspects of the interface between international business – primarily in the guise of the MNE – and the governments of the countries which are host to its activities, within a changing world economic and political scenario. The chapter sets out to examine why, how and in what ways this interface has been shaped by, or has shaped, the events of the past twenty-five years, and speculates a little about the prospects for the remainder of the twentieth century.

ANTECEDENTS OF THE MNE

The Multi-Plant Enterprise

The MNE is the modern equivalent of the multi-plant domestic enterprise which dates back more than a century. In particular, the years following the Civil War saw the transformation of many regional American corporations into national corporations, and the emergence of multi-plant establishments, under the same ownership, in different parts of the USA. And it is, perhaps, worth recalling that the spread of Northern US companies into the south was regarded by some observers at the time with almost the same suspicion and unrest as that exhibited more recently by some Southern (developing) countries towards international corporations from the Northern hemisphere.

A useful starting point to any understanding of the modern MNE is to regard it as an extension of the domestic multi-plant firm (Caves, 1982). In both instances, a company seeking to service a market beyond its immediate catchment area must have some kind of advantage, which we shall call an ownership-specific advantage (Dunning, 1981, 1988) over and above that possessed by its competitors, or potential competitors, producing in that market. In both instances, too, it must be more profitable to supply the market from a foreign, rather than a domestic, location, and for the firm possessing the advantage to use it itself rather than sell the right to do so to other firms.

The growth of the multi-plant and/or multi-activity domestic enterprise in the second half of the last century may be explained by a series of separate, but interconnected, events. The first was the introduction – in both Europe and the USA – of the joint-stock company and the principle of limited liability, which, by lessening the risk for entrepreneurial capital, aided the finance of the technological and organizational advances of the time, and paved the way for the growth of the large business corporation (Chandler, 1977). The second event was the emergence of technology, including organizational technology, as the major vehicle of economic development.

From earliest times, economic progress has been conditioned by the availability of human and natural resources, and the efficiency by which these resources are administered to meet man's demands. In the first stage of development, typified by a Robinson Crusoe type economy, technology is primitive, and is freely available or easily copiable; the economic system is elemental, and man's standard of living essentially rests on the abundance of natural resources immediately available and his capacity to convert these resources into finished products. To make progress from such a situation one of two things is normally necessary. First, the economy must obtain the goods it needs but is unable to produce for itself from elsewhere; second, ways must be found of increasing the quality and productivity of its own resources.

Trade, technological advances and improvement in economic management have proved important vehicles of growth in the past, and, in some countries, for example, Japan, have more than compensated for deficiencies in natural resources. What is less obvious is that, as the more accessible non-renewable resources are depleted and the benefits of trade become fully exploited, the role of technology and organization becomes more decisive. Now technology has several unique features. Like natural resources its use has to be organized, but, unlike them, it has to be created in the first place.[1] Moreover, technology is frequently mobile across space, and often assumes the characteristics of a public good (in the sense that once produced it can be made available to additional consumers at a zero or low marginal cost). Because of these properties, society has devised various mechanisms, including the patent system, to allow the generators of some kind of technology privileged rights to its use, at least for a period of time – that is, the technology becomes ownership-specific. Not all types of technology, of course, are patentable or need to be patented. For example, the system (and often customer) specific computer technology of a company like IBM requires an extremely costly infrastructure which competitors find difficult to emulate. But it is the gain or erosion of such property rights, and the efficiency of their usage, which explain much of the birth, growth and death of firms in modern industrial society.

There are three main types of ownership (O) advantages which give both domestic and multinational firms an edge over their competitors.

International Business in a Changing Environment

The first is an exclusive or preferential access to a particular input or market (which might be directly acquired or negotiated with independent buyers or sellers); where the firm owns these rights it may have the option of leasing them to other firms either in its home or a foreign country. The second advantage is the possession of a unique intangible asset, for instance, a patent or a trade mark. Such an asset is locked into the firm and is often the output of its own research and development or marketing department, or the accumulation of managerial expertise. Like the first, however, it is often capable of being transferred to other firms, by way of a technical service agreement, managerial contract and the like.

The third *O*-specific advantage is different from the other two and reflects the ability of hierarchies to organize related productive activities more efficiently than the market. It stems not so much from the possession of a particular asset but from the economizing of transaction costs when such transactions are under the same governance. Such an advantage includes better access to, and ability to assimilate, information flows; the economies of synergy and the spreading of overhead costs; the capacity to practise price discrimination; the diversification of risks; the ability to protect property rights; and the efficient scheduling of production consequent upon internalizing intermediate goods or services markets. For example, a branch plant of an existing firm can benefit from the research and development or marketing facilities of its parent company, which a *de novo* competitor would have to reproduce for itself. Because of their high transaction costs, the rights to these assets cannot be bought and sold, that is, externalized, in the same way as can the first and second kind, for their value depends on their being centrally co-ordinated and controlled. Nevertheless, they often confer an important economic leverage on the firms possessing them, which, according to many economists,[2] is the main *raison d'etre* for the existence of large diversified firms, including MNEs.

The last reason for the growth of multi-plant firms over the last century has to do partly with the economies of product or process specialization and partly with the supplying of distant markets from alternative production sites, that is, what we might call location-specific factors. Again there is a parallel between domestic multi-plant and MNE activity; the basic question is the same – where is it best to site a plant to supply a market? The literature on the subject offers three sets of answers. The first is where costs are lowest. Given that technology is firm- rather than branch- (or plant-) specific, then production costs will be determined by spatial differences in the prices and productivity of factor inputs, while transfer costs will vary according to distance, the nature of the product being marketed and government imposed inducements to, or restrictions on, trade. However, the point worth stressing is that multi-plant operations are likely to be pronounced when the ownership advantages of a firm are of a kind which favour the geographical separation rather than the concentration of production units. The second answer to 'Why multiplant firms?' is that a physical presence of a firm in a market may

12 *Multinationals, Technology and Competitiveness*

improve a firm's competitive viability and may make it more difficult for a prospective competitor to enter that market; a lot of import substituting foreign direct investment, as described in the product cycle literature (Vernon, 1966, 1974, 1979), originates in this way.

Thirdly, firms may produce in different locations to minimize transaction costs over space, and to take advantage of international product and process specialization. In this respect, improvements in transport, initiated by railroads in the nineteenth and aircraft in the twentieth centuries, have had a decisive impact on the location of economic activity. But, no less dramatically, so have advances in communications and data transmitting technology. While, in one way, such innovations have worked alongside new product and process technology to centralize value-adding activity, in another, by reducing obstacles to the movement of goods, people and information, they have contributed to its spatial diversification.

The International Trading Enterprise

Let us now turn to consider another antecedent of the MNE which is still very much a part of international business: the trading company. Trade is usually the first introduction of a firm into the international economic arena; indeed, domestic trade, in the form of exports from a production unit located in one part of the country to a customer in another, tends to precede the establishment of production units in the latter region. The reasons for this are straightforward. Initially, an enterprise, because of its uncertainty about market prospects, or its ability to produce in an unfamiliar environment, is reluctant to incur the heavy setting up and monitoring costs which FDI usually involves. So the first step from a domestic to a foreign market tends to take the form of trade – either of intermediate or of final products. However, trade, like international production, requires a firm to possess one or two types of advantage over a firm in the country to which it is selling. Either it must have access to country-specific resource and organizational mechanisms not available to firms in the buying country and not transferable between the two countries, *or* it must possess ownership-specific advantages which, although they may reflect the economic institutional and cultural characteristics of the country from which they originate, are capable of being deployed in another country. Just as economic growth is increasingly dependent on advances in technology and organizational systems, so the pattern of trade is increasingly reflecting the mobile ownership advantages of firms, rather than the immobile resource endowments of countries. But, whereas in the case of the first kind of trade resources have to be used where they are located, in the second this is not necessary, and trade will be replaced by foreign production, wherever the location-specific endowments (which require to be combined with the ownership advantages of firms) most favour foreign countries.

Driven by purely economic considerations, business corporations would prefer to ignore political boundaries and view the world as a

International Business in a Changing Environment   13

single, integrated market. And it is true that national frontiers do not necessarily herald a discrete change in the amount or disposition of factor endowments. The 49th parallel and many borders in Western Europe make little *economic* sense. Resources are more unevenly distributed within the USA than, for example, between Washington and British Columbia or Michigan and Southern Ontario. In such cases, there may be a greater economic affinity between firms on one side of their national border and markets on the other, than between the same firms and distant parts of the domestic market.

If we interpret economic distance as the cost of overcoming the obstacles of space between an enterprise's place of production and its markets, including the transaction cost of surmounting language, cultural and other barriers, then, given the size and nature of the markets, the enterprise will normally seek to service those nearest to it. Governments may increase or lessen this distance. In the past, economic and political ties and a common legal and commercial system between metropolitan European powers and their colonies helped to lower spatial costs; export-free zones are performing this function today and trade and monetary integration, as it exists within parts of the EEC, has a similar effect. Import controls or political differences, for example, vividly demonstrated between East and West Germany or South and North Korea, work in the opposite direction. Both by the economic systems they operate and the development and other strategies they pursue, governments may exercise a decisive influence on transfer costs and the profitability of international business.

The purpose of government intervention in economic distance is primarily to alter patterns of resource allocation in pursuance of social and strategic objectives. Sometimes the intervention may be directed to encouraging import substitution activities; sometimes to strengthening the competitive viability of indigenous vis à vis foreign enterprises; and sometimes to gain tax revenue or protect the balance of payments. A great deal of foreign direct investment in the post-war period, especially in developing countries, has been prompted by host government intervention, either in response to penalties imposed on trade or to incentives to local production; likewise, governments, by regulating the conditions for FDI have sometimes fostered non-equity transfers of technology via licensing, management contracts and the like.

Scholars interested in comparative economic systems find it is helpful to classify countries by use of (what is called) the ESP paradigm.[3] Countries differ from each other, for example, in respect of their stage of development or propensity to attract international business, according to their economic *environment* (E), *systems* (S), and *policies* (P). By *environment* is meant the resources, including existing technology, available to a particular country and the ability of its enterprises to use these to service domestic or foreign markets. By *system* is meant the organizational framework within which the use and allocation of these resources is decided. Is it, for example, the market which is the main administrative mechanism or is it some form of government fiat or some

ENVIRONMENT (*E*)

Components:
- Human resources
- Natural resources
- Stage of economic development
- Cultural/historical background

Outcomes:
- Level and structure of output (primary, industrial service, specializations)
- Attitudes to work, wealth, foreigners, etc.

SYSTEM (*S*)

- Capitalist (free enterprise)
- Socialist
- Mixed
- Alliance with other countries

- Structure of decision taking
- Propensity to engage in international commerce
- Resource allocation controlled by market
- Nationalization

POLICIES (*P*)

- Macro economics (fiscal, monetary, exchange rate)
- Micro economics, (industry, trade, competition)
- General (education, consumer protection)
- Specific to FDI

- Extent and form of government intervention
- Controls
- Performance requirements

Figure 2.1   *The ESP Paradigm*

combination of the two? What is the role of the government in affecting the transaction costs of different organizational forms? *Inter alia* the answer to these questions will affect the creation of *new* technology, and will be determined, in part at least, by political circumstances and by cultural and social attitudes. By *policy* is meant both the strategic objectives of governments and the measures taken by them or related institutions to implement and advance these objectives, within the system and environment of which they are part. Figure 2.1 sets out the main attributes of the ESP configuration and their respective outcomes.

Clearly, the three elements of the paradigm are interlinked; each affects and is affected by the other. A change in government policy may dramatically recast the economic system, as, for example, in the cases of Chile and the Republic of China, while over a longer period government involvement in educational and research and development programmes

International Business in a Changing Environment

may no less impinge on the environment. A detailed appraisal of the ESP characteristics of countries takes us a long way to understanding the likely interaction between MNEs and the nation-states in which they operate.

Most of the literature on international economics tends to concentrate on the *environmental* influences of trade and foreign direct investment. Certainly, the classical and neo-classical trade models assume a market system in which there is atomistic competition, no government intervention, zero economic distance and technology which is freely and instantaneously transferred across national boundaries. Later theories acknowledge market imperfections and, implicitly at least, by accepting the possibility of ownership-specific advantages – including scale economies – and positive transaction costs, some of the characteristics of a mixed economy. From the start, explanations of international production have more explicitly taken system and policy factors into account. For example, in a survey of the forty-four most commonly quoted factors said to determine the investments of firms in developing countries, one half were found to be directly related to system or policy variables and the remainder to environmental variables (Root and Ahmed, 1978). Although the survey was primarily concerned with their locational choice, the ESP paradigm is no less relevant in explaining differences in the ownership advantages of MNEs of different nationalities and the modalities by which these advantages may be used.

Let us recap our thesis up to this point. MNEs possess many of the characteristics of multi-plant domestic firms and of firms engaged in international trade. The fact that a corporation locates part of its income generating activities outside its national boundaries, that is, engages in international production, does not really affect the nature of the beast. It must still possess certain advantages over firms which might seek to serve the same market; it must also be worthwhile to use these itself, rather than lease them to other firms (that is, the net benefits from internalization – which may include risk reduction – are expected to exceed those offered by the market); and it must be profitable to produce at least part of its output in a foreign, rather than a domestic, location. What primarily distinguishes *international* from *domestic* corporations is the configuration of the ESP variables facing the two groups of firms and the way in which this impinges on the OLI (ownership, location, internalization) advantages just described. The form and structure of these OLI advantages then determine the extent and pattern of multiplant operations. This suggests that any explanatory model of international production must take account of new variables, and particularly those to do with location-specific systems and policies, which do not usually vary between regions *within* a country, for example, those to do with operating in different political, currency and tax regimes; while others, which also influence the siting of domestic economic activity – communication and labour costs etc. – take on different values.

16 *Multinationals, Technology and Competitiveness*

MULTINATIONAL ENTERPRISES AND HOST COUNTRY INTERACTION: THE LAST THIRTY YEARS

Using this kind of approach, let us now turn to examine some aspects of the interaction between MNEs and the countries in which they have operated in the last thirty years or so. We can identify three fairly distinct stages in this interaction. While the precise timing of each stage may differ between companies and countries, by and large, the first lasted from the early 1950s to the mid 1970s; the second from the mid 1960s to the mid 1970s and the third from the mid 1970s to date. For reasons which will become apparent, we shall call them respectively the honeymoon, the confrontation and the reconciliation phases.

The Honeymoon Phase

Any partnership, and particularly one which is intended to be lasting, starts off with each partner having a great expectancy of what the other can offer, although this is sometimes more a matter of faith than anything else. And certainly, if love is not blind, mutual attraction does tend to wear rose-coloured spectacles, which magnify the good and overlook the less desirable features of one's partner. So it was with the early post-war interface between MNEs – or foreign direct investors as they were then known – and the countries in which they operated. From the viewpoint of both newly emerging developing nations and war-ravaged Europe, the capital, technology, managerial skills and entrepreneurship of US firms were sorely needed. However, owing to a shortage of dollars and an inadequate international market for these assets, these could only be obtained via equity investment, that is, their transfer remained internalized within the transferring firm. During these years, US economic and technological hegemony was at its peak, and American corporations dominated international production just as UK firms had dominated world trade a century and a half before. At the same time, US manufacturers were looking for new markets for their products, (particularly in the late 1950s, when some of the steam had gone out of the domestic economy) and new sources of materials to supplement indigenous supplies.

On the face of it, it seemed a perfect partnership between US investors and host countries, although in some cases it was Hobson's choice for the latter, as at the time only MNEs possessed many of the assets or markets they needed. And it was this very monopoly which gave rise to the first signs of discontent in the relationship. Nevertheless, in the 1950s and early 1960s at least, all (or most) was sweetness and light, and with the international economic climate, fashioned at Bretton Woods and Havana in the mid 1940s ensuring exchange rate stability and a well-ordered trading regime, the scenario for international business was more promising than at any time since before the First World War.

One other thing is worth mentioning. Most MNEs in those days were

International Business in a Changing Environment

quite small, and involved in many fewer countries than they are today. Most manufacturing affiliates, too, were set up as import-substituting ventures, and were truncated replicas of their parent companies acting independently of each other and closely identified with the interests of the host country. Only in the primary goods sectors had foreign corporations evolved anything approaching a global product or marketing mandate, or was there much intra-firm trading. The main impact of such corporations in these years was, then, in the assets they provided, rather than the way in which these and local resources were allocated.[4]

The Confrontation Stage

As a marriage passes out of its honeymoon stage and becomes more firmly established, the partners are better able to assess how far each is *in fact* able to satisfy the other's aspirations. Sometimes this learning process affects the attitudes and behaviour of one or both of the partners; sometimes the character of the relationship changes; sometimes the balance of influence shifts. One thing is certain however: after a time, each partner becomes aware of the weaknesses as well as the strengths of the other, and the costs as well as the benefits of the relationship.

The most far reaching changes in the international economic climate of the 1960s and early 1970s stemmed directly from the growing political independence of many developing countries, a better identification of their economic goals and a more realistic perception of their capacity to achieve these goals.

This national self-awareness, coupled with a Keynesian approach to economic management and the setting up of new economic systems and policies, was occurring at a time when MNEs were gaining a substantial foothold in many host countries. As more emphasis began to be given to such developmental goals as satisfying basic needs, advancing self reliance, improving the balance of payments and raising the level of technological capacity, so FDI became evaluated in these terms – and not surprisingly, in one direction or another, was found wanting. Gradually, it dawned on governments that the kind of contribution which MNEs might make to development was not always or necessarily that which they most needed. To be sure, foreign firms provided technology, but was it always the appropriate kind or at the right price? True, their affiliates might help to save imports, but did they always buy as much from local producers as was socially desirable? Admittedly, they might export part of their output, but was not this restricted to markets designated by their parent company? Agreed that they created employment, but were not their production methods more capital-intensive than those of indigenous firms, and did they always recruit or train local management as well as they might?

On top of this, MNEs were perceived to transmit a way of life which was not always welcomed and, through advertising and other promotional means, adversely influence social and cultural values. By their presence and behaviour they could drive out, or preclude the entry of,

18 *Multinationals, Technology and Competitiveness*

indigenous competitors, while, in refusing to transfer high value-added activities from their home countries, and/or by internalizing knowledge and information transfers, they could lessen the chances of a host country achieving even a modest technological capability. Finally, because of their monopoly power they were able to earn high economic rents, and so the local net output created by them might be minimal and in some cases even negative.

These were years, too, when the management style and organizational strategy of some of the larger MNEs was changing. As the activities and geographical spread of their foreign affiliates increased, so did the tendency of corporations to adopt a more centralized and multidivisional control structure, while decisions about capital investment, product range, sourcing and markets were more likely to be taken from a regional or global perspective. The trend, too, towards the international standardization of some products, and specialization of processes and markets, placed an increasing premium on quality control, the continuity of output, the protection of proprietary rights and transaction cost economizing, all of which encouraged a more integrated governance structure of MNEs and conferred upon them O advantages of the third kind described on p. 11

In the later 1960s, fixed exchange rates held good, world economic growth continued apace and inflation was generally under control. But the system was under great strain, particularly when the US balance of payments position turned sour and the US dollar lost some of its appeal as a reserve currency. Two events in the early 1970s – the devaluation of the dollar and the huge price rise of oil by the Organization of Petroleum Exporting Countries (OPEC) – heralded a watershed in post-war international economic relations. These events, together with the growing frustration of many developing countries with the inability of the existing economic order to reduce the income gap between themselves and the developed nations, sparked off a period of intensive North/South confrontation. Though much of the debate was rhetorical, it did create an uncongenial climate for international business. In the first half of the 1970s MNEs came under increasing scrutiny and attack. Not only were they criticized on the grounds of their unacceptable behaviour[5] and uneven contribution to economic development but also because they were perceived to be an expression of a no longer acceptable international economic system; if the system could not be changed, *inter alia* because of the inadequate bargaining strength of developing countries, then at least some redress might be taken against one of its institutions, – the MNE.

This flexing of muscles by many countries, including some developed countries such as Canada and Australia, was both understandable and inevitable, even though the actions taken were often imprudent and counter-productive.

The early 1970s were the 'high noon' of confrontation between several nation-states and MNEs. The measures taken by governments are well known and already part of history:[6] they ranged from outright expropri-

International Business in a Changing Environment 19

ation of foreign assets of MNEs, through restricting the level and direction of new investment, to laying down comprehensive performance criteria for foreign affiliates, and aiding indigenous firms to compete more effectively against foreign affiliates.

The response of the MNEs – which has not been so well documented – was predictable. Where their subsidiaries were already fully integrated into the local economy (as in the case of many older import-substituting ventures), but were still earning an economic rent, they absorbed the costs of intervention – but thought twice before investing any new capital. In other cases, however, their options were wider; these ranged from restricting the transfer of technology or the introduction of new products to circumventing controls on income flows through transfer pricing manipulation; from switching – or threatening to switch – production to a more congenial environment to trying to persuade their home governments to use their economic or political leverage against offending host governments.

In the main, this kind of reaction enraged host countries even more, especially where, in order to compete for the same foreign investment, they were forced to pay even higher economic rents. So harmonized regional action as, for example, taken by the Andean Pact countries and the EEC, and an international consensus in the form of the Commission on Transnational Corporations (TNCs),[7] and other UN bodies, was urged to strengthen the negotiating and bargaining power of host nations, and also to provide more information about MNEs and their role in the development process. Some of us involved in these early discussions saw the Commission on TNCs, in particular, as a kind of marriage guidance counsellor, which might provide a forum for a dialogue between MNEs and governments so that each might be better informed of what the other expected and had to offer and also be more appreciative of the interaction between each other's policies and strategies.

Reconciliation

As often happens, just as one is beginning to find a solution to a particular problem the problem becomes less pressing or ceases to exist. The latter 1970s saw governments learning from the experiences of the previous decade, refining, modifying and extending policy instruments better to harness the contribution of foreign direct investment – witness the very sophisticated machinery now used by some Latin American and East Asian countries in their dealings with non-resident companies. While, at an international level, attention has centred on drawing up codes of conduct or guidelines of behaviour for MNEs and improving the flow of information about their activities. There are now encouraging signs that governments have made progress in their understanding not only of the costs and benefits of different types of MNEs and foreign direct investment but of the costs and benefits of obtaining resources through alternative routes. If the 1960s and the early 1970s were years of disillusionment regarding the net benefits of international business, the later 1970s brought no less disenchantment with the gains offered by unbundling the package of resources provided by MNEs. However, the result of a sometimes costly learning process has been a more enlightened appraisal of the alternative forms of resource importation, and a more positive and constructive set of policies towards MNEs. At the same time, MNEs have become more cognisant of the ways in which their operations might not always work in the best social interests of the countries in which they operate. A new and better trained breed of managers and civil servants has emerged, and the focus of bargaining has moved to promoting a more harmonious and mutually beneficial relationship between the parties concerned, rather that of extracting the most economic rent out of each other.

These shifts in attitudes have been sparked off and shaped by changes in the ESP configuration of countries and the OLI configuration of firms. We would simply emphasize four such changes. First, and most important, there has been a widening of the sources of many of the assets which, in the 1960s, were largely monopolized by US and some European MNEs. The markets for many kinds of technology, management skills and capital have become less imperfect, and hence the incentive to internalize their sales has lessened. Second, the 1970s and 1980s have witnessed considerably higher levels of unemployment, more competition for the kind of resources which MNEs have to offer and lower rates of growth than the 1960s, and, as a consequence, host countries have become more sympathetically disposed to inward direct investment. Third, and allied to the first, an increasing number of countries are themselves engaging in FDI – South Korea, Brazil, Hong Kong, Singapore and Taiwan are among some recent examples[8] and, as a result, we see movements in disembodied intangible assets beginning to resemble those of goods embodying these assets, with intra-industry international production developing along the lines of intra-industry trade (Dunning, 1988). Fourth, while we observe a substantial growth of all types of non-equity or contractual resource exchanges, we also see more integration between the activities of some MNEs, which has occurred in spite of the volatility of exchange rates and an unstable monetary environment of the latter 1970s. This has led some countries to ask themselves how far they want to be locked into the kind of international economic order that the division of labour imposed by MNEs seems to require. For the dilemma is that the more unique the contributions of MNEs are to development the less amenable they are to government control.

There is, of course, a political dimension to what has happened in the last decade. With a few exceptions – the French elections being a noticeable example – governments have moved to the right, and with this policies have been modified and more emphasis has been placed on the market as an allocative mechanism.[9] Moreover, countries which have grown the fastest in the past decade are generally those which are favourably disposed towards inward direct investment and accept the need to be economically interdependent with the rest of the world. But

International Business in a Changing Environment 21

governments come and go, and policies, and even systems, come and go with them. The scholar evaluating the ESP paradigm from a longer term perspective has to try to discern broad trends and, with the usual caveats, we would argue that the happenings of the last decade, viewed in this context, do allow us to make certain observations about the likely course of international business.

TOWARDS A NEW UNDERSTANDING BETWEEN MNEs AND GOVERNMENTS

The last few years have seen signs of a more mature and positive relationship emerging between MNEs and governments. Each now knows the conditions under which either may, or may not, be expected to contribute to the other's well being. But because the economic and social goals, the ability to achieve these goals, and the bargaining power of countries, differ, it follows that one might expect a wide divergence of policies directed towards the involvement of MNEs. Moreover, there is nothing permanent about an ESP configuration of a particular country; the opening up of some Eastern European countries and mainland China to international business is testimony to this. Similarly, MNEs vary in size and strategy and the OLI values affecting their behaviour will change over time.

One of the lacunae in the literature on international business is a dynamic approach to its role in economic development. What we believe is needed is a reinterpretation of W. W. Rostow's model of the economic growth process – first presented in the late 1950s (Rostow, 1959) – and an extension of Hollis Chenery's analysis of transitional growth and world industrialization (Chenery, 1977, 1979) explicitly to incorporate the various modalities of international economic involvement. In formulating such an approach, we believe some use can be made of the ESP/OLI paradigms and, that, although the value of the explanatory variables affecting the configuration of each may fluctuate wildly both between countries and over time, some useful hypotheses might be made about the interaction of international business and the stage and direction of economic development.

Elsewhere (Dunning, 1981, 1988), we have put forward the concept of an international direct investment development cycle (or path). Put in its simplest terms it comes down to this. In the initial stage of economic development there is only a very limited role for foreign business, however rich a country may be in natural resources, basically because of the lack of domestic markets, the inadequacy of its commercial, technological or educational infrastructure, its inferior organizational capacities, and its immature or inappropriate economic policies. In the second stage of development when GNP per head in 1985 values reaches around the $500 mark – but occasionally well before, for example, India – foreign business may be attracted by the prospects of larger domestic markets and better production capabilities, while import substituting investment may be aided by local governments imposing import controls, and by foreign firms anxious to gain a presence before their competitors. On the other hand, in the case of countries whose prosperity relies more on the export of primary products, then *ceteris paribus*, improved infrastructure facilities – particularly roads, docks, airports and tele-communication facilities – may be sufficient to lower the costs of production and marketing to an economic level. However, as with import substitution investment, firms may wish to internalize the tech-nology transferred, not only to maintain product quality and protect property rights but also to exploit the gains of integrating new activities into the existing operations, for instance, to guarantee supplies. At this stage of development, information markets are likely to be extremely imperfect, and consequently, the transaction costs of contractual resource flows will be high. Finally, depending on the availability of cheap and well motivated labour, in some larger industrializing econo-mies MNEs may begin assembling and processing goods for export to industrialized countries.

It is at this point that most explanations for the determinants of international production seem to stop; indeed, their interest is largely confined to discrete acts of investment rather than to the process by which the pattern of foreign involvement is built up (Kogut, 1983). But let us take our examination a step further. When one looks at the role of MNEs in developed countries one observes similar types of import substitution and export oriented investment taking place, although the sectors in which MNEs dominate may be different. One also sees a different type of investment, however, which, like intra-industry trade, is primarily a phenomenon of the advanced industrialized countries; this is rationalized investment – of the Ford, Philips Eindhoven and IBM type – which is geared to exploiting the advantages of product- or process-specialization, scale and scope economies and the economies of synergy. Unlike import substituting investment, rationalized or efficiency-seeking investment requires to be centrally co-ordinated, and the resulting pattern of resource allocation may not always be consistent with indi-vidual host country goals.

The link between the role of MNEs in developing and developed countries lies in the interface between MNEs and the development process via the ESP variables. Ignoring the role of government for the moment, factors such as size of country, structure of resources and economic distance from the main centres of technology and markets play a crucial role in influencing the OLI configuration of both foreign and domestic firms. But we would expect that as a country moves along its development path, its indigenous firms would begin to generate their own ownership advantages in those sectors which required the type of resources in which it has, or is developing, a comparative advantage. At the same time, expanding markets and the changing costs of a country's endowments might increase the demand for new products which required the kind of resources which foreign firms were best able to provide, either by trade or foreign production. On balance, we would

International Business in a Changing Environment

anticipate that, as it approaches economic maturity, a country would become *more* rather than less involved in international production, though its *balance* as a net inward or outward direct investor would very much depend on the structure of its resource endowments vis-à-vis the rest of the world (for example, Canada compared with that of Japan).

What is perhaps more difficult to predict is the *form* in which the changing advantages of international business will be exploited. The choice between trade and foreign production is not the real issue, although in passing one might suggest that, as countries develop, the case for international production based on differential factor endowments weakens; instead, the options rest increasingly on differences in technology and consumer tastes between countries, and the opportunity for the economies of scale and scope.

We earlier argued that the growth of MNEs – especially in the late 1950s and early 1960s – rested on advances in the technology and organization of intra-firm information flows over space, and on the continued imperfections of markets. The relative decline in the MNE as a resource or rights transferor (that is, its acting as an arbitrager in shifting resources from where they earn less to where they earn more) over the past fifteen to twenty years may then be put down either to its reduced efficiency as an organizational unit or to a lowering of the transaction costs of the external market. The evidence strongly supports the latter hypothesis; indeed, advances in intra-firm communication and information technology have continued to favour multinational hierarchies. The widening of alternative sources of technology, however, the decline in the transaction costs of intermediate goods and services, especially some primary products, mature or standardized technology and some kinds of information, have all combined to make licensing agreements, managing contracts, turnkey operation and other non-equity resource flows more viable than once they were.

However, this tendency has not occurred in all countries or in all sectors of activity; indeed, in those sectors at the vanguard of technological progress, for example, fibre optics, telematics, microchips and bio-technology, the markets for new technology remain as imperfect as ever, and MNEs continue to dominate. Moreover, as we have seen, as firms grow they tend to generate the kind of *O*-specific advantages which are not readily marketable. Since the production and trade of products based on these advantages is mainly between developed countries, it is not surprising that the 100 per cent-owned affiliate still flourishes in these areas. It also remains the main mode of involvement in sectors in which the advantages of internalization are strong (for example, Japanese trading companies are 100% owned, even if their manufacturing associates are not, as are most export-platform affiliates).

From this viewpoint, the future of international business – like its past – rests on the extent, pattern and geographical distribution of technological and organizational advances. Recent innovations in data retrieval, storage and dissemination systems – particularly transborder information flows – suggest that the boundaries of large firms will be pushed further out and that hierarchies will be even easier to manage. However, human factors – for example, the huge costs associated with human error and disruptions in large organizations – and government intervention – for example, in breaking up or controlling conglomerates – may have the opposite effect. Innovations of new products and processes will continue, but their direction and rate – as opposed to the dissemination of *existing* technology – may well condition the extent to which contractual resource flow will replace direct investment as the main vehicle of resource transference. At the same time, the likely spread of ownership advantages among firms of different nationalities, and the growth of intra-industry production, suggests that a lot of international subcontracting will be internalized as firms wish to exploit non-marketable advantages.

What, now, of the role of governments in the development process? More than anything, governments have influenced the modality of resource transference across boundaries, and sometimes (and Japan and Korea are classic cases), through their educational, technological and industrial strategies, the ownership advantages of their countries' own firms as well. Governments also affect international business by the economic systems they operate, the work, cultural attitudes and social values they fashion, and the particular policies they pursue. We have seen that these change with the ideologies of governments,[10] and there is only a faint suggestion that S and P variables vary with economic development, with industrial maturity being associated with less rather than more state intervention in trade and investment.

More important, perhaps, is the extent to which countries wish to be interdependent or independent of each other. With so many uncertainties (for instance, economic and political stability and the future of non-renewable resources), but with the growing internationalization of ideas, customs and technology, most countries pursue a schizophrenic course; they want the benefits of cross-border interdependence but not the costs. Most noticeably, they wish to maintain their economic and political sovereignty. The trade-offs vary, too, according to the relative bargaining powers of MNEs and host countries, and the way in which the advantages and disadvantages of interdependence change over time. Thus, regional integration is a recognition of the benefits of large markets, while a self-sufficient energy or science and technology policy suggests that countries also value some degree of economic autonomy.

After a century of unparalleled economic expansion and the acceptance of the benefits of interdependence, the inter-war years saw most countries adopting a much more insulated stance, with governments seeking more control over their own destinies. The post Second World War period up to 1971 tried to capture some of the spirit of the nineteenth century by emulating the conditions which made for its prosperity, but these conditions had their costs, and it was these costs which countries were seeking to minimize in the 1970s as they moved towards a new mercantilism, with economic stability tending to give way to self-reliance as the main driving force in many parts of the developing world.

International Business in a Changing Environment 25

SOME OBSERVATIONS ON THE FUTURE OF MNEs: GOVERNMENT RELATIONSHIPS

Underlying the changes in the international economic climate described above there do seem to be a number of irreversible trends. Governments are much more active in the areas of social programmes, defence and environmental protection schemes and, in spite of political swings, are likely to continue to be so. In the international arena, a policy of controlled geocentricism seems the most probable future scenario, with nations seeking to benefit from economic co-operation with the rest of a shrinking world, and, at the same time, either separately or through sympathetic sectoral or regional groupings, to influence supranational decisions and minimize the adjustment costs of industrial restructuring. Even for very large countries, a policy of economic isolationism will become increasingly more difficult to sustain. All this, of course, places an enormous burden on existing regional and international organizations, which are likely to take on board increasing co-ordinative responsibilities, particularly in the energy and environmental fields.

In summary, then, it seems likely that the response to international business from countries and international organizations will increasingly parallel that towards trade, and that, in due course, similar mechanisms will be devised to provide an orderly framework for international production and resource transference, as GATT provides for trade in goods. For the foreseeable future, however, control will continue to be exerted through the unilateral policies of governments – aided by more intensive monitoring of corporate behaviour – codes and guidelines, the goodwill of companies, the actions of organized labour, and, not least, by competition.

Within such a scenario we would expect international business to flourish, but its character to change and its organizational structure to become a lot more diversified. The integrated MNE would remain a dominant force in technology and information-intensive sectors, but probably would not be the typical foreign investor of the future. With the advent of telematics, the opportunities for smaller firms to international-ize their operations will increase. At the same time, there might be an extension of functional internalization based on either equity participa-tion (as exists in banking and import and export merchanting) or through contracts (as exists in the hotel industry). There might be, too, a growth of time-limited equity arrangements, particularly in the less technology-intensive import substituting sectors, with MNEs from Japan and the more advanced developing countries playing an active tutorial role (Kojima, 1978), while MNEs in high technology sectors from developed countries are likely to display a greater propensity towards strategic alliances and collaborative arrangements, in order to strengthen their global marketing capacities (Ohmae, 1985; Contractor and Lorange, 1987).[11]

At the same time, as mergers and rationalizations are part of domestic economic life – particularly in times of structural change – as long as imperfections remain in international capital and foreign exchange markets, we would foresee an increase both in the exit and entry of MNEs and of transborder acquisitions, with one type of MNE, the multinational conglomerate, behaving more like an institutional portfolio than a direct investor. Finally, we would envisage a greater role for governments as initiators, and the international capital markets as financiers, of projects in which foreign firms will act more as contractors or subcontractors than as entrepreneurs. Gone are the days when foreign companies *own* country-specfic natural resources which are the basis of that country's comparative trading advantage with the rest of the world. This indigenization of assets will become more widespread in some manufacturing and service sectors – with the role of the foreign direct investor becoming increasingly that of a catalyst for self-development rather than that of an economic imperialist.

More generally, in many ways, the international economic climate of the last two decades of the twentieth century will be very different from that of the third quarter. Then the emphasis was on technological innovations and productivity improvements, spurred on by the need to cope with rising living standards and manpower shortages; these generated ownership-specific advantages of a capital- or technology-intensive kind. In the foreseeable future, in an industrialized world of limited growth and substantial unemployment, and one which is concerned with environmental factors and the depletion of non-renewable resources, and in a developing world increasingly conscious of its need to satisfy basic needs, the innovatory emphasis may well be on materials and energy saving, and on increasing agricultural output.

If this diagnosis is correct, it may be that the type of technological advances of the 1980s and 1990s will require different organizational forms to exploit them. As some countries move towards a post-industrial stage of development, more innovations will occur in the service sector. Already this has happened in the spheres of banking and finance, insurance, telecommunications, medical services and data provision and transmission (Quinn, 1987). It is by no means certain that the resource endowments needed for these innovations and their development will be those which generated their predecessors, nor that the hierarchical structure of firms evolved during the 1960s and 1970s will be suitable for the remaining years of the twentieth century.

All this suggests a constantly shifting role for MNEs in the world economy and the form of their involvement. This is no less true of the domestic business sector in many countries, however; very few firms supply the same product or markets that they did fifty years ago. Yet whatever the problems of size and diversification, for every firm that cannot manage to cope efficiently, another can – spurred on by some new technology or organizational advance which it can accommodate within its hierarchy. That, perhaps, may prove to be the criterion of change; new innovations, institutions and ideas on the one hand, and the willingness of countries to be economically interdependent on the other.

Twenty years ago, some commentators, notably Howard Perlmutter

International Business in a Changing Environment   27

(1966) were forecasting a world dominated by the leading 200 or 300 MNEs by the 1990s. Today, perceptions of the future of international business are very different. Due to the increasing speed at which technology is disseminated, it may be that some retrenchment or realignment of the multi-plant phenomena and the ownership of foreign assets is on the cards. Add to this the possibility that the technologies of the future will require a different form of governance for their commercialization, then it is at least possible that some of the giant MNEs of today will be the dinosaurs of tomorrow. This does not necessarily augur a decline in international business. Rather, it suggests that the MNE of the 1960s as a packager and a transmitter of resources may no longer be as unique or appropriate an organizational form as it has been in the past, and that the future will see the ingredients of growth differently bundled and channelled through the market and by co-operative arrangements between independent firms as well as by foreign direct investment.[12]

CONCLUSIONS

We conclude this chapter by observing one particularly disturbing feature of the world economy in the 1980s, which, to a large extent, is a response to the events of the past decade. This is the drift to protectionism by the industrialized developed countries. This drift does not primarily take the form of restrictions or traditional non-tariff barriers but of domestic interventionist policies by governments which affect the kind and standard of goods and services produced, their means of procurement and the terms on which they are traded.

Such protectionism is reminiscent of the beggar-my-neighbour trade policies of the inter-war years but goes well beyond these. In the 1930s, non-resident companies tried to overcome trade obstacles by setting up local producing facilities. This seems to be re-occurring in the 1980s, particularly with respect to Japanese penetration of European and North American markets. However, unlike the situation in the inter-war years, governments today are major (in some cases the only) purchasers of goods and services, particularly those supplied by MNEs in high technology industries.

Now, while GATT rules generally forbit member governments to impose discriminatory import duties, and the OECD guidelines for MNEs endorse the principle of equitable treatment between national and foreign-owned firms, it is not difficult to find ways around their rules and guidelines, particularly where sensitive areas of national security are involved. And it is worth observing that the impact of many of the new technologies, for example, telematics, microchips and biotechnology, straddles both private and public domains, and that commercial and social interests are becoming more difficult to disentangle. While the movement towards deregulation in some service sectors is likely to make for more foreign direct investment, the pressure to mitigate the inroads of competition from Japan, and the newly industrialized countries in manufacturing goods, could lead to governments introducing protectionist policies which might jeopardize the fabric of international production built up by MNEs during the last two decades. Indeed, whereas in the 1960s and 1970s the main battleground of the MNEs was in the developing world, in the 1980s this battleground has removed to Europe, the USA and Japan. Dare one hope that the combined wisdom of individual governments, international agencies and MNEs may be deployed, not only to avoid conflict but to promote positive industrial, trade and investment policies which will allow international business to adjust to the economic challenges of the future as it has done so successfully in the past?

NOTES

1 That is to say technology is the output of natural resources; it is a secondary rather than a primary resource, although once produced it fundamentally affects the efficiency of natural resource usage.
2 For example, Chandler (1977); Williamson (1981); Casson (1987).
3 As developed by Koopman and Montias (1971).
4 Chapter 3 takes this point up in more detail.
5 The most blatant example being the ITT intervention in Chilean politics.
6 See, for example, the various reports of the UN Centre on Transnational Corporations, especially UNCTC (1978, 1983, 1988), Boarman and Schollhammer (1975) and Lall and Streeten (1977).
7 The UN's preferred nomenclature for MNEs.
8 For an examination of MNEs from developing countries see Wells (1983), Lall (1983) and Kahn (1987).
9 Though often within the framework of a well-defined and articulated economic and industrial economic strategy, for example, as in the case of Japan.
10 The relation between country-specific ideologies and national competitiveness is examined by Lodge and Vogel (1987).
11 Which route is chosen depends on how far the benefits of internalization can be captured in a contractual agreement.
12 The increasing relevance of the non-equity forms of resource transference is now being explored by the OECD Development Centre. (See, for example, Oman (1984).)

Chapter 3

Market Power of the Firm and International Transfer of Technology

INTRODUCTION

This chapter examines some ways in which the international transfer of technology may be affected by the economic power of the transmitting enterprises. The chapter takes a historical perspective on this issue, and examines power from a strictly microeconomic stance. Power is defined as the economic leverage which firms have over their own (and other firms') behaviour. In neo-classical economics, the source of such discretion is the economic rent earned by firms. Such rent may be derived from the exclusive or privileged possession of an asset or right, or from the governance of a number of separate, but interdependent, activities. When buying inputs and selling outputs in a perfect market, a firm is assumed to have no economic leverage, except over whether or not to produce. In imperfect competition, it is assumed to have more latitude; for example, a single-product monopolist may restrict output below, or raise price above, the competitive level; a horizontally or vertically integrated monopolist may have wider options which stem from the economies of scope and the ability to co-ordinate interrelated value-adding activities (Williamson, 1981).

Industrial economics looks at the power of firms from a broader viewpoint. It examines not only a firm's own product and pricing strategy but also the effect which this may have on the market environment in which it operates. Thus, by acquiring some monopolistic advantage, a firm may be able to impose certain conditions on its buyers which it could not do in a spot market; similarly, by gaining exclusive distribution rights, it might be able to influence selling terms, and to preclude the access of its rivals to such markets. By a variety of anti-competitive tactics, a multi-activity monopolist may be able to drive single-activity competitors out of the market. Firms may pursue such practices unilaterally or by collusive or cartel arrangements.

The neo-classical treatment of economic power in most microeconomic texts is deficient in a number of respects. First, it tends to focus on the asset power of the single-product firm and ignore the transaction

30 Multinationals, Technology and Competitiveness

economizing activities resulting from product, process, or market diversification. Yet in practice, almost all enterprises engage in multiple activities. They do this because they believe that they are better able to control price, quality, or the flow of inputs than the market. This, in turn, implies that the latter form of governance of economic activity is inefficient, that is, that market failure exists. But quite apart from the incentive to internalize, the fact that firms are mutli-transactional may give them a certain discretion over the nature and terms of any *one* transaction.

To distinguish this kind of leverage from *asset* power we shall call it *transaction* power, and the proposition of this chapter is that firms may deploy such leverage to influence the international transfer of technology in exactly the same way as they may affect the disposition of a particular asset.

The second aspect of power concerns the way in which it is used. The assumption of neo-classical economics is that all firms are profit maximizers and will behave accordingly. But where a firm is in a position to earn surplus profits, it may decide to 'buy' other goals with all or part of that surplus; and the result may be a different disposition of resources than the profit maximizing model predicts. Such goals include growth (beyond the profit maximizing output), earning only a satisfactory profit discretionary investment (including that of technology creation) or X-inefficiency (that is, other than cost-minimizing efficiency). One variant of X-inefficiency is that firms which transfer technology to other countries via foreign direct investment may not always adapt that technology (or make use of local factor inputs) in a way which maximizes profits of the local affiliates, let alone advance the developmental goals of the host country.

Thirdly, economic power is usually treated in a static rather than a dynamic context. Indeed, much of the literature does not concern itself with such questions as 'What is the optimum rate of growth of a firm?', or 'What is the organizational response to a change in environmental risk?'. This is clearly unsatisfactory when considering the market for technology or technological assets, and the necessity of a supplying firm to secure a reliable return on its unique skills or knowledge (Vernon, 1983). Moreover, where the market for the technology is imperfect and is governed by a foreign institution, the way in which such an institution takes decisions on the production, dissemination and location of technology is of crucial importance.

Finally, neo-classical economics tends to ignore government fiat as an alternative to either private hierarchies or the market as a resource allocator. But, in so far as they are able to bargain away part or all of economic rents of firms, or, by affecting their behaviour, influence whether the rents are earned in the first place, governments may act as counteracting forces to hierarchies in the latters' use of economic power.

We conclude that a firm's economic power depends on the uniqueness of the assets it possesses, the number and kind of internal transactions it undertakes, and the externalities to which they give rise. The manner in

Market Power and Technology Transfer 31

which the power is exercised depends on the goals of the enterprise, the tactics the enterprise adopts to achieve these goals, and the extent to which government fiat or other mechanisms are able to constrain its behaviour. Both the origin and use of economic leverage will depend on country, product and firm-specific characteristics. Thus, the market for a particular piece of technology, for example, a drug formula, may operate effectively within a given country but be very imperfect between one country and another. It may be expected to vary according to the nature of the technology being transferred, for instance, whether it is idiosyncratic or standardized, new or old, codifiable or tacit, and the size and strategy of the investing firm (Teece, 1981a and b). In the case of established MNEs, there is also a strong suggestion that the extent and pattern of their existing international involvement is also relevant (Davidson and McFetridge, 1984). Finally, home and host governments may exercise a decisive influence on the way in which technology is traded.[1]

We now examine some of the ways in which changes in the asset and transaction power of companies have affected the extent and pattern of transborder flows of technology and technological capacity. We shall deal briefly with five phases – which broadly correspond to the main thrusts of technological advance and the internationalization of activity of firms over the last 150 years.

PHASE 1: THE INDUSTRIAL REVOLUTION
– TO AROUND 1870

In this era the first in which technology[2] was traded internationally to any extent, there was little activity on the part of MNEs.[3] At the same time, there was a good deal of expatriate direct investment, particularly of European migrants in the USA, while foreign capitalists and traders from developed countries were active in promoting and financing mining and agricultural ventures in developing countries. Although a new wave of technological advances was emerging towards the end of that period, most cross-border technology flows were based on the 'interrelated and mutually reinforcing' innovations of the Industrial Revolution (Rosenberg, 1981). Not surprisingly, these usually originated from the UK which, until the early 1820s, was responsible for nearly one-half of all major inventions, discoveries and innovations (Streit, 1949). But by the mid-nineteenth century, most of these had been disseminated to the rest of Europe and the USA, and by 1875 Britain's technological leadership was being strongly challenged by France, Germany and the USA.[4]

The reason for this speedy transfer of knowledge is usually put down to its fairly uncomplicated state, its low transaction costs, and the fact that it could be easily copied, learnt, or embodied in human capital; moreover the major recipient countries, that is, France, Germany and the USA, generally had the necessary skills and technical infrastructure to assimilate, service and adapt foreign technology. History recalls that attempts by the UK government to control the outflow of technology and safeguard its own industries' monopolistic position generally failed. Sometimes knowledge was transmitted via migrant labour, and sometimes by entrepreneurs and innovators in the belief that industrializing 'late-comers' offered better prospects for the use of their inventions than the UK.[5] The early US brewing, textile, jute, silk, carpet, pottery, cutlery and metal-using industries were largely dominated by European expatriates, individuals or firms, many of whom brought their machinery, equipment, drawings and patterns with them (Coram, 1967; Wilkins, 1988).

Until the mid-nineteenth century, most businesses were small, owner-managed and single-product; the age of the joint stock company and managerial capitalism was only just beginning to dawn. Few firms had any transaction power, and, with one major exception, there was little vertical integration. Some commentators (for example, Chandler, 1976) have argued that the desire to retain family control of a business, and a compact, tightly organized national distributional network, lessened the incentive of UK firms to exploit transactional and organization economies, which their US counterparts managed to do so successfully. The exception was that of some primary-product foreign investments. To fuel and efficiently schedule their domestic manufacturing activities, and to cater for rising living standards, UK companies had to be sure of supplies of raw materials and foodstuffs. At first, these were bought by spot or contract transactions, but as orders became larger, suppliers, mainly due to lack of capital and technology, found them more difficult to meet; while buying firms, as their sunk and operating costs increased, and small variations in output resulted in disproportionate fluctuations in profits, began to integrate backwards to insure themselves against supply irregularities.

The need to economize on international transactions and reduce environmental risks led directly to the birth of the modern MNE. At the same time, MNEs possessed asset power in the form of capital, technology, market access and managerial expertise. Early venturers of this kind included both manufacturers, such as Lever and Cadbury, and trading companies such as Shaw, Jardine Matheson, Wallace, Butterfield and Swire (UK tea and rubber estates and timber forests in the East), Atkins (US sugar plantations in Cuba) and Litvinoff (Russian tea factories in China).[6] United Kingdom and European entrepreneurs and capitalists also gained control of foreign mines; this was a different mode of entry, but a no less important antecedent of the MNE. For the entrepreneur cum speculator was often a marriage broker bringing together local resources, foreign capital, and technology; UK companies such as Rio Tinto Zinc and many US oil companies started in this way.

Most of these early investments in natural resources were located in developing countries. Economic governance was exerted both by the home country (for example, jurisdictional or administrative discrimination by colonial powers against other foreign investors – as practised

Market Power and Technology Transfer 33

especially by the French and Japanese)[7] and by the foreign firms themselves, through (a) the asset advantages they possessed, and (b) their ability to internalize decision taking and hence force affiliates to behave in a way consistent with the interests of the enterprise imposed few constraints on the activities of foreign investors. They were thus able to take advantage of these market imperfections to promote their wider goals.

PHASE 2: 1870–1914

There were two reasons why this period is best regarded as the one in which the modern MNE grew from infancy to adolescence. In the first place, it was one of extensive technological progress, quite different in kind to that of the first Industrial Revolution. In the second place, the new technologies required more hierarchical forms of governance for their efficient exploitation and dissemination. Indeed, without parallel advances in organizational, transport and communications technology, new products, such as the internal combustion engine and electrical generator, and new processes based on volume production and the interchangeability of parts, could never have been profitably commercialized. The story is well known and is best told in the writings of Chandler,[8] although he tends to emphasize only one aspect of the increased economic leverage these events created.

The USA was the source country of the second Industrial Revolution. The innovations on which it was based reflected that country's particular resource and market characteristics. There were several distinctive features about the new technology, compared with that which preceded it. First, it was usually more costly to produce, yet less costly to reproduce; this necessitated new institutional mechanisms (for example, the patent system) to enable the innovator both to recoup his sunk costs and to protect him from having his invention pirated by competitors. Second, it needed large standardized and stable markets to cover its costs; in the case of consumer goods, this led to the introduction of branded products, protected by trademarks, and underlined the importance of a stable flow of raw and semi-processed materials and parts. Third, the externalities associated with the new technology were often widespread; much of it, for example, required the co-ordination of separate production processes, and, at least in the fabricating industries, the assembly of interchangeable parts.

These technological advances led to the emergence of new industries supplying four types of products; first, branded consumer goods, for instance, cigarettes, soup, confectionery, canned goods and medicines; second, tropical agricultural products, such as bananas, pineapples, coffee, etc. which, due to improvements in quality control, transportation and temperature-controlling techniques, could be transported and stored over long distances; third, mass-produced metal products such as sewing machines, typewriters, refrigerators, etc.; and fourth, standardized heavy machinery and capital goods, for example, electrical equipment, basic chemicals. Almost without exception, these products required new organizational modes for their efficient production and marketing. In particular, they favoured firms which were in a position to exploit the economies of large-scale production and gains from vertical integration. Growth through transaction economizing and risk internalization, as well as through the creation of acquisition of asset power, was then the order of the day. Hence the output of firms not only became more concentrated, it changed in character. Because of the higher transaction costs of the new technology, and the fact that it could not be as readily absorbed as human capital, it was less easily transmittable between countries than that which preceded it.

While, from the start, the foreign activities of some MNEs were integrated with their domestic operations, this was not the normal pattern of events. Most manufacturing affiliates were set up in response to import restrictions imposed by host countries; in such cases, foreign production by MNEs replaced part of their domestic production. Such economic leverage as a firm possessed over its foreign rivals existed *prior* to the firm becoming an MNE, although sometimes where foreign production led to additional internalizing advantages, transaction power was enhanced. However, for the most part, these defensive investments were located in developed countries; they were mainly of the 'greenfield' kind and, prior to 1914 at least, involved fairly small amounts of capital. Although some of the investing companies were forerunners of today's giant manufacturing MNEs, their economic muscle at the time rested primarily in their exclusive or privileged possession of property rights. Even then, however, an aspect of transaction power was beginning to show itself. As described in the writings of Vernon and his colleagues (see especially Vernon, 1966, 1983; Knickerbocker, 1973), the market structure of many of these newer industries was oligopolistic, and the foreign strategy of the constituent firms was often designed to protect their overall competitive position. In such cases, the motive for investing abroad was not only to earn profits but also to preclude rival firms from gaining a foothold in a foreign market, or in response to their penetration of the firm's own markets, or potential markets. Sometimes, protection was demanded of host governments by MNEs as a condition for entry; in such conditions, the transfer of technology frequently led to a suboptimum market structure in the host country. And although MNEs transferred the necessary product or process technology, very rarely was technological *capacity* exported. In the main, foreign subsidiaries were treated as domestic branch plants located in an alien environment. Usually their range of activities was truncated, and not always were these suitably modified to meet local input and market needs. This not only resulted in X-inefficiency, but, where their presence spoiled the market for indigenous competitors, also stifled the development of local technological capability.

Yet, notwithstanding the growth of these investments, it is estimated that in 1914 63 per cent of the international direct capital stock was in

Market Power and Technology Transfer 35

developing countries (Dunning, 1983), and the great proportion of this was outside the manufacturing sector. As in Europe and the USA, about 15 per cent was in railroads and public utilities, but vertically integrated European and US resource-based investments, particularly in the European colonies, Asia and the Caribbean, were expanding fast, and the years prior to the First World War saw the emergence of companies such as the United Fruit Company (US) which had every bit as much power as their modern day equivalents. No less important were the risk-minimizing backward integrations by manufacturing companies. The introduction of the motor vehicle and the vulcanization of rubber prompted companies such as the United Tyre Company to search for new sources of natural rubber, particular in Latin America and Malaysia. Internalization of the coffee, tea, sugar and tropical fruit markets was undertaken by processors and merchants, and by groups of entrepreneurs. Hard mineral, for example, tin companies pursued a similar strategy, as did the rapidly expanding oil firms.

So gradually, although the movement did not reach its peak until after the First World War, most of the capital-intensive primary-product sectors in developing countries became not only owned by foreign companies but co-ordinated with their domestic operations. It was this governance over successive stages of production and marketing that gave them their economic strength, as much as any asset advantages they possessed. Moreover, the companies behaved as integrated entities, serving the interest of the parent group of which they were part rather than that of their subsidiaries – except where the two were coincidental. Technology was transferred as long as it served these interests, but the authority of the MNE rested in its ability to extract an economic rent from its system of interdependent activities. The fact that it often gained exclusive concessions to mines, or engaged in agricultural operations, frequently made countries hostage to its operations. However, as in the first phase, there was little evidence of host governments intervening in order to curb this economic power, or to further harness it to national objectives; one suspects, however, that in those countries dominated by vertically integrated resource-based MNEs, this reflected a lack of bargaining strength rather than a mutuality of interests between the MNE and host governments.

PHASE 3: 1919–1939

Although the economic climate for international direct investment was less congenial in the years following the First World War, the total stock of the foreign capital stake (in money terms) rose by 75 per cent between 1914 and 1938, and there was a substantial growth of the number of foreign affiliates, particularly in the manufacturing sector of developed market countries where import controls were restricting trade flows. These were also years of an aggressive thrust overseas by manufacturing MNEs to secure access to primary products for their domestic factories,

36   *Multinationals, Technology and Competitiveness*

for example, oil, rubber and non-ferrous metals, and to meet expanding consumer goods markets.

From our perspective, the period saw an increase in the market power of MNEs in two respects. First, because the economic viability of many of the new process technologies rested on a large and stable demand for their products, and because many national markets were fragmented, depressed or growing insufficiently to accommodate these advances, there was a major movement towards the rationalization of firms and the formation of international cartels (Casson, 1987). This led to an intensification of industrial concentration, a more oligopolistic market structure and an increase in the transaction power of firms. Though such a change in the organization of production affected both declining and expanding industries, its impact was most marked on those with the greatest propensity for foreign production.

Second, although international cartel arrangements in some primary-product sectors made foreign direct investment unnecessary, in others (and especially those which tended to be dominated by a small group of firms from one country), the preferred modality of expansion (or protection of existing interests) was vertical integration. During these years, the transaction costs of many intermediate-product markets were rising as a regular flow of some raw materials was becoming more difficult to sustain; and, to protect themselves against such uncertainties and/or to exploit the benefits of market failure, firms were encouraged to internalize spot or contractual exchanges. These were also used as anti-competitive devices to forestall new entrants from acquiring such inputs. In such instances, the power of the MNE rested not only in the unique resources which it supplied but also in its control over distribution channels, and sometimes of shipping and other transport facilities. The technology which it provided was determined by its global interest rather than that of any particular recipient affiliate; the extent to which host governments had bargaining capacity to influence the terms of the technology transfer had then to be set against the sovereignty exercised by the MNEs as an integrated unit. Managerial and organizational innovations – and in particular the introduction of the multidivisional (or M-form) structure and improved financial control systems by such companies as DuPont and General Motors in the 1920s[9] – gave further impetus to the replacement of markets by hierarchies in these years.

Once again, developing countries bore the brunt of events, partly because of the character of the technology associated with the sectors in which foreign firms were involved in developing countries, partly because the markets for technology and primary products in those countries were either non-existent or undeveloped, and partly because the gains from internalization were especially noticeable in these sectors. We have suggested that the way in which such discretionary power is used rests both on the extent to which the MNE is able and willing to make surplus profits, and on the way in which these are spent. But there does seem to be evidence that part of the 'potential' surplus profits of MNEs in these years was spent on not transferring the kind or amount of

Market Power and Technology Transfer 37

technology which would have occurred had the affiliates been self-contained profit centres; and certainly – although this became more apparent in later years – by not engaging in secondary processing activities and, by the fact of their presence, making it uneconomic for indigenous firms so to do.

In summary, then, the inter-war years saw a slower pace of technical advances than the pre–1914 period; yet there was rather more international transfer of the results of the earlier advances.[10] In some branches of manufacturing and, for instance, in the basic chemicals and metals sectors, where knowledge was already reasonably dispersed among industrialized countries, such international transfers took place predominantly through cartel agreements; in others, where a firm or group of firms of a particular nationality dominated the world market, FDI was the preferred vehicle. Thus, in some newer industrial sectors, such as motor vehicles, domestic electrical applicances, packaged foods, etc., US firms gained a dominant foothold in the inter-war years, and, by 1939, had gained access to most large markets; however, their source of strength mainly rested in the unique technology and/or trademark transferred within an oligopolistic market framework. Such MNEs were rarely integrated in their product or process structure, and the discretion which they had on internal transactions was fairly limited. This, however, was not the case for a lot of the technology transferred to developing countries; here, the investment was more supply oriented and was as much geared to economizing on the transaction costs of imperfect product markets as to anything else.[11] Market power was then of a different kind and affected the bargaining power of firms and countries.

During the inter-war years, some governments became more interventionist, partly in response to the general move towards protectionism, and partly as a consequence of world recession. However, although governments' economic policies affected the behaviour of MNEs, as did their rather more liberal attitude towards the formation of international cartels, they still made little effort to influence directly the activities of foreign affiliates or the distribution of any surplus profits earned by them.

PHASE 4: 1945–65

In the first two decades following the Second World War, the rate of increase in international production was greater than at any time before or since, being twice that of world output and half as much again as world trade. During these years the technological hegemony of the USA reached its peak. However, unlike the technology of Phase 1, its markets, and particularly its overseas markets, were highly imperfect, and hence the owners of this technology found it more to their interest to internalize its use than to sell this right to other firms. At the same time, as a result of initiative of the GATT and the International Monetary Fund (IMF), international commerce flourished. Nevertheless, a shortage of US dollars in most countries made it necessary for American firms

38 *Multinationals, Technology and Competitiveness*

to service these foreign markets via foreign production rather than by exports.

By the early 1960s, the 187 largest US MNEs were setting up more than 300 new manufacturing subsidiaries in Europe each year – three times the number in the 1950s and ten times that in the inter-war years (Vaupel and Curhan, 1974). By 1965, UK and Continental European MNEs were also rapidly increasing their penetration of European markets, stimulated by regional economic integration. There was also some market-oriented activity by European and US MNEs in other developed countries, notably Australia, Canada and the USA.

For the most part, these early post-war manufacturing investments were substitutes for exports rather than part of an international marketing strategy by MNEs. And, although many of the leading MNEs were involved, there were a large number of smaller firms also prompted to go overseas. Out of these, some of today's largest and most successful international companies emerged. But, at the time of entry, their main competitive advantage lay in their ownership of superior intangible assets rather than in synergistic economies arising from product or process diversification. Again, the period typified the stage of the product cycle where production was being transferred from home to host country but where the product had not yet reached its standardized or mature state, or local firms had entered the market. One very clear illustration of this type of asset power was the penetration of the European drug industry by US MNEs in the later 1950s and early 1960s; another was the later pattern of entry by American firms in the semi-conductor industry (Lake, 1979).

As the years went by and US MNEs gained a firmer foothold in many high-technology industries in Europe, increasing concern was expressed by a number of host countries – as, for example, articulated by Servan-Schreiber (1968). The concern was partly about the price paid for the technology, but also about the apparent inability of European industry to respond to the stimulus of foreign direct investment. Far from acting as tutors to European firms, US MNEs seemed to be driving them out of business. Quite apart from political or strategic considerations, it was feared that Europe was in danger of becoming a manufacturing satellite of the USA, with a major share of the technological capacity being located in the home country. If, for any reason, US investment should be withdrawn, Europe would be left with little capability to generate its own innovations. Here, the discretionary power of the MNE was felt to be the barriers to entry it erected to the production of indigenous knowledge wherever (1) affiliates dominated the local market, and (2) it chose to centralize its technology-creating activities in the home country. Indeed, it might even use its entry into a local market to further this goal, for example, by buying up high technology firms and transferring the research and development (R & D) back to the parent company. Put another way, as technology became a more important ingredient of economic efficiency, its internalization by the firm producing it and the

Market Power and Technology Transfer 39

economics of the location of R & D were viewed with increasing anxiety by many host countries.[12]

It is also worth emphasizing that, although there were joint ventures and non-equity transfers of technology in the first half of the post-war period, the strongly preferred mode of transmission was the 100 per cent-owned subsidiary. From the firm's viewpoint, this was thought to be the best way of protecting its technological strengths against abuse or dissipation, and advancing its product and/or market strategy. In several oligopolistic sectors, this led to a marked bunching of the activities of MNEs, for instance, in semi-conductors and pharmaceuticals by US firms in Europe (Lake, 1979). From the viewpoint of most host countries, finance capital as well as technology was needed, and in those years only passing attention was paid to the possible drawbacks of FDI. In the early country studies of Dunning (1958), Brash (1966) and Safarian (1966), little attention was paid to the discretionary power of foreign MNEs, except in so far as this might impinge upon the domestic market structure.

What has been written about the transfer of technology to developed countries applies with even more force to that transferred to developing countries, except that, in the latter case, the technology was generally more mature and standardized. Nevertheless, in many instances, the technological, commercial and educational infrastructure was inadequate to protect the transferring firm against market failure, while host governments had neither the desire nor the ability to encourage the externalization of such a transfer.

For the most part, however, the major developments of the 1950s and 1960s in developing countries were centred on MNE activity in resource-based industries. In Chapter 1 we referred to the honeymoon relations between countries and companies in this era, but these did not extend to some investment in minerals and raw materials. For here the tie between imperialism or colonialism and the activities of companies from metropolitan powers was perceived to be too close for comfort! So, as the colonies gained their independence, it was not surprising that they looked critically at the kind of economic relations which reminded them of their past. Many were also aware that, if they had any bargaining power with the outside world at all, it rested in their possession of natural resources. The perception was that as long as these resources were in foreign hands, sovereignty could never be achieved. So over the years, both by unilateral policy, encouraging or forcing divestment or exerting more control over the way in which resources were exploited, or by improving the terms of the exploitation, and by multilateral persuasion (including guidelines and codes of conduct), the economic governance of MNEs *qua* MNEs was weakened. At the same time, if countries did not want foreign control over their resources, they still needed external capital, technology and markets to help them exploit these resources. The belief that the transfer of these resources could be disinternalized, that is, either acquired on the open market or through non-equity foreign involvement, or reproduced through indigenous capacity, underlay this change in attitude towards MNEs.

40 *Multinationals, Technology and Competitiveness*

In some cases this belief was warranted, but usually it was not. The need for developing countries to generate an ability to adapt imported technology, and to develop more appropriate technology, has been persuasively argued by Stewart (1981). In general, during the initial period in their dealings with MNEs, host governments persistently overestimated both the entrepreneurial initiative of their own firms, and their capability not only to know from where technology could be obtained but also to buy it at the right price, organize it with other factor inputs and to adapt it to local needs. This was, and to a large extent still is, the unique contribution of the inward direct investment, that is, the provision, organization and management of a system of interlocking technologies, management and marketing skills.

In conclusion, the first part of the post-war period saw the dominating role of US MNEs and a particularly favourable international climate for foreign direct investment. But in the early 1960s two anxieties began to be raised. The first concern, mainly raised by developed countries, was regarding the ability of foreign (mainly US) companies both to extract monopoly rent from their asset power and to control the amount and type of technology transferred and the conditions attached to it. By contrast, in resource-based developing countries, concern was directed to areas of their perceived comparative advantage, that is, the production of primary products. Here, it was feared not only that MNEs might not always pursue production and marketing strategies in the interest of recipient countries, but, by choosing to process minerals, raw materials and foodstuffs in their home countries, that they were also limiting the possible benefits of technology transfer. In this connection, faced with the colonialism of the past and newly found political independence, some developing host countries took rather more drastic steps than their European counterparts in their exercise of bargaining power, and the late 1950s and 1960s saw a spate of nationalizations and expropriations.[13]

PHASE 5: 1965–85

In many respects, the last twenty years have been the most interesting regarding the evolution of the MNE and its position in the world economy. No less interesting has been the marked and rapid growth of the technological ability of countries and the extended sphere of government fiat.

Let us very briefly recount the main events of the period. First, although there has been a slowing down in the rate of increase in MNE activity, there has been an acceleration in the extent of technological creation and dissemination. This speeding up, however, only applies to some parts of the world, and for most of the period respresents a catching up process with the USA. By the late 1970s new industrial leaders such as Japan were generating their own advances, for instance, in the fields of computer and robot technology, consumer electronics and optic firms,

Market Power and Technology Transfer

while the USA, possibly stimulated by greater competition to its own MNEs, and compensating for the declining investment in defence and space research, was making marked advances in micro-chip, biotechnology, and information technology. Those years have also witnessed increasing competition among MNEs, and a reduction in the transaction costs of most kinds of technology. Moreover, the sources of commercial information and knowledge have widened, while the capacity of both developed and developing countries either to generate their own technology or to use the technology available on the market has improved dramatically, particularly in the larger Latin American and rapidly industrializing Asian developing countries. Again, as regards much of the earlier investment in manufacturing industry by MNEs, the products initially supplied and their technology of production have now become standardized; as a result, price competition has become more widespread and MNEs are less able to exert their asset power.

These and other related events have had two consequences: first, they have reduced the transaction costs for the transfer and/or creation of many kinds of knowledge; second, they have improved the bargaining capabilities of host governments vis-à-vis MNEs. As a result, in many sectors, particularly those producing standardized products with mature technology, contractual resource flows, such as technical assistance agreements, management contracts, turnkey operations, etc., are replacing FDI as the main modality of foreign involvement. In retrospect this was to be expected, and it is entirely consistent with the idea of a technology cycle put forward by Magee (1981), although the extent to which it has occurred is dependent on both industry and country-specific circumstances.

At the same time, the concentration among MNEs, as opposed to that of particular products supplied by MNEs, has continued to increase. This is partly explained by the continual innovation of MNEs into new product or process lines. But it is also a consequence of their diversification in order to exploit transaction cost economies. This, in turn, has taken several forms. The first has been diversification through innovation, where new and old products exist side by side. The second is where new products or processes are acquired through takeovers or mergers. Both of these give rise to transaction cost economies by widening the range of products or associated activities. The third is by backward or forward process diversification. The fourth is a relocation of some activities which has had the effect of vertical diversification between parent and subsidiary, that is, the rationale of export processing zones and the centralization of technology creating activities in industrially advanced countries. The fifth is less diversification *per se* as a rationalization of existing diversification, but, in some respects, it is the most interesting of the reasons for the growth of MNEs. This is typified by what has happened to the EEC and other free trade areas. Here, affiliates are treated as part of an integrated production and marketing mandate for the region, and to take advantage of the economies of scale, each plant is assigned a specific function or functions which are not

42 *Multinationals, Technology and Competitiveness*

duplicated elsewhere. Trade takes place between the affiliates, either of intermediate or financial products. The division of labour practised by IBM, Philips, Ford, International Harvester, and Honeywell falls into this category. In such cases, the MNE has the fiat not only over what should be produced and where, but also over the kind of technology which is transferred, the markets to be served and the terms on which these exchanges take place. Following its counterpart in the primary product sector, the discretionary power of the manufacturing MNE has shifted from its monopoly over the assets or over rights being transferred to the economies of integration or scale derived from the international allocation of its activities. Each plant or firm is treated as a branch whose interests are subordinate to the whole.

It may be asked as to whether or not this matters. For surely the MNE is simply doing what the market should be doing. Rather than produce A, B and C in countries X, Y and Z, each for sale only to the local market, does it not make sense to produce A in X, B in Y, etc., and sell each to all countries? The answer depends on the difference it makes as to who *owns* these separate facilities. If each were operated as a separate entity and the results were exactly the same, the answer would be No. But, if being under the same governance it does, then the answer may be Yes. Caves (1980) argues that it does matter, and that MNEs, by their co-ordination of interdependent activities, help to make resource allocation more efficient than it would otherwise be. Williamson (1981) also emphasizes the role of MNEs as transaction cost economizers across national boundaries. An alternative hypothesis is that while MNEs may perform a useful arbitrage function, wherever transaction power is used to advance defensive oligopolistic behaviour or promote behaviour or to advance the interests of the MNE at the expense of one of its affiliates, the net benefit accruing to particular host countries may be minimal.[14]

Which of these views is correct is a matter for empirical investigation, and is strongly dependent on the strategic behaviour of both governments and MNEs. What cannot be ignored, however, are the distributional consequences of the action of MNEs, and the effects which these may have on the economic and social goals of individual countries. In other words, the integrative behaviour on the part of an MNE will only produce a pattern of international economic activity acceptable to all countries in which it operates if its objectives are the same as those of these countries, and it either operates in a near-perfect market or is shown to be a more efficient allocator than the market. Certainly, the location of technological capacity would be evaluated from this perspective, yet the MNE cannot be expected to allocate its activities so as to promote each and every country's dynamic comparative advantage. *Inter alia* the costs of economic restructuring and resource adaptation may be too great for it to bear. Social costs and benefits are not the same as private costs and benefits; hence, the disposition of resources as perceived by governments and by international companies may be very different.

The conclusion to be drawn from the above paragraphs is that the

Market Power and Technology Transfer 43

hierarchical leverage of the modern manufacturing MNE in particular foreign markets is as different from that of its nineteenth-century equivalent as is the hierarchical leverage of a huge conglomerate in a particular domestic market from a small single product firm. Furthermore, in the absence of government fiat, the consequences of such power for the flow and terms of international technology transfer are likely to be very different from those which might arise if such transactions were conducted between independent parties. With the gradual widening of the transactional role of companies through internalization of intermediate product markets or by product diversification, the focus of discretionary behaviour has switched from the proprietary possessions of any one asset to that which results from the organization of bundles of assets which are synergistic to each other. Such corporate integration has two effects. First, subsidiaries are no longer allowed to operate on an 'every tub has its own bottom' policy; each is judged not by its own profits but by the contribution it makes to the profits of the group as a whole. Second, the MNE's control over the technology transferred will be guided less by what is the appropriate technology to produce this or that particular product and more by the appropriate range of products or processes to produce. This may or may not be what the host country desires any more than the technology MNEs transfer to produce a particular product. However, while in the first case the host country may be able to get what it wants from the spot market, in the second this may not be feasible since its capacity is limited to producing part of a product for which the investing firm supplying is the purchaser.

Rationalized or efficiency-seeking manufacturing investment of the kind just described often originates as import substituting investment; as yet, it is still largely confined to Europe and Latin America, but it may well extend to the Asia-Pacific region in the 1980s. Added to the export platform investment of the region, where a different sort of *dependencia* is created, MNEs continue to exert considerable control over the international transfer of technology. In some cases, for example, in Europe, regional integration has helped curb the adverse effects of corporate integration; in others, for instance, in the Third World, the former may have strengthened the latter (UNCTC, 1982). Within a particular country, however, strong indigenous competition, and government encouragement to foreign affiliates to engage in the sort of activity which is consistent with its long-term economic goals, are the most effective counteracting powers to that of the MNEs. This, however, is often easier said than done. Moreover, not only are developing countries faced with this problem but also some smaller developed countries, notably Canada, where the debate over the role of US subsidiaries in technology transference and generation is still very much alive. At one time it was felt that subsidiaries should be encouraged to do more R & D. This helps to upgrade local labour, but the output is still retained in foreign hands. Current thinking is to encourage more indigenous research in selected areas where Canada sees her future comparative advantage (Rugman, 1981, 1986a).

44   *Multinationals, Technology and Competitiveness*

It is true that, looking back over the last twenty years, governments, either unilaterally or multilaterally, and by a variety of control devices ranging from legislation to codes of conduct, guidelines and monitoring performance of foreign affiliates, have sought to reduce the adverse effects of MNE behaviour. Yet, it is by no means certain that governments have always been the main, or even an important, cause of what has happened; much more important has been the general improvement of markets for many kinds of technology, and the realization on the part of many MNEs that relinquishing some part of rights in foreign countries does not necessarily reduce their capacity to capture the full economic rent on that technology. Even less is it likely that power resides in the control of technology, or, indeed, in many aspects of behaviour of foreign affiliates which have caused code makers so much anguish. What one has seen in the last decade or more is the growth of integrated MNEs in the manufacturing sector, and some service sectors such as banking, hotels and advertising, which surpasses, in terms of control over the assets transferred, anything which took place earlier in the natural resource sector; yet this new form of the 'visible hand' is very much more difficult for governments to get to grips with, without detriment to some of their long-term economic goals.[15]

At least in one respect, however, the leverage of the host government is increased: that is, where prosperity of the parent system is dependent on any one affiliate, the costs of disruptions in that affiliate may make the MNE more, rather than less, vulnerable to the actions taken by host governments. But power to disrupt is very different from the ability to encourage MNEs to conform with long-term industrial and technological strategy. Indeed, it is such a strategy, which has not always been well formulated or articulated, that is becoming one of the focal points of concern of many industrialized and industrializing countries in the 1980s.[16] For the rest, we would foresee a gradual dissemination of an increasing proportion of the world's technological stock, with a fall in the discretionary power of any one institution to exert monopoly rents from its own part of that stock. This proportion will obviously vary according to the speed and distribution of technological advance but, with the growth of the NICs, the hope for the least advanced developing countries is that the kind of technology they need will be increasingly obtainable from many MNEs (including those from other developing countries) and/or in the market place. The real constraint on economic progress is likely to be in the ability of the acquiring countries to absorb, adapt and maintain that technology to their own requirements.

NOTES

1   For an analysis of country-specific factors affecting the balance of equity and non-equity involvement by foreign firms, see Contractor (1980) and Dunning (1988).

2   We use technology in the broadest sense to embrace all forms of knowledge

Market Power and Technology Transfer 45

which may affect the production and transactional capabilities of the user firm.

3 For a succinct review of the early history of MNEs, see Wilkins (1974b) and Wilson (n.d.).

4 According to Streit (1949), of the 327 important inventions discovered between 1750 and 1850, Britain was responsible for 38 per cent, France for 24 per cent, Germany for 12 per cent, and the USA for 16 per cent. In the following half-century, the corresponding figures were 16 per cent, 19 per cent, 21 per cent and 32 per cent. See also Dunning (1988), Chapter 3.

5 In the case of the American republic, very generous incentives were offered to British firms and personnel to set up business (Coram, 1967).

6 For further details, see, e.g. Wilkins (1974b), Nicholas (1982) and Stopford (1974).

7 For example, Svedberg (1982) reports that 'at certain times and within some of its colonial territories, all foreign investment from the non-Francophone world was excluded'.

8 See especially Chandler (1977, 1986).

9 As described in Chandler (1977). The 'M' form of organization was not adopted widely by US firms until the 1945–60 period and not until late in the 1960s by European companies. Franko (1976) suggests that the initiation of the EEC and the post-war penetration by US MNEs were important contributing factors to the reorganization which has since taken place.

10 In product cycle terms, firms were moving from the innovation to the commercialization stage via foreign direct investment rather than by exports.

11 To some extent, this applied to foreign investments in manufacturing which grew out of trading investment; this form of involvement was preferred to licensing and other contractual arrangements, because there was insufficient technological capacity to guarantee product quality and/or patent protection.

12 It is interesting that other writers (e.g. Baranson, 1976) have argued that US foreign investment in high technology industries has helped erode the home country's comparative advantage. See also chapters by Dunning and Hawkins in Sagafi-Negad, Moxon and Perlmutter (1981).

13 As described in UNCTC (1978). In this period, not only did host governments see more clearly than ever before the ways in which MNEs might misuse their economic power (in terms of the resource allocative activities of their affiliates and the extraction of economic rent), but, for the first time, they took steps to minimize these abuses. During this era both developed and developing countries became more selective regarding the entry conditions for foreign direct investment and imposed constraints on the conduct of foreign affiliates. However, while most developed countries focused on controlling the asset power on MNEs by the above measures and by fostering indigenous competition, some developing countries were forced to resort to nationalization and expropriation of foreign affiliates in key sectors in order to stop what they perceived to be a misuse of both asset and transaction power.

14 For a critical view of the internalization policies of MNEs, see a paper by Constantine Vaitsos for the UNCTC (UNCTC, 1982).

15 For a discussion of the effectiveness of unilateral and multilateral policies towards foreign direct investment, according to the 'response elasticity' of the investing company (which itself is a function of the asset and transaction power), see Chapter 14 of Dunning (1981).

16 Particularly in the case of some newly industrialized countries seeking to upgrade their industrial structure, while the developed countries are seeking avenues to exploit their comparative advantage.

Chapter Four

Multinational Enterprises, Technology Transfer and National Competitiveness

INTRODUCTION

This chapter considers some aspects of the impact of international technology transfers and the activities of MNEs on the competitiveness of home and host economies. We use the word technology in the generic sense to embrace all forms of know-how, including software technology, such as organizational and managerial skills, which may affect the production function and transactional efficiency of firms.

International production involves technology transfers which take place within the same enterprise; in such cases the ownership of the technology remains with the transferor. This is likely to result in different patterns of resource usage and allocation from those which would result in an arm's length transaction for two reasons. First FDI almost always involves the transfer of a package of interrelated technologies (for example, a particular drug formula is likely to be accompanied by processing and marketing know-how); second, by internalizing sales or purchases, which would otherwise be undertaken by independent economic agents, FDI saves on transaction costs.

Unlike an external transfer of technology, one within the MNE impinges not only on the production of individual processes of goods or services but also on the type of goods produced and on the synergistic effects between multiple activities within the firm.

SOME THEORETICAL ISSUES

In a closed economy, made up of a large number of single-activity[1] firms producing under perfectly competitive conditions, each firm would be maximizing its own technical and price efficiency, that is, it would be producing on the right production function, minimizing its costs and selling its output at prices which allow it to earn only normal profits. Moreover, in the absence of any kind of barriers to entry, the disposition of resources between firms would be at its optimum, that is, it could not be improved by any marginal redeployment. Each resource within the economy would be doing the task which it was *comparatively* best suited to do; market failure – in the sense *either* that any one firm possessed some degree of monopolistic leverage, based upon the privileged possession of a particular asset or group of assets, *or* that transactions of any good or service undertaken by the market could be more efficiently undertaken by private administrative hierarchies – would not exist.[2]

Next, suppose there are two economies with similar features to those just described, except that the pattern of resource endowments in each is different. One might be relatively labour abundant and the other relatively raw material abundant. Assume, too, that the resources are immobile between the countries but the products produced by them are not. Technology is assumed to a costless and freely mobile intermediate product. In such a case, neo-classical trade theory suggests that each country could improve its economic well-being by a reallocation of its resources until the comparative advantage of each was adjusted to the new opportunities offered by trading its products with the other. Observe, however, that one implication of such trading is that the competitive position of individual sectors of any one economy (that is, their contribution to the GNP) may have changed; this does *not* mean that they have become less or more efficient; simply that, for the maximum combined output of the two economies to be achieved, a redeployment of resources is necessary.

Even this simple illustration suggests that there is no absolute criterion by which competitiveness of a firm or an industry – or indeed a country – may be judged; it all depends on the opportunity costs of the resources involved. As the number of trading countries is increased, so further realignment of resources is likely to occur. At the same time, the share of any one country of the trade of all countries is likely to fall because more countries are trading. The fact that the UK's share of world manufacturing exports has fallen over the last half-century need not, in itself, be a cause for concern; neither need its falling export share of particular products. To be meaningful, national competitiveness must be related to some perceived optimum or best attainable X- and sectoral efficiency, rather than to the perceived performance of another country. It is only the difficulty of making this evaluation, while comparative performance data on other firms, industries, or countries are often available, that leads one to measure competitiveness in this way. And certainly where care is taken to compare like with like, such comparisons may yield useful results.

In practice, of course, the assumptions underlying the analysis of the previous two paragraphs do not apply. For various reasons, including those to do with imperfections of markets and the different objectives of firms, both X-inefficiency and structural misallocation of resources do exist in an economy. At an international level, natural and artificial barriers to trade, and government intervention in the pricing and output decisions of firms,[3] weaken the application of the principle of comparative advantage as a guide to the desired pattern of resource allo-

MNEs, Technology Transfer and Competitiveness

cation between countries, or as an indicator of performance in particular sectors. Moreover, efficiency considerations are not the only criteria used by governments for evaluating the welfare effects of resource allocation; questions of equity and sovereignty may be no less relevant. Competitiveness in such situations becomes an extremely elusive concept to define.

When one introduces dynamic elements into the picture, for example, technological innovations, the situation becomes even more complex. This is primarily because of the nature of technology. Neo-classical economics assumes it to be a free intermediate product, instantaneously transferable between firms and over space. But this is obviously not the case. Technology is often expensive to produce and, although once produced it takes on many of the characteristics of a public good, it is often quite costly to transfer and disseminate (Teece, 1977). Moreover, due to patent legislation and other barriers to entry, a lot of technology once produced becomes the specific property of economic agents, and, should the owner so choose, may not be made available to other firms or countries. So production functions of firms producing similar goods may differ both within and between countries, and X-inefficiency may arise, which will last as long as one firm retains an advantage over another and keeps it to itself.

The concentration of the ownership and production of technology and technological capacity – as, for example, described by Mansfield (1974) – has been shown greatly to affect both the performance of firms and industries and also the distribution of economic activity between countries. We are not concerned at this point as to the mechanism by which this is achieved. Here, it is worth observing that technological advances not only affect products produced by firms and the efficiency with which they are produced but also the scope of firms' activities and the way in which these are organized.

Indeed, some commentators (for instance, Chandler, 1977) would assert that the impact of technology on the way in which output is organized *among* firms has been a more important factor affecting industrial and national competitiveness than its impact on the productive efficiency of individual producers. The clearest outcome of organizational change has been the growth of large firms, by way of the diversification of activities which would otherwise be co-ordinated among independent firms by the market. This has been brought about, first, by the growth of market failure in intermediate products, and end products requiring after-sales servicing and maintenance and, with this, the consequential increase in buyer or seller firms by some form of vertical integration. Second, due *inter alia* to the nature of production processes, particularly the growth of tangible and intangible overheads of a firm, capable of being put to alternative use at low or zero marginal costs, there has been growing interdependence and complementarity in the use of some resources. This has prompted firms to capture the benefits of synergy and utilize surplus capacity by widening the scope of their activities in a way in which the market (or brokers in the market)

50 *Multinationals, Technology and Competitiveness*

cannot. Within an economy, the pursuance of these goals may lead to the concentration of firms, while technical economies of scale or improvements in production functions may lead to the concentration of plants or the output of a particular product.

Because of the leverage which both asset and transaction power confers, its impact on competitiveness is difficult to isolate. Suffice to say that, from the mid-nineteenth century onwards, advances in technology have not only pushed the limits of plant size outward, but, in order to employ their fixed assets properly, firms have been forced to protect their supplies and markets by vertical integration, and to engage in more output diversification.

Even so, in an economy which engages in no trade in (disembodied) technology, and in which there is no inward or outward direct investment, both the efficiency of a given activity and the allocation of resources between different activities reflects the extent and distribution of asset power and the way in which goods and services are transacted, that is, within private hierarchies, by government measures or by the market. Moreover, since consumers have different tastes and value product variety, markets are often not large enough for firms to produce at the optimum scale of plant within a competitive market structure; since, too, product innovation may best be undertaken under non-competitive conditions, it may be exceedingly difficult to interpret the extent to which either micro or macro competitivenss may, or should, be improved. Neither are we convinced that the usual measures of competitiveness are meaningful for policy-makers. We shall return to this point later.

TECHNOLOGY TRADED THROUGH THE MARKET

Taking things as they are, what difference does it make to an economy if it can import and export knowledge and engage in international production?

Let us first consider knowledge traded on the open market between independent firms. Knowledge, of course, may be embodied in goods or traded as an intermediate service. In practice, there may be no hard and fast dividing line between technology as an input into a production function, for example, a particular component for a machine, and something which changes that function. For often, accompanying intermediate products and capital goods, will come instruction manuals, after-sales servicing and maintenance facilities, and often management and technical assistance as well.

Assuming one can delineate technology as an intermediate service in its own right, however, the main effects of opening it up to trade are threefold. First, it may improve X-efficiency of the recipient firm; second, because its impact will not fall evenly in the economy, it will cause a reallocation of resources between sectors; third, it may alter the competitive position of sectors between countries and thus cause a

MNEs, Technology Transfer and Competitiveness

further reallocation of resources to profit from international trade. In a world of rapid technological change, yet one in which at least some resources are non-tradeable, these effects, in the short run at least, may be destabilizing.

A number of writers have attempted to incorporate technology in their explanations of trade between countries. These vary from the neo-technology and product-cycle theories (Hufbauer, 1970; Vernon, 1966), which purport to explain how the structure of trade will vary according to a country's capabilities of generating technology – treating such capabilities like other resources – to those which examine the impact of technology transfer on the welfare of sending and recipient nations.

Among the latter, one might especially mention Kiyoshi Kojima in his efforts to formulate a macroeconomic theory of FDI (Kojima, 1978). In fact, although Kojima uses FDI as the modality of international technology transfer, most of his analysis is equally applicable to externalized transfers. This is because he is primarily interested in evaluating the impact of FDI on the productive efficiency of the recipient country rather than on the consequences of bypassing intermediate product markets to minimize transaction costs and capturing any external benefits associated with such transactions. Nevertheless, he argues that this might not operate in either the home or the host country's interests in cases where the investment is undertaken either in response to government intervention in the market, for example, by way of trade barriers, export subsidies, foreign investment controls, etc., or as a form of defensive oligopolistic strategy practised by MNEs to safeguard their international market positions. In such instances, it is possible that the wrong kind of technology is transferred – wrong in the sense that neither international resource allocation nor X-efficiency is improved. Moreover, any anti-competitive tactics by MNEs may have undesirable effects on the industrial structure of the host country which, in turn, may inhibit indigenous technological capacity – as is claimed to be the case in Canada, for instance.

Kojima also argues that transfer of technology under these conditions is quite different from that which is intended to take advantage in changing comparative advantage. In this case vertical FDI may assist the development of sectors in host countries by providing them with capital and technology necessary efficiently to exploit those indigenous (and immobile) resources in which they are well endowed. At the same time FDI helps release capacity in the home country for it to concentrate on the production of goods which require resources in which they have a comparative advantage.

Here FDI is regarded as a conduit by which mobile factors of production (for instance, capital) and/or intermediate services (for instance, technology) are steered internationally to those locations which offer the immobile resources which can be combined most effectively with these factors. Although technology is not perceived as a free good, it is thought of as something which can be readily transferred at a price, either through the market or internally within the organization owning

52 *Multinationals, Technology and Competitiveness*

the technology. To this extent, it is the distribution of country-specific immobile endowments, together with the world availability and price of the mobile factors, which determines international resource allocation.[4]

The impact of international transfer of technology on national competitiveness then rests on:

(1) the conditions under which technology is transferred;
(2) the organizational form of its transference; and
(3) the absorptive capacity and economic characteristics of the sending and recipient countries.

Under near competitive conditions, trade in technology can only act to improve the quantity or quality of goods produced in the world, and, over time, to increase the welfare of both host and home countries as they seek to reallocate their resources to meet new patterns of comparative advantage. As in other kinds of trade, any problems which might arise from technology trade are not ones of efficiency but of equity, and, as long as the technology is transferred via the market, there will be no sovereignty issues, except in so far as the transfer results in a redistribution of economic power between nation-states (Gilpin, 1975).

The extent to which a country's competitiveness is affected by trade in technology will also depend on its existing technological capabilities and economic performance. In some cases, the effects of technology will be primarily on restructuring with comparatively minor benefits to national welfare; in other cases, where a country has been performing well below its economic potential, the technological impact may be pronounced – for good or bad.[5] Hence, in the 1960s, we saw the inflow of US technology into Germany and Japan having a much more dramatic effect on the prosperity of those countries than its equivalent in the UK; similarly, in the 1970s, technological imports have had a much greater impact on the economies of South East Asia than their counterparts in Southern Europe, most of Africa, and Latin America. But here there are other country-specific factors to take into account, such as those identified in the environment system and policies (ESP) paradigm and outlined in Chapter 1.

Technology obtained through the market initially affects the X-efficiency of the recipient firm; normally one would expect a buying firm to go on purchasing technology as long as its price (or marginal cost) is less than the marginal revenue it expects to gain from its use. But there may be structural consequences as well. To yield the fullest benefits, the market may need to be large, and there may have to be appropriate back-up facilities, for example, for its efficient absorption, deployment and maintenance. In smaller recipient countries, this may lead to industrial rationalization via mergers and takeovers, which could lessen competition. In other cases, technology imports might stimulate other indigenous firms which do not have the capacity to produce the technology for themselves to acquire it through the licensing route.

A second-stage effect of the import of technology is the way it spills

MNEs, Technology Transfer and Competitiveness 53

over to the rest of the economy outside the recipient firm – mainly through competition and subcontracting. The literature – particularly the earlier literature on FDI – provides copious examples of the way in which host countries have gained through the dissemination of such technology;[6] it is worth noting, however, that the effect of externalized technology flows, for example, through licensing, management contracts, technology-assistance agreements, franchises, etc., have not been studied in the same way Several OECD studies of the impact of MNEs on the technological and scientific capacity of the computer, pharmaceutical and food products sectors concentrate on the way technology transferred by MNEs has affected the growth and structure of the recipient industry – a kind of *horizontal* impact. *Inter alia* they show that a lot depends on the existing structure of the industry (or some perceived 'optimum' structure), given the potential markets and supply of inputs offered by the recipient economy. The *vertical* impact of MNEs, for example, on subcontractors and industrial purchasers, is considered in early studies of Dunning (1958), Brash (1966) and Safarian (1966), and in many sectoral case studies since.[7]

In practice, the success or otherwise of technology trade, as with foreign technology incorporated into domestic production, rests on the capacity of the recipient economy both to absorb it and to make the consequent necessary structural adjustments in its resource usage. As another OECD study has shown (OECD, 1981), much depends on the macroeconomic employment and industrial and competition policies pursued. It also depends on the speed at which the effects of the new technology are felt.

Two often voiced concerns on the part of developing countries are, first, the undesirable effects of importing the wrong kind of technology at too high a price, and, second, the fear of the disruptive effects of the uncontrolled export of technology on domestic employment, and the failure of the home economy to promote adequate or appropriate training, redeployment and relocation policies. It is worth observing that this is partly a country-specific factor and is related both to the prosperity of the country and its institutional flexibility, the better records of adjustment of Japan and Sweden compared with the USA being cases in point. This issue is explored in more detail in Chapter 8.

It is also worth repeating that part of the problem of technology transfer lies in its distributional consequences. To this extent, technology export is like a capital export; it benefits the owners of the asset rather than those of other factors of production, though it may, through its efficiency, structural and spillover effects also benefit the latter. When the returns to technology are captured in the profits or dividends of the exporting firm (as property income) it does not appear as part of the gross domestic product (GDP); indeed, this might fall as GNP rises. We believe that the concept of national competitiveness should be defined in terms of GNP rather than GDP, and return to this point in a later section of this chapter.

TECHNOLOGY TRANSFERS WITHIN THE MNE

Let us now consider transfers of technology within the MNE. Here, technology remains the property of the transferor; it is for the owner concerned to do what he or she likes with it. The difference this makes captures the essence of the difference between internalized and externalized technology flows.

Why, then, should an exporter of technology wish to use the technology transferred differently from an independent technology importer? Why, indeed, should there be a wish to internalize the sale? That internalized technology transfer is still the preferred modality of commercial transfers is shown by the fact that about 75 per cent of the royalties and fees for technology received by UK and US firms are from the foreign affiliates in which they have a direct investment stake; only the balance represented arm's length transfers, and even in these cases it is not unusual for conditions on the use of the technology to be part of the terms of sale.

The literature suggests that a firm may wish to maintain control over the use of technology exported partly to avoid the transaction costs and/or risks associated with its sale to an independent firm and partly so it may internalize any gains such an export may bring to the rest of the enterprise (that is, external to the particular transfer and/or the recipient firms); these are the economies of synergy or complementarity between separate activities.

Transaction costs of using the market, which result from some type of market failure, are greatest where the technology is idiosyncratic and non-codifiable, where *ex ante* the benefits are difficult to identify, where the risk of dissipation is high, where price discrimination cannot be practised, where there are high search and/or negotiating costs, where it is difficult to enforce contracts or monitor the activities of purchasers, and/or to guarantee quality control necessary to protect the supplier's reputation, for example, in the case of trademarks. These costs tend to be high in the case of new and advanced technology and where the transactions are between countries at different stages of industrial development, and with different cultural and social perceptions, business customs and legal systems. The risks attached to the erosion of proprietary rights, the creation of which often involves the investment of substantial R & D, cause firms to internalize their foreign transfers, via foreign production rather than licensing.

The desire to minimize transaction costs of international markets in intermediate products and services is the chief reason for FDI compared with non-equity technological transfers; of itself, it may not cause the recipient's resource allocation or X-efficiency to be any different from a licensing or franchising arrangement. On the other hand, where the owner of the technology genuinely believes that the kind of technology which needs to be transferred cannot be externalized, or can only be deployed to the best advantage of the transferor by FDI, then the transfer will have a different effect on the recipient firm and the sector of

MNEs, Technology Transfer and Competitiveness 55

which it is part. This particularly applies in the case of production or organizational systems – or where the know-how transferred cannot be easily codified.

The second reason why FDI may be a preferred route for technology transfer is that the goals of the purchaser may be inconsistent with those of the seller. This is not just a question of the price paid for the technology. Where, apart from the profits earned, the actions of an affiliate are perceived not to affect the rest of the organization of which it is a part, then control by the parent company is only needed to ensure the efficiency of the affiliate is maximized. Where, however, to achieve an MNE's overall objectives, a resource-allocative strategy is called for which may not necessarily advance the interests of its affiliate, then clearly governance of that affiliate is required for a different reason. When might this dichotomy of interests occur?

Consider just three examples. The first is where an MNE operates just one foreign affiliate which manufactures an identical product (for instance, a toilet soap) to that produced in the home country, and sells it in the local market. Let us suppose that, left to itself, the subsidiary would purchase a particular type of packaging machine from a local supplier; however, the parent firm may decree that it buys a dearer packaging machine from its own workshops simply because the loss of the profit is more than outweighed by the profit earned on the machine. A further reason for preferring the latter action might be where a higher than arm's length transfer price for the export of the machine was perceived to be in the parent company's best interest, perhaps for tax purposes.

The second example concerns the decision of whether to manufacture a particular product in country A or country B. On strict cost minimization criteria, country A may offer the best opportunities, but, again, should the spillover effects on the rest of the organization be more favourable if production is sited in country B, then this latter location may well be preferred.

The third example is the more typical of the essence of multinationality. Where the parent company has a particular product, process and marketing strategy for a particular region of the world, any transfer of technology is related to that strategy. This strategy may be very different from that for a particular country in isolation from the rest of the region or world. In essence, corporate integration follows regional or international integration. When the economics warrant it, this may result in a very different division of labour or specialization from where each affiliate has to satisfy only its domestic market with a range of products. It is based upon taking advantage of economies of plant scale and the organization of the location of production so as to achieve world profit maximization.[8] The transfer of technology will then be in accordance with this strategy and may be different than if the plants were autonomous or self-contained units. The development of intra-European plant specialization by American MNEs consequent upon the advent of the EEC is the best example of a strategy designed to capture both the advantages of scale

56 *Multinationals, Technology and Competitiveness*

and of synergy. Backward and forward vertical integration has the same intention, though the nature of transactional gains may be different.

The question may then be asked: How far is such a strategy very different from that which would have occurred in any case? Is the development of horizontal hierarchies less the result of FDI *per se* and more a response to regional integration which makes such rationalization profitable? In other words, supposing the plans now under the ownership of an MNE were under separate ownership, would the result be any different? As the previous chapter has shown and according to Caves (1980) and Williamson (1981) the answer is probably 'yes'.

Caves argues, from some research on US MNEs in Canada, that the common governance of resources had made for a more efficient disposition of investment due to the lower transaction costs and greater externalities than would accrue in the case of independent firms.[9] Williamson, while accepting the possibility of increased monopoly power which arises from product or process integration, asserts that there is only a slight likelihood of this outweighing the efficiency effect associated with avoiding the costs of the market. Both writers, of course, tend to view efficiency gains from a world aspect, rather than that of an individual country. Both, too, pay little heed to the impact of MNE activity on dynamic comparative advantage.

It is these elements which commentators, most critical of the control exerted by MNEs (Hymer, 1970; Vaitsos, 1979), tend to emphasize – particularly with respect to the location of technological capacity, restrictions placed on the use of technology transferred and the inappropriateness of that technology. Sometimes, of course, there are other than economic efficiency criteria involved in this criticism[10], but in most cases it is argued that the international division of labour practised by international oligopolists will not necessarily be that which optimizes world welfare in a static or dynamic sense, let alone that of a particular nation-state.

In consequence, as an agent for transferring technology, the MNE may occasion a different level and pattern of resource allocation than that which would result from externalized transfers or, indeed, from indigenously created technology. This is because the know-how transferred, and the terms on which it is transferred, will be evaluated by what is good for the parent group, and the motives for such a transfer are less to promote the productive efficiency of the transferee and more to economize on the cost of international market transactions by internalizing these within the MNE. The more geographically diversified or integrated the firm is, the more likely its growth, and hence its technological strategy, will be influenced by these latter gains as opposed to minimizing X-efficiency.

THE INFLUENCE OF MNEs ON NATIONAL COMPETITIVENESS

How, then, might the MNE influence a country's competitiveness? First consider the competitiveness of the recipient nation. Depending on the role and direction of government intervention, the stage of its economic development, its structure of markets and nature of international competition faced by MNEs, the inflow of technology may or may not raise X-efficiency and reallocate resources in accord with the principle of comparative advantage. Where it does, it immediately draws the host economy more fully into international commerce and makes it more economically interdependent.

Where, however, the wrong economic signals are given by host governments, and MNEs operate within a monopolistic or oligopolistic environment with their goals geared more towards protecting market shares rather than to profit maximization, then technology imports may both lower X-efficiency and lead to a sub-optimum allocation of resources between firms or sectors. Moreover, even if X-efficiency were raised, if the whole of the gains are recouped by the foreign firms, then the host country is not better off.

From a dynamic perspective, the tendency of the international division of labour fashioned by private enterprise is to perpetuate the existing allocation of resources, except where the marginal private costs of reallocation are more than covered by the anticipated gains. But the price of restructuring economic activity, for example, upgrading and relocating human capital and the capital costs of penetrating new markets, may sometimes be too great for private enterprise to bear. Hence, for an industrializing country to make any technological progress requires not only 'tutorial' technology to be acquired from abroad but for the host government to undertake the necessary investment in educating and training the labour force, and providing the infrastructure for privately financed technological capacity. (It is worth recalling that all industrialized countries spend very large sums of public money in the support of private R & D.) No less may public assistance be required in the restructuring of mature industrialized countries in their efforts to cope with shifts in comparative advantage away from some of the products in which they excelled in the past.

The dilemma is that, if foreign affiliates gain a foothold in the supply of products incorporating the technology of their parent companies, then, although the recipient country may have a potential comparative advantage in producing these products, because of the high costs of entry and/or market limitations, there may not be the incentive for local firms to do so. Encouraging the MNE to decentralize R & D may be one way out of the dilemma, but only in so far as this aids the development of local innovatory capacity.

There are some exceptions to this among both developed and developing countries, and it is certainly true that a growth in intra-industry FDI has led to some dispersal of technological capacity among the larger industrialized countries. For every UK and Germany, however, there are many more Swedens and Canadas – and Canada in particular is reappraising inward direct investment from the viewpoint of how this affect's Canada's long-term dynamic advantage and industrial competitiveness.

A nation bent on economic self-determination and technological autonomy is not likely to accept the kind of argument set out above, for the simple reason that it believes that any benefits of international specialization are more than outweighed by its costs. For, quite apart from any loss of sovereignty which economic interdependence may bring, the assumptions underlying the principles of classical and neo-classical comparative advantage do not apply in the modern world, nor do they allow for the possible improvements in resource capability through technological innovation.

Countries, indeed, may behave like firms when they find the transaction costs of international involvement too high. Either for political or economic reasons, they may seek to avoid these costs by trading internally. Such perceived costs include the risk of economic instability, often related to high adjustment costs consequential upon changes in supply or demand conditions; uncertainty surrounding the terms of trade; being locked into an unacceptable international economic order and international division of labour, particularly with respect to the procurement of essential raw materials or intermediate products, and/or access to markets, and the political costs of an uneven international distribution of economic power. A policy of isolationism uses the weapon of government regulation to internalize the perceived transaction costs of imperfect international markets. A closed economy has little worry about national competitiveness, except in so far as it judges the performance of its industries in the light of their counterparts in other countries. Even a quasi-closed economy, for example, the Soviet Union, cannot properly gauge its competitiveness, since the usual yardsticks of market prices for valuing inputs and outputs do not apply.

As an economy becomes more open, it implicitly embraces the costs and benefits of international market forces and/or hierarchies as alternative resource allocation mechanisms. One particularly interesting stage is that of regional integration, where governments of participating countries within a particular region agree to relinquish part of their regulatory sovereignty concerning the disposition of resources within the region to market forces, international hierarchies, or supra-national regional authorities.

The interaction between government measures, international hierarchies and markets, and technology transfer (and its effect on national competitiveness) has been inadequately explored in the literature. Here, we are postulating that one not only needs to consider the type and modality of technology transference in relation to the existing resource disposition within a country but also the broader questions relating to economic environment, system, and policies (all country-specific factors) of the sending and recipient countries – the ESP configuration mentioned

MNEs, Technology Transfer and Competitiveness 59

earlier. These latter considerations impinge on the extent to which the technology can be absorbed and disseminated, its effect on industrial structure and restructuring and, through these, on national competitiveness.

Besides the OECD studies mentioned earlier, several studies on the impact of the inflow of technology on competitiveness[11] suggest that stage of development, and especially industrial and technological infrastructure, size of country, degree of openness (measured by percentage of GNP accounted for by international trade), the economic system, and policies pursued by country – especially with respect to education, R & D, competition, industrial organization and FDI – all play an important role.

MEASURING AND INTERPRETING NATIONAL COMPETITIVENESS

We now turn to some considerations affecting the measurement and interpretation of a country's competitiveness. In a closed economy, a common measure of the real value of its resources and the efficiency with which they are used is the value of GDP per head.[12] This is defined as the output produced within the national boundaries of a country divided by the population of that country. The contribution of any sector to GDP is shown by the share of that output accounted for by the sector; the performance or efficiency of a sector is usually measured by its (average) profitability of productivity.

In an open economy, but without any international capital movements, the GDP is equal to the value of output produced within the economy for domestic sale plus exports less imports; this allows us an additional dimension of competitiveness, that is, the performance of the economy or a particular sector, relative to that of other economies or sectors, and/or the extent to which any one sector is a net exporter.[13] If one then wishes to answer the question, 'What is the appropriate allocation of resources between sectors and economies?', one has to normalize trade shares of sectors by average export share, thus obtaining a revealed comparative advantage index (RCA) as defined by Balassa (1965).[14] It should be noted that for this index to be a guide to policy, some assumption has been made about X-efficiency in each sector. The normal supposition is that each firm in each sector is operating at full X-efficiency, that is, on its production frontier, and that resources are appropriately allocated between firms within sectors. In practice, this may not be the case, and a country's GDP may be more appropriately increased by raising the efficiency of firms within particular sectors rather than by allocating more resources to sectors which are perceived to be relatively the most efficient.

Where available, details of the cross-border transfers of disembodied technology between independent parties are contained in the normal trade statistics. However, these are rarely attributed to particular sectors

60 *Multinationals, Technology and Competitiveness*

selling the technology and are never classified in the same detail as the traded goods embodying that technology. Where technology is classified as an intermediate good, it is possible to examine the performance of a country as a producer and trader in technology; what *is* difficult to establish is the extent to which particular sectors which have a comparative advantage in the goods embodying technology derive that advantage from the production of the technology *per se* or the subsequent processes of production.

When a country engages in international investment, then the distinction between GDP and GNP becomes much more important. GNP is output produced by the residents of a country both inside and outside its national boundaries. It is equal to GDP plus income earned overseas by its own residents less income accruing to foreign residents earned within its domestic territory. In theory, the GDP of a country could be zero if the total income of its residents was derived from its overseas assets.

This difference between domestic and national value-added is also relevant at a sectoral level. Take the example of an industry that exports nothing but engages in a great deal of foreign production, for which the return to the investing firm and country takes the form of profits, interest and dividends. In terms of its share of the domestic value-added of the industry, or its revealed comparative advantage in international markets, its performance would be very poor. But recalculating value-added on a national basis, its contribution (when compared with its equivalent in other countries) might be very considerable. Similarly, any international competitiveness index based solely upon the imports and exports of goods may be very different from one which also takes account of the imports and exports of disembodied technology, and the profits and dividends resulting from inward and outward direct investment. Both from a national and a sectoral viewpoint, then, it is important to be clear as to whether one is interested in the value-added activities generated within a national territory independently of *who* produces it, or by that generated by the residents or institutions of a particular country independently of *where* it is located.

Perhaps we might further illustrate this point by referring to some data which are discussed at some length in Chapter 5. In 1957, some 37.0 per cent of the combined exports of Europe and the USA in high and medium technology-intensive manufacturing industries[15] were accounted for by firms based in the USA; by 1965 this proportion had fallen to 27.3 per cent and by 1982 to 25.6 per cent. *Prima facie*, this would suggest that the USA's competitive position in these sectors vis-à-vis that of Europe had fallen considerably. However, when one compares the exports of European *owned* (resident) firms from Europe with the exports of American owned (resident) firms from in the USA and Europe,[16] the respective figures are 42.6 per cent, 35.7 per cent and 35.9 per cent. If one was further to add the exports of disembodied technology (in the form of royalties and fees), between non-affiliated US and European firms to these data, then the figures for 1965 and 1982 would rise a further percentage point.[17]

MNEs, Technology Transfer and Competitiveness   61

According, then, to which interpretation of output one chooses, one's conclusion about a nation's competitive ability may differ. Perhaps, to avoid confusion, one should always prefix 'competitiveness' by 'domestic' or 'national'. But it should also be noted that differences may arise according to whether the *enterprise* (or groups of enterprises) or the *country* is taken as the unit of account.[18] To the firm, market share, growth of sales and profitability are the kind of indices it uses to measure performance independently of the location of activity; to the country, it is value-added, that is, contribution to GNP in relation to the resources used. Hence, as far as FDI is concerned, the home country is only interested in that part of its firm's activities which accrue to it in the form of interest, profits and dividends and as a feedback to the profitability or wealth of the parent company.

SOME EVIDENCE CONCERNING THE IMPACT OF THE TRANSFER OF TECHNOLOGY THROUGH MNEs ON EUROPEAN COMPETITIVENESS UP TO THE MID–1970s

The data presented in Chapter 5 also throw some light on the impact of the transfer of technology through MNEs on the domestic competitiveness of Europe and European firms in the 1960s and early 1970s. Obviously, in so far as a particular sector can better penetrate a foreign market than previously, its dynamic X-efficiency has improved.[19] A lower import penetration should suggest a similar result. Export data show that the most marked improvement in European competitiveness since 1955 has been in the technologically advanced sectors; these are also those in which US FDI is most heavily concentrated. It is also clear that, up to the mid–1960s at least, in most R & D-intensive sectors, for instance, micro-electronics, pharmaceuticals, etc., the US affiliates made most of the running in this improvement.[20] Government measures may have played their part by setting the right ambience for such investment. But in the last fifteen or so years, European indigenous firms, spurred on by the competition from US affiliates and the growing dissemination of technology through licensing and other means, have stepped up their own innovatory activities and have regained some of the markets earlier lost.

As Chapter 6 will show, the extent to which FDI has this effect on a country's competitiveness in part depends on its technological capacity and market structure at the time the investment is made and the extent to which parent MNEs continue to generate new innovations. As is also shown by differences between British and French reactions to inward US investment – especially in the early 1980s – FDI is also influenced by government policy, and especially the extent to which this encourages indigenous firms (including those which are themselves MNEs) not only to be more efficient in the output they produce but also to generate the technological capacity necessary to reproduce that output.

The impact on the competitiveness of indigenous firms (including their own ability to compete as foreign producers), also depends on the strategy of the inward investors and the extent to which the country is part of a customs union of a regional trading bloc.[21] Take the case of Europe again. During the 1950s and early 1960s, US MNEs mainly invested in individual European countries to supply the domestic markets of these countries; the UK was an exception as it provided an entré into the non-dollar Commonwealth market. Much of this early FDI was import-replacing and corresponded well to the post-export phase of the product cycle. However, with the growing stake of US companies in Europe and the removal of trade barriers consequent upon the formation of the EEC, US firms began to rationalize their activities and to engage in product or process specialization in their European plants. Instead of each plant supplying its own market with several products, it concentrated on supplying all (or several) countries in Europe with only one, or a reduced range of, product. In consequence, not only did FDI lead to more exports and imports, it also caused a shift in the revealed comparative trade advantage of particular sectors. The nature and direction of the shift reflected industry- and country-specific factors, the extent of the free trade area and the strategy of individual MNEs.

The changing role of MNEs (via their effect on production efficiency and transaction cost economizing) on the competitiveness of recipient economies is best illustrated in the case of those industries in which there are substantial economies of scope and of plant specialization, for example, motor vehicles, domestic electrical appliances, agricultural machinery and pharmaceuticals. *Inter alia*, this is shown by the very substantial intra-firm and intra-industry trade and direct investment in these sectors in the 1960s and 1970s, both by US and European MNEs. The response by indigenous firms has depended on their ability to adopt a similar strategy or compete with a more limited range of products.

But just as intra-industry trade is not primarily based on the disposition of resource endowments,[22] neither is the pattern of competitiveness resulting from some kinds of international production of MNEs. One writer (Krugman, 1981) has coined the term 'inter-trade' to embrace two rapidly growing types of trade; the one based on *inter*-industry (vertical) specialization of production, for example, as practised by MNEs between their plants in industrial and in newly industrializing developing countries; and the other on *intra*-industry (horizontal) specialization as practised by MNEs within the EEC, LAFTA and North America, to exploit the economies of plant specialization. In each case, the transfer of technology via MNEs and the control of that technology once transferred are crucial elements in determining which countries and sectors gain or lose by the transfer; in each case, too, the pattern of domestic competitiveness in home and host countries is affected by government policy towards industrial restructuring and the nature of the competition which exists between foreign and indigenous companies.

As (some) MNEs become more globally oriented in their marketing and production strategies, so their role in forging linkages between technology creation and transfer, and the competitiveness of nation-

MNEs, Technology Transfer and Competitiveness

states in which they participate, will change. Some of the pertinent issues are taken up in Chapters 6, 9 and 11. Suffice to observe, at this point, that the increasing propensity of large MNEs, especially in technologically advanced industries, to form strategic alliances with each other (Contractor and Lorange, 1988) is both changing the structure of international competition and, by dint of a new kind of cross-border interdependence, forcing governments to redefine their economic boundaries and industrial strategies. The emergence of hierarchical galaxies, comprising multi-technology core firms, surrounded by satellite specialists and suppliers – often located in different countries – is creating a new kind of competitive advantage of firms, which is only country specific in so far as governments are able to provide or support the provision of the infrastructure and supply of suitably trained manpower necessary for a strong indigenous technological capacity. Increasingly, one suspects, in advanced industrial economies at least, the role of *natural* resources in determining the structure of economic activity and comparative advantage will take second place to *engineered* resources,[23] and that the organization of technology creation and dissemination and the willingness of a community to invest in technology, are *the* crucial variables influencing its supply.

SUMMARY AND CONCLUSIONS

Let us now draw the threads of our argument together. Competitiveness is a function of the ability of firms to produce particular goods and services, and the extent to which countries or firms, relative to other countries or firms, have a natural or engineered resource or resource usage advantage in particular sectors. In neo-classical (for example, Heckscher-Ohlin-Samuelson) trade models, technology is assumed to be a free and instantaneously transferable good, intermediate and final product markets work perfectly, all firms are single product profit maximizers, and there is no government intervention. In such conditions, there is no X-inefficiency, transaction costs are zero and all countries produce the kind of goods requiring resources in which they have a comparative advantage. Neither is there any place for trade in technology by FDI. The introduction of a new technology may affect the production frontiers and X-efficiency of firms, but assuming the technology is sector-specific or, at least, affects different sectors differently, its main result will be to alter the pattern of comparative advantage of sectors and countries, and so induce the redeployment of economic activity.

The fact that technology is rarely a free good creates a barrier to its dissemination; this may lead to differences in production functions and X-efficiency between firms and countries, and, hence, a different pattern of resource allocation than the neo-classical model would suggest. Where, too, intermediate or final product markets are imperfect and there are economies of plant size, there may be good reason why the location of

64   *Multinationals, Technology and Competitiveness*

certain activities should be centralized in certain countries. The incorporation of differences in consumer tastes, the economics of scope and the value of product differentiation, open up the possibility of another kind of trade, that is, intra-industry trade (for example, large cars are exported from the USA to Europe and small cars are exported from Europe to the USA). Technological advances, coupled with advertising, may affect the extent and form of product differentiation, the nature of competition between firms and subsequently the ability of any one firm, sector or country to supply a particular market. When account is taken of the impact of government measures on the disposition of resources, it is difficult to adhere to the assumptions underlying the Heckscher-Ohlin-Samuelson model.

Now to all these factors add the component of FDI. FDI is exported control over the use of assets transferred; such control will vary according to the nature of the assets and the strategy and competitive position of MNEs, but it is likely to be geared to the interests of the MNE as a whole. This may affect both the vertical and horizontal distribution of economic activity of an economy and its competitiveness; though how such competitiveness is affected it is not easy to say. Much, as we have already suggested, depends on the technological capabilities of the inventing and recipient countries, the kinds of technology transferred by MNEs and the role of the subsidiaries or contractees of MNEs in the latters' global production and marketing strategies. Generally, one would expect X-efficiency to be raised; one would also anticipate that where the markets for the unique assets possessed by the MNE are highly imperfect, the internal or hierarchical governance will lead to an improvement in the efficiency of resource allocation. On the other hand, efficiency may not be the only criterion for measuring the social benefits of FDI, and it may also be reasonable to suppose that where MNEs operate within an oligopolistic environment they will not necessarily behave in a way which advances economic welfare of either home or host countries. In such cases, government measures may be necessary to counteract the actions of private hierarchies and simulate a situation that might have existed in a perfect market.

Faced with the Hymer/Vaitsos view of MNEs as oligopolists who behave in a way inimical to economic efficiency and welfare, or the Williamson contention that large, integrated companies are likely to be more efficient transactors of resources, only empirical research can establish which is the correct position. As usual, one suspects that circumstances will dictate which view is likely to be the most valid. However, one conceptual difficulty is that while Hymer and Vaitsos seem to judge the efficacy of FDI in terms of some ideal alternative, Williamson evaluates it in terms of the best practical option.[24] What is not in dispute is that, through corporate integration, the impact of MNEs on the transfer of technology, industrial structure and competitiveness has often been decisive. This conclusion holds good for both inward and outward direct investment.[25] In some cases corporate and regional integration have gone hand in hand; in others the MNEs have

MNEs, Technology Transfer and Competitiveness 65

been both the main architects and beneficiaries of integration (UNCTC, 1982).

We conclude this chapter on a more normative note. Assuming, for the moment, the absence of government measures and regulations, can one indicate under what conditions MNEs may aid competitiveness and what might be done to encourage this? We have said that in their absence and accepting the benefits of economic interdependence, countries gain by specializing in the production of those goods and services which require *immobile* factor endowments in which they have a comparative advantage. We have argued that MNEs are a vehicle for moving *mobile* resources – mainly capital and technology (including management and organizational skills) – around the world. Now technology is not a homogeneous good; its attributes reflect the (immobile) resources and market needs of the countries in which its producer resides and/or serves. Even today, apart from some small European countries, and outside the primary sector, most MNEs still largely produce in, and sell to, their home countries.[26] So countries relatively well-endowed with capital but short of labour may generate capital-intensive labour saving innovations, while those relatively well-endowed with labour but short of materials may generate labour-intensive material saving technology. For this reason alone, one would expect the direction of Japanese competitiveness in mobile resources to be different from that of US competitiveness.

Admittedly, not all technology is transferable across national boundaries (Lall, 1980b); but a lot *is*, either through the market or by the innovating company. In some cases, the transfer of technology may have to be internalized simply because there is no international market for it. Much organizational technology is of this kind. For example, the MNE's ability to allocate and integrate the production and sale of many products in many different countries affords it an important ownership advantage over its non-MNE competitors. This advantage, however, is non-marketable; it reflects the MNE's particular ability to reduce the transaction costs on separate, but interrelated, activities, and to exploit market imperfections, and/or government intervention.[27]

So countries which possess these various kinds of technology, but are relatively disadvantaged in the immobile resources necessary to produce products and services embodying the technology, will find it profitable to export that technology 'disembodied', either by FDI or via the market, according to which route allows them to appropriate the highest economic rent. Assuming full employment in both home and host countries, this will enable the immobile resources to be shifted into other sectors which, when combined with either domestic or foreign originated technology, will supply goods to which they are comparatively better suited. Thus inward FDI should bring in the kind of technology in which the country is comparatively disadvantaged but used with resources with which the country is comparatively well-endowed.

In reality, of course, there are a whole set of obstacles to prevent a juxtaposition between the *O* advantages of MNEs and the locational

66 *Multinationals, Technology and Competitiveness*

advantages of countries being deployed in the way suggested. Full employment may not exist, government measures may affect the price and productivity of factors or the purchasing power of consumers; the oligopolistic behaviour of firms may distort market structure and price and output decisions; economic uncertainty and political risk may play havoc with resource-allocation decisions. The goals of countries may include many other variables than the purely economic.

But one has to start somewhere in any analysis, and the link between technology, industrial structure and competitiveness may well be the disposition of immobile but specific intangible assets between firms of different nationalities and the immobile but non-specific resources between countries; with the modality of the transfer of the former, and the effect this has on X and allocative efficiency being of critical importance.

Alternatively, one could begin by assuming a set of national goals, and then examine the consequences of introducing the above variables and the way in which they advance or inhibit these goals. Or one might examine how far the existing competitiveness of a country might be improved by more, by less or by a different kind of trade and international production.

It is this latter exercise which the Japanese and Koreans seem to be tackling the most seriously. As far as we are aware, Japan and Korea are the only two countries which explicitly incorporate foreign direct investment production into their industrial and technological strategies, although several others, for example, Singapore, Taiwan, Canada and Belgium, are now beginning to do so. This is shown by the Japanese government's efforts to encourage the outflow of capital and technology in those sectors in which Japan is perceived to be losing her comparative advantage and encouraging capital and technology into those sectors in which its comparative advantage is thought to be increasing.

But as regards most other countries – including the two largest foreign direct investors (the USA and the UK) – while there is a great deal of talk about structural adjustment to new patterns of international division of labour, there has been little attempt to include non-trade international involvement in the reckoning. Too often technological, industrial, trade and FDI policy are isolated from one another; instead they should be considered as related aspects of a common strategy to ensure the most efficient allocation of resources in an economy, and how these can best adapt to innovations, changes in population and tastes and social planning throughout the world.

NOTES

1 By single activity we mean the production of a particular good or service in which no internal transactions of intermediate products are involved.
2 See Chapter 2 for an elaboration of the distinction between the *asset* and *transaction* power of the firm.

MNEs, Technology Transfer and Competitiveness 67

3 Obvious examples are import tariffs and export subsidies.

4 We shall take up this point later in this chapter.

5 This point is dealt with in some detail in Chapter 6.

6 For an examination of the conditions under which technology imports are most likely to be disseminated see Wilkins (1974a).

7 See especially Germidis (1980), UNCTC (1981), Lim and Fong Pang Eng (1982), Landi (1985).

8 Or some other goal or combination of goals set by the MNE, e.g. maintenance of market share, growth of sales.

9 This is quite apart from the gains in productive efficiency noted again by many researchers on FDI. See, e.g. Parry (1980).

10 To do with the fashioning of consumer tastes and culture, the distribution of incomes, sovereignty, etc.

11 As summarized, e.g. in Parry (1980), Lall and Streeten (1977), Stobaugh and Wells (1985).

12 This means that GDP per head can be increased by raising the value of its resources (e.g. technological capacities) or by improving the efficiency with which the resources are used.

13 Usually measured by exports-imports/exports plus imports.

14 For a definition of RCA, see footnote 5 to Chapter 9 (page 200).

15 Defined as those in which the proportion of sales accounted for by R & D in the USA was 2.0 per cent or more.

16 Unfortunately, no data are available on the exports of European-owned (resident) firms in the USA, but these are thought to be very small.

17 These differences would be much greater if one could take a value-added figure of exports to correspond to what is essentially a value-added figure for technology.

18 For an interesting analysis of the competitive position of US economy with that of US multinational firms, see Lipsey and Kravis (1985, 1987). For a discussion of the ownership advantages of UK firms and the locational advantages of the UK economy, see Chapter 10.

19 An exception is where the price of exports does not reflect the true costs of production, e.g. in the case of dumping.

10 For details of the impact of MNEs on the UK, the semi-conductor and the pharmaceutical industries, see Lake (1976b).

21 This is the subject of a special issue of the *Journal of Common Market Studies* (December, 1987). See also Pelkmans (1984) and Robson (1987).

22 Although how much partly depends on the fineness of the industrial classification.

23 By natural resources we mean the available manpower and physical assets of a country; by engineered resources we mean the way in which these assets may be increased in their income-generating capacity by such means as investment in education and training; investment in R & D; the provision of efficient organizational and support facilities, e.g. telecommunications, etc.; and the attitudes of both consumers and the business community to wealth creation and the distribution of income. The final point to observe is that governments may and do play a crucial role in influencing the extent to which a community is able and willing to engineer resources. For an elaboration of this point, see Scott and Lodge (1985).

24 Though neither pay much attention to government fiat as another form of organization.

25 For a view on how US MNEs have affected the domestic competitiveness of US firms, see Bergsten, Horst and Moran (1978).

26 About 29 per cent of all production by the largest 490 industrial firms in 1982 was undertaken outside their home country (Dunning and Pearce, 1985).
27 For example, international differences in taxation, managed exchange rates, export subsidies, tariff barriers, etc.

Chapter Five

Inward Direct Investment From the USA and Europe's Technological Competitiveness

INTRODUCTION

In a paper presented to the International Economic Association in 1969, which was subsequently published in a volume edited by Charles Kindleberger and Andrew Shonfield (1971), the author sought to estimate the extent to which the technology and managerial gap between the USA and Western Europe, which was causing concern to many European commentators in the late 1950s and early 1960s,[1] had been reduced between 1955 and 1965, and what role (if any) US manufacturing subsidiaries had played in this.

Using the theoretical framework of the produce cycle (Vernon, 1966), the paper argued that, owing *inter alia* to the shortage of US dollars and the desire to gain a foothold in an industrialized region with great potential for growth, US manufacturing firms, which had evolved strong competitive advantages vis à vis European firms during the Second World War, were encouraged to exploit these advantages from a European rather than a US production base. The paper further asserted that this penetration by US affiliates had three related effects. First that it slanted the structure of European industry towards the production of technology-intensive products more, or faster, than would otherwise have been the case; second, that in some sectors it acted as a competitive spur to indigenous European technological capacity; and third, that it helped improve the performance of European located firms in the exports of high technology products, vis à vis US located firms.

This chapter extends the previous statistical analysis to 1982 and adopts a slightly different theoretical underpinning, that is, the eclectic paradigm of international production as developed by the author and set out in Dunning (1977, 1981, 1988).[2] This paradigm states that the level and structure of international economic involvement of enterprise (and hence of countries) is dependent on the following.

70　　　　　　　　　*Multinationals, Technology and Competitiveness*

(1) The extent to which such enterprises, relative to those other nationalities, possess, or can co-ordinate more efficiently, a collection of unique intangible assets or *ownership-specific* advantages, for example, patents and trademarks, management and organizational skills, preferential access to inputs and/or markets and the economies of size and scope.

(2) Whether the enterprises owning the assets are best able to appropriate their economic rents by selling the right of the use of the assets to other enterprises, or by exploiting the intermediate products themselves, that is, *internalizing* their markets; this choice depends largely on the relative transaction costs and strategic advantages of using external and internal markets.

(3) The immobile and specific resource endowments of home and foreign countries, which will determine the attractiveness of alternative *locations* for at least *some* of the production of intermediate as well as finished products based on these assets; such variables include materials, wage and energy costs, transport costs, tariffs and non-tariff barriers, and government intervention.

According to the eclectic paradigm, the international economic involvement of a country may be measured by its visible exports, plus the foreign production of their MNEs, together with the foreign earnings from the export of intangible or invisible assets (or their rights) to unaffiliated foreign firms, for example, royalties and fees, less the equivalent imports of these items. However, the *form* of involvement will depend on the advantages offered by the home country vis à vis any particular foreign country as a value-adding base, and the extent to which transaction costs favour the market or the hierarchical route to exploiting ownership-specific advantages. In turn, the significance of these determinants will vary according to *country-*, *industry-* (or activity) and *firm-*specific factors.

The eclectic paradigm may be applied to different types of FDI and forms of international production, but, as the value of its determinants will be strongly influenced by the structural factors just mentioned, it follows that no one explanation can account for all forms of international involvement.

In this chapter, we are especially interested in a dynamic interpretation of the eclectic paradigm, and in changes in ownership, location and internalization advantages over time. In particular, we need to distinguish between the competitiveness of firms of a particular nationality, irrespective of where the firms are undertaking production, and that of countries, irrespective of the nationality of firms producing in the country.[3] For example, an improvement in the net export performance of the USA in the chemical industry might suggest that US-*owned* firms have become better able to penetrate foreign markets than their international competitors. But a no less plausible inference might be that the USA has become a more attractive location (relative to other countries) to produce chemicals, *or* that the profits to be gained from exporting chemicals have risen relative to the fees from selling the rights to produce chemicals to firms in other countries, or a combination of each of these. In turn, such changes reflect differences in the value of ownership, location or internalization advantages of producing chemicals in the USA and by US firms at home and abroad.

Until recently, the only dynamic approach to our understanding of FDI was the product cycle model (PCM), although Vernon himself now accepts that this is just one possible explanation of how a country's international economic involvement may change over time, and is by no means applicable worldwide (Vernon, 1979). Market size and growth constituted the dynamic element of the theory, which offered a useful explanation of the expansion of US FDI in Europe in the 1960s. Due to the disposition of the endowments of its home country (for instance, high incomes earned in the USA) firms of one nationality are likely to generate or acquire particular kinds of intangible assets more than those of other nationalities. Initially, the innovating firms prefer to internalize the use of their advantages, since it is presumed that their uniqueness makes the market for their rights highly imperfect, that is, that their transaction costs are very high, while the economics of production suggests that, initially at least, this should be sited near the innovating activities. From this it follows that a firm in the first phase of its technology cycle is unlikely to be internationally involved. However, this may change as the firm looks beyond the local market for additional sales, and as the possibility of foreign competitors generating or acquiring similar assets grows.

The eclectic paradigm interprets the next stage of the product cycle as a shift of locational advantages away from the innovating to a foreign country, which is spurred on by a fear of some erosion in the ownership advantages of the innovating firm by other MNEs or foreign firms entering the market. While the PCM has little to say about the choice between using external markets as a modality for the export of the intangible asset (or right to its use) it is implied that, at this stage, the latter route is thought the more likely to guarantee a regular and reliable return on its sunk costs.[4] However, as the unique qualities of the asset are eroded, for example, as the technology and/or management skills become standardized and more easily codified, and/or are copied or assimilated by other firms, then the contractual route of transfer may become more viable, and the form of international involvement changed with it.

The next phase of the product cycle arises if and when the location-specific endowments of the foreign country become sufficiently favourable to allow the affiliate of the innovating firms to export, sometimes in competition with its parent, even to its own home market. The alternative possibility is that the presence of the MNE in the foreign market stimulates local competition and that, in due course, the original ownership advantage of the former is completely eroded.

The eclectic paradigm is more generally applicable to the different

72 — *Multinationals, Technology and Competitiveness*

types of FDI and forms of international involvement than is the PCM and it can also be applied more directly in an analysis of the consequences of inward investment. The PCM, for example, is not very helpful (and was never claimed to be), for explaining FDI in the primary goods sector, for, in this case, exports and foreign production do not compete with each other. The eclectic paradigm, however, can explain why a firm should wish to by-pass the market for its purchases of raw material or intermediate products. Supply uncertainty is just one example of the unacceptable transaction costs of the latter route.

Such resource-based investment was typical of much early FDI, but with the growth of markets and firms (accompanied by a rising cost of R & D and the development of managerial hierarchies) especially in the post-war period, the emphasis shifted to market-oriented FDI, and became concentrated in manufacturing in the developed countries. With regard to US involvement in Europe, the trend led to the evolution (out of import substituting investment) of rationalized, or efficiency-seeking investment. Such investment is intended to capture the gains from the international division of labour, that is, those to do with product or process specialization and the economics of scope and synergy, which arise from producing in economies with a different structure of factor endowments, market characteristics and government involvement; it is typified by MNEs such as Ford, IBM, International Harvester and Honeywell, which engage in corporate integration across European boundaries, and in so doing gain both in production and transaction efficiency. Such co-ordinating economies do not easily fit into the PCM – as it concerns itself with a single economic activity rather than a multiple of activities by firms. The eclectic paradigm, however, explains them by the presence of additional ownership advantages, (which are not saleable on the open market), based upon the common governance of production facilities in different locations.[5]

Because of changes in the size and nature of the European market (particularly that of the EEC) brought about by regional integration, it is not difficult to understand how a group of self-contained production outlets, originally designed to supply the local market with a range of products previously exported from the home country, might be translated into a group of interdependent value-adding activities, each designed to supply a regional market, with a single or limited range of products. Of course, the economics of such corporate integration will depend on a variety of industry-, country- and firm-specific characteristics, while its geographical distribution will depend on location-specific factors (Dunning and Robson, 1987). Unlike import substituting investment, however, it does tend to generate more imports *and* exports for the involved country; examining one without the other would give a false impression of a country's comparative advantage.

The eclectic paradigm also provides a more comprehensive analytical framework in which to examine the extent to which inward investment may play a dynamic role in enhancing the ownership advantages of

Inward Investment and Europe's Competitiveness 73

indigenous firms through its effect on the host country's entrepreneurship and technological competitiveness, together with the existing location-specific advantages which local firms were initially unable to exploit. The possibility of the international transfer of technology, which is dealt with in the product cycle literature, being diffused within the recipient country, is thereby increased. Alternatively, indigenous firms may seek to import the technology through licensing or co-operative agreements. The industry technology cycle, as described by Magee (1977) suggests this may occur as the technology initially transferred within the MNE becomes less idiosyncratic and more standardized. Arm's length purchases of technology as a means of advancing export competitiveness may then be expected to follow inward direct investment, and become relatively more important as the transaction costs associated with its transfer are reduced.

The consequences of US foreign direct investment in European industries has been extensively documented; Dunning (1958, 1971b), noted the higher productivity of US affiliates in the UK vis à vis indigenous producers in a series of industries in the 1950s and early 1960s, and the US Tariff Commission Report (1973) confirmed these findings for a wide range of European industries. Moreover, such subsidiaries tended to be concentrated in the newer technology-intensive faster growing and export-oriented industry. They helped form many linkages with local firms. Through the technological multiplier, they created a competitive spur to indigenous firms, and, through lowering costs, released resources and encouraged innovations on the part of customers and suppliers as well as the direct rivals of the US-based firms.[6]

As a general rule, Hymer and Rowthorn (1970) found that the Americans felt challenged as the technological gap narrowed, in spite of the fact that the European subsidiaries of US firms were growing faster than non-US firms in Europe. Selective industry studies (see, for example, Lake (1976a and b) on the UK pharmaceutical and semiconductor industries) have shown that, in certain cases, the direct presence of US affiliates has exerted considerable competitive pressure on host country firms to undertake R & D, and to introduce the most recent technology, resulting in a change in industry structure and growth. In such sectors, rivalry between US firms and other foreign companies, as well as host country firms, has accelerated the rate of technology transfer. In those countries and sectors in which indigenous firms were well placed to respond, the increasing use of new technology in Europe led to its being adopted by European firms; while Dunning (1971a) found that the share of technology-intensive exports in total European manufactured exports rose between 1955 and 1965. One test to determine which sectors or countries witnessed growing ownership-specific advantages on the part of European firms is the extent to which the share of the technology-intensive exports accounted for by US affiliates, after rising initially, grew at a slower rate or even fell.

74   Multinationals, Technology and Competitiveness

THE CHANGING COMPETITIVE POSITION OF EUROPEAN INDUSTRY

Using the theoretical framework just described, we now examine some of the changes in the competitive position of the USA and Europe in technology-intensive industries in the period 1955–82, and the extent to which this has been influenced by the presence of US subsidiaries in Europe and of European subsidiaries in the USA. To do this comprehensively would require data on export and import of goods, and rights to assets (especially technology), and direct investment by US firms in Europe and European firms in the US. Unfortunately, data constraints force us to limit our analysis to five sets of statistics. These are:

(1) The relative share of European and US exports, as a combined measure of the location-specific (L) advantages of Europe and the USA *and* the ownership-specific (O) advantages of European and US firms.[7] This measure is supplemented by another, that is, the ratio between the European direct investment stake in Europe and the US direct investment stake in Europe. Both are measures of competitiveness, and it might be hypothesized that they should move in similar directions, that is, when the European share of exports is rising so also should the ratio between outward and inward investment.

(2) The growth of worldwide sales of the largest US and European companies; this reflects rather more the O advantages of firms than the previous set of data as a substantial part of the output (38 per cent in the case of US firms and 57 per cent in the case of European firms in 1982) is exported or produced outside their home countries.

(3) US direct investment in, and US exports to, Europe which, assuming each to be alternative means of servicing the European market, may be used to gauge the relative advantages of a US or European location.

(4) The share of total European exports by US affiliates, which, assuming these might otherwise have been supplied by European firms, is an index of the relative O advantages of the two groups of firms, and gives us some idea of the role played by the internalized transfer of intangible assets from the USA to Europe in influencing Europe's *trading* performance.

(5) The ratio between receipts of and payments for technology and managerial services of the USA and selected European countries, as an index of the technological capacity of these countries.

We first consider Europe's trading position vis à vis that of the USA. We take three main groups of products, which are classified in Tables 5.1 and 5.2 according to their R & D intensity. The definitions of the categories employed and data sources for this and subsequent tables are given in an Appendix to this chapter (see p. 102). To ensure consistencies

Inward Investment and Europe's Competitiveness

Table 5.1 *Changing Share of EEC, European and US Exports According to Degree of Research Intensity 1955–85*

| | As % of European plus US exports | | | |
	1955	*1965*	*1975*	*1985*
Group 1 products				
(High research intensity)				
EEC	36.0	46.3	49.8	46.9
Europe	63.1	70.2	73.8	72.1
USA	36.9	29.8	26.2	27.9
Group 2 products				
(Average research intensity)				
EEC	33.4	48.3	54.5	55.5
Europe	59.3	72.2	75.5	79.8
USA	40.7	27.8	23.1	20.2
Group 3 products				
(Low research intensity)				
EEC	53.1	51.4	51.0	56.3
Europe	63.9	74.8	80.0	86.5
USA	36.1	25.2	20.0	13.5
All products				
EEC	39.8	49.6	51.5	52.9
Europe	67.4	74.7	77.4	79.5
USA	32.6	25.3	22.6	20.5

Source: United Nations *Commodity Trade Statistics* 1955, 1965, 1975 and 1985.
(For details of industries comprising Groups 1–3, see Table 5.2 and the Appendix to this chapter.)

of interpretation over the period under review, we also distinguish between the original six founder members of the EEC and the rest of Western Europe. The data show that, between 1955 and 1985, the percentage of European plus US exports accounted for by European countries rose from 67.4 per cent to 79.5 per cent, with the largest part of this increase coming in the first decade, and with EEC countries achieving slightly higher rates of growth than other Western European countries.[8] For the period as a whole, Europe's export performance improved most markedly in Group 2 and 3 products, although in some Group 1 products, for example, aircraft, the share of EEC exports rose substantially.[9] However, in two of the most technology-intensive sectors, instruments and electrical machinery, the combined European plus US exports actually declined between 1955 and 1985; in addition, during the final decade, some of the earlier loss of markets by the USA in the electrical machinery, drugs and rubber product sectors was recouped.

The fact that Europe's export performance in Group 1 products has slipped back relative to that of the USA since 1975 suggests that the USA may be regaining some of its technological prowess. Indeed, the rise in US exports of Group 1 products between 1975 and 1985 was more than

Table 5.2 Growth in Exports of Selected Products: USA, Europe and the EEC 1955–85

	USA 1955–65 (1955=100)	USA 1965–75 (1965=100)	USA 1975–85 (1975=100)	USA 1955–85 (1955=100)	EEC 6 1955–65 (1955=100)	EEC 6 1965–75 (1965=100)	EEC 6 1975–85 (1975=100)	EEC 6 1955–85 (1975=100)	Europe 1955–65 (1955=100)	Europe 1965–75 (1965=100)	Europe 1975–85 (1975=100)	Europe 1955–85 (1955=100)
Aircraft	150.2	564.5	232.2	1,970.5	2,169.4	330.3	487.7	34,163.6	522.9	345.6	461.9	8,324.4
Instruments	497.4	445.0	341.3	7,535.7	292.8	462.5	264.5	3,561.4	310.7	468.9	274.8	4,006.9
Agricultural machinery	517.4	332.1	76.5	1,312.3	701.7	540.5	148.3	5,600.0	652.5	432.9	132.9	3,762.6
Office machinery	436.6	568.4	711.7	14,046.2	577.3	516.4	405.9	12,102.0	464.8	560.5	465.3	12,137.9
Electrical machinery	215.0	467.8	306.5	3,083.8	366.5	537.9	203.7	4,013.9	301.6	545.8	217.5	3,579.1
Chemicals: drugs	112.4	342.6	322.2	1,240.0	315.1	518.7	221.8	3,613.8	259.8	516.8	230.4	3,089.6
Other chemicals	240.3	366.7	236.0	2,079.4	305.4	559.3	236.9	4,045.0	273.6	546.2	244.7	3,658.1
All Group 1	228.7	438.8	259.8	2,606.5	352.9	536.7	229.3	4,342.1	305.7	524.1	237.7	3,809.1
Motor vehicles	146.0	510.7	193.5	1,442.8	435.2	555.5	222.2	5,368.6	342.9	497.0	221.4	3,773.3
Other non-electrical machinery	193.2	414.0	165.5	1,323.4	331.9	566.9	170.3	3,202.2	272.1	522.6	174.7	2,484.6
Rubber products	128.2	392.3	224.1	1,125.3	262.6	608.5	219.1	3,500.0	282.4	589.7	219.7	3,637.3
Petroleum products	71.4	222.4	98.5	156.4	194.3	659.0	211.3	2,705.2	187.1	681.4	259.2	3,303.9
All Group 2	158.4	429.1	167.1	1,135.5	336.0	575.6	197.1	3,812.0	281.5	534.6	204.8	3,082.8
Fabricated metals	179.8	344.9	151.3	938.0	246.4	511.0	178.6	2,249.3	216.5	513.7	181.1	2,013.9
Primary metals: non-ferrous metals	268.8	254.0	146.5	1,001.6	257.8	310.9	219.3	1,759.1	249.8	336.2	218.1	1,833.1
Stone, clay and glass	93.3	394.8	49.9	184.0	214.9	478.0	125.2	1,285.9	209.6	463.0	142.0	1,378.2
Printing and publishing	141.8	277.7	203.9	802.8	238.4	452.3	207.0	2,232.9	198.9	468.3	204.6	1,905.7
Tobacco products	240.7	246.6	233.4	1,390.2	351.0	428.3	204.4	2,149.3	326.7	446.8	207.7	3,024.3
Food and drink	196.3	327.3	222.6	1,430.3	592.8	573.6	256.8	8,872.2	231.2	469.3	215.8	2,333.3
Textiles and clothing	134.2	392.5	122.5	645.1	265.7	485.8	191.1	2,465.9	246.7	432.6	190.4	2,031.9
Lumber and wood products	129.5	296.0	166.8	639.5	206.0	381.0	197.6	1,549.0	178.2	391.4	199.8	1,393.9
Furniture and fixtures	154.9	611.9	168.0	1,584.3	338.5	649.3	233.7	5,138.6	243.9	669.9	237.4	3,881.6
Paper and allied products	197.2	373.3	160.6	1,185.7	295.0	569.2	268.6	4,504.6	232.4	601.1	239.6	3,348.3
All Group 3	149.5	362.9	134.9	731.7	207.7	452.9	183.5	1,725.0	205.3	440.0	189.7	1,713.6
All products	177.1	407.7	187.6	1,354.4	284.5	510.1	197.3	2,862.9	251.2	488.3	207.4	2,544.1

Source: United Nations Commodity Trade Statistics 1955, 1965, 1975 and 1985.

Table 5.3 *Growth in Exports of European Countries and the USA by Broad Industrial Groups 1955–85*

	Group 1 1955–65 (1955 = 100)	Group 1 1965–75 (1965 = 100)	Group 1 1975–85 (1975 = 100)	Group 1 1955–85 (1955 = 100)	Group 2 1955–65 (1955 = 100)	Group 2 1965–75 (1965 = 100)	Group 2 1975–85 (1975 = 100)	Group 2 1955–85 (1955 = 100)	Group 3 1955–65 (1955 = 100)	Group 3 1965–75 (1965 = 100)	Group 3 1975–85 (1975 = 100)	Group 3 1955–85 (1955 = 100)	Total 1955–65 (1955 = 100)	Total 1965–75 (1965 = 100)	Total 1975–85 (1975 = 100)	Total 1955–85 (1955 = 100)
United States	228.7	438.8	284.6	2,855.9	158.4	429.1	167.1	1,165,7	149.5	362.9	134.9	713.7	177.1	407.7	198.4	1,432.1
EEC 6:	352.9	536.7	229.3	4,342.1	336.0	575.6	197.1	3,812.0	207.7	452.9	183.5	1,726.3	284.5	510.1	200.1	2,903.4
Germany	326.0	517.5	231.7	3,409.0	349.7	493.8	197.8	3,415.5	268.9	540.2	189.1	2,746.5	315.9	514.5	204.8	3,328.7
France	352.5	542.0	250.8	4,790.1	266.2	712.4	167.9	3,182.1	177.6	429.3	175.8	1,340.7	228.8	522.2	191.8	2,291.4
Italy	576.0	486.8	243.6	6,772.1	414.0	583.7	193.4	4,676.8	275.7	435.2	234.4	2,811.4	359.9	490.5	222.6	3,927.6
Netherlands	370.6	554.1	212.0	4,352.0	240.2	781.0	236.0	4,432.8	242.5	456.9	160.7	1,780.4	276.4	538.7	196.9	2,932.2
Belgium and Luxembourg	289.1	669.8	187.7	3,628.7	460.1	620.5	214.2	6,104.9	209.4	378.7	149.6	1,186.0	248.5	472.1	174.7	2,049.6
United Kingdom	212.4	379.4	256.7	2,067.9	182.9	324.4	164.2	974.1	138.5	296.3	176.2	723.1	171.4	329.6	197.5	1,115.8
Denmark	412.5	514.3	221.3	4,680.9	308.4	521.3	197.3	3,171.0	295.2	333.7	185.4	1,824.5	328.8	389.4	195.2	2,501.4
Other Europe	242.6	499.5	257.9	3,125.1	212.2	454.9	292.4	2,822.2	201.1	416.6	216.9	1,817.7	208.7	447.4	246.2	2,299.2
Europe	305.7	524.1	237.8	3,809.1	281.5	534.6	204.8	3,082.8	203.3	440.0	189.7	1,713.6	251.2	488.3	207.4	2,544.1
TOTAL	277.0	498.5	237.9	3,284.1	233.7	505.1	195.9	2,312.4	196.0	423.8	179.8	1,493.8	228.1	468.2	201.7	2,154.4

Source: United Nations *Commodity Trade Statistics* 1955, 1965, 1975 and 1985.

78 — Multinationals, Technology and Competitiveness

double the increase of that of Group 2 and 3 products, while in the case of EEC exports it was about one-third greater. It would seem that while, in general, the trend towards closing the technological gap between European and US industries was sustained throughout the three decades under · examination, it not only slowed down in the latter ten years, but, in the case of some of the most R & D-intensive sectors, the gap began to widen again.

Table 5.3 shows that, within Europe, export growth rates varied widely, but with two exceptions[10] only the UK performed less well than the USA for all periods in all groups (except Group 2 for 1955–65). However, relative to its European competitors, the UK achieved the most pronounced growth in exports of Group 1 products in the 1975–85 period; Italy and the Netherlands achieved the highest growth rate for Group 1 products between 1955 and 1975; while France and 'other' European countries, along with the UK (for example, Sweden) achieved the most creditable performances in the following decade. Exports of Group 2 products has risen fastest in Luxembourg, Italy and the Netherlands. As with Group 1 exports, the non EEC European countries (as a group) have achieved faster rates of growth in their exports than EEC countries since 1975. For the period as a whole, Italy recorded the most impressive increase in exports, with Germany and the Netherlands not far behind. Both the UK and other European countries have done much better during the last ten years of the period than in the first twenty years.

An analysis of the percentage distribution of exports by principal product groups (not presented in tabulated form) lends further support to this hypothesis. The deviation around the mean percentage of the total exports by Europe and the USA accounted for by Group 1 products averaged 26.0 per cent in 1955, 18.5 per cent in 1965 and 15.7 per cent in 1975; however, it widened again to 21.7 per cent in 1985, mainly as a result of above-average export growth recorded by the USA.[11] This suggests a convergence in the structure of manufacturing exports between European and US producers. Particularly noteworthy is the reduction in the dispersion *within* the three main groups between 1955 and 1985. For all countries, for example, the share of Group 3 exports fell from 49.5 per cent in 1955 to 38.4 per cent in 1975, and 34.3 per cent in 1985, while that for Group 1 exports rose from 22.0 per cent to 28.5 per cent to 33.6 per cent and that of Group 2 exports from 28.5 per cent to 33.1 per cent to 32.1 per cent over the corresponding period. Moreover, countries whose share of Group 1 and 2 exports has risen the most are those whose export growth has been the most impressive.

THE GROWTH OF THE LEADING US AND EUROPEAN FIRMS

Data from Dunning and Pearce (1985) on the sales of the largest US and European industrial-owned firms, within a constant sample of the 483 largest industrial firms, over the period 1962–82, reveals that the increase

Table 5.4 *Rate of Growth of Sales, 1962–7, 1967–72, 1972–7, 1977–82, For Constant Sample of Firms, By Industry and Country*

	USA				Europe			
	1962–7 1962 = 100	1967–72 1967 = 100	1972–7 1972 = 100	1977–82 1977 = 100	1962–7 1962 = 100	1967–72 1967 = 100	1972–7 1972 = 100	1977–82 1977 = 100
High research intensity								
Aerospace	168.4	97.4	184.9	183.9	142.5	118.8	199.4	199.2
Office equipment (including computers)	223.9	180.9	181.6	196.1	134.2	172.2	169.9	165.2
Electronics and electrical appliances	173.1	177.3	154.6	155.8	157.0	212.6	196.3	166.1
Measurement, scientific and photographic equipment	238.3	151.5	187.9	188.3	N.S.A.	N.S.A.	217.9	136.6
Industrial and agricultural chemicals	167.6	144.0	202.0	147.7	154.3	212.4	218.3	148.9
Pharmaceuticals and consumer chemicals	185.4	174.3	192.5	166.4	189.1	192.3	183.0	160.2
Motor vehicles (including components)	146.7	162.5	182.9	101.7	159.8	208.8	216.7	148.8
Total	167.0	155.9	180.9	146.2	157.2	205.7	208.3	155.0
Medium research intensity								
Industrial and farm equipment	176.0	158.4	195.5	141.1	128.9	174.0	181.5	150.7
Shipbuilding, railroad and transportation equipment	140.1	88.1	179.2	150.2			166.8	139.6
Rubber	137.0	144.2	161.2	109.0	148.7	167.4	178.9	157.3
Building materials	133.9	189.7	164.3	128.8	149.4	129.7	207.7	165.2
Metal manufacturing and products	136.5	147.8	173.4	135.1	142.2	172.2	202.2	146.9
Total	144.8	148.7	176.7	133.3	140.9	171.3	196.9	150.1
Low research intensity								
Textiles, apparel and leather goods	152.9	148.4	148.6	143.7	141.2	178.0	145.7	113.4
Paper and wood products	155.9	171.3	180.3	133.1	174.4	224.7	185.5	139.6
Publishing and printing	180.4	152.7	173.9	217.3	135.6	130.0	197.9	174.5
Food	138.5	154.1	179.3	154.2	133.3	173.5	180.3	157.3
Drink	177.5	190.9	195.3	198.3	155.7	139.0	141.1	175.0
Tobacco	139.5	185.0	207.8	208.0	152.9	236.1	202.9	193.3
Total	146.3	161.0	178.7	158.8	140.6	181.6	176.9	158.8
Petroleum	154.6	163.7	295.4	202.2	142.0	187.0	324.4	223.5
Other manufacturing	160.2	164.6	179.3	162.0	100.7	120.3	208.7	179.2
TOTAL	156.3	156.9	198.7	161.3	145.5	188.4	215.6	168.5

N.S.A. = not separately available.
Source: Dunning and Pearce, 1985, Table 6.5, p. 125.

80 *Multinationals, Technology and Competitiveness*

in sales of European firms over each of the four quinquennia outpaced that of US firms. The data set out in Table 5.4 also show that the relative growth performance of the European firms was most impressive in the 1967/77 decade, and, except in the aerospace and office equipment sectors, the European firms did relatively better in the high research-intensity sectors, especially between 1967 and 1972, than their US counterparts. In the last quinquennium, however, the growth of US firms has outpaced that of European firms in three of the seven high research-intensive sectors, and only in motor vehicles have the European firms performed notably better. Of the European firms, those from France, Germany and Sweden each recorded substantially above average rates of growth and those from the UK substantially below average rates of growth between 1962 and 1977. In the last quinquennium, however, the growth of UK firms has outstripped that of other European and the US firms in all sectors.

These data are reinforced by the results of a study by Franko (1985) which deals only with the largest share of world markets of twelve firms in eleven manufacturing sectors. The study concludes that, in all but computers and office equipment sectors, the share of the leading US firms relative to that of other nationalities fell between 1960 and 1980, but that between 1980 and 1982 the USA recovered part of its lost share in six of these sectors and in two others maintained its 1980 share. Franko also found that growth rates were positively and significantly related to R & D intensity and that in sectors in which US firms experienced major losses of market share in the 1970s, their R & D intensive was low in comparison to their European and Japanese competitors

THE CONTRIBUTION OF US MANUFACTURING SUBSIDIARIES TO EUROPEAN EXPORTS

We now turn to consider the extent to which the growing participation of US firms in European industry has affected the ownership of European manufacturing exports. For a host of reasons, many of which have been discussed in the relevant literature (Dunning, 1972; see also Chapter 11 of this book), the increasing attractions of a production outlet in Europe, resulted in a sharp rise in the ratio between the sales of US affiliates and exports from the US between 1955 and 1975. Since that date (and data are only available up until 1982) US exports to Europe have increased more than the value of sales of US affiliates in Europe. Table 5.5 sets out the figures. Certainly the earlier period, the over-valuation of the US dollar, the formation of the EEC, and the growing rationalization of production of US firms in Europe all contributed towards a higher sales/export ratio. Between 1975 and 1982, however, the volume of intra-industry trade between the USA and European countries increased sharply, while the value of the $ relative to many European currencies fell back. Special factors, for example, the marked reduction in US investment in France, following the socialist policies of M. Mitterand,

Table 5.5   *Ratio of Sales of US Manufacturing Affiliates to Exports from USA 1957–82*

	Europe 1957	Europe 1966	Europe 1975	Europe 1982	EEC 6 1957	EEC 6 1966	EEC 6 1975	EEC 6 1982	Germany 1957	Germany 1966	Germany 1975	Germany 1982	France 1957	France 1966
Chemicals and allied products	2.33	3.69	7.43	5.13	1.23	2.91	6.87	5.00	1.07	3.83	8.70	6.42	2.38	4.85
Rubber products	2.70	5.17	12.30	3.73	1.28	3.21	11.19	N.A.	N.A.	N.A.	8.16	N.A.	N.A.	4.52
Non-electrical machinery	1.78	2.61	3.90	3.56	1.64	2.96	4.45	4.37	3.86	3.79	5.54	6.67	1.70	3.27
Electrical machinery	5.95	3.37	5.46	1.31	5.44	3.59	7.04	1.31	9.13	N.A.	7.44	1.95	6.08	N.A.
Transportation equipment	6.97	7.75	6.55	5.81	5.88	7.85	8.53	5.07	N.A.	N.A.	14.12	10.67	4.46	N.A.
Groups 1 and 2	3.25	3.92	5.51	3.52	2 48	3.83	6.25	3.72	5.87	5.83	8.27	5.80	2.62	4.19
Paper and allied products	0.37	1.49	3.52	N.A.	0.30	1.54	3.47	N.A.	0.40	1.11	2.15	N.A.	N.A.	1.94
Primary and fabricated metals	0.94	3.26	6.55	4.93	0.68	2.19	7.04	3.73	0.64	2.38	10.88	5.91	1.13	2.08
ALL PRODUCTS	2.56	3.72	5.47	3.55	2.01	3.51	6.27	3.73	3.90	5.10	7.98	5.91	2.33	3.84

Table 5.5   *continued*

	France 1975	France 1982	Belgium, Luxembourg and Netherlands 1957	Belgium, Luxembourg and Netherlands 1966	Belgium, Luxembourg and Netherlands 1975	Belgium, Luxembourg and Netherlands 1982	Italy 1957	Italy 1966	Italy 1975	Italy 1982	UK 1957	UK 1966	UK 1975	UK 1982
Chemicals and allied products	10.46	7.44	0.70	1.56	5.01	3.41	1.20	4.45	7.45	6.31	11.75	7.98	12.67	8.24
Rubber products	13.74	N.A.	2.33	N.A.	11.69	N.A.	N.A.	2.64	8.64	N.A.	7.32	22.33	22.08	N.A.
Non-electrical machinery	4.53	3.37	0.50	1.84	3.50	2.87	0.74	2.66	4.14	5.83	5.22	4.68	5.99	4.02
Electrical machinery	7.86	0.88	4.19	N.A.	8.94	0.26	4.4	5.22	5.34	2.20	30.00	N.A.	4.06	0.97
Transportation equipment	10.32	1.90	2.06	N.A.	2.38	0.11	N.A.	3.15	3.60	1.31	41.53	N.A.	14.12	12.18
Groups 1 and 2	7.13	2.96	1.30	1.93	4.51	2.18	1.44	3.66	5.03	4.03	11.99	8.22	8.15	4.38
Paper and allied products	4.24	N.A.	0.36	2.16	7.31	N.A.	N.A.	1.38	2.87	N.A.	0.51	1.37	2.33	N.A.
Primary and fabricated metals	5.44	2.99	0.42	2.07	5.28	2.39	0.46	2.18	5.67	4.64	1.80	6.56	7.47	6.99
ALL PRODUCTS	6.85	2.99	1.14	1.95	4.41	2.16	1.17	3.15	4.93	3.71	6.95	7.48	7.67	4.43

N.A. = not available.
Source: United Nations *Commodity Trade Statistics* 1955, 1965, 1975 and 1985 and US Department of Commerce, *US Direct Investment Abroad 1982*, Benchmark Survey (published in 1985), Survey of Current Business, November 1966, October 1970, August 1974, November 1966, February 1977, and US Tariff Commission Report 1973.

Inward Investment and Europe's Competitiveness 83

and the industrial and labour problems of the UK which culminated with 'the winter of discontent' in 1979, were also relevant. Overall, the table shows that the relative importance of the US presence has risen more noticeably in the initial six EEC countries (apart from France), and least in the UK where it has actually fallen. Among industrial sectors, the high and medium technology-intensive sectors seem to have recorded a slightly smaller increase in the propensity to favour a European location, and it is in the electrical and electronic equipment sector where the most dramatic increase in US exports to Europe has occurred.

A word of caution against reading too much into these figures should be made here. Local sales of US affiliates may include imports of intermediate products from their parent companies, while part of these sales may be exported. In the case of rationalized affiliates, it is less likely that their exports will be substitutes for US exports than in the case of import-substituting investments. However, even in the latter case, as various surveys have shown (Bergsten, Horst and Moran 1978; Hood and Young 1980) exports and sales of foreign subsidiaries often complement each other; for example, the latter may help to create a demand for goods from the parent company which it is nòt economic to produce locally.

To consider the extent to which Europe has acquired technology through the operation of US firms, another set of data relates the presence of US affiliates in Europe to Europe's share of exports of high and medium technology-intensive goods. How far, indeed, can any reduction in the technological gap between the USA and Europe – as suggested by various indicators of technological maturity – be put down to technology transferred *internally* by US firms or *externally* through the market, and/or from the competitive stimulus to indigenous firms given by US affiliates? How far indeed can an improvement in the competitive performance due to the presence of such affiliates be regarded as an indicator of added technological capacity?

In tackling these questions, let us first look at the contribution of US affiliates to the changing share of European exports. Table 5.6 classifies European exports into those supplied by US affiliates and those supplied by other firms in Europe (including the affiliates of other foreign – Japanese – firms). It reveals that, in 1957, US affiliates accounted for 3.8 per cent of the combined European and US manufacturing exports; this compares with 63.8 per cent for other firms in Europe and 32.3 per cent for firms located in the USA.[12] The respective proportions for Group 1 and 2 products were 5.6 per cent, 57.4 per cent and 37.0 per cent. If one attributes the exports of US affiliates to those of their parent companies, then it can be seen that, in 1957, 36.2 per cent of exports were supplied by US-owned firms and, as Table 5.6 shows, in some industries (for example, the transportation sector) the attribution of exports by *ownership* of firms rather than *location* of production makes a lot of difference.

Naturally, which method of classification one uses depends on what one is trying to show. For our purposes, we are interested in identifying

Table 5.6 *The Contribution of US Affiliates in Europe to Total European and US Exports of Selected Manufactured Products 1957–82*

	(1) Other firms in Europe %	*(2)* US affiliates in Europe %	*(3)* USA %	*(4)* (3) ÷ (2) %	*(5)* Other firms in Europe %	*(6)* US affiliates in Europe %	*(7)* USA %	*(8)* (7) ÷ (6) %	*(9)* Other firms in Europe %	*(10)* US affiliates in Europe %	*(11)* USA %	*(12)* (11) ÷ (10) %	*(13)* Other firms in Europe %	*(14)* US affiliates in Europe %	*(15)* USA %	*(16)* (15) ÷ (14) %
	1957				*1965*				*1975*				*1982*			
Chemicals and allied products	64.3	3.1	32.6	35.7	67.6	7.0	25.4	32.4	67.2	14.2	18.6	32.8	64.6	13.8	21.6	35.4
Rubber products	58.8	7.4	33.9	41.2	65.1	14.4	20.5	34.9	70.8	16.6	12.6	29.2	N.A.	N.A.	14.7	N.A.
Non-electrical machinery	56.6	2.7	40.7	43.4	63.0	6.1	30.9	37.0	62.1	11.4	26.5	37.9	62.1	10.6	27.3	37.9
Electrical machinery	63.7	3.4	32.9	36.3	69.7	5.1	25.2	30.3	71.1	6.5	22.4	28.9	64.8	5.6	29.6	35.2
Transportation equipment†	46.0	16.3	37.7	54.0	58.7	16.8	24.5	41.3	62.9	12.1	25.0	37.1	65.5	10.0	24.5	34.5
Groups 1 and 2	57.4	5.6	37.0	42.6	64.3	8.4	27.3	35.7	65.1	11.5	23.4	34.9	64.1	10.3	25.6	35.9
Food products	63.4	0.6	36.0	36.6	63.5	1.0	35.5	36.5	64.2	2.0	33.8	35.8	68.9	4.4	26.7	31.1
Paper and allied products	78.9	0.5	20.6	21.1	75.8	0.8	23.4	24.2	77.8	6.3	15.9	22.2	N.A.	N.A.	14.7	N.A.
Primary and fabricated metals*	81.8	1.8	16.4	18.2	84.0	2.7	13.3	16.0	85.9	3.5	10.6	14.1	86.3	3.3	10.4	13.7
Group 3	73.4	1.1	25.5	26.6	72.8	1.7	25.5	27.2	76.7	3.1	22.2	25.3	77.1	3.9	19.0	22.9
ALL PRODUCTS	63.8	3.8	32.3	36.2	67.3	6.1	26.6	32.7	68.2	8.8	23.0	31.8	65.6	8.5	25.9	34.4

† Only motor vehicles
* Excluding non-ferrous metals
Source: United Nations *Commodity Trade Statistics* 1955, 1965, 1975 and 1985 and US Department of Commerce, *US Direct Investment Abroad 1982*, Benchmark Survey (published in 1985), Survey of Current Business, November 1966, October 1970, August 1974, November 1966, February 1977, and US Tariff Commission Report 1973.

Inward Investment and Europe's Competitiveness

proxies for technological competitiveness. Now, it might be reasonably argued that if the exports of affiliates largely embody production technology imported from their parent companies, then an increase in such exports will not necessarily involve an improvement in the technological *capacity* of the host country. An increase in exports of indigenous firms would suggest that this was more likely to be the case, although even in this case the technology used could have been imported under licence. In this connection, it is clearly important to distinguish between *the ability to produce goods* and the *ability to reproduce technology* as an indicator of a country's technological capabilities.

This point is highlighted when one observes what has happened since 1957. Take, for example, changes in the US and European share of Groups 1 and 2 products. By 1982, the total European share of these exports had risen to 74.4 per cent, from 63.0 per cent in 1957, while the US share had fallen from 37.0 per cent to 25.6 per cent. However, a significant part of the European improvement in export competitiveness appears to be due to the contribution of US affiliates; for example, the share of these affiliates rose by 4.7 per cent while that of other European-based firms rose by 6.7 per cent. If one were then to add this former percentage to US exports, then as columns 4 and 12 in Table 5.6 show, the share of exports attributable to US firms fell only from 42.6 per cent to 35.9 per cent between 1957 and 1982. For individual industries, the role of US affiliates varies considerably. While in chemicals and electrical machinery, the share of exports of non US-owned firms in Europe hardly rose between 1957 and 1982, that of the US manufacturing subsidiaries increased from 3.1 per cent to 13.8 per cent in the former case, and from 3.4 per cent to 5.6 per cent in the latter. By contrast in the transportation equipment sector, the share of non-US-owned firms in Europe moved sharply up from 46.0 per cent to 65.5 per cent, while that of the US subsidiaries dropped back from 16.3 per cent to 10.0 per cent. In non-electrical machinery and food products, the share of both groups of firms has increased.

With one or two exceptions, the trend towards an increased participation by US subsidiaries in European exports was fairly consistent, although until 1975 (perhaps, contrary to what one might have expected) US firms enjoyed a slightly higher share of the additional exports from Europe in the second ten years than the first (12.3 per cent in 1965–75 compared with 10.7 per cent in 1957–64). However, between 1975 and 1982, with the exception of the food products sector, non US firms appeared to have held their own with US subsidiaries in the export market, although in Groups 1 and 2 industries both appear to have lost out to US exports.

While the data set out in Table 5.6 are not inconsistent with the PCM, the extent of increase in the share of European exports by US affiliates is somewhat surprising. One might have reasonably hypothesized that indigenous European firms would have reacted to the presence of US affiliates by improving their own technological capabilities and competitive efficiency. This has clearly happened in some sectors, for example,

Table 5.7 *Share of Majority-Owned Affiliates of US Firms in Total Exports of European Countries 1957–82*

	Europe 1965 %	Europe 1975 %	Europe 1982 %	EEC 6 1966 %	EEC 6 1975 %	EEC 6 1982 %	Germany 1966 %	Germany 1975 %	Germany 1982 %	France 1966 %	France 1975 %	France 1982 %
Chemicals and allied products	9.4	17.5	17.6	7.9	18.3	18.1	2.0	5.3	11.9	7.1	13.3	12.0
Rubber products	18.1	19.0	N.A.	18.1	22.9	N.A.	0.0	3.0	N.A.	17.9	27.2	N.A.
Non-electrical machinery	8.9	15.5	14.6	11.6	14.0	15.0	6.7	7.9	10.8	22.9	14.5	26.0
Electrical machinery	6.8	9.0	8.0	7.2	9.8	8.1	4.4	7.6	8.0	7.6	7.8	5.6
Transportation equipment	22.2	16.1	13.3	15.8	13.2*	11.2	23.7	20.2	19.4	1.9	6.9	2.3
Groups 1 and 2	11.5	15.1	13.8	11.2	14.4*	13.5	9.4	10.0	13.5	11.1	11.6	11.2
Food products	1.6	3.1	6.0	3.0	3.5	5.8	6.4	4.0	5.9	1.2	1.4	3.5
Paper and allied products	1.1	7.5	N.A.	6.2	6.6*	N.A.	1.1	2.6	N.A.	3.4	4.4	N.A.
Primary and fabricated metals	3.1	3.9	3.7	1.2	2.2	3.5	1.1	1.4	4.3	0.6	3.4	2.5
Other manufacturing	3.8	3.8	7.8	3.0	3.3	5.7	2.8	4.2	4.5	3.3	6.9	8.0
Group 3	3.0	3.9	6.3	2.5	3.0*	5.1	2.2	2.4	4.6	1.7	3.8	5.0
ALL PRODUCTS	7.2	9.8	10.4	7.0	9.4	9.7	7.0	7.4	10.4	6.3	8.0	8.3

Table 5.7 *continued*

	Italy 1966 %	Italy 1975 %	Italy 1972 %	Netherlands 1966 %	Netherlands 1975 %	Netherlands 1982 %	Belgium and Luxembourg 1966 %	Belgium and Luxembourg 1975 %	Belgium and Luxembourg 1982 %	UK 1966 %	UK 1975 %	UK 1982 %
Chemicals and allied products	5.8	11.7	10.5	17.8	39.6	33.5	28.4	38.7	32.3	16.2	26.1	20.3
Rubber products	N.A.	3.7	N.A.	N.A.	N.A.	N.A.	57.7	N.A.	N.A.	21.0	20.0	N.A.
Non-electrical machinery	8.4	7.7	9.8	N.A.	22.3	16.4	37.3	72.1	36.4	20.6	31.9	20.5
Electrical machinery	13.6	10.0	8.3	2.7	3.0	3.4	14.5	39.1	25.2	20.3	12.7	9.4
Transportation equipment	N.A.	1.7	0.9	N.A.	N.A.	2.1	20.4	N.A.	0.03	32.8	29.9	25.4
Groups 1 and 2	6.9	7.3	7.7	12.0	N.A.	19.9	26.9	N.A.	20.6	23.1	27.1	19.4
Food products	2.5	1.2	1.3	4.4	5.6	10.4	2.6	5.3	5.6	9.4	2.3	7.8
Paper and allied products	18.3	24.4	N.A.	12.1	N.A.	N.A.	8.9	N.A.	N.A.	2.6	7.2	N.A.
Primary and fabricated metals	1.8	2.8	1.7	5.9	4.3	6.3	0.4	2.5	2.9	9.1	10.8	10.4
Other manufacturing	1.6	1.8	1.9	5.3	1.7	N.A.	3.1	2.0	2.4	9.3	10.7	19.4
Group 3	2.1	2.4	1.8	5.3	N.A.	9.3	1.6	N.A.	3.3	9.0	8.8	14.4
ALL PRODUCTS	4.4	4.9	4.4	7.8	13.1	15.3	10.6	18.9	11.2	17.9	19.7	17.5

* Excluding Benelux transportation equipment
† Excluding Benelux paper and allied products
Source: United Nations *Commodity Trade Statistics* 1955, 1965, 1975 and 1985 and US Department of Commerce, *US Direct Investment Abroad 1982*, Benchmark Survey (published in 1985), Survey of Current Business, November 1966, October 1970, August 1974, November 1966, February 1977, and US Tariff Commission Report 1973.

88 Multinationals, Technology and Competitiveness

transportation equipment and pharmaceutical products, but not in others. Perhaps more illuminating in this respect is Table 5.7 which sets out data on the contribution of US affiliates to the exports of individual European countries. Here, there are two particularly striking features. The first is that between 1966 and 1975 there was a sharp difference in the role of US subsidiaries in the larger and smaller industrialized economies. While for the UK, Germany, France and Italy, the share of exports by US affiliates remained about the same, for Belgium and the Netherlands it increased sharply. Secondly, however, in the following decade this situation was reversed. In all major countries, the share of US affiliates in their manufacturing exports rose, while those in Belgium and the Netherlands dropped back a little. The increased share of US affiliates was particularly marked in the chemicals industry of Germany and the non electrical machinery and food industry of France and the food industry of the UK. By contrast, in the electrical equipment industry there was a decline in the export contribution of US affiliates.

The competitive response from firms in the UK, Germany, France and Italy to the presence of US affiliates is illustrated by the fact that the growth in the total exports of Groups 1 and 2 products from these countries in 1965–75 exceeded the growth in the sales of US affiliates of such products in the same countries in 1966–75, whereas the growth of exports in 1955–65 lagged behind the growth in affiliate sales in 1957–66 in all the European countries for which separate data are available. Thus, while the share of US affiliates in total European exports rose sharply in all countries between 1957 and 1966 (from 3.8 per cent to 7.0 per cent in Germany, 1.0 per cent to 6.3 per cent in France, 2.3 per cent to 10.6 per cent in Belgium and Luxembourg, and 11.7 per cent to 17.9 per cent in the UK), this was not repeated in the larger European economies over the following nine years. As can be seen from Table 5.6, in 1966–75 indigenous firms performed especially well in transportation equipment and food products in Germany, in non electrical machinery in France, in non electrical and electrical machinery and food products in Italy, and in rubber tyres, electrical machinery, transportation equipment and food products in the UK. In the subsequent seven years, however, US affiliates seemed to recapture some of their share of some export markets, although during this period the proportion of imports accounted for by US affiliates also rose.[13] These data suggest that while in the case of the larger industrialized countries the presence of US affiliates has acted as a spur to the technological capacity of indigenous firms, partly because the local markets have been sufficiently large to allow both foreign and indigenous firms to produce at an economic scale, in the smaller countries the size of the domestic market may have inhibited indigenous competition, and particularly in high technology industries in which there are substantial economies of scale. The fact that, more recently, the exports of US affiliates have risen faster than those of indigenous firms may be put down to the larger amount of intra-European trade conducted by such affiliates, and the growth in rationalized investment.

Inward Investment and Europe's Competitiveness

Though the product classification which we have adopted is too broad for any firm conclusions to be drawn about the technological impact of US firms in Europe, the suggestions we have offered are supported by studies carried out at a rather more disaggregated level. Illustrative of these are research conducted by Burstall, Dunning and Lake (1981) and Burstall and Senior (1985) on the impact of MNEs on the technological capacity of the pharmaceutical industry in OECD countries. (See also Chapters 6 and 7 of this book.) The studies quite clearly demonstrate that, whereas in the UK with its thriving indigenous pharmaceutical sector foreign (and particularly US) firms have had a stimulating effect on indigenous technological innovation – and hence on the international competitive position of UK-owned pharmaceutical companies, the smaller European countries, and especially the Scandinavian countries and Ireland, relied almost completely on foreign firms for the import of both innovatory capacity and production technology associated with the intermediate and final processes of drug manufacture. A related report on the impact of MNEs in the food processing industry (OECD, 1979b) also confirms that, following the rapid expansion of US food companies in Europe in the 1960s, from around 1968, certain European companies, in particular large UK firms, began to respond through their own internationalization strategies, based largely on the development of new products and diversification into new food subsectors. Lake's (1976a) study of the semiconductor industry also suggested that, amid rapid technological change spreading out from the USA, firms based in the largest European markets had been best placed to retain their position, given the fundamental importance of economies of scale and the introduction of new projects into larger markets at a relatively early stage.

In terms of the eclectic paradigm, these findings are consistent with the hypothesis that the initial O advantages of US affiliates will be sustained or eroded according to how far the local market can support indigenous competition, which, in turn, is determined by:

(1)   the initial technological capabilities of such competition;
(2)   the presence or absence of the economies of size of the *firm*;
(3)   whether or not the production process can be distintegrated;
(4)   the advantages of relocating these between the home and host country; and
(5)   the extent to which market failure encourages a firm to internalize these advantages rather than sell the right to use them to indigenous European firms.

These points are taken up further in Chapter 6.

The evidence of Tables 5.6 and 5.7 suggests that while, for the most part, US firms have generally retained their competitive position vis à vis European firms since 1955 in the high technology industries – and they have done so in part by the relocation of some of their value-adding facilities to Europe, they have surrendered some of their share in world

90 *Multinationals, Technology and Competitiveness*

markets in the medium- and low-technology sectors to their European counterparts. The data further suggest that it is the larger European economies, all of which are now members of the EEC, which have most improved their export competitiveness. However, as a location for producing goods based on these advantages, Europe has become relatively more attractive, while separate evidence confirms that production within US MNEs has been expanding faster than production of European firms licensed to independent US firms.[14]

THE CHANGING PATTERN OF THE US/EUROPEAN DIRECT INVESTMENT IN MANUFACTURING

The data set out in the previous section need supplementing to complete the picture. For example, if indigenous firms in the larger European economies have increasingly relied on licensing agreements with US firms, this might explain the improvement in technological capacity suggested by their rising export shares. Alternatively, if European-based firms have come to rely more on FDI rather than exporting in order to service markets abroad, then our conclusions might be strengthened. Such fragmentary evidence as may be adduced supports the results so far presented. Data on the stock and changes in the stock of manufacturing investment by US companies in Europe and European companies in the US since 1960 are set out in Table 5.8. These reveal that the stock of European investment in US manufacturing industry rose by nearly three times the rate of US investment in European manufacturing between 1962 and 1985; and that, whereas in 1962 the value of the former was 37 per cent that of the latter, in 1985 it was marginally greater. However, most of the surge of interest by European investors in the US did not occur until the later 1970s. It was in 1979 that the US dollar began to depreciate markedly against the European currencies, and the shift of

Table 5.8 *US Direct Investment in European Manufacturing Industry and European Direct Investment in US Manufacturing Industry 1962–85*

	Stock $ million				Changes in share		
	(1) *USA in Europe*	*(2)* *Europe in USA*	*(3)* *1/2*		*(4)* *USA in Europe*	*(5)* *Europe in USA*	*(6)* *5/6*
1962	4,883	1,797	2.72				
1965	7,606	2,167	3.51	1962–65	2,723	370	7.36
1970	13,819	4,091	3.38	1965–70	6,213	1,924	3.23
1975	26,013	6,673	3.90	1970–75	12,194	2,582	4.72
1977	30,469	9,267	3.29	1975–77	4,456	2,594	1.72
1982	37,786	33,032	1.14	1978–82	7,299	23,765	0.31
1985	45,214	46,515	0.97	1983–85	7,428	13,486	0.55

Source: *Survey of Current Business* (various editions).

Inward Investment and Europe's Competitiveness 91

locational advantages towards the US as a production base became marked. At the same time, the improving competitive performance of European relative to US firms (Dunning and Pearce, 1985) gave added impetus to the latter's presence in the USA.

Between 1982 and 1985, the pace of new European investment in the USA decelerated, as the decline in the value of the dollar was halted; on the other hand, in all but the most technology-intensive sectors the competitive position of European firms continued to improve, while the rejuvenation of the US economy relative to the sluggishness of the European economy encouraged more capital inflows into the USA. Moreover, in some of the high technology sectors European firms were investing in the USA to gain an insight into the latest technological developments.

Few data are available on the composition of the European–US international investment position before 1977. However, Table 5.9 reveals that over the eight-year period after that date the most pronounced improvement in the growth of European investment in the US occurred in the food and kindred and other manufacturing industry (including motor vehicles) sectors, while US firms in Europe recorded the most substantial increase in their European investments in the food and kindred industries, machinery and chemicals. While these statistics are too aggregated to tell us much about the changing technological strength of Europe vis à vis the US, they do support rather than refute the hypotheses so far considered.

THE TECHNOLOGICAL BALANCE OF PAYMENTS: THE USA COMPARED WITH EUROPE

It might also be expected that an improvement in the technological *capacity* of Western Europe relative to the United States would show itself in an improvement in its technological balance of payments and rate of increase in new patents. We looked into three sets of data: (1) the growth of receipts of royalties and fees of European countries relative to that of the USA; (2) the balance of technological payments of the two groups of countries; and (3) the ratio between the receipts of European firms from US firms, and that of payments made by the former to the latter.

Unfortunately, most data on royalties and fees do not separate payments or receipts made between affiliated and unaffiliated firms. The former, which account for the bulk of such fees (about 75 per cent in the case of US and UK transactions) are known to be affected by intra-firm pricing practices which may have little to do with the value of the technology transferred. Where possible, we shall use only payments between non-affiliated firms.

First, considering the growth of all kinds of royalties and fees, between 1960 and 1975 those received by a group of ten European countries rose significantly faster than those received by firms in the USA (Poznanski,

Table 5.9　*The Euro–US Investment Stake Position*

	European stake in USA ($m)			US stake in Europe ($m)			Ratio of European to US stake	
	1977	*1985*	*% growth (1977 = 100)*	*1977*	*1985*	*% growth (1977 = 100)*	*1977*	*1985*
Manufacturing								
Food and kindred	992	10,439	1,052.3	2,288	4,532	198.1	0.43	2.30
Chemicals	3,965	17.150	432.5	5,698	8,319	146.0	0.70	2.06
Metals	747	2,783	372.6	1,981	1,971	99.5	0.38	1.41
Non-electrical machinery }	1,710	6,509	380.6	7,299	12,039	164.9 }	0.17	0.41
Electrical machinery				2,858	3,824	133.8		
Transportation }	1,853	9,634	519.9	4,534	4,104	90.5 }	0.18	0.66
Other				5,811	10,425	179.4		
Total	9,267	46,515	501.9	30,469	45,214	148.4	0.30	1.03
Other								
Petroleum	5,523	25,437	460.0	13,629	22,638	166.0	0.40	1.12
Banking	N.S.A.	5,963	N.S.A.	2,021	6,326	313.0	N.S.A.	0.94
Finance and real estate	3,272	20,129	615.2	5,674	15,628	275.4	0.58	1.29
Wholesale trade	N.S.A	12,533	N.S.A.	7,874	12,428	157.8	N.S.A.	1.01
Total*	14,487	74,391	513.8	32,083	61,548	191.8	0.45	1.21
ALL SECTORS	23,754	120,906	509.0	62,552	106,762	170.7	0.38	1.13

* Including all other non-manufacturing activities
Source: US Department of Commerce, 1981, 1984, 1985; *Survey of Current Business* August 1985, 1986.

Inward Investment and Europe's Competitiveness 93

1981). The UK, German, French and Swiss rates of growth were the most impressive. Second, the same source reveals that the ratio between receipts and payments for royalties and fees improved in the case of the UK, Germany and Belgium but worsened in the case of other European countries and the USA.

Separate data for technology transactions between unaffiliated firms suggest that, between 1967 and 1985, receipts of royalties and fees by European firms from US firms rose 3.01 times while payments made by European firms to US firms rose 3.15 times. (US Department of Commerce, various dates). Corresponding figures for the UK were 2.78 and 2.50 and for other European countries 3.17 and 3.40. As between affiliated firms, receipts by European-based companies have fluctuated considerably since 1967, but rose sharply in the mid-1970s, and dramatically so in 1978, though payments made to US firms rose more steeply over the period as a whole.[15]

The third set of data, presented in Table 5.10, set out the growth of receipts and payments of royalties and fees *in manufacturing industry* between *unaffiliated* firms for three European countries and the USA, between 1965 and 1975. The statistics show that the fastest rates of growth of both receipts and payments have occurred in the European countries (particularly in Germany), but that only in the case of the USA and Germany has the rate of growth of the former exceeded that of the latter. Of the more technology-intensive sectors, the most pronounced improvement in Europe's net technological capabilities is recorded by the chemicals industry; indeed, by 1975, the royalty receipts of German-based firms from unaffiliated foreign residents were equal to those of US-based firms.

This is interesting, as the chemicals sector is one in which the share of US affiliates in total European exports has increased between 1965–75 (see Table 5.7). This could mean that European, and especially German, firms have increasingly come to rely on FDI and licensing agreements with foreign firms as a means of exploiting their O advantages abroad, but it could also reflect an increase in intra-industry foreign direct investment between Europe and the USA. In the one technology-intensive sector in which the export performance of German-based firms improved vis à vis the US affiliates, that is, transportation equipment, the royalty receipts of German firms clearly rose faster than their payments (and continued to do in the following decade). This lends further support to the suggestion that the O advantages of German firms have improved. However, in the case of food products in Germany, royalty payments have risen markedly faster than receipts, though both remain at a comparatively low level. The inference is that at least part of the higher export share of German firms in food products has been due to a rise in the arm's length technology transactions with foreign firms. A similar pattern emerges in the case of the UK, where it appears that indigenous firms have continued to rely on foreign technology in the electrical engineering and food products sectors, but have more clearly improved their position in the transportation equipment sector.

Table 5.10   *Growth of Royalties and Fees of the US and Selected European Countries 1977–85*

					(1965=100)			
	USA		UK		Sweden		West Germany	
	Receipts	*Payments*	*Receipts*	*Payments*	*Receipts*	*Payments*	*Receipts*	*Payments*
More technology-intensive sectors								
Chemicals and allied products	174.3	151.9	235.1	488.8	381.8	321.4	426.4	285.0
Mechanical and instrument engineering	223.3	275.0	328.9	141.1	407.1	413.3	451.2	453.1
Electrical engineering	215.6	500.0	375.3	495.7	314.3	176.9	398.6	426.2
Transportation equipment	190.0	266.7	73.1	31.6	14.3	925.0	241.8	168.3
	202.1	197.2	253.5	279.8	332.8	353.3	377.1	319.5
Less technology-intensive sectors								
Food, drink and tobacco	137.5	133.3	296.5	485.7	200.0	550.0	266.6	480.0
Primary and fabricated metals	162.1	33.3	2,300.0	372.7	116.6	241.2	1,366.7	341.7
Textiles, leather, clothing and footwear	21.4	100.0	32.4	237.5	150.0	700.0	250.0	200.0
Paper, printing and publishing	350.0	200.0	863.2	643.5	350.0	183.3	433.3	900.0
Other manufacturing industries	438.5	187.5	1,108.5	478.7	357.1	500.0	896.0	766.6
	205.2	120.0	500.4	484.7	217.2	325.0	752.5	633.3
All manufacturing	203.0	177.1	322.0	327.5	297.9	346.3	402.0	347.0

Source: Data compiled from various government sources by Jeremy Clegg, now at the University of Bath. Where possible the data conform to the US definition of royalties and fees.

Inward Investment and Europe's Competitiveness 95

Data available since 1975 are more patchy, but in the case of West Germany royalty receipts from non affiliated companies rose by 58 per cent between 1976 and 1982, while royalty payments rose by 28 per cent. The corresponding percentages for the UK were 43 per cent and a decline of 29 per cent, and for the USA 100 per cent and 54 per cent.

A final index of technological capacity which we might briefly examine is the number of patents granted.[16] We have chosen to compare the patents granted in the USA to US and European residents. Over the period 1963–9 there were an average 46,763 patents granted to US residents, compared with 5,799 to residents of the original six members of the EEC, 2,473 to UK residents and 1,723 to 'Other European' residents. By 1983, patents granted to US residents had declined to 32,732, a fall of 30 per cent, while those of EEC residents had risen to 8,773 (an increase of 51 per cent), those to UK residents had declined to 1,923 (a fall of 22 per cent), and those to 'Other European' residents had increased to 3,037 (an increase of 16 per cent). All of the increase in patents granted occurred in the first part of the period. Indeed, between 1975 and 1983, the total number of patents granted in the USA fell by 21 per cent compared with an increase of 12 per cent in the preceding decade.[17]

In 1965, patents granted to all European residents were 16.8 per cent of those made available to US residents; the corresponding proportions for 1975 and 1983 were 22.4 per cent and 22.7 per cent. This suggests that most of the relative improvement in Europe's patenting situation occurred in the first half of the period under review.[18] Table 5.11 also shows that the increase in patenting was most pronounced in the case of German, Italian and French firms.

Relative to the *average* change in the number of patents granted, those awarded to European countries showed the most marked improvement in the low research-intensive (for example, Group 3) sectors; but in some Groups 1 and 2 sectors, for example, motor vehicles, they also performed well.

CONCLUSIONS

In this chapter we have examined some changes in the competitive position of European countries vis à vis the USA, between 1955 and the 1980s, using the framework of the eclectic paradigm of international production. The data suggest that, in the first decade, locational advantages strongly favoured the servicing of the European market from a European base; and that the strong O advantages of US firms (vis à vis their European rivals) explained the increasing share of European output and exports accounted for by the subsidiaries of US firms. Partly as a consequence of the dissemination of new technologies and of competitive pressures generated by these firms, and partly to the natural course of industrial recovery after the war, new O advantages were created by European firms, with a resulting improvement in their

Table 5.11 *Growth in Patents Taken out in the USA Classified by Country of Origin 1965–83*

	US origin			UK origin			German origin			French origin			Italian origin		
	1	*2*	*3*	*1*	*2*	*3*	*1*	*2*	*3*	*1*	*2*	*3*	*1*	*2*	*3*
Instruments	123.2	74.2	91.4	143.1	77.5	110.9	157.5	105.4	166.0	177.2	98.1	173.8	243.0	91.8	223.1
Electrical machinery	91.1	76.6	69.8	106.2	61.8	65.6	176.7	90.0	159.0	150.8	105.6	159.2	181.6	84.3	153.1
Radio and TV equipment	103.4	105.4	108.9	125.0	60.0	75.0	190.0	113.2	215.0	112.5	188.9	212.5	100.0	100.0	100.0
All chemicals	119.8	70.2	84.1	156.9	68.3	107.1	208.1	77.6	161.5	228.0	73.3	167.1	164.0	79.1	129.8
Drugs	193.9	85.5	166.4	285.7	131.7	376.2	328.1	112.4	368.7	314.3	89.4	280.9	285.7	160.0	457.1
Other chemicals	115.5	65.7	79.4	149.4	60.4	90.2	202.4	74.7	151.3	217.7	70.9	154.3	156.1	68.9	107.5
Transportation equipment	100.3	57.4	57.6	96.7	61.1	59.1	186.1	92.2	171.6	153.7	66.7	102.5	124.0	80.6	100.0
Aircraft	80.0	73.5	59.1	69.3	69.2	48.0	141.2	130.6	184.3	114.7	94.9	108.8	100.0	100.0	100.0
Motor and other transport	105.9	54.0	57.2	112.2	58.3	65.5	200.6	83.5	167.5	90.3	58.5	98.8	128.6	77.8	100.0
Non-electrical machinery	88.7	65.6	58.1	99.3	59.5	59.1	163.5	89.0	145.4	178.3	68.7	122.6	165.8	96.1	159.3
Rubber and plastics	110.6	52.1	90.8	169.1	65.0	109.9	184.9	116.7	215.9	225.6	72.2	162.8	139.1	87.5	121.7
Petroleum	94.2	101.7	95.8	95.4	52.4	50.0	100.0	161.5	161.5	200.0	137.5	275.0	100.0	300.0	300.0
All Groups 1 and 2	100.7	71.7	71.6	117.3	64.5	75.7	177.4	89.7	159.1	181.0	80.4	145.5	151.1	97.6	147.5
Fabricated metal	93.7	65.3	61.1	123.3	60.5	74.6	185.4	90.4	167.6	156.6	88.6	138.7	257.1	70.4	180.9
Primary metals	105.3	77.5	81.6	118.2	64.1	75.8	162.5	76.9	125.0	150.0	70.4	105.6	200.0	87.5	175.0
Stone, clay and glass	108.0	82.3	88.9	228.6	58.3	133.3	204.4	15.2	235.6	148.1	115.0	170.4	183.3	63.6	116.7
Food and drink	142.2	59.6	84.7	444.4	42.5	188.9	241.7	69.0	166.7	300.0	125.0	375.0	100.0	150.0	150.0
Textiles	112.7	72.3	81.5	166.7	56.7	94.4	207.4	83.9	174.1	175.0	114.3	200.0	50.0	150.0	75.0
All Group 3	99.6	68.3	68.0	150.2	58.5	87.8	188.9	91.0	172.0	158.9	93.8	149.1	208.1	75.3	156.8
ALL PRODUCTS	99.8	70.1	70.0	123.0	63.2	77.8	177.6	89.7	159.4	175.1	80.0	140.0	172.4	84.6	145.9

Table 5.11 *continued*

	Dutch origin			Belgian and Luxembourg origin			Other European origin†			Total all countries		
	1	*2*	*3*	*1*	*2*	*3*	*1*	*2*	*3*	*1*	*2*	*3*
Instruments	153.4	111.5	171.1	188.4	61.5	115.9	229.3	76.2	174.8	148.4	86.6	128.5
Electrical machinery	138.9	95.0	132.1	113.6	96.0	109.0	122.3	84.5	103.4	111.2	88.1	97.9
Radio and TV equipment	175.0	142.9	250.0	200.0	100.0	200.0	200.0	91.7	183.3	139.4	118.8	165.7
All chemicals	104.2	96.9	101.1	194.6	69.4	135.1	204.7	58.3	119.4	148.2	74.1	109.8
Drugs	150.0	100.0	150.0	200.0	116.7	233.4	200.0	111.1	222.2	235.2	99.5	233.9
Other chemicals	101.1	95.5	96.6	194.1	65.1	126.5	206.2	53.8	111.0	142.8	71.5	102.0
Transportation equipment	150.0	125.0	187.5	175.0	100.0	175.0	126.6	89.9	113.8	117.1	72.6	85.0
Aircraft	100.0	100.0	100.0	0.0	0.0	0.0	93.7	106.7	100.0	94.7	94.5	89.5
Motor and other transport	183.3	127.3	233.3	175.0	100.0	175.0	127.8	87.1	111.4	123.6	67.8	83.8
Non-electrical machinery	123.6	95.6	118.2	166.7	73.3	122.2	168.3	68.7	115.6	108.6	74.3	80.7
Rubber and plastics	140.0	171.4	240.0	233.3	107.1	250.0	202.4	91.8	185.7	135.5	90.7	122.8
Petroleum	66.7	150.0	100.0	∞ *	300.0	∞ *	250.0	120.0	300.0	99.1	104.6	103.7
All Groups 1 and 2	126.4	101.8	128.7	172.0	75.6	130.1	173.6	70.8	123.0	123.0	80.0	98.2
Fabricated metal	170.4	91.3	155.6	214.3	73.3	157.1	178.4	75.0	133.8	109.7	72.6	79.7
Primary metals	300.0	83.3	250.0	166.7	110.0	183.3	226.1	73.1	165.2	142.1	82.9	117.9
Stone, clay and glass	200.0	150.0	300.0	66.7	66.7	44.4	254.2	70.5	179.2	134.3	91.8	123.4
Food and drink	360.0	55.6	200.0	∞ *	150.0	∞ *	426.5	73.0	337.5	170.7	65.4	111.7
Textiles	100.0	100.0	100.0	50.0	200.0	100.0	107.1	166.7	178.6	136.5	85.0	116.1
All Group 3	197.7	93.1	184.1	141.7	91.2	129.2	198.6	77.2	153.4	119.6	76.4	91.3
ALL PRODUCTS	133.9	100.8	135.0	136.7	78.8	124.4	176.3	71.6	126.2	121.1	78.7	95.3

Notes:
[1] 1965–75 (1965 = 100)
[2] 1975–83 (1975 = 100)
[3] 1965–83 (1965 = 100)
  * zero in 1965
  † Swedish, Swiss, Austrian, Danish, Norwegian, Portuguese, Irish, Spanish, Greek, Lichtenstein
Source: The Office of Technology Assessment and Forecast, US Patent and Trademark Office.

competitive position. First, there was a dramatic rise in R & D expenditure and the number of patents registered. This was followed by an improvement in the relative growth of European firms, in their export and net export performance, and then by a substantial increase in European investment in the USA. United States subsidiaries contributed to an industrial renaissance, which was most marked in the medium to low research-intensive sectors. And while all the data, including movements in direct investment capital, point to a reduction and, indeed, in some cases a closing of the technological gap between the USA and Europe, in the most technologically advanced sectors, especially micro-electronics, computers, telecommunications and bio-technology, the USA has remained very much in the lead. The data presented suggest that the 'catching up' process was largely completed by the early 1970s (in the UK it occurred a good deal earlier), since when the differential in growth (especially in Groups 1 and 2 industries) between European and US industries has been much less pronounced. Within Europe, however, there have been some quite marked differences as several of the previous tables have shown.

The extent to which US direct investment in Europe held back or contributed to European recovery is a moot point. In the short run it undoubtedly contributed to the recovery – as the production and export data show. In the long run, however, the evidence is mixed. In some industries European firms have caught up with, and in some cases (or subsections) overtaken, their US counterparts. In others, the added competitive strength afforded to US companies as a result of their European presence has probably raised new barriers to the expansion of European companies, in addition to those already imposed by the European economic and political structures and institutions. This has been most noticeable in the case of smaller European countries, whose initial market size (prior to the advent of the EEC) limited the number of companies which could economically supply particular products.

Some further aspects of the impact of US FDI on the technological capacity of European countries (and especially the UK) are taken up in the following chapters. For the moment we would suggest that the relative merits of the 'open door' policies towards FDI of most European countries and the 'door ajar' policy of the Japanese for most of the post-war period, have not yet been analysed with any rigour. But a cursory examination of the Japanese data on R & D patents, production and exports suggests that their relative improvement since 1968 has been much more pronounced than that of European companies in Groups 1 and 2 industries, and that, in some sectors, for example, robotics, semi-conductors and computers and biotechnology, at least some of their firms are technologically on a par with their US competitors.

Let us now draw together some other conclusions of this chapter. We summarize these under four main headings.

Inward Investment and Europe's Competitiveness 99

(1) *The improvement in Europe's goods trading position vis à vis the USA.*
    (a) The improvement is especially marked in the EEC countries before 1965, and in the medium research-intensive product range;
    (b) It has led to a rising share in total European exports to technology-intensive products, which have served as growth leaders;
    (c) The USA has best maintained its share in the export of high technology products.

(2) *The tendency for US firms to exploit their O advantages in Europe through foreign production rather than through exports.*
    (a) The rise in the local production/export from US ratio has been most marked in the smaller European countries in the decade 1965–75. In the later period, American exports rose faster than US production in Europe. *Inter alia*, this reflected the decline in the value of the US dollar, particularly in the earlier part of this period;
    (b) The rise in the local production/export from US is also partly due to an increase in rationalized investment, which is less substitutable for US exports than markets seeking investment.

(3) *The relationship between the presence of US affiliates and the improvement in the European export share.*
    (a) Although the total US share of all US and European exports has fallen, the share of US affiliates in Europe has risen;
    (b) In the larger European countries (the UK, Germany, France and Italy) the exports of indigenous firms have kept pace with the exports of US affiliates later in the period, especially, for example, in the transportation equipment sector;
    (c) These countries have also witnessed a generally rising ratio of outward/inward FDI and receipts/payments of royalties and fees, especially in the case of Germany, and particularly here in the chemicals sector in which her firms appear not to have relied on exports in their operations abroad to the same extent as have US affiliates.

(4) *The improvement in the balance of Europe's direct investment and relationship with the USA in Europe's technological balance of payments with the USA.*
    (a) Europe's direct investment in the USA has risen faster than US investment in Europe, particularly since 1977. In 1985, European firms had a larger capital stake in US manufacturing industry than US firms in European manufacturing industry. In that latter year, of the main industrial sectors, only in the electrical and now electrical goods and machinery and transportation equipment sectors, did US firms have a substantially bigger stake in Europe than European firms in the US.
    (b) European receipts of royalties and fees from the USA rose faster after 1965 than payments of royalties and fees to the USA.

100 *Multinationals, Technology and Competitiveness*

(c) However, both receipts and payments for technology rose faster in Europe than in the USA. In the chemicals sector, indigenous firms may have begun to improve their position through licensing, or have become involved in more cross-licensing agreements amidst an increase in intra-industry FDI.

(d) In the transportation equipment sector, the technological improvement of firms based in the larger European countries is clearly confirmed in a rising ratio of receipts/payments of royalties and fees.

(e) The patents registered by European firms in the USA have increased relative to those registered by US firms. The relative improvement was most marked in the 1965–75 period and in the medium to low technology-intensive sectors.

NOTES

1　Notably as expressed in *The American Challenge* by Servan Schreiber (1968).

2　See Dunning (1972) for an earlier discussion of the implications of an enlarged EEC for US direct investment in Europe.

3　This important distinction is made elsewhere in this book (e.g. Chapters 5 and 10) and by Lipsey and Kravis (1985, 1987).

4　That is, as a risk avoiding strategy. For an examination of institutional response to international risk, see Vernon (1983).

5　These are not confined to production economies; some MNEs which do not rationalize their products or processes may nevertheless integrate other activities, for example R & D, purchasing, advertising, management recruitment and marketing. For an examination of the consequences of a common ownership of production facilities on resource allocation and efficiency, see Caves (1980). For an empirical study of the changing European development strategies of US-owned manufacturing companies in Scotland, see Hood and Young (1980).

6　For an earlier investigation of these effects in Europe see Dunning (1970).

7　Calculations were also done on net exports (exports less imports) and broadly the same results obtained.

8　Between 1955 and 1965, the ratio between the percentage increase in European exports and that of US exports was 1.42; in the two subsequent decades it was 1.19 and 1.1. The corresponding ratios between EEC and all European exports were 1.13, 1.04 and 0.95.

9　The relative European/US growth ratios for this period 1955/85 were 1.46 for Group 1 products, 2.71 for Group 2 products, and 2.34 for Group 3 products.

10　For Group 2 products for 1955/65 and Group 3 products for 1975/85.

11　In 1975, Group 1 exports accounted for 50.2 per cent of all US exports, compared with 35.0 per cent in 1975; the corresponding percentages for European countries were 30.5 per cent and 26.6 per cent.

12　Including the affiliates on non-US MNEs.

13　Mainly because of the increasing product or process specialization between the European affiliates of US firms and between these and their US parent companies. This was particularly noteworthy in the motor vehicle industry.

Inward Investment and Europe's Competitiveness 101

14 This is illustrated by comparing the growth of the sales of US MNEs with that of licensing fees from unaffiliated foreigners, on the assumption that licence fees represent a roughly constant proportion of sales in the period concerned. The total sales of US affiliates in Europe grew by 6.7 times between 1966 and 1982, while US receipts of royalties and fees from unaffiliated European residents rose by 3.2 times between 1967 and 1982.

15 Between 1967 and 1977 royalties and fees paid by US affiliates in Europe to their parent companies rose by 268.2 per cent, while those between unaffiliated European and US firms rose by 126.2 per cent. This would seem to suggest that the incentive to disinternalize knowledge transfer over the period has fallen; while this may have been the case in high technology sectors and those which have been subject to rationalization of their European activities, one also suspects that during the earlier part of the period US affiliates were not charged arm's length prices for the technology transferred from the USA, but that over the years this has increasingly been the case.

16 We recognize the danger of reading too much into these statistics. For example, patents granted may not be taken out; they may represent scientific or technical knowledge of little direct technical use; the strategies of MNEs may obscure the relationship between technology flows and patent activity, and so on.

17 In the same period patents granted to Western European residents rose by 73 per cent, while those granted to US residents fell by 0.2 per cent.

18 Data (which are not directly comparable to those presented in Table 5.11) suggest that the increase in patents to Western European residents in the period 1955–65 was four times greater than that to US residents. Taken as a whole, the data suggest a strong 'catching up' but not surpassing the US element in them.

APPENDIX DEFINITIONS OF CATEGORIES OF TRADE DATA USED

Industry	Group 1 SITC rev 2 (1982 and 1985 data)	SITC rev 1 (1955–1975 data)
Transportation equipment:		
aircraft	792	734
Instruments	87 + 88	86
Agricultural machinery	721 + 722	712
Office machinery	75	714
Electrical machinery	75 + 76 + 77	72 + 714
Chemical and allied:	5	5
Chemicals:		
drugs	541	541
Chemicals:		
other	5–541	5–541
Group 2		
Transportation equipment:		
motor vehicles	78	732
Other non-electrical machinery	71 + 72 + 73 + 74 – 721 – 722	71 – 712 – 714
Rubber products	62 + 893 + 233.1	62 + 893 + 231.2
Petroleum products	323 + 334 + 341	321 + 332 + 341
Groups 1 and 2		
Non-electrical machinery	71 + 72 + 73 + 74	71 – 714
Transportation equipment	78 + 79	73
Group 3		
Fabricated metal products	69	69
Primary metals:		
non-ferrous	68	68
Primary metals:		
ferrous	67	67
Stone, clay and glass products	66 – 667	66 – 667
Printing and publishing	892	892
Tobacco products	12	12
Food and drink	0 – 001 + 11	0 – 000 + 11
Textiles and clothing	61 + 65 + 84 + 85 + 266 + 267	61 + 65 + 84 + 85 + 266 + 267
Lumber and wood products	63 + 82	63 + 82
Paper and allied	64	64
Other manufacturing	667 + 81 + 83 + 89 – 892 – 893	667 + 81 + 83 + 89 – 892 – 893
Primary and fabricated metals	67 + 68 + 69	67 + 68 + 69

The classification of products into Groups 1, 2 and 3 is based on the following definition:

Group 1 products include those in which R & D expenditure as a percentage of sales in 1962 was 4 per cent or more, or where scientists and engineers employed in R & D were 2 per cent or more of total employment.

Group 2 products include those in which the corresponding percentages were 2 per cent but under 4 per cent and 1 per cent but under 2 per cent.

Group 3 products include those in which the corresponding percentages were under 2 per cent and under 1 per cent.

Figures were taken from Table 1 of Gruber, Mehta and Vernon (1967).

Chapter Six

The Changing Role of MNEs in the Creation and Diffusion of Technology

INTRODUCTION

This chapter discusses some aspects of the changing role of MNEs as producers, transferors and disseminators of technology and technological capacity,[1] and how their activities may affect the international competitiveness of countries. The argument adopts the theoretical framework of the eclectic paradigm of international production developed in previous chapters, and relates this to the concept of technological cumulation (Pavitt, 1987).

The central theme of the chapter is that the steady growth of MNEs, especially since the 1950s, has been associated with new (and closer) relationships between the international creation and dissemination of technology. Such creation and dissemination may occur across or within the national boundaries, and within or between firms.[2]

The chapter begins with a brief historical review of the changing nature of technological innovation. In particular, it examines the proposition that there has been a fundamental shift of emphasis from technology being perceived by the firm as a specific and single-purpose input, requiring little co-ordination with other technologies, towards it being perceived to be more general and multipurpose, and often needing to be used with other technologies for its effective deployment. The rise of such technological interdependence means that it is no longer appropriate to think simply in terms of a sequence which runs from technology production to transfer and diffusion. The successful creation and application of new technology is becoming increasingly dependent upon its ability to relate to other related technologies within the firm, and of parallel technologies developed elsewhere by other firms. It is also difficult to separate individual innovations from the way in which they are organized by firms, and from the multiple use of the same technology to produce different products or processes across national boundaries. This is one major reason why the product cycle (Vernon, 1966, 1979) and the industry technology cycle (Magee, 1977) type of hypotheses are today inadequate in explaining the complex

104   *Multinationals, Technology and Competitiveness*

modern role of the MNE as both a source and a recipient of innovative change.

The next section considers the recent behaviour of MNEs in greater detail. In particular, it is contended that the extent to which they create and disseminate technology and technological capacity depends upon their international competitive position, and the extent to which their production and marketing activities are globally integrated. Some evidence of the significance of technology creation is a competitive force behind the international expansion of MNEs (through generating new O advantages) is reviewed. The evidence for the relationship between this and technology transfer and dissemination is more tentative.

The influence of the foreign investment strategy of MNEs on internal and external technology dissemination is then discussed. A distinction is drawn between resource-based, import-substituting and rationalized types of MNE activity. The part played by these different activities in the global operations of the MNE concerned will affect the degree and form of technology dissemination between subsidiaries. In addition, it is contended that the strength of local competitors, the nature of the linkages with local firms, the structure of the relevant domestic markets and host country government policies, are among the determinants of the amount and speed of technology transfer and diffusion.

The chapter concludes by examining some of the implications of the increasingly footloose nature of many kinds of economic activity, for individual countries that wish to create and sustain indigenous technological capacity. We shall argue that because of the shift towards technological systems or galaxies, the growing linkages between technological developments are likely to entail an increasing interdependence between innovation in different countries. The way in which these developments are allied to patterns of cumulative causation in the international competitiveness of industries is discussed.

THE HISTORICAL TREND TOWARDS TECHNOLOGICAL SYSTEMS

The production and efficient deployment of technology lie at the heart of the growth of most MNEs. Historically, product and process innovations are an essential source of the competitive advantages of firms. Since they arise from the exclusive or privileged possession of a specific asset, they have also been called 'asset' advantages. There is considerable evidence that many MNEs which maintained successful foreign manufacturing facilities abroad before 1914 depended upon specialized product- or process-innovative strengths. Sanna Randaccio (1980), Buckley and Roberts (1982), Archer (1986) and Wilkins (1988) consider the case of European direct investment in the USA before 1914, while Wilkins (1970) describes the foreign expansion of US MNEs in the same period. Chapter 3 of this volume has provided further evidence on the historical

MNEs and Technology Creation and Diffusion 105

role of technology as an *O*-specific advantage fashioning international production.

We have already argued in Chapter 2 that the success of the modern MNE rests on its ability to create or acquire and effectively organize advantages of a transaction cost minimizing kind. In the present context, this type of advantage arises from the role of the firm as a co-ordinator of economic activities requiring different technologies, rather than as a producer of a single product using one particular technology, and that the technologies can only be exploited by the firm producing at different points of the value-added chain or on different value-added chains. The technological complementarity which exists between certain groupings of products and processes is a case in point. Here, Rosenberg (1981) has described how innovative success in related activities, and how the possibility of new applications of any particular innovation, may stimulate complementary innovations. However, close links are required between the creation and use of technology (which is an iterative process), and these links are often maintained more efficiently within the firm or the MNE. Historically, MNEs have increasingly been able to provide such linkages, and to benefit as a result from transaction cost or governance advantages, as the costs of managing larger and more complex firms have fallen (Casson, 1983).

In the past, the relative significance of asset-based (*Oa*) and transaction cost-based (*Ot*) advantages in MNE activity has depended on the overall rate of product and process innovation, and the comparative efficiency of markets and hierarchies as transactional agents. At times, when the pace of new innovations has been especially strong (as in the industrialized world in the 1890s and in the 1950s), then *Oa* advantages played a more prominent role in the internationalization of firms and industries. However, in other periods, the extent of the leadership of particular MNEs over their rivals, in terms of specialized technological strengths, has been much more limited. At these times, MNEs have become more dependent upon other *Oa* advantages, or upon a more careful co-ordination of their international activities.

However, apart from such fluctuations in the balance between *Oa* and *Ot* advantages, there has been an historical shift towards the latter in the organization of MNEs. *Inter alia*, this is associated with the development of integrated technological systems by MNEs, which, to be efficiently exploited, need to be under the control of the same hierarchy. In part, this is the natural outcome of the growth of such industrial firms, and the progress of technological innovation itself, which continually forges new links between established productive experience and potential new applications for the underlying skills and process technology. Moreover, not only has technology become less activity-specific but it has increasingly affected the capacity of firms to co-ordinate different and/or geographically diversified activities. In other words, technology, and its organization has become a generic competitive advantage, not very different in kind from management or entrepreneurship.

This transformation in the extent to which technological innovation is organized within the firm or the MNE can also be attributed to changes in the international economic and political environment. In a purely technological sense, there may well have been benefits from a closer spatial integration of production in the inter-war period, especially between Europe and the USA. However, in these years such a development was inhibited by the height of protectionist barriers (and their increase in the 1930s), and by the political and exchange risks encountered by any MNE that co-ordinated production across potentially hostile countries. Since 1945, the liberalization of trade in manufactured goods between the industrialized countries (particularly within Europe), and the relative political stability of the same regions, has helped to encourage the establishment of global networks of trade and production, within the industrialized and the newly industrialized world.

The change in the international environment has further compelled a move towards integrated technological systems. The advantages which stem from such centralized co-ordination have helped to strengthen the position of many MNEs vis-à-vis uninational firms, who are constrained to follow seriously only those activities in which their own countries have an existing or potential locational advantage. In turn, those MNEs which have remained strongest in the creation of new technology, as well as in its use and dissemination, have generally been those best able to sustain the fastest growth rates of all. The best illustration of this is the emergence of many Japanese firms as important MNES, which have developed a unique capacity for linking import and dissemination of foreign technology to the creation and transfer of new indigenous technology. While Japanese firms accounted for 9.1 per cent of all patents granted in the USA to foreign residents in the period 1963–9, they accounted for a massive 36.5 per cent in 1983,[3] and this improvement was matched by an increase in the Japanese share of the sales of the world's largest 483 industrial firms, from 6.0 per cent in 1962 to 12.1 per cent in 1982 (Dunning and Pearce, 1985). Innovation is now clearly tied to technology creation, organization, transfer and use.

THE DEPENDENCE OF INTERNATIONAL TECHNOLOGY TRANSFER AND DIFFUSION ON THE STRUCTURE OF INDUSTRIES

The extent of international technology dissemination will vary between an industry in which one leading MNE predominates (say, IBM in computers), and an industry in which groups of major rivals coexist (say, pharmaceutical MNEs based in the USA, Germany, Switzerland and the UK). In the former case, technology will be rather more centrally controlled, and its dissemination will tend to run in just one direction. Innovation diffusion outside the MNE is limited to a range of more specialized companies, which typically compete in market segments in which the leader is less involved. In the latter case, the transmittance of technology within the MNE may well run in more than one direction, and it may further diffuse to other MNEs as an input to their own technology creation and transfer.

The location of poles of innovatory capacity in an international industry may affect the nature of the competitive advantages of firms (determining which countries are sources of the strongest MNEs), as well as influencing the location of MNE activity. A shift in the location of innovatory capacity will strengthen the position of the firms, which will increase their stake in the creation of technology. A contemporary example of this is the gradual movement of Japanese firms from the adaptation of existing, to the innovation of new, technology in a number of sectors (such as motor vehicles and consumer electronics).

Meanwhile, over the last decade at least, MNEs based in Europe and the USA have tended to place an increasing emphasis on the more effective use of existing technologies rather than the creation of new technologies. This has required them to give more weight to better organizing and managing technology, one consequence of which has been a trend toward the rationalization of international activity (creating advantages of transaction cost kind through improved co-ordination). The implication is that although US and European MNEs may have slowed down their technology creation (at least relative to Japanese firms), their use and dissemination of technology – both cross-border and within the countries of their affiliates – may well have increased. Firms which become more competitive through their ability to locate and relocate productive activities to the best advantage, while developing the benefits of the common governance of their full range of activities, may well need to increase the transfer of technology between activities and locations. Whether this increases the international dissemination of technology depends, in part, on the capabilities and location of competitors, suppliers and customers.

Despite this shift, most MNEs continue to link technology transfer (and imitation or diffusion from other firms) to efforts toward fresh innovation. In a recent study, based on some field research (Wyatt *et al.*, 1985), when ninety-five leading MNEs were asked to rank different means of maintaining their international competitive advantage, technological superiority was believed to be most important for the sample as a whole. Using data on their patenting activity in the USA, it is also possible to identify the sectoral pattern of the technological advantages of the firms for each industrialized country, using data on their patenting activity in the USA (Soete, 1980). From these data, it is also possible to indicate the types of sectors in which particular countries appear to have particularly strong technological advantages, relative to their major foreign competitors. Cantwell (1985), for example, has shown how, in the early 1980s, established technological advantage calculated in this way has remained especially important for the competitive success of firms from Germany, the UK, the USA and Japan. For the companies of these four countries, the index of technological advantage is significantly

108 *Multinationals, Technology and Competitiveness*

correlated with the industrial distribution of their share in total international manufacturing activity.

We have suggested that the extent and speed of international technology dissemination by MNEs depends upon the structure of the industry in question, the strengths of the constituent firms and their geographical configuration. Consider first an industry which is located in a number of countries, each of which is home to a group of highly innovative firms. This base of technology creation helps to support a network of exports and international production in each case, though, for the reasons outlined above, each firm also becomes dependent upon the co-ordination of connected activities. Over the last twenty-five years, this is the kind of industry that has been characterized by the rise of the cross-hauling of investments between those countries harbouring the strongest firms. Such countries become hosts to the greatest levels of international production as well as being homes to MNEs of their own. We have offered some explanations for this phenomenon in a previous chapter; such intra-industry trade and production are also usually accompanied by intra-industry technology flows as well.

It is in this kind of industry that those countries that have become poles of innovation tend to build up a position of absolute advantage in international trade or as hosts to foreign-based MNEs. This position is achieved by the continuous innovation and growth of production of such a country's own firms and also of the affiliates of foreign MNEs, which adapt their technology in the light of local knowledge and customer requirements. Indeed, one reason why MNEs may invest heavily in such an advantaged country is to take advantage of the agglomerative economies offered by a flourishing innovatory environment. By so doing they may advance the technological capacity of the country. The firms of each country tend to embark on a path of technological accumulation which has certain unique characteristics (Pavitt, 1987). Moreover, the kinds of linkages that grow up between competitors, suppliers and customer in any one country are also, to some extent, peculiar to that country, and imbue the technology creation of its firms (which depends on such linkages) with distinctive features. For these reasons, other MNEs often need to be on-site with their own production and their innovatory capacity if they are properly to benefit from the latest advances in foreign technological development.

By contrast, where the technological capacity of a host country is weak in the sector concerned, the investments of MNEs may drive out local competition and reduce local technological capability still further. Foreign-owned affiliates tend to import a higher proportion of their inputs than do indigenous firms, particularly in the early years of their operations, or where they constitute part of a globally integrated network. Even where host governments set targets for a gradual increase in the local sourcing of components – particularly those which involve high value-added activities (for example, tubes for TV sets, wafers for microchips, chemicals for pharmaceuticals, etc.) – subsidiaries of foreign

MNEs and Technology Creation and Diffusion

companies supplying the parent MNE may be established to fulfil this function.[4] While this may result in a greater international dissemination of technology, it is quite possible that the design, research and development work remains concentrated in the parent company. Indeed, in supply activities upstream from the original investment (for example, in the motor vehicles or electronics components sectors), this is potentially very serious, as the expanding global sales of supplying MNEs allows them to increase their own technological capacity at the expense of local suppliers who are then driven out even more effectively.[5]

In today's international economic environment, MNEs that operate in industries characterized by strong, oligopolistic (or technological) competition normally need a direct presence in each of those countries which hold leading positions in the development of their industries and of associated technologies (Ohmae, 1985). Whether or not this is achieved depends on the strengths of the existing technological capacity of the countries, the policies of these countries regarding inward trade and investments, the strategy and competitive position of the individual MNEs, and the economics of the location of research and development. By contrast, MNEs which are among the world technology leaders are not so concerned with attempting to feed off parallel technologies developed by other firms. In so far as they need to do so, they are content to imitate promising new ventures or, within limitations, perhaps to buy out smaller but innovative competitors. In the case of this kind of MNE, in so far as R &D facilities are decentralized at all, they tend to be located primarily by cost considerations, and there may be little immediate dissemination of technology. The latter situation is today rather more prevalent among US MNEs (and perhaps in the future among Japanese MNEs) than it is among European MNEs. As a rule, European MNEs (and, of course, Third World MNEs) are the most likely to want access to a range of alternative technologies generated outside their home countries, to link together more firmly the creation and dissemination of their own technologies.

However, since it is the US data that are the most readily available, the hypothesis that where international technological competition is greatest then technological interdependence and dissemination will be greater, is most easily tested in the case of US firms. First, let us define the revealed technological advantage (RTA) of US companies as follows (Soete, 1980; Cantwell, 1985):

$$\text{USRTA} = \frac{\text{USP}_i/\text{TP}_i}{\Sigma_i\text{USP}_i\Sigma_i\text{TP}_i}$$

where USP_i represents the number of patents granted in the USA in industry i to US residents, and TP_i denotes the total number of patents granted in the USA in industry i to residents of all countries. The USRTA index has as many observations as there are industries in the sample. The index measures the share of patents for which US firms are responsible in each sector, relative to the US share in total patenting activity across all industries. Hence it consists of a distribution of values which vary around unity, according to whether US firms are relatively technologically advantaged or disadvantaged in each industry. It is clear that the index is normalized for industry-specific differences in the propensity to patent which affect the firms of all countries.

Now, consider further the revealed technological advantage of foreign affiliates of US-based MNEs, which is defined as followed:

$$USFARTA = \frac{FAP_i/FP_i}{\Sigma_i FAP_i/\Sigma_i FP_i}$$

where FAP_i shows the number of patents granted in the USA in industry i to the foreign affiliates of US firms, while FP_i indicates the number of patents granted in the USA in industry i to all foreign-located firms. In this case, interest centres on the industrial distribution of the patenting activity of US-owned foreign affiliates as a share of all foreign patenting activity within the USA. One difficulty with this measure in the present context is that the decentralization of technological capacity within the MNE (as captured by a decentralization of R & D), may not be reflected in the decentralization of patenting activity. Indeed, Etemed and Sequin Dulude (1985) argue that patents are more frequently pooled by MNEs as a means of ensuring a greater strategic control over technology.

The view advanced in this section is that, where US firms are technologically weak, they are unlikely to be able to establish technological capacity abroad, but that, where they are pre-eminent in their industries they will not have the incentive to disseminate technology. The hypothesis is, then, that US MNEs are most likely to invest heavily abroad in R & D sectors where they are confronted with major international rivals whose home countries are sources of innovative activity. This view has also been expressed more generally by Graham (1985) in respect of those sectors where US-owned foreign affiliates are most likely to develop some independent technological capacity. This, then, suggests an inverted U-shaped relationship between USFARTA index and USRTA which was tested by fitting a quadratic function of the following form:

$$USFARTA_i = \alpha + \beta\, USRTA_i + \gamma USRTA^2 + \delta USINT_i + \epsilon_i$$

The variable UNINT is an index of the internationalization of US industries; it is the production of US-owned foreign affiliates divided by domestic US production in the sector in question. It proved important to allow for this additional influence which affects the extent of decentralization of innovative activity. The following regression line was fitted using twenty-seven industry observations for the period 1977–83 (except for the UNINT index, which was calculated for 1983):

MNEs and Technology Creation and Diffusion

$$USFARTA_i = -16.702 + 37.270^* \, USRTA_i - 19.61^* \, USRTA_i^2 + 1.030^{**}UNINT_i$$
$$(-2.04) \quad (2.23) \quad\quad (-2.31) \quad\quad (3.85)$$

$R^2 = 0.454$, $F = 6.38$, * = significant at the 5 per cent level on a two-tailed t-test.
** = significant at the 1 per cent level on a two-tailed t-text.

The negative sign on the coefficient on $USRTA^2$ supports the hypothesis that the function reaches a maximum rather than a minimum point. The coefficients on the independent technological advantage variables are significantly different from zero at the 5 per cent level.

This result provides some support for the hypothesis that the R & D of MNEs is more decentralized where international technological competition is greater. However, a more complete test of this idea awaits the collection of evidence on the geographical and industrial distribution of R & D carried out by US-owned foreign affiliates.

THE DEPENDENCE OF INTERNATIONAL TECHNOLOGY CREATION AND DISSEMINATION ON THE GLOBAL INVESTMENT STRATEGY OF MNEs

For MNEs to be successful in technology-intensive industries, they must not only be productive innovators but successful commercializers and users of that technology. This suggests that they must have, or be able to acquire, the complementary assets needed for commercialization (Teece, 1986) and be able to disseminate among their user subordinates. However, the form that this dissemination takes is closely allied to the prospects for an MNE's diffusion to *other* firms producing in the host country. The implications of transferring technology by way of a co-operative agreement with another firm (whether this takes the form of a joint venture, or some kind of contractual agreement such as the licensing of an unaffiliated company) will be different from the implications of a transfer controlled within the MNE.

The reasons why MNEs may enter into collaborative arrangements are discussed by Cantwell and Dunning (1985) and Contractor and Lorange (1988). Broadly speaking, MNEs more readily transfer technology in this way where their main O advantages derive from their possession of a specific asset or grouping of assets; where the local partner has some synergistic contribution to make (which might include some technological contribution, especially in the case of joint ventures or cross-licensing agreements between MNEs); where the technology is of a mature or standardized kind and is easily codifiable, or is of secondary concern to the major activities in which the MNE is engaged; or where political pressure encourages such arrangements. In the first three cases the diffusion of technology from the affiliates of MNEs to other local firms is likely to be more pronounced due to the very conditions which brought about a co-operative agreement in the first place.

112   *Multinationals, Technology and Competitiveness*

To put this in context, it is important to understand why technology transfer is more frequently internalized within the MNE. Firstly, where technology is not mature or standardized it is not easy to determine its price in an external market (that is, the MNE wishes to ensure that it appropriates a full rent on its O advantages of an asset kind). Secondly, technology dissemination may well involve external economies to the rest of the owning firm which require close co-ordination and feedback between the parties concerned (so the MNE is able to benefit from O advantages of a transaction cost kind). This second factor has become increasingly important, and it is bound up with the need of the MNE to retain control over technology transfer in order to link it more effectively to technology creation through drawing on the feedback that it receives from the transferee. Thirdly, there may be risks (for example, of infringement of property rights) associated with an arm's length transaction which the selling firm is not prepared to bear.

The costs of technology transfer are more significant than is commonly thought (Teece, 1977), and, as market failure may be greater across borders than within a country, the costs of international dissemination between independent firms are especially high. In international dissemination, the technology must be adapted to conform to foreign work practices and existing technology, and to accommodate differences in the infrastructure of the countries within which it must function. In addition, there may be high travel and communication costs involved in the initial establishment of a new technology acquired from abroad (Hirsch, 1976). These costs can be reduced where transfer takes place within the MNE. One reason is that the implementation of technology and the transfer of know-how is greatly facilitated by a close co-operation between the creators and users of technology. One aspect of this is the interactive links between capital goods producers and users that are built into the infrastructure of all industrialized countries (Rosenberg, 1976).

The efficient creation and/or absorption of technology can only be achieved if the environment offers the right market conditions for the supply and use of inputs necessary to it. Innovation is an ongoing process, and it must be sustained to make technology viable at each stage; any given technology is not a static blueprint to be taken off the drawing board and applied at will. This connection between the design, production and use of technology requires a co-ordination which the market is not well suited to achieve. However, if the transfer of technology by an MNE to its subsidiaries is also to give rise to its diffusion within their host countries, this requires some capacity on the part of these countries to absorb and utilize this technology. This is the main reason why innovation diffusion is often harder to achieve in a less developed country.

External technology diffusion is more likely to occur where some related technological capacity already exists among local firms. Otherwise the presence of MNE subsidiaries may act solely as low value

MNEs and Technology Creation and Diffusion 113

satellites of their parent companies. With reference to the 'Le Defi Americain' (Servan-Schreiber, 1968) that threatened the long-term competitiveness of European firms in the 1960s, Cantwell (1985) found that a necessary condition for indigenous revival in Britain, Germany and France was the existence of strong technological advantages on the part of local firms. In such cases, inward direct investment led to technology diffusion, and the competitive stimulation of a new wave of local innovation; the pharmaceutical industry provides an excellent illustration.

In these instances, the investments of US MNEs in Europe were mainly of an import-substituting kind and, by example and competitive stimulus, technology was diffused to their local competitors. Indeed, it was often the potential for such diffusion or imitation which gave the impetus to the displacement of US exports by local European production on the part of US MNEs in the first place. However, import substituting investment also carries with it the possibility of innovation diffusion to local suppliers and customers. It is usually associated with backward technology dissemination from assembly operations to their local component suppliers. This happened in the 1950s and 1960s, and also more recently in the case of Japanese manufacturing investment in the UK, especially in the consumer electronics sector (Dunning, 1986). As innovation diffusion proceeds, subsequent inward MNE investment (or subcontracting arrangements) takes place in more technology-intensive or higher value-added activities at an earlier stage of the vertically integrated chain.

A similar pattern of increased local vertical integration as diffusion proceeds is sometimes observed in the case of MNE investments of a resource-based kind. However, resource-based investments normally lead to forward rather than backward diffusion of technology, for example, into secondary processing activities which may be established locally. This is particularly the case where the cost of transporting the raw materials is greater than the cost of transporting the intermediate or final products. This is more likely to be achieved through national technology diffusion and subcontracting (as opposed to an extension of MNE investment and technology transfer) where the MNE has some monopsonistic power and where the co-ordination with further processing and marketing is not difficult to accomplish.

The exception in the case of resource-based MNE investment is that undertaken in export processing zones, in which the 'resource' being exploited is cheap labour. This is akin to import substituting investment in as much as any subsequent technology diffusion is likely to be upstream in further preparation for the MNE's marketing network abroad. However, MNE investments aimed at taking advantage of cheap labour, or the availability of other local resources in developing countries, have not often led to much technology diffusion to independent firms, except in the electrical and electronics goods sector. All too frequently the technology transferred from MNEs to their subsidiaries and the spillover effects of the latter's presence are confined to low

114 *Multinationals, Technology and Competitiveness*

value-added activities; indeed, where such investment inhibits the development of indigenous firms, which might have produced at other points along the value-added chain, it may actually diminish local technological capacity.

This type of export platform investment in the developing countries is a special case of rationalized investment, in which the affiliate in question is integrated into a global network of activity within the MNE. This kind of investment has grown significantly since the early 1970s, as MNEs have increasingly come to rely upon O advantages of a transaction cost kind through global organization and management. Although international technology dissemination may sometimes be greater within such a system, the extent of diffusion through linkages with host country firms is likely to be less than in the case of import substituting or most resource-based investments. This is because the main linkages of the affiliate are with other parts of the MNE, and in this sense *inter*-border corporate integration may be at the expense of *intra*-border sectoral integration.

However, even in the case of a rationalized investment, it is quite possible that certain activities may be subcontracted locally to other firms. In this situation, it might be supposed that technology diffusion (in both directions) will be greater where the component suppliers are themselves MNEs. Hence, with reference to recent Japanese involvement in the UK colour television sector, the component suppliers such as Phillips and Plessey are as powerful as the CTV companies to whom they sell, unlike in Japan where subcontractors tend to be small and highly specialized. However, much depends upon the strength of the O advantages of these competitor firms. One of the complaints frequently voiced by the UK component suppliers is that they are inhibited from being genuinely global (and hence competitive with other MNEs) because they are prevented from having full access to one of the main growth markets, namely Japan (Dunning, 1986).

The extent to which technology diffuses to other firms in consequence of an MNE investment depends upon the impact on competitors that have local operations, and upon the impact on suppliers and customers, which in turn relates to the strategic decision of the MNE to buy in certain inputs locally rather than importing them. It also depends upon which products the MNE decides to produce locally, and the technology the MNE choses to use in its local operations. The potential for domestic diffusion may be greater where it locates more technology-intensive or higher value-added activities in the host country, and this kind of decision may well be influenced by the state of local industry and by the industrial policies of the local government.

In sum, technology dissemination will be affected by the number and strength of indigenous competitors, the form of linkages with local firms, the structure of the relevant domestic market's host country government policies towards sourcing inputs and encouraging a higher local proportion in value-added, local technological capacity and infrastructure, local managerial skills and the destination of exports from the MNE affiliate.

THE POLICY IMPLICATIONS OF THE CLOSER RELATIONSHIP BETWEEN THE INTERNATIONAL CREATION, TRANSFER AND DIFFUSION OF TECHNOLOGY

The emergence of globally oriented MNEs, within which the international dissemination of technology is now more linked to its creation, has led to an increased mobility of certain types of economic activity – and particularly that in medium and high technology-intensive activities.

The increasingly footloose nature of international production and of innovatory activities is likely to reinforce patterns of cumulative causation within countries. Those countries which are growing more rapidly, upgrading their industrial structures and devoting more resources to the encouragement of indigenous technological capacity (for example, by a well formulated industrial strategy, and an educational policy designed to meet this strategy) are more likely to attract inward MNE investment in technology-intensive activities, and to benefit from the dissemination outside the recipient affiliates. By contrast, countries which are losing international competitiveness are more likely to attract MNE satellites concentrated in assembly and low value-added activities; however, since these affiliates are able to import the O advantages of their parent companies, they may still be able to drive out their local competitors. In so doing they will reduce the technological capacity of indigenous competitors (and that of their suppliers) and, hence, reduce their capacity for domestic technological dissemination consequent upon inward investment. It is this possibility which in the case of recent Japanese direct investment in the UK and the US has been labelled the 'Trojan horse' effect.

Approaching the argument from the role of outward direct investment, where domestic firms hold an internationally strong competitive position, they can usually afford to invest more in technology creation which, through backward linkages, may benefit their domestic suppliers. This, in turn, will strengthen the latter's competitive capacity to supply the affiliates of foreign firms requiring their products. More subcontracting work is then given to domestic suppliers by foreign affiliates, which further strengthens their technological capacity. In this scenario, outward and inward investment are complementary forces making for an improved international competitive situation of the country concerned. But the link to this success is technology creation and dissemination via the MNE.

In summary, then, where economies become convergent in their technological capabilities, aided and abetted by intra-industry trade and production, MNEs may assist in the transfer and diffusion of technology between them. Through cross-investments and spillover effects there is more international diffusion of technology, while technology creation in each country becomes more closely intertwined. Thus, in the context of national economic policy, the MNE may play a dual role. On the one hand, it may serve to increase technological divergences between coun-

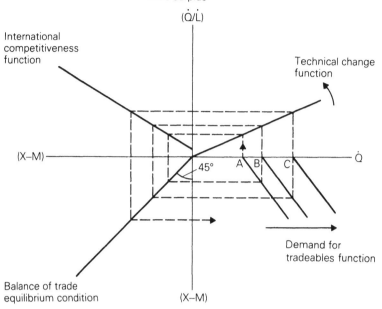

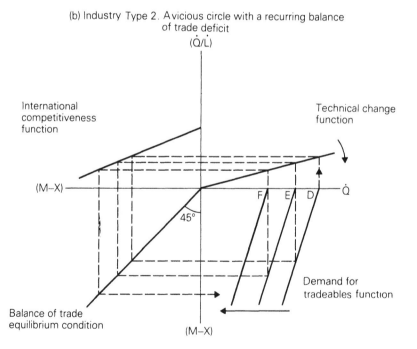

Figure 6.1 *Cumulative Causation in International Trade, Production and Technology Dissemination*

MNEs and Technology Creation and Diffusion

tries; on the other, it may strengthen the technological linkages between them. Whether countries are brought closer together or pushed farther apart, the interdependence between them is increased, and the development of technological systems or galaxies within MNEs reinforces such interdependence between innovation in different countries.

Consider, now, how the technological activities of MNEs may intensify cumulative causation, but operate in different directions in different industries in the same country.[6] Figure 6.1 helps to illustrate how patterns of cumulative causation in international trade become established in the first place.[7] Diagram (a) shows a 'virtuous circle' and diagram (b) a 'vicious circle'. In the present context, any country may have some industries that fall into one group, some that fall into the other, and some which fit in somewhere between the two.

At the top right-hand quadrant is the technical change function which relates the proportional rate of growth of output, Q, to the proportional rate of growth of productivity (Q/L). The output of the industry in volume or constant price terms is denoted by Q, while the number of workers employed is represented by L, and the proportional growth rates are defined as follows:

$$\dot{Q} = \frac{1}{Q}\frac{dQ}{dt}$$

$$\dot{L} = \frac{1}{L}\frac{dL}{dt}$$

$$(\dot{Q}/L) = \dot{Q} - \dot{L}$$

The technical change function shows that higher rates of growth of industry output are associated with higher rates of growth of productivity. This is because the faster growth of output is linked to more rapid technological progress, so that employment growth does not rise by as much as output growth. The greater the technological capacity of the industry, the steeper will be the slope of the technical change function, as the growth of output rises more through innovation. The analogous relationship at a macroeconomic level is known as Okun's law, which suggests that for an economy as a whole a 3 per cent rise in output is in general accompanied by a 1 per cent fall in unemployment.

In the top left-hand quadrant is the international competitiveness function. This suggests that a higher rate of productivity growth is associated with a larger balance of trade surplus (exports minus imports, $X - M$), or with a smaller balance of trade deficit $(M - X)$. Two assumptions are implicit in the derivation of this schedule. First, it is assumed that capital per worker grows at the same rate as productivity (output per worker), so that the capital-output ratio is constant. The reason is that technological change is, to some extent, embodied in new capital equipment. Secondly, it is assumed that, while the wage rate rises

118 Multinationals, Technology and Competitiveness

faster with faster productivity growth, the increase in the growth of wages lags behind the increase in productivity growth. Taken together, these assumptions mean that a higher rate of productivity growth leads to a fall in unit costs, and an increase in profitability and international competitiveness.

A simple balance of trade equilibrium condition is placed in the bottom left-hand quadrant $(X - M = X - M \text{ or } M - X = M - X)$. in the bottom right-hand quadrant is the export demand and demand for imports function. As international competitiveness rises, and export and domestic demand increases (as imports fall), entrepreneurial expectations of future demand improve and investment rises further, in turn increasing the growth of output. Hence, the function is drawn to show that higher net export demand is associated with higher investment and a faster growth of output (and vice versa). However, this is not the end of the story. A more rapid growth of output occasioned by more favourable demand conditions leads to an increased requirement for imported component parts. In other words, in case (a) a higher rate of growth of output leads to an increased demand for imports to support faster rising domestic production, and this pushes the balance of trade back towards equilibrium. This is represented by an outward or rightward shift in the net export demand line, as imports begin to rise at the new rate of growth of output.

It is now clear how a pattern of cumulative causation may become established. Suppose an industry can be depicted by Figure 6.1(a) (Industry type 1) and that it begins with a rate of growth of output at point A. This is associated with a sufficient rate of innovation and productivity growth so that the sector is internationally competitive, and it begins to build up a balance of trade surplus as a result. The rate of growth of output rises to a level equivalent to B, and with this imports begin to rise and the export demand function shifts to the right. However, the faster rate of growth of output is associated with a still more rapid rate of innovation and productivity growth, such that the balance of trade surplus reappears and is even larger than it was previously. This generates a still faster rate of growth of output, at C, and a virtuous circle sets in. In the case of (b) (Industry type 2), cumulative causation operates in the reverse direction, and it moves from D to E to F as the growth of domestic production slows down and balance of trade deficits become larger and larger.

The question might be asked: If this accurately reflects the state of certain industries in the real world, what is to stop this dynamically unstable process from exploding? Here, two possibilities may arise. First, in the case of a virtuous circle, supplies of suitable skilled labour may begin to dry up, causing the wage rate to rise faster than the growth of productivity. Second, this increase in real wage costs may induce a more labour-saving type of technological change such that capital per worker starts to rise faster than productivity, and the capital-output ratio rises. Moreover, as innovation along the prevailing 'technology paradigm' (Dosi, 1983) becomes increasingly difficult, productivity growth

MNEs and Technology Creation and Diffusion 119

falls below the rate of growth of capital per worker for this reason as well. Both these possibilities can be represented by an upward shift in the international competitiveness function in Figure 6.1(a), which has the effect of slowing down the upward spiral of activity, and, within limits, of shutting it off altogether. These arguments can be applied in reverse to explain the stemming of a vicious circle when, for instance, excess supplies of labour cause real wages to fall back and the international competitiveness function of Figure 6.1(b) to shift down.

The role of MNEs suggested earlier can now be incorporated into this model. Inward MNE investment is likely to be attracted into innovative industries caught up in a virtuous circle, and is likely to be associated with local R & D facilities and an increase in indigenous technological capacity. In doing so, foreign-owned affiliates may increase local technological dissemination to suppliers and customers and, by increasing competition, spur local rivals to a higher rate of innovation. Indeed, firms in these industries are probably investors in their own right. The rise in technology creation which accompanies outward and inward direct investment is represented through an upward rotation of the technical change function in Figure 6.1(a). The technological activity of MNEs, and its local dissemination, reinforces the industries' virtuous cycles.

By contrast, inward direct investment may still take place in declining sectors, but it is likely to be in low value-added subsectors of the industry, importing the more high value-added intermediate products. By dint of their higher efficiency, or by deliberate strategy, the foreign affiliates may cut in the markets of local competitors. Indeed, the foreign MNE may be able to finance an increased level of R & D within its parent company from its increased global sales, including its greater market share in the host country. Meanwhile local firms whose markets are cut back may lack the resources to 'go global' themselves, and are consequently compelled to cut back their R & D expenditure. If, in addition, the government of the home country of the MNEs prohibits or creates obstacles against investment by foreign firms in its own domestic market, this constitutes the type of 'technological protectionism' of which the Japanese are sometimes accused (Spencer and Brander, 1983). In these circumstances, inward direct MNE investment is liable not only to drive out local competitors but also to restrict the technology creation of local suppliers, even if more technology disseminates to them from the MNE. For both these reasons, domestic technological capacity is reduced, generating a downward rotation in the technical change function in Figure 6.1(b), and compounding the vicious circle in the local industry.[8]

Studies of US direct investment in Europe in the 1950s and 1960s, and of Japanese investment in the UK in the early 1980s, provide ample evidence of cases where new competitive stimulus helps set in motion or intensifies a virtuous circle, and cases where it drives out local firms and sets in motion a vicious circle of increasing dependency on external sources of supply. Much depends on the initial technological capacity and

120   *Multinationals, Technology and Competitiveness*

international competitiveness of the country and sector in question, and this influences the motivation underlying the MNE investment. Until now, the literature on MNEs and international technology dissemination has not paid attention to this issue, as it has been concerned with the immediate form or impact of technology transfer in a static framework, rather than the unfolding dynamic process which it opens up.

Two UK industries which help to illustrate the role of the location of technological activity by MNEs in cumulative causation are the pharmaceutical and motor vehicles sectors.[9] The UK pharmaceutical industry has become caught up in a virtuous circle since the rise in inward US MNE investment twenty or so years ago, together with its favourable competitive impact (Lake, 1976a and b). The R & D of local UK firms – many of which are active MNEs in their own right – has increased tremendously, as well as the location of R & D facilities on the part of foreign affiliates of MNEs (as described by Brech and Sharp, 1984), and the technological capacity of the UK industry has benefited accordingly. By contrast, the UK motor vehicle industry has undergone a rapid decline since the 1960s, as its international competitiveness has fallen back. In part, this has been due to the increasing global integration of the industry, in which UK affiliates of foreign firms have been linked into MNE networks whose major technological capacity lies outside the UK (Foreman-Peck, 1986); in part it also reflects the inability of the major UK firms to secure a sufficiently high share of the international vehicles market which could fund their own innovatory activities. The net result has been for the UK's technological base in this sector to be squeezed, and this has, equally seriously, spilled over to component suppliers. This type of industry, characterized by a vicious cycle, is reminiscent of Hymer's (1976) theory, which views FDI as having an anti-competitive effect on the structure of local industries.[10]

The major policy implication of the changes described in this chapter is that governments are likely to have to rethink their industrial and technology policies in the light of the activities of MNEs. Technology is not a natural resource; it has to be created and sustained. Increasingly, governments, by a variety of policies, are determining the amount of technology produced and designated in their territories. A government which creates a basis for the domestic location of investment and living standards should have some guidelines for the way in which domestic industry can be restructured in the light of its previous experience. This is the kind of outlook which has been embodied in Japanese (and latterly that of the Singaporean and South Korean) government policy in order to engineer the continual upgrading of domestic industry and the further progression of technological development. Investment in 'sunrise' sectors is welcomed through favourable institutional arrangements, while firms in 'sunset' industries are encouraged to relocate their activities in other South East Asian economies at an earlier stage of development. Clearly, if other governments were to follow a similar course of action, the selection of 'sunrise' industries would differ between countries, depending not only upon their stage of development

MNEs and Technology Creation and Diffusion 121

but also upon their existing technological strengths with a capacity to support further innovation.

Governments can encourage new investment and technology dissemination in those activities in which the prospects for innovation diffusion are greatest, while allowing MNEs to strengthen innovative linkages between technology creation in the domestic economy and other countries which have similar or related advantages. What is clear is that governments cannot ignore the implications of recent developments, both in international innovation and in the cross-border organization of its fruits, in which technology creation and dissemination have become progressively more intertwined, with globally oriented MNEs at the forefront of this process.

NOTES

1 By technological capacity we mean the assets required to produce technology. Technology is a flow of ideas, information and knowledge generated from this capacity. Technology is itself defined as the ability to create output or produce a given output more effectively. It embraces the 'how' of the production process throughout the value-added chain.
2 Note that some commentators distinguish between international transfer and diffusion. Wilkins (1974a), for example, suggests that a technology transferred across national boundaries by an MNE (whether to an affiliate or to a licensee) is only diffused to other firms if it 'spills over' to suppliers or customers in the host country, or if it is imitated by other, indigenous, firms. We shall treat this international diffusion as a particular type of dissemination that takes place within a country and between independent firms.
3 According to the US Office of Technology Assessment and Forecast (unpublished data).
4 As a result of Nissan's investment in the UK, several Japanese component suppliers are setting up plants.
5 Recent studies on the effects of MNEs on the local firms that supply their affiliates are provided by Lall (1980), Landi (1985) and Dunning (1986).
6 The following section summarizes an argument that is set out in greater detail in Cantwell (1987b).
7 This issue, and the policy implications for individual countries, before the MNE is brought into the story, is discussed further by Kaldor (1985), Vandenbroucke (1985), and Eatwell (1982).
8 In the language of the eclectic paradigm, inward investment will be attracted where there are strong specific advantages of the host country, both for the generation of technologically oriented O specific advantages of its own firms and for the utilization of such advantages possessed by foreign-owned MNEs. Inward direct investment will help create or sustain a virtuous circle when it interacts with local competitors to add to indigenous production and technological capacity; it will intensify a vicious circle, which not only drives out local competitors but, by concentrating the high value activities (e.g. innovatory) in the home countries, reduces the production capabilities and hence the L advantages of the host country.
9 Other UK industries in which there is a substantial amount of inward investment fall in between the two extremes but veer towards one or the

other. As a broad generalization, the impact of both inward and outward direct investment seems to have been most favourable in the processing industries and least favourable in the fabricating industries. Whether the recent Japanese investment in motor vehicles and industrial electronics changes this position remains to be seen.

10 The analysis set out in the following paragraphs is taken up in more detail in Cantwell (1988). See also Chapter 7 of this book.

Chapter Seven

International Direct Investment in Innovation: The Pharmaceutical Industry

INTRODUCTION

To a quite unusual extent, the pharmaceutical industry organizes its activities along transnational lines. This is not merely true of production and marketing but also of research and development (R & D). Most large drug companies have research centres of one kind or another in a number of countries, and, to an increasing extent, the products currently arriving on the market have been developed as part of an integrated global, rather than a national or regional, innovatory programme.

How has this process of decentralization come about? What forms has it taken? What have been the motives behind it? What costs and benefits has it entailed for the companies and countries involved? In attempting to answer these questions, this chapter draws upon information collected in the course of two inquiries into the role of multinational enterprises (MNEs) in the pharmaceutical industry; one conducted for the OECD (Burstall, Dunning and Lake, 1981) and another for the EEC (Burstall and Senior, 1985).

The chapter is divided into four main sections. The first describes the extent and pattern of R & D activities undertaken by pharmaceutical MNEs. The second examines the factors making for the decentralization of these activities and the choice of country in which R & D is located. The third section suggests some gains and losses to companies and countries resulting from the internalization of R & D; and the last pays special attention to the UK's situation and the way in which current government policy is affecting the R & D strategies of UK- and foreign-based MNEs.

THE SCALE OF INTERNATIONAL INVESTMENT IN PHARMACEUTICAL R & D

In spite of the high cost of R & D in the pharmaceutical industry, and the economies of scale associated with it, it is not unusual for a major drug

Table 7.1 *Location of R & D Facilities of the Leading Thirty Pharmaceutical Companies in 1985*

Company	France	Germany	Italy	UK	Switzerland	Other Europe	USA	Japan	Other
Bayer (US)	x	x	x	x		x	x	x	x
Merck, Sharp and Dohme (US)	x			x		x	x	x	x
American Home Products (US)							x		x
Hoechst (German)	x	x		x			x	x	x
Ciba-Geigy (Swiss)	x		x	x	x		x	x	
Pfizer (US)	x	x		x			x	x	
Lilly (US)	x			x			x		
Hoffman Laroche (Swiss)	x			x	x		x	x	x
Sandoz (Swiss)					x		x		x
Bristol-Myers (US)	x						x	x	
Smithkline (US)				x		x	x	x	x
Abbott (US)			x				x		
Takeda (Japanese)								x	
Warner-Lambert (US)		x		x			x		
Boehringer-Ingelheim (German)	x	x	x				x	x	
Upjohn (US)	x			x			x	x	
Johnson and Johnson (US)				x		x	x		
Glaxo (UK)			x	x			x		x
Squibb (US)	x	x		x			x		
Rhone-Poulenc (French)	x			x					
Cyanamid (US)			x	x			x		
Schering–Plough (US)	x				x		x		x
ICI (UK)	x			x			x		
Wellcome (UK)				x			x		
Beecham (UK)				x					
Dow (US)	x		x	x			x		
Schering, AG (German)		x						x	
Fujisawa (Japanese)								x	
Sankyo (Japanese)								x	
Shionogi (Japanese)								x	

Source: Author's estimates.

Table 7.2   *Estimated R & D Expenditure by Pharmaceutical Companies in Various Countries in 1982 ($ million)*

| Country of expenditure | Nationality of company | | | | | | | | | |
	Belgium	France	Germany	Italy	Netherlands	UK	Switzerland	USA	Japan	Total
Belgium	30	10						30		70
France		400	50			20	20	80		600
Germany	15		700					50		800
Italy		10	20	120		20	30	50		230
Netherlands					80			10		90
UK		20	20		10	400	20	120		600
Switzerland			10				450			475
USA		10	100		10	50	250	2,000		2,500
Japan			20				30	100	700	850
Total	45	450	950	120	100	500	800	2,500	700	6,300

Note: Because of problems of allocation, columns and rows do not total. In addition, these estimates are based on data from a variety of sources and involve a considerable element of guesswork.

Source: Author's estimates.

126 *Multinationals, Technology and Competitiveness*

firm to conduct research in several countries. Table 7.1 shows the location of the R & D laboratories of the world's top thirty companies. It can be seen that, apart from the Japanese firms whose international operations are generally very limited, these enterprises normally decentralize at least part of their R & D activities.[1] It should be noted that the local testing of new drugs is not included in these activities.

Merely to enumerate these laboratories, however, can be misleading. Their capabilities may vary greatly. At one extreme, they may be freestanding research complexes able to carry out all stages of product innovation. At the other, they may be limited to specialized functions, for example, process or product adaptation to meet the needs of local markets. Our inquiries suggest very strongly that a firm will normally conduct the most sensitive and demanding types of work in centres located in its country of origin. Only a few of the top thirty companies own laboratories conducting basic research situated elsewhere.

To put a figure on the foreign research effort of these firms is difficult. Some more or less informed guesses are presented in Table 7.2. As a group, the Swiss companies spend the highest proportion of their research funds abroad; in the early 1980s, this approached 40 per cent of the total, most of which went to their laboratories in the USA. American member firms of the Pharmaceutical Manufacturers Association spent about 20 per cent of their combined R & D budget in 1980 outside the USA, with about three-quarters going to Western Europe and most of the rest to Japan.

Companies based in the EEC show a more varied pattern. Taken together, British firms are now probably spending upwards of 20 per cent of their research funds abroad, a substantial proportion being placed in their US subsidiaries. The same is true of their German rivals. French and (still more) Italian companies, however, have a much less international approach to research, as do those of the smaller European countries. Japanese MNEs currently do almost all their research at home.

The position of the host nations also merits attention. In most countries – Switzerland is the most important exception – a significant part of pharmaceutical research spending originates with the local affiliates of foreign multinational companies. In Italy the proportion is more than 40 per cent, and in France and the UK about 30 per cent. Elsewhere it is lower but still appreciable: 20 per cent in Japan and the USA, and 10–15 per cent in Germany and the Netherlands. (The balance between inward and outward direct investment in R & D activity is discussed later in this chapter.)

The extent to which R & D has been internationalized has increased during the past decade. The proportion of the research budget spent abroad by major American drug firms almost tripled between 1970 and 1980. Although there are no quantitative data on their European counterparts, there is little doubt that they, too, have done likewise. In particular, investment by UK MNEs in fine chemicals and pharmaceutical activity in the US has dramatically risen in the last decade (see

Table 7.3 *International Biotechnology Agreements 1981–First Quarter of 1986*

	Acquisition	Venture capital/ equity investment	Contract R & D	Joint R & D	License/ production	Distribution/ marketing	Joint production/ marketing distribution/ establishment of new firms	Total types of agreements*	Total number of contracts
Belgium	1	1	1	3		1	2	9	9
Denmark		1	2	2	1	1	1	8	7
Finland			1		1	3		5	3
France	4	1	6	3	4	6	5	29	21
Germany	1	1	7	6	14	18	3	50	31
Italy		3	1	3	2	1	1	11	10
Netherlands	2	3		2		2	1	10	9
Norway		1						1	1
Spain		1		1			1	3	2
Sweden	3	3	5	4	5	6	3	29	19
Switzerland	1	2	11	4	5	6	5	34	26
UK	4	11	4	5	4	5	5	38	35
Total Europe	16	28	38	33	36	49	27	227	173
Japan	2	24	30	24	40	59	24	203	141

* Some contracts may involve more than one type of agreement.

Source: This table is based on data compiled by Rachel Schiller, Office of Basic Industries, International Trade Administration, US Department of Commerce.

128 *Multinationals, Technology and Competitiveness*

Chapter 11). Research has followed the same path as production and marketing, though not to the same extent and at a later point in time.

In the 1980s, there have been an increasing number of cross-border collaborative agreements concluded between MNEs, particularly in biotechnology, in which the pharmaceutical industry is becoming increasingly involved. Some details of such agreements involving US firms are set out in Table 7.3.[2] As will be seen, about one-third relate to R & D. Examples include Ciba Geigy (Switzerland) teaming up with Chiron Corporation (USA) to develop vaccines for AIDS and other adult diseases, Genetech (USA) and Speywood Laboratories (UK) are co-operating to develop Factor VIII, and Genex (USA) is undertaking contract research for Mitsui Toatsu Chemicals (Japan) to develop a microbial strain that produces human urokinase. Japan, indeed, has concluded almost as many international agreements in biotechnology as the USA; 203 over the period 1981 to 31 March 1986, compared with the USA's 227 (Yuan, 1987).

MOTIVES FOR INTERNATIONAL INVESTMENT IN RESEARCH

An MNE may engage in foreign R & D activities for a variety of reasons (Hakanson and Zander, 1986). Usually, the initial entry is either by way of an acquisition of a firm already undertaking R & D, or the setting up of technical support facilities. In a study conducted by Ronstadt (1977), almost one-half of the R & D laboratories originally established as *transfer technology* units were found to have evolved into *indigenous technology* units. In certain cases the driving force was circumstances that no longer exist: thus, the Swiss majors began their involvement with the USA as a hedge against a possible world war. In general, however, the decision to move abroad or to expand an existing laboratory is strongly influenced by certain common factors, some of which were internal to the firm and some of which result from action by the governments of host nations.

The most powerful reason for decentralizing R & D is the desire to exploit the pool of research talents of another country 'to tap into another scientific culture', as one researcher director has put it. In a comment on the setting up of Hoechst's overseas R & D activities, Garies (1971) noted that although economies of scale dictated a centralized R & D function, the desire to profit from the talents of foreign chemists and pharmacologists, and the need to be part of the communities at the forefront of pharmaceutical research, were powerful decentralizing forces. In operational terms, this means forming close relationships with local universities and other public research centres and using the special skills and insights of local scientists. This cannot be done at a distance or second hand. It is best achieved by creating a local research centre of genuine innovative capacity, which can interact fruitfully with the national scientific community. Clearly this is an

Investment in Innovation: The Pharmaceutical Industry 129

expensive course of action which only a few companies (and countries) can afford.

Commercial reasons often play a part in the decision to begin R & D abroad. Availability and cost of research scientists is obviously a critical consideration, while a large national market may require particular products in particular forms. Generally it is best to develop these products on the spot and in close association with the local production and sales personnel. There is an obvious analogy here with the product cycle (Vernon, 1966, 1979). In addition, it is sometimes said that, other things being equal, doctors are more willing to prescribe drugs which have some local content. Such requirements can, however, be met by relatively simple facilities and represent a much lower level of commitment and expenditure on the part of the parent company than does a major centre. Major centres are, of course, much more common. Most foreign-based R & D facilities engage in technical support activities, formulae or process adaptation and product development. A few MNEs engage in some international rationalization of R & D, and the pursuance of specialized research programmes. Country-specific characteristics are often relevant in this connection. For example, research into tropical diseases peculiar to particular countries or areas may be best carried out in those particular locations; on the other hand, many drugs needed by developing countries fall into the category of orphan drugs, so named because the markets for them are too small to allow private firms to recoup their R & D costs.

Pressures and/or support from host governments are also important. Many national administrations are anxious to build up their national capacities for pharmaceutical innovation, in effect, as a form of import substitution. They use a variety of instruments for this purpose, cash or in-kind grants for R & D, procurement preferences and domestic content requirements. In the UK, for example, the permitted rate of return on capital for drug companies depends, *inter alia*, on their innovatory activities in the UK. Similarly in France, the prices which foreign drug firms are allowed to charge are based on the extent to which they produce in the country; once again, spending on R & D is taken into consideration. Measures of this kind are common in both the developed and the developing world, and cannot but have an effect on locational policies.

Other forms of government action are less important. Controls over the introduction of new drugs vary considerably in extent and severity from country to country. At the present time, however, many products have to be sold worldwide to recoup their development costs, and the incentive to shift research to permissive nations is reduced. Nevertheless, in recent years American companies have often chosen to introduce their latest drugs in Europe rather than in the more restrictive regulatory environment of the USA, and this has undoubtedly influenced their levels of spending abroad. Although sometimes appreciable in their effects, tax concessions and subsidies do not seem to have played much part in decisions to move research to other countries.

MNEs may pursue various strategies towards the international organi-

130 *Multinationals, Technology and Competitiveness*

zation of their research activities. Hood and Young (1982) distinguish between three main types of R & D laboratories which a foreign subsidiary might house. These are (1) laboratories whose primary function is to assist the production and marketing facilities in a host country to make effective use of technology and ideas imported from the parent company; (2) locally integrated laboratories which, while remaining predominantly oriented towards the sources and needs of the host country, undertake some product of process adaptation, development and design work, and (3) the international interdependent laboratory which, though located in a particular host country, undertakes R & D on behalf of the global needs of the MNE.

A related classification to that of Hood and Young is made by Ghoshal and Bartlett (1987) who delineate the innovatory activities of MNEs according to where the R & D is undertaken and for what purpose. Thus, they define local-for-local R & D activities as those in which a particular national subsidiary of the MNE creates and complements innovations entirely at a national level. Where these innovations are found to be applicable in multiple locations, they become local-for-global activities. By contrast, a centre-for-global innovatory strategy is that in which a central R & D laboratory creates a product, process or system for worldwide use, while global-for-global innovations are those which are created by pooling the resources and capabilities of many different R & D units to arrive at a jointly developed general solution to a worldwide problem (Ghoshal and Bartlett 1987, p. 11).

The great majority of the leading pharmaceutical companies identified in Table 7.1 (see p. 124) still undertake most of their basic R & D activities in their home countries, and operate or support locally integrated laboratories in other developed countries, and in India and Brazil. The European MNEs tend to be less ethnocentric in their R & D strategies than either the American or the Japanese; and a number, for example, Ciba-Geigy, Welcome and Hoechst undertake some fundamental (and usually specialized) research in at least some of their foreign R & D laboratories. Increasingly, however, there appears to be a shift in the organization of R & D among pharmaceutical MNEs of all nationalities from a local-for-local to a local-for-global stance, and from a centre-for-global to a global-to-global stance. Among the reasons for this are: the continued growth of world demand for drugs and an increasing internationalization of their production; the steeply rising cost of R & D; the trend towards cross-border corporate alliances (particularly in the more complex areas of physio-chemical and biotechnology research); the increasing spread of scientific and technological capacity; and advances in transborder data transmitting facilities.

THE CHOICE OF HOST COUNTRY

Companies do not, of course, consider the possibility of starting research abroad in the abstract: they usually have a host country or countries in

Table 7.4 *Opportunities for R & D: Host Country Characteristics 1985*

Country	Strength of scientific community	Commercial characteristics		Regulatory regime	
		Size of local market	Price level	Control over new drugs	Encouragement to maximize local R & D activities
Belgium	Medium	Small	Low	Moderate	Yes
France	Medium	Large	Low	Moderate	Yes
Germany	High	Large	High	Moderate	No
Italy	Medium	Medium	Low	Moderate to easy	?
Netherlands	Medium	Small	High	Moderate to severe	No
UK	High	Medium	Medium	Moderate to severe	Yes
USA	High	Very large	High	Severe	No
Japan	Medium	Very large	High	Severe	No
Third World countries	Low[1]	Small[1]	Variable	Easy[1]	Often

[1] India and Brazil are exceptions where there is some indigenous scientific capacity and the size of the market is medium. Control over new drugs is moderate and there is a strong encouragement of foreign MNEs to decentralize their R & D activities. At the same time, in both countries a major effort is being made to build up indigenous innovatory capabilities.

Source: Author's estimates.

132 *Multinationals, Technology and Competitiveness*

mind. The choice between alternatives is necessarily complex. But it seems likely that local strength in scientific capability, a large local drug market, and incentives or pressures from host governments comprise the main locational variables affecting R & D investment. At the same time, the history of the company, its current competitive strengths and weaknesses and its international strategy also come into play. It is therefore interesting to see how thirty years of multinational activity in the field of research have worked out for the principal host countries.[3]

Focusing first on the UK – which we discuss in more detail later in this chapter – Table 7.4 shows the presence of a very strong scientific community. The pricing system is generous as pricing systems go (although it has become less so since 1983), and actively encourages foreign companies to expand their local activities. Testing and other controls over the introduction of new drugs are strict but applied in a relatively flexible way. The national drug market is of moderate size. Britain is a favourable site for foreign MNEs to conduct R & D, and several have built up centres of considerable size and innovative capacity. United States' firms are particularly prominent, but German, Swiss and French companies are also active. There is strong evidence to suggest that the high quality of British science and higher educational facilities has been the main reason for this development.

France, on the other hand, seems, in certain respects, less well placed. The French scientific community does not command the same international respect as that of the British, French drug prices are low, and relations between government and industry are strained. At the same time, the French pharmaceutical market is a large one, and successive administrations have put considerable pressure on foreign MNEs to maximize the value-added component of their local operations. As a result, investment in R & D by foreign firms is considerable. However, the bulk of these research centres are used for local product development or for specialized kinds of research, and few if any have a serious capacity for innovation.

Germany has attracted less attention from foreign MNEs than might have been expected. German science has an excellent reputation, the internal market is the largest in Europe, and the regulatory regime is benign. It is, however, an expensive place to do research, and the markedly non-interventionist attitude of the German government may have had an effect. The same is true of Switzerland, where the indigenous demand for drugs is, in any case, quite small. The foreign research centres in Belgium and Italy have largely come about as a result of the acquisition of innovative local firms by foreign companies.

The USA is particularly well placed to attract foreign investment in pharmaceutical research. It not only dominates the world of science but also forms the largest national market in the world. Controls over the introduction of new drugs are extremely strict, but prices are uncontrolled. Apart from safety considerations, American governments leave the industry to its own devices. Many foreign MNEs have set up research

Investment in Innovation: The Pharmaceutical Industry 133

establishments in the USA, several of them being of the greatest importance. The Swiss multinationals predominate, but more recently German and British firms have expanded their American activities.

Japan is a large, rapidly growing and more or less isolated drug market. Research carried out in Japan by companies from abroad has expanded considerably during the past decade. In part, this has resulted from increased general investment in the Japanese pharmaceutical sector, but there is also considerable interest in Japanese expertise in such fields as anti-cancer drugs and biotechnology.

It is also instructive to glance at countries which are unattractive as locations for research. Most Third World countries are in this position. They are generally weak in fundamental knowledge – India is one exception – and often provide a hostile political climate. Their only interest is as sources of exotic compounds of animal or vegetable origin, or as sources of diseases which are endemic to their part of the world. Few foreign companies are keen to place research centres in these nations, and where they have done so it is often as a result of political pressure (Burstall, 1979). The new World Health Organization (WHO) special tropical disease programme offers opportunities for collaboration in research between private companies and the public sector, but in recent years it has not been well supported by governments (NEDO, 1987a).

The foregoing review suggests a number of general conclusions. First, from the standpoint of the MNE, there is no single reason which explains why one country is chosen rather than another as a location for R & D activity. A research centre in nation A may be there because local science is strong, or in nation B because of arm twisting on the part of the local government or in nation C because the multinational took over a local firm in order to penetrate the national market.

Second, it seems that different motives lead to different results. If the desire to exploit local scientific talent is an important consideration, then laboratories with a capacity for innovative work may well emerge. If, however, political pressures or purely commercial motives are uppermost, then local R & D may be limited in scope. It is quite possible for the same volume of inward investment in research to produce widely divergent outcomes.

GAINS AND LOSSES: A GENERAL REVIEW

What have been the rewards and penalties for the internationalization of pharmaceutical research? The evaluations of the industry must necessarily differ from those of governments. In turn, a government's views will vary according to (1) whether it is the donor or the recipient, (2) its strategic and developmental goals, (3) the strength of its indigenous industry and (4) its policies towards inward and outward direct investment.

134   *Multinationals, Technology and Competitiveness*

Table 7.5   *Some Possible Gains and Losses from the Internationalization of R & D*

Protagonist	Gains	Losses
Multinational company	●Greater efficiency in product innovation and/or development ●Improved access to local markets.	●Reduced economies of scale.
Host nation	●Improved employment ●Access to high technology and related scientific skills ●Strengthened links with other sectors.	●Damage to indigenous companies ●Dilution of control over local innovative capacity
Donor nation	●May strengthen overall position of indigenous companies.	●Possible loss of employment. ●Reduction in local innovative capacity.

Source: Author's estimates.

The Position of the Industry

Taking first the industry's perspective, it is possible that a company might both gain and lose by spreading its R & D over several countries (see Table 7.5). It could gain in terms of the efficiency with which it develops or modifies its products and taps into a larger pool of scientific talent and entrepreneurial stimulus. It could lose by failing to realize economies of scale and the scope of centralized R & D as fully as would otherwise be the case.

There is evidence of both positive and negative effects, but on the whole it seems probable that the former predominate. As far as innovative research is concerned, there are dis-economies as well as economies of scale, and for many companies the point of diminishing returns has already been reached in their original centre. Moreover key scientific talent, such as the users of such talent, are geographically more dispersed than they have ever been (Doz, 1987). Increasingly, large pharmaceutical companies are finding it desirable to have an R & D presence at or near the main innovatory centres in the USA and Europe. When a new establishment is to be set up, there are good reasons, which have already been discussed, for placing it in a different culture. Those who have done so seem to be pleased with the outcome. Equally, product development for substantial markets, for example, in Japan, almost always requires some local input and, therefore, some local facilities.

The losses to a company come if and when it is obliged to expand its local R & D beyond the level that it considers to be economically or strategically appropriate. This may have happened on occasion – the

Investment in Innovation: The Pharmaceutical Industry

definition of 'appropriate' is necessarily flexible – but that it has been a critical factor may be doubted. As yet, the additional investment required by a local research centre has usually been fairly modest. In effect, it is a condition of operating in an otherwise worthwhile market, and it is a price that companies seem willing to pay. Remarkably few of them have chosen to withdraw from a country when this particular pistol has been held to their heads. At the same time, they may limit the nature and form of their R & D activities, and, in particular, confine their more sensitive and innovatory research to their domestic laboratories.

The Position of Host Nations

A host nation faces a different set of costs and benefits. By attracting foreign investment in R & D it gains in terms of employment and access to foreign know-how and specialized skills. The demands of the incomers may stimulate the growth of related parts of the economy. Backward linkages to the universities and to the suppliers of specialized goods and services are especially important.

On the debit side, the position of indigenous companies may be adversely affected through unacceptable competitive pressure for limited human resources. Local control over the national capacity for pharmaceutical innovation may be diluted. This is particularly the case when an innovative local company is acquired by foreign interests, as has happened in Belgium, Italy and Denmark. Even with goodwill on both sides, the interests of the company and the host nation may be in conflict.

Once again the balance appears to lie on the positive side. There is little evidence that the presence of foreign-owned research centres has weakened local industries. The British experience suggests that shortages of skilled personnel or specialized services have not been a limiting factor for either indigenous or foreign companies. Indeed, it is highly probable that demand has stimulated supply.

The issue of national control is more contentious. A substantial proportion of the innovative capacity of several European countries is in foreign hands. This is a legitimate cause for anxiety. It is, however, fair to say that this has not happened in the nations whose record of innovation is genuinely outstanding. Rather, they have attracted investment by foreign MNEs while their own firms have continued to flourish and expand.

The reason for this state of affairs is simple. The major drug companies developed in nations where the social, economic and cultural infrastructure is favourable. A foreign multinational will look for the same underlying factors in selecting a host country. It is strength that attracts, not weakness.

The Position of Donor Nations

If there are distinctive gains from being a recipient of inward research investment, the position of the countries whose firms provide the investment is less clear.

136 *Multinationals, Technology and Competitiveness*

At first sight it might appear that they must lose. Work which is done abroad is not done at home. Employment suffers, and the national capacity for innovation is reduced. Much anxiety has been expressed about these possibilities, especially in the USA. A closer examination suggests, however, that there are advantages as well as disadvantages for the donor nation.

A country gains by having strong rather than weak drug companies. With the rising costs of R & D – it has recently been estimated that it can cost up to $54 million to develop a major new drug (*Economist*, 1987) – it is essential that they produce and market on a global basis. They will, however, place most of their really high value and innovatory intensive manufacturing activities in their country of origin. These activities will grow in importance with the firms. Up to a point, therefore, a company will gain by expanding its foreign operations.

Do such arguments apply to R & D? Within limits, the answer is 'yes'. Much development work has to be done near the market. If undertaken at home it would be less effective and the company would suffer. The situation with regard to innovative research is less certain. Even here, however, a laboratory may well gain by exposure to different ideas and techniques.

Once again there is a parallel with the product cycle theory. Just as the manufacture of novel goods initially takes place at home, and is only later shifted abroad to exploit local advantages in production, so with R & D. Innovation is concentrated in the country of origin, while the work of adaptation to local markets takes place elsewhere. In both cases the object is to maximize the profits generated by the innovation.

A nation would unquestionably lose capacity if a major firm were to move all its research abroad. It is highly probable that it benefits when selected parts are transferred to other countries.

THE UK PHARMACEUTICAL INDUSTRY

We now turn to examine some of the issues raised in this chapter from the perspective of the UK pharmaceutical industry.

Some Statistics

In 1980, according to the Association of the British Pharmaceutical Industry (ABPI), 69 per cent of the sales of the ethical proprietaries supplied to the National Health market in the UK were supplied by affiliates of foreign MNEs. In the same year, about one-half of the sales of the major UK-owned pharmaceutical companies were produced by their foreign subsidiaries. The position as regards R & D is rather different; only about one-third of R & D undertaken in the UK is by non UK-owned companies, while UK-owned MNEs undertook nearly four-fifths of their R & D in the UK.

However, perhaps of greater relevance to the present discussion is the extent to which the UK, relative to other countries, is a favoured location for R & D activities on the part of domestic and foreign-based

Investment in Innovation: The Pharmaceutical Industry

MNEs. Data produced by OECD and the National Economic Development Office (NEDO 1987a) suggest that, in the late 1970s, the UK accounted for 3.5 per cent of the non-communist world consumption and 5 per cent of its production of pharmaceutical products. However, the UK was host to 11.5 per cent of the value of R & D activity of UK- and foreign-based companies, so clearly, compared to its consumption and production of pharmaceuticals, the UK has revealed a comparative advantage in high value activity. In 1985, British discoveries accounted for five out of the ten top selling medicines in the world (NEDO, 1987a). The proportion of the UK workforce in pharmaceuticals employed in R & D activity rose from 10.2 per cent in 1967 to 16.6 per cent in 1981. Of the 30 largest pharmaceutical MNEs in 1982, 16 had R & D facilities in the UK, compared with 23 in the USA, 11 in France and 7 each in Italy and Germany. Of the 48 major R & D establishments in the world with fundamental research capacity, 31 per cent are in the UK, 13 per cent in Germany and 6 per cent in France (Brech and Sharp, 1984). In the 1980s, the UK has consistently earned a surplus on its technological balance of payments account.

The Attractions of the UK

The reason for the attractions of the UK as a research base have been described earlier in this chapter, while in the previous chapter we argued that the UK pharmaceutical industry is a good example of the operation of the long run process of cumulative technological causation at work, leading to a virtuous circle of inward investment, innovation, domestic competitiveness and growth.[4]

In a paper presented to an Office of Health Economics conference on 'The Sunrise Industries' in 1984, Professor Bruce Williams argued that there were two reasons for the relative decline of much of UK industry in the twentieth century. The first was that it failed to appreciate the need for a holistic and integrated approach to the production chain from purchasing, through research and development, to manufacturing, testing and marketing. Too often it seemed, UK firms concentrated their efforts on innovating new products and production methods but paid insufficient attention to their commercialization or marketing. Put slightly differently, UK firms paid too little heed to minimizing the transaction costs associated with their innovatory and production programmes. The second reason he pinpointed was the inability of the British educational system to provide for the changing needs of industry, one result of which was that the best graduates preferred careers in the professions, the civil service and the City of London.

An examination of the pharmaceutical industry suggests that neither of these constraints applied. Like other processing sectors in which the UK also excels the industry has long taken a co-ordinated approach to innovation, production and marketing, *inter alia*, as witnessed by its well developed links with university and medical schools at the beginning of the value-added chain to its interface with medical practitioners and

138   *Multinationals, Technology and Competitiveness*

pharmacists in the marketing of its products. Moreover, the scientific infrastructure and regulatory environment for the testing of drugs has been generally favourble, as (until 1983) had been the scheme adopted by the UK government (the Pharmaceutical Price Regulatory Scheme – PPRS) for setting maximum profit targets for companies supplying the National Health Service. Finally, the structure of the industry, consisting as it does of several large companies, including MNEs or subsidiaries of MNEs and a large number of smaller firms, has been sufficiently competitive to encourage both innovation by indigenous companies and the dissemination of imported innovation (Burstall, Dunning and Lake, 1984). Lake (1976b) concluded that the impact of US pharmaceutical investment in the UK had speeded up the rate of indigenous technological development and had led to an improved competitive position in world markets.[5]

The Impact

These circumstances have led to the UK being an attractive base for innovation in pharmaceuticals. The question now arises: To what extent has the internationalization of research been beneficial from the viewpoint of the UK? Can one identify the optimum amount of research which should be done in the UK? Let us consider four possible scenarios, which are set out in Figure 7.1.

Scenario 1 corresponds to a situation in which every MNE, be it British- or foreign-owned, concentrates all of its innovatory activities in its home country. Scenario 2 represents the state of affairs in which UK firms decentralize at least some of the R & D outside their home country but foreign firms do not, while Scenario 3 shows the converse situation. Scenario 4 corresponds to the realities of the present day. Given that Britain is an attractive place for foreign companies to locate R & D facilities, what would be the advantages and disadvantages for British firms and for Great Britain as a whole if the pattern of R & D location moved in the direction of Scenarios 1, 2 or 3? From a company standpoint, Scenario 1 would bring with it distinct losses compared with Scenario 4. It would be more difficult to exploit other scientific cultures and to modify products for local markets. Foreign firms would, of course, suffer from the same problems. From the national point of view, employment would be reduced – there is currently more inward- than outward-innovating activity by pharmaceutical MNEs – with possible adverse feedback effects on the universities and other providers of specialized services and manpower. National control over the UK industry would, however, be somewhat strengthened, since innovative capacity would be entirely concentrated in locally owned firms and within the UK.

In Scenario 2, the outcome is seen to be rather different. The international competitive strength of UK companies is improved, but the amount of R & D undertaken in Britain falls. National control is also reduced. In this alternative, UK pharmaceutical companies may gain,

Investment in Innovation: The Pharmaceutical Industry

Scenario 1: All Companies Do All R & D in Home Country

Gains	*Losses*
● Increased control over use of R & D capacity.	● Loss of capacity to innovate and develop products for local market. ● Reduction in volume of R & D. ● Negative feedback on universities, other parts of industry and the economy.

Scenario 2: UK Companies Do R & D
Worldwide; Other Companies Do R & D in Home Country

Gains	*Losses*
● Capacity for innovation and development of UK firms improved relative to that of overseas competitors.	● Reduction in R & D activity with corresponding loss of employment. ● Negative feedback on university, other parts of the industry and the economy. ● Possibly more redirection of R & D activity to main centres of innovation (e.g. the USA).

Scenario 3: UK Companies Do All R & D in Home Country; Other Companies
Do R & D Worldwide

Gains	*Losses*
● Increase in R & D and rise in UK employment. ● Positive feedback to universities, other parts of the industry and the economy.	● Possible loss of capacity for innovation and development of indigenous companies if outcompeted by foreign firms.

Scenario 4: All Major Companies Do R & D Worldwide

● This is the situation at the moment, but, of course, the UK could gain or lose R & D capacity according to its location attractions vis-à-vis its major competitors.

Figure 7.1 *Possible Gains and Losses Resulting from Change in Location of Innovatory Activities by MNEs*

but the country loses. The reverse is true of Scenario 3. The volume of pharmaceutical research carried out in Britain rises and national control over the industry is increased. The competitive position of the UK firms falls, however, as their innovative capabilities are reduced.

These explorations are, of course, quite tentative, and we have not attempted to quantify the outcome. It is, however, possible to come to certain conclusions. The first is that, providing the UK can offer the right kind of locational attractions for R & D, Scenario 4 is probably the most likely to ensure the continuation of the virtuous cycle of technological accumulation referred to earlier. Scenario 2 is the least desirable, particularly if other countries are seen to offer better opportunities than

140 *Multinationals, Technology and Competitiveness*

the UK for innovatory activities on the part of British MNEs. The second is that in this matter the interests of the industry are not *necessarily* identical with those of the country. Steps that strengthen a company may reduce employment or dilute national control. This is not to say that they will; rather, it is to suggest that a potential dilemma could exist.

Our second conclusion is that the actual state of affairs, if not optimal, is at least one which offers advantages to all parties. As we have already seen, the amount of pharmaceutical research undertaken in Britain is substantially higher than would be the case in two of the three alternatives which we have identified. National control over the industry is very considerable, since British firms continue to do the bulk of their research in the UK, and to account for the majority of spending there. At the same time, these companies are strongly competitive and seem likely to continue to be so.

The Future of Innovatory Activities and UK Government Policy

What now of the future? We would make three points. First, although R & D activity by MNEs tends to be more concentrated than production, the pattern is changing. In 1982, for example, US firms undertook 18.4 per cent of their pharmaceutical R & D outside their home countries, double that in the early 1960s. Partly, this is a deliberate company policy as production and markets have become geographically more dispersed (Dunning and Pearce, 1985), and partly it is a response to government persuasion. But for reasons set out in Chapter 11, we believe that R & D activities may become more footloose in the future, and that the role of government in influencing this location will increase.

Having said this, is the competitive position of UK MNEs improving or deteriorating? And what of the UK as a base for R & D? An examination of the sales and employment of MNEs of all nationalities (Dunning and Pearce, 1985) suggests that UK MNEs have been expanding their share of the output of the world pharmaceutical industry. However, there were suggestions that these same MNEs are increasing the proportion of their value-adding activities, including R & D, which they undertake outside the UK, while foreign-based MNEs are switching innovatory and manufacturing activities away from the UK to a European location.

We believe this to be a signal to governments to recognize the crucial role which their policies play in influencing the production and transaction costs of the pharmaceutical firms, and to acknowledge that this is not something for which the firms themselves have sole responsibility. Many of the country-specific advantages which currently influence the loction of R & D activity have been 'created' or 'engineered' by governments, and often the social net benefits of such activities are likely to be greater than the private net benefits.[6] Such advantages include the availability of suitably trained chemists, pharmacologists, biotechnicians, etc.; a strong interface between the academic and industrial scientific community, and an environment in which the 'customer contract' principle

Investment in Innovation: The Pharmaceutical Industry 141

can flourish;[7] active and well supported co-operative research institutions; realistic regulatory and safety provisions, a patent system and pricing drugs which gives the deserved impetus for innovatory activities; and the provision of the communications infrastructure necessary to operate an efficient globally oriented industry.

However, with its higher education and R & D cuts in the 1980s, its reduction of the industry's target rate of return in 1983 from 25 per cent to 17 per cent, a price freeze, its curtailing of the industry's freedom to charge promotional expenses against profits and the introduction of a 'limited list' of medicines for which the National Health Service is prepared to pay, the UK government has hindered rather than advanced the attractiveness of the UK as a site for R & D for pharmaceutical MNEs.[8]

One hopes that these measures will not reverse the cumulative technology cycle (described in Chapter 6) which has worked in favour of the UK throughout the last two decades. The lesson yet to be learned by the US administration to developments in the biotechnology field seems even more serious. Although US firms still largely dominate this sector, their leadership position is being threatened by a gamut of regulations and an ethnocentric attitude towards the international role of their own companies (Yuan, 1987). Also, compared with governments of other countries, including the UK, the support given by the US government particularly to the funding of applied R & D and in streamlining of drug legislation (for example, with respect to the processing of new drugs) is very limited. These points are taken up in a more general context in Chapter 11.

CONCLUSIONS

Most large industrialized countries are both donors and recipients of R & D activities by MNEs, and this chapter concludes by striking a trial balance, to show, in a very tentative way, which country has won and which lost in this complex process of change.

The UK and France have most assuredly gained, although in different ways. In both countries the volume of research spending is higher than would otherwise have been the case. The UK has come off best, in that it has attracted considerable investment in basic and innovative work. That carried out in France is generally of a more downstream nature.

The United States has broken even. The development of foreign research facilities by American firms has been largely balanced by European investment in the USA. This appears to be true both in quantitative and in qualitative terms.

Switzerland has been a net loser in that Swiss companies have invested heavily abroad, especially in the USA, while few foreign firms have done so in Switzerland. It seems probable, however, that the Swiss majors have been strengthened by their international research strategies.

Most other countries show small positive or negative balances. Rela-

142 *Multinationals, Technology and Competitiveness*

tive to their size, Belgium and Italy show large positive balances, but this is due to the special factors discussed earlier.

This pattern is what might have been expected. A donor nation is one with large indigenous companies. It has such companies for the same reasons that make it attractive to foreign firms. Inward and outward flows of research funds are therefore linked.

Could this situation change? This seems improbable. For the past twenty years stability has been the central characteristic of the pharmaceutical industry. There has been change, but of degree rather than kind. The factors that make a country a major donor or recipient of R & D activities are of a fundamental nature and unlikely to change in the short run. We expect the process of internationalization to continue, but along established lines and at a measured pace. Much, however, will rest on the strategy of Japanese pharmaceutical companies, and particularly on the extent to which they may decide to increase their foreign production by acquiring European or US firms.

Should governments worry? Probably not. Most countries break even in the trend to the internationalization of R & D. Even where there are losses, they may be made up by indirect benefits. The pharmaceutical industry operates on a worldwide basis and any calculus of national welfare must begin from this point.

NOTES

1 Partly, at least, the propensity of a company to decentralize R & D will depend on the amount of R & D it undertakes. This in turn will be related to its size. Japanese pharmaceutical firms are generally small and fragmented. In 1985 only one Japanese company, Takeda, featured among the top twenty drug firms in the world (it was ranked number 17). However, under pressure from the Japanese government, the top fifteen Japanese drug companies have more than quadrupled the proportion of capital expenditure devoted to R & D (*Economist*, 1987).

2 These also include agreements made by non-pharmacutical, e.g. chemical and genetic engineering, companies.

3 For a study of the UK situation, see Brech and Sharp (1984).

4 To quote from Cantwell (1988):

The activities of transnational enterprises (TNEs) accelerate the process of cumulative causation between competing locations. They do so by increasing the general international mobility of industrial production, and by making more likely the geographical separation of the research intensive and assembly types of production. Their activities have the effect of raising the slope of the technical progress function in dynamic locations while lowering it in stagnant production sites, and of increasing the speed with which the tradeables demand function is capable of shifting. Both these effects serve to reinforce the operation of virtuous and vicious circles in different countries. In short, the research intensive production of TNEs is attracted to the major sites of innovation in an international industry, but this in turn serves to strengthen innovation and the growth of production in the countries in question (as well as the competitive position of the TNEs

Investment in Innovation: The Pharmaceutical Industry 143

themselves). This secondary spiral of cumulative causation strengthens the primary spiral associated with the existence of international trade, converting a long-run process into a rather more immediate one.

Host countries attracted inward TNE investment where they have innovative domestic industries, and the TNEs concerned also establish local R & D facilities to support research intensive forms of production, and to gain further access to local scientific and technological experience, and methods of work. In doing so, foreign TNE entry increases local research capacity, and may also increase the extent of technological dissemination to local suppliers and customers. By increasing the technological competition faced by indigenous firms in the same sector local rivals may be spurred on to a higher rate of innovation. The combined effect is to raise the local technical progress function, thereby increasing the size of the local trade surplus and output growth. This type of sector is as a rule home to TNEs of its own, and their outward investment plays a similar role to the inward investment of foreign TNEs in this respect. By locating research intensive production in other important centres of innovation abroad, and assembly and allied outlets in other countries, the firms of the most dynamic countries sustain more effectively the global basis for increased research activity at home. They are able to integrate complementary foreign technologies, and to devise more broadly based technological systems in their domestic innovation.

5 Later data show that the UK increased its balance of trade surplus in pharmaceutical products from $156 million in 1965 to $1,052 million in 1982 (Burstall and Senior, 1985).

6 Defined as the difference between the costs of creating human and/or physical capital and the benefits. The costs are likely to be mainly fixed costs while the benefits are recurrent over a long period of time.

7 The 'customer contract' principle was put forward by Lord Rothschild who suggested that a particular government ministry might request a Research Council to commission research in a certain area, thus responding to the perceived need of the community as a whole. A recent NEDO report (NEDO 1987b) argues the need for a more formalized institutional structure to allow this principle to operate effectively.

8 Although it should be noted that other European governments have also taken similar – if not quite so harsh or widespread – measures.

Chapter 8

The Consequences of the International Transfer of Technology by MNEs: A Home Country Perspective

INTRODUCTION

In the past two decades, a good deal of attention has been focused on the consequences of the international transfer of technology (and other resources) on recipient or host countries.[1] But it has only been since the mid–1970s that some of the implications of this transfer for the exporting or source countries have been seriously discussed. This has been prompted primarily by a growing sense of concern, articulated by politicians, businessmen and academics alike, that the industrialized developed world – as represented mainly by the OECD countries – is either benefiting insufficiently from the export of technology or technological capacity[2] or being adversely affected by it. That these concerns are being expressed at a time when host countries, particularly developing countries, are taking action to control the amount and form of technological imports and to tilt the terms of trade in their favour has led some observers to be pessimistic about the prospects for the international transfer of technology, at least as between North and South. From a time in the mid–1950s, when the exchange of technology was generally thought to be a positive sum game, with both exporting and importing nations benefiting, the early 1980s, by contrast, were producing situations in which both parties perceived themselves to be worse off as a result of the transfer. Though *prima facie* implausible, such a result is theoretically feasible, particularly where the parties to the exchange aim to maximize relative rather than absolute economic gains, and/or have different political or cultural perceptions.

Apart from inter-government grants and loans, the main institution for the transmission of resources in the post-war period has been the MNE operating through a network of foreign affiliates[3] and contractual relationships with foreign firms. In such cases the transfer of technology is internalized in the sense that there is no change in its *ownership*, and the transferor continues to exercise a *de jure* direction over the use made

Transfer of Technology and Home Countries 145

of the resources. It is the nature and effects of this control, and the fact that technology is transmitted as part of a package of resources, that distinguishes this vehicle of transference from that of arm's length exchange between independent sellers and buyers. It is the identification and evaluation of the consequences which arise from the transfer and dissemination of technology on the part of MNEs that is the subject of this chapter. The presentation proceeds as follows. First, the main causes of concern, expressed by home countries, about technology exports to host countries will be described. Second, the extent and pattern of these exports over the last two decades and the role of MNEs in promoting them are summarized. Third, the effects these have had on the economic goals of home countries are considered. Fourth, there will be a discussion of some of the policies pursued by home governments and those which might be pursued to further technology transfer by their own MNEs.

THE PROBLEM STATED

The initial interest of most policy-makers in developed market economies (DMEs)[4] in the effects of technology exports by their own MNEs arose in the late 1970s, as a result of such circumstances as a slowing down of international economic growth, a downswing in technological innovation, rising domestic unemployment, stagnant industrial productivity and widespread inflation, all of which are viewed as symptoms of a decline in international competitiveness. Such concern has been most often voiced in Sweden, the USA and the UK, the three DMEs which have experienced the most dramatic fall in their share of world trade in manufactured goods and *relative* industrial status vis-à-vis both other industrialized countries and the rest of the world.[5]

Coincidental, and partly related to these trends, has been the increasing effort of developing countries to shift the balance of economic and industrial power from the North to the South. Illustrated by the philosophy and intent of the New International Economic Order, and the Lima Declaration of UNIDO in 1975 which *inter alia* aims to increase the share of world industrial production by developing countries to 25 per cent by the year 2000, attempts by such countries to pursue a policy of rapid industrialization are taken as signals by the DMEs that the order of economic interdependence, fashioned at Bretton Woods and Havana, is no longer acceptable, and that some developing countries – particularly the so-called NICs – are a force to be reckoned with. Taken together with the expansion of alternative sources of technology, for example, from Eastern Europe and some developing countries (Lall, 1979), the established industrial powers fear not only an erosion of their industrial hegemony but an undermining of their economic structures.

This might not matter so much within a framework of nations at similar stages of economic development and a common political ideology, such as broadly exists within the OECD. But outside it, for the most part, that is not the case. The political perceptions and economic philosophy of

146   *Multinationals, Technology and Competitiveness*

many developing countries anxious to acquire technology are sufficiently divergent from those of most technology exporting countries as to make the latter worried lest the added economic leverage which the technology brings might be used to the detriment of their strategic and other aspirations. Here, as has been pointed out by Hawkins and Gladwin (1981), a conflict may arise between humanitarian, economic and political goals of the home countries. The matter is further complicated by the effects which some kinds of non commercial technology transfers or sharing may have on the home country's commercial technological capacity. The export of weapons by the USA may help support innovation in the military aircraft and missile industries, with consequential spillover effects on the domestic aerospace and electronics industries. Just as the cut-back in the US space research programme has reduced the flow of commercially useful technology, so any retrenchment of defence spending, including arms exports to friendly nations, could have similar effects.

While no commentator would go as far as ascribing all the current economic difficulties of the DMEs to the growing competitive strength of the NICs, and still less to the transfer of technology by MNEs to these countries, some, most noticeably Baranson (1979), Gilpin (1975), Scott and Lodge (1985) and some of the labour unions, assign it a major role, at least from a US perspective. There are two main thrusts to this allegation. The first is that MNEs, by engaging in FDI, have diverted their energies away from technology-innovating activities in their home countries. It is pointed out that, since the early 1970s, the amount of GNP allocated to R & D (and particularly non defence-related R & D) in the USA has fallen relative to that of its major competitors; that, whereas in the early 1960s the USA accounted for 75 per cent of the world's industrial R & D, by the early 1980s this proportion had fallen to about one-half, and that while the share of new patents registered in the USA by US-owned firms fell from 78.7 per cent in 1965 to 57.8 per cent in 1983.

The second (and main) charge against technological exports is that they improve the international competitiveness of firms in the recipient country at the expense of firms in the sending country. Thus, while between 1960 and 1980 the USA's trade balance in R & D-intensive manufactured goods increased, her share of world high technology exports – notably electrical and electronics components – was substantially eroded. A similar picture emerges for most Western European countries. This, in turn (so the argument goes), erodes the market base of the technology-exporting firms and makes the rising costs of R & D more difficult to recoup. In the case of labour-intensive industries, the effect is more dramatically and immediately felt on domestic employment. In the context of North/South technology transfers, the debate has been less to do with falling export shares in the DMEs and more with increasing import competition faced by them; none the less, it is a variant of the 'we want to sell more milk and fewer cows' type of argument.[6]

These, then, are some of the main concerns currently felt to a greater

Transfer of Technology and Home Countries 147

or lesser degree by all developed countries. How far are they justified? How far can they be attributed to the activities of MNEs? What, if anything, can be done about them?

THE CONDITIONS OF TECHNOLOGY TRANSFER

We take, as a starting point, the proposition that firms will only transfer proprietary technology if they believe it to be to their overall benefit. Where a firm sells or leases technology to other firms, it is presumed that the terms and conditions of the exchange will fully compensate it for the opportunity costs of supplying that technology. In some cases a transfer will only take place subject to the fulfilment of restrictive constraints on the part of the transferee. Thus, a license to exploit a patent may only be granted on the understanding that the licensee will only market the good embodying the technology in his own country, or if certain production methods and material specifications are adhered to, or if a satisfactory standard of maintenance and after-sales servicing is guaranteed, or if specific tie-in arrangements are accepted. Where a firm is transferring the technology to one of its own affiliates, then, subject to the regulations and policies of the host governments, it has full and continuing control over its use. *A priori*, one may assume that, from the transferring firm's viewpoint, in the short and medium run, at least, the transfer is expected to be beneficial. In the long run, as the previous chapters have shown, the matter is less certain, as it is possible that, as a result of the competitive stimulus from FDI, indigenous firms may become technologically more progressive and out-compete the foreign affiliate.[7]

Depending on whether its sale is internalized or externalized, there are various gains to the transferor from the transfer. To the firm selling under contract, these primarily comprise the revenue it receives from the sale of technology. As long as the marginal revenue exceeds the marginal opportunity costs[8] (including externalities) of supplying the technology, the firm will find the transfer worthwhile. In practice, for many firms selling technology that would have been produced in any case for use by the firm at home, the costs reduce to the marginal negotiating and transaction costs; in other instances and for technology supplying specialists in particular, for example, construction contractors, project engineers, systems analysts, petrochemical consultants, etc., the resource costs of producing the technology are relevant (Graham, 1981; Teece, 1977, 1981b). To the MNE, transferring (or sharing) technology by the direct investment route is frequently the preferred means of capturing the full economic rent of the technology and unique ownership advantages transferred with it.[9] The gains from the transfer are those which accrue to the enterprise as a whole; they include not only the profits earned on the capital invested but all the other benefits which arise from foreign production, including the securing of new markets which help spread the R & D and other overhead costs of the parent company, thus helping the MNE to maintain and extend its competitive strength.

148 *Multinationals, Technology and Competitiveness*

But MNEs may also transfer technological capacity and, by so doing, advance the ability to the recipient country to produce technology for itself. This may be done either because it is cheaper to set up new R & D facilities abroad, rather than expand facilities in the home country, or because there are some kinds of R & D best done in the host country, or because difference in factor endowments and/or markets enable the host country to specialize in particular kinds of R & D in different countries. Examples of this latter kind of R & D include that into tropical diseases by pharmaceutical companies in tropical locations, new methods of cultivating or blending tea and tobacco in tea and tobacco producing regions, and research into labour-intensive production technologies, for example, for the production of motor vehicles, machine tools and processed foods in low labour cost countries. Again, quite apart from the efforts of host governments to attract such technological capacity, MNEs will tend to locate their R & D activities in countries which they think will best advance their own interests.[10]

Excepting, then, cases of business misjudgement, to suggest that a home country may not benefit from an export of technology on the part of its firms is to suggest the social opportunity costs of such exports transfer exceed the private opportunity costs. This may be so; one only has to look at the different goals between MNEs and home countries. MNEs are primarily interested in making profits independently of where these profits are earned. They will consequently engage in foreign production and transfer the necessary technology with this objective in mind. Investigating countries, on the other hand, are interested in the activities of MNE affiliates from a wider perspective; their goals include the growth of GNP, maintaining full employment, controlling inflation, building up indigenous technological capacity, promoting the most efficient structure of resource allocation, and so on. There is no presumption that, in achieving their own objectives, firms will necessarily be advancing those of their home countries.

At the same time, it would be wrong to judge the macroeconomic consequences of a transfer of technology by an MNE by its microeconomic opportunity costs, *or* to attribute such costs to the MNE. Let us give a simple example. Suppose that, as a result of the transfer of technology by their parent companies, US affiliates in South Korea are able to outcompete domestic producers in the supply of colour television to the US market, and that jobs are displaced in the US television set industry. Suppose also that those made unemployed do not find other work. Then the immediate gains to the USA of the transfer of technology will be the profits, net of foreign tax, earned by the foreign affiliates and any reduction in the price of television sets passed on to the US consumers, while the opportunity cost will be any loss in the GDP caused by unemployment. To the MNE, on the other hand, the effect of the transfer may be higher sales and profits than otherwise would have been possible.

It is obvious that this conclusion *may* be entirely false. It may be quite wrong to attribute any fall in domestic employment to a foreign capital

Transfer of Technology and Home Countries

outflow simply because, in its absence, the investment might have been undertaken by other firms, which would not only have resulted in the same fall in domestic jobs and output but would have meant that the US economy would have lost the profits which otherwise would have been earned by its own MNE. Moreover, the resulting unemployment may only be temporary and, over time, the labour displaced may be employed in more productive activities, either in the same firm, or elsewhere in the economy, so raising rather than lowering the GDP.

The word 'may' has been used throughout the previous paragraph because, whatever the theoretical validity of the argument, the actual effects may be very difficult. For a host of reasons, labour displaced by a transfer of technology may not be easily re-employed and the costs of adjustment assistance may more than outweigh the benefits; while the argument that the recipient economy will obtain the technology it needs in any event and out-compete US producers cuts little ice with those who argue that this can be counteracted by import controls.

All this, of course, approaches the question of microeconomic standpoint. Depending on their consequences on the host countries, however, it is not only the costs and benefits of the investing firms which have to be taken into account. Studies carried out in the UK and USA[11] suggest that the main beneficiaries of outward direct investment are often the suppliers of capital equipment and intermediary products to the foreign affiliates.[12] All, or part, of these exports would have been lost without the foreign investment, as investment by firms of other nationalities would have led to these goods being bought from their home countries. On the other hand, the extra output abroad may not only replace domestic output by the investing MNE but that of its domestic competitors as well. Again, the effects depend critically on the assumptions made about what would have happened, in both the home and host countries, in the absence of such a transfer of technology and as a consequence of it.

It is worth observing that, in the neo-classical literature, provided that there are no market distortions, a transfer or dissemination of technology between countries will normally increase world real output, by raising both allocative and technical efficiency. Moreover both technology exporting and importing countries will benefit, although some redeployment of resources may be necessary. The difficulty of using this approach in the current context is that the assumptions underlying it are unrealistic. MNEs do not normally transfer technology in a competitive market situation; neither are governments able to ensure that, come what may, full employment is always achieved. Moreover, the welfare functions of countries embrace goals other than the maximization of output, which could be adversely affected by the transfer of technology. It may be that the transfer of technology is not as beneficial to the home country as it could be, precisely because of market distortions. In such an event, rather than control the outflow of technology, policy might be better directed to removing the distortions.

So far, much of this argument has implied that the technology being transferred by MNEs will be used to produce competitive goods to those

150 *Multinationals, Technology and Competitiveness*

produced by the transferring firm or country. With investment designed to substitute for exports – so called import-substituting investment by the recipient country – a lot of technology will be of this kind. But even here, experience has shown that where a foreign affiliate is set up to produce one line of goods, its presence may stimulate the imports of other lines of goods from the home firm or country; this has proved to be especially common in the case of firms producing consumer goods, for example, colour television sets, motor vehicles, man-made textiles, processed food products, cosmetics and pharmaceuticals.

With other kinds of foreign activity, technology may be used to produce complementary, or even quite unrelated, goods to those produced by the transferring firm or country.[13] In such cases, output and employment in the home country may be increased and its technology base strengthened. Investment by MNEs in trade and distributive activities is of this kind: while it may improve the marketing competence of recipient firms, it may directly increase the exports of goods from the home country. Investment in building and construction, capital equipment and energy ventures, and by chemical and engineering consultancies, may have the same effect. In other words, a disembodied transfer of technology may give rise to the transfer of technology embodied in goods. It is, of course, a moot point how far technology *is* transferred through goods, but, for the purpose of this analysis, we shall treat such exports as a benefit to the home firm and country.

The transfer of technology through international vertical backward integration by MNEs in resource-based industries may also result in a spinoff in technological capacity in the home country, depending on the extent to which secondary processing activities are undertaken in host or home countries. Even if there is a transfer of expansion of technological capacity, imports of capital equipment are likely to take place, and these are more likely to be obtained from the home than from other countries. In some service industries, for example, banking and international tourism, similar externalities are likely.

Finally, there are multiplier effects of the income generated from the transfer of technology, whatever its kind. In the nineteenth century, these yielded substantial benefits to the UK economy. Rising incomes of recipient countries generated by the exports of British capital and expertise provided markets for UK-manufactured goods which helped to finance new investment and, through the economies of firm size, reduce the prices of goods supplied to home markets. Although there is no economy currently as internationally dominant as the UK once was, depending on the domestic value-added of foreign affiliates and the recipient country's marginal propensity to import from the investing country, gains may accrue to the latter. Work done by Hufbauer and Adler (1968) and Bergsten, Horst and Moran (1978) suggests that, for the US economy, these consequences are often significant.

It must be admitted that some of the effects on the home country ascribed to the transfer of technology by MNEs would be better ascribed to FDI in general. Our defence of the present approach is that the unique

Transfer of Technology and Home Countries 151

ingredient of most kinds of FDI *is* technology, be it the technology of product, materials production, management, organization or marketing. Without this component, direct investment would become portfolio investment. The main incentive for a firm to internalize the flow of resources across national boundaries is to capture the full economic rent on the package of technological ingredients which are specific to it. It is no coincidence that MNEs tend to dominate in industries supplying products with a high technological content and that, because of the benefits from internalization, they are the main products and trans-mitters of technology.[14]

Nevertheless, accepting that the focus of interest is often on the effects of transfer of technology *per se*, it is reasonable to look at the extent to which MNEs do transfer technology across national boundaries, and see how this affects the host country and what the short- and medium-term repercussions are on the exporting countries. The previous paragraphs have suggested certain principles which will determine these effects. These include, first, the market conditions in which the transfer of technology takes place; second, the form of technological transfer, and in particular whether it is likely to complement or substitute that produced at home; third, the strategies of the investing or technological exporting firms; and fourth, the goals of home and host governments, and the policies pursued by them to achieve these goals.

MULTINATIONAL ENTERPRISES AND TECHNOLOGY TRANSFER TO DEVELOPING COUNTRIES

The Role of MNEs

What, then, has been the extent and significance of technological transfer by MNEs to developing countries?

The most widely published indicator of the extent of foreign involve-ment by MNEs is value of outward direct investment. Figures supplied by the US Department of Commerce (1987) show that, at the end of 1984, the cumulative value of direct investment by MNEs of all nationali-ties was $600 billion. Between 1967 and 1984, the FDI stock increased by an average of 10.8 per cent per annum and, in the latter year, accounted for about 7.0 per cent of the GNP of Development Assistance Countries (DAC).[15] For most of the period, the value of international production exceeded that in international trade, although the relative significance of the former decreased in the early 1980s with the dramatic fall in the growth of outward direct investment.[16] In the case of the USA, the foreign direct capital stake to export of goods ratio in 1983 was just over 1.5: 1; for the UK in 1984 it was just under 1.5: 1.

In 1985, about 96 per cent of the foreign investment stake was owned by MNEs from developed countries, and about three-quarters of this was located in the other developed countries. The latter ratio has steadily increased since 1967, when it was 70 per cent. Receipts from technology exports to developing countries from some leading OECD countries[17]

152 *Multinationals, Technology and Competitiveness*

also increased relative to the flow of FDI. However, these technology exports represented only one-sixth of all such exports from these same OECD countries; moreover this ratio has also steadily declined. These data suggest that technology exported by OECD MNEs is primarily to other OECD countries and not to developing countries. It is also worth observing that investment flows, particularly in recent years, have become more symmetrical among the OECD countries. Whereas, in the late 1950s, the USA was, by far and away, the dominant capital exporter, with all European countries and Japan importing more capital than they exported, the last decade has seen the rate of FDI in the USA growing much faster than that of foreign investment from the USA (UNCTC, 1988).[18] Since, like trade, inward and outward direct investment flows are not entirely unrelated to each other, the critics of outward technology flows would do well to take account of the possible effects of controlling such flows on inward direct investment.

As recipients of FDI and technology, developing countries may be divided into a number of fairly distinct groups. First there are the OPEC countries which, in 1983, accounted for one-fifth of the foreign capital stake in developing countries, and whose imports of technology are heavily biased towards petroleum and petroleum-related activities. Second, tax haven countries accounted for a further 12 per cent: here, there was little, if any, technological transfer. Third, there are the mainly industrializing countries of which eleven accounted for 41 per cent of the total foreign stake in 1983. These include the larger NICs[19] whose imports of technology are largely directed to the manufacturing sector.[20] Fourth, there is a mixed bag of developing countries which mainly attract foreign capital and technology to specialized resource sectors and to fairly standardized import substituting manufacturing activities. By area, Latin America and the Caribbean accounted for 53 per cent of the total foreign investment in developing countries in 1983, in Asia for 20 per cent and Africa for 15 per cent. For manufacturing industry alone, the respective proportions were 61 per cent, 18 per cent and 6 per cent (Dunning and Cantwell, 1987).

How important are the affiliates of MNEs to the economies of developing countries? Tables 8.1 and 8.2 set out some details of the shares of foreign affiliates in the manufacturing sector of a sample of developing countries. They reveal that their contribution is, in general, more important in Latin America than in Asia;[21] details on African countries are too scant to be reliable, although it is known that FDI in Africa is much more oriented towards natural resource-based activities than is the case in other developing regions.[22] Of the African countries with a sizeable manufacturing sector, the participation of foreign-owned firms is known to be significant in Cameroon, Central African Republic, Congo, Gabon, Ghana, Kenya, Nigeria and Zaire (Dunning and Cantwell, 1987). The data also show that the degree of MNE participation appears to be negatively associated with the host country's contribution to total manufacturing exports and bears little relationship to the rate of increase in these exports between 1965 and 1985.[23]

Table 8.1 *Participation Rates of MNE Affiliates in Manufacturing Sectors of Selected Developing Countries and Manufacturing Exports 1965–85*

| | Output | Employment | Exports | Total manufacturing exports | | | |
| | | | | 1985 ($m) | 1985 ÷ 1976 Value | 1985 ÷ 1965 Value | 1976 ÷ 1965 Value |
	(Per cent accounted for by MNE affiliates)						
Latin America							
Argentina	29.4 (1983)		24.9 (1977)	1,423	1.5	16.9	12.0
Brazil	32.0 (1974)	23.0 (1977)	37.2 (1978)	8,911	4.1	66.5	21.0
Chile		15.4 (1979)[1]		255	1.8	9.1	4.1
Colombia	43.4 (1974)		14.4 (1978)	611	1.6	17.5	11.4
Mexico	27.0 (1972)	21.0 (1970)	35.0 (1973)	7,129	3.4	43.2	14.0
Peru	21.2 (1975)	13.5 (1975)	8.0 (1978)	236	2.3	47.2	20.2
Asia							
Hong Kong	13.9 (1981)	9.8 (1984)	16.5 (1984)	27,540	3.5	27.7	7.9
India	7.9 (1979)[2]			5,890	2.1	7.1	3.5
Korea (South)	19.3 (1978)	9.5 (1978)	24.6 (1978)	27,669	4.1	266.0	65.0
Malaysia	39.8 (1975)	19.7 (1975)		4,404	5.5	58.7	11.8
Pakistan			8.0 (1973)	1,731	2.6	9.1	3.6
Philippines	78.0 (1974)	8.6 (1976)		2,534	4.2	58.9	14.1
Singapore	62.9 (1982)	72.1 (1982)	72.1 (1982)	13,317	4.6	39.4	9.7
Taiwan		16.6 (1981)	25.6 (1981)				37.1
Thailand	18.2 (1971)	8.9 (1970)	22.7 (1971)	2,583	5.1	86.1	42.2
Africa							
Ghana	67.0 (1969)			26	2.2	3.7	1.7
Nigeria	70.0 (1968)[3]			78	4.2	4.6	2.2
Zimbabwe	70.0 (1982)[3]			167	n.a.	1.4	n.a.
Southern Europe and the Middle East							
Greece	25.5 (1977)	21.34 (1977)	18.5 (1977)	2,241	1.8	50.9	28.7
Israel		28.0 (1976)		5,212	2.8	18.5	6.7
Portugal	19.6 (1978)	12.9 (1981)	25.0 (1981)	4,412	3.6	12.4	3.5
Spain	74.6 (1977)	46.6 (1977)[1]	51.1 (1977)	17,227	2.9	45.1	15.8
Turkey	7.8 (1977)	5.7 (1977)	6.1 (1977)	3,849	8.3	349.9	42.7

Notes:
[1]Employment in foreign affiliates as a percentage of all employment in all industry.
[2]This figure would increase to 31.4% (in 1980) if the share of output of foreign owned companies was expressed as a proportion of that of medium and large non-government public limited companies.
[3]Per cent of assets not output.
Sources: Dunning and Cantwell (1987); World Bank (1987).

154   *Multinationals, Technology and Competitiveness*

Table 8.2   *Ranking of Countries in Selected Developing Countries According to Degree of MNE Penetration in Manufacturing Industry and Export Performance*

Degree of TNC penetration	Developing countries	A^a	B^b	C^c	D^d
1 High	Brazil	6.5	21.0	4.1	66.5
	Colombia	0.4	11.4	1.6	17.5
	Ghana	0.0	1.8	2.9	3.7
	Malaysia	3.2	11.8	5.5	58.7
	Philippines	1.8	14.1	4.2	58.9
	Singapore	9.7	9.7	4.6	39.4
	Spain	12.6	15.8	2.9	45.1
		34.2	12.8	3.6	46.4
2 Medium	Argentina	1.0	12.0	1.5	16.9
	Chile	0.2	1.8	4.1	9.1
	Greece	1.6	28.7	1.8	50.9
	Mexico	5.2	14.0	3.4	43.2
	Nigeria	0.0	2.2	4.2	4.6
	Peru	0.2	20.2	2.3	47.2
	Portugal	3.2	3.5	3.6	12.4
		11.4	8.3	2.7	22.5
3 Low	Hong Kong	20.1	7.9	3.5	27.7
	India	4.3	3.5	2.1	7.1
	Israel	3.8	6.7	2.8	18.5
	Korea	20.2	65.0	4.1	266.0
	Pakistan	1.3	3.6	2.6	9.1
	Thailand	1.9	42.2	5.1	86.1
	Turkey	2.8	42.7	8.3	349.9
		54.4	8.6	3.6	30.5

Notes:
[a]= Share of total manufacturing exports from countries listed in 1985.
[b]= 1976 ÷ 1965 manufacturing exports.
[c]= 1985 ÷ 1976 manufacturing exports.
[d]= 1985 ÷ 1965 manufacturing exports.
Sources: Dunning and Cantwell (1987); World Bank (1987).

Interesting as these data may be, more relevant to our present theme is the effect that the transfer of technology by MNEs may have on the *structure* of industry in developing countries. In this connection, recently published data reveal that, within manufacturing industry, the pattern of involvement by MNEs in developing countries is broadly comparable to that in developed countries (Dunning and Cantwell, 1987; UNCTC 1988). There are differences *between* countries within the developing world, and particularly among the NICs, but in both groups of countries MNEs play their most important role in those sectors characterized

Transfer of Technology and Home Countries
155

either by above average technological intensity or product differentiation, for example, the chemical, engineering, motor vehicles and food, drink and tobacco industries. By contrast, indigenous firms in both groups of countries dominate in labour-intensive industries producing goods which require fairly standardized technology, for example, textiles, wearing apparel and leather products.

The importance of foreign affiliates of MNEs in high and medium technology industries suggests that the transfer of technology by MNEs by this route has helped to build up these sectors in these countries. However, there are some notable country differences. In Singapore in 1985, for example, foreign corporations accounted for 98 per cent of the assets in the textiles and 82 per cent of the assets in the clothing industry. Though lower, the figures are also significant in other South East Asian countries, notably Thailand, Taiwan and South Korea. Japanese companies are known to have a particular strength in the textiles industry. In 1985, their share of all FDI in this industry was more than twice their average share of foreign direct investments in developing countries; however, part of the explanation for the Japanese involvement is their strength in the man-made fibres sector which is more appropriately classified within the chemical industry.

Types of Foreign Investment and the Nature of Technology Transfer

It would be unwise to read too much into the kind of data just presented. One important deficiency is that the contribution of the foreign affiliates of MNEs is usually expressed in terms of gross sales rather than local value-added. By itself, this may tell us nothing about the extent and form of the production undertaken, or about the important technology content. The pharmaceutical industry provides a good illustration of this. There is very little R & D in pharmaceuticals done in developing countries by MNEs, and in only a few of the larger NICs are pharmaceutical chemicals produced in any quantities. By far the greater part of the value-added created by foreign affiliates of MNEs consists of labour-intensive formulae or dosage preparations and the packaging of the final product. It could well be that within the sectors dominated by MNEs the operations actually carried out in developing countries are labour-intensive, while in the developed countries they may be capital- or technology-intensive.

Much, of course, will depend on the type of foreign investment undertaken, its position in the product cycle and the policies pursued by host governments. Import-substituting activities normally start with simple finishing operations to a product which is mainly made elsewhere, and gradually work backwards to other, and technologically more intensive, manufacturing stages. By contrast, investment in resource-based industries may start with extractive activities but later extend forward to secondary processing operations. Investments intended to take advantage of cheap and abundant supplies of semi-skilled labour may initially be directed to labour-intensive production processes and later embrace the more capital- or technology-intensive processes. Nevertheless, though the particular processes undertaken by MNEs may not be technology-intensive, the final output produced may be classified to an industry normally regarded as such. Technology aids the use of all factor endowments, but it does not necessarily make for a more technology-intensive industrial structure.

As far as the transfer of technological capacity is concerned, data on US MNEs show that, of the R & D undertaken by them, only 6.4 per cent was located outside the USA in 1982 and only 0.33 per cent in developing countries.[24] Most of this was concentrated in a small number of industrial sectors that have a high level of product differentiation in consumer products or specific requirements for adaptation to local conditions of production factors.[25] Other estimates suggest that the developing countries only account for 2 per cent of the world R & D compared with 12 per cent of world manufacturing production and 10 per cent of manufacturing exports. MNEs may also advance foreign technological capacity by training programmes and skill development. OECD and ILO studies suggest this has been quite important in some industries (for example, rubber tyres, petrochemicals, pharmaceuticals, constructional engineering and hotels), but in others (for instance, textiles and clothing) the development of indigenous skills, at least in East Africa, has been largely due to local efforts.

The conclusion suggested by these data is that although MNEs may transfer most of their technology within industries classified as high or medium technology-intensive, in some cases, at least in developing countries, the technology will be used to improve the efficiency of labour-intensive processes of production rather than promote the development of technology-intensive sectors. This is most likely to occur in the so-called high technology industries in which some form of international specialization of products or processes is practised, and where intra-firm transactions also tend to be concentrated.

The Nature of Competition Between Developed and Developing Countries

Table 8.3, which is derived from a study done for the ILO (Sabolo and Trajtenberg, 1976), sets out the breakdown of activities of foreign affiliates of MNEs in developing regions in 1970; *inter alia* it reveals that resource-based and local market-oriented investments were far more important than labour-oriented investments in three of the major region lists. In Asia (which included India) labour-oriented activities were of equal importance with the other two groups; the evidence suggests that, in the 1970s, they became considerably more significant.

For the purpose of our analysis, this distinction is an important one. Not only may the *raison d'être* for FDI be very different, but so might its consequences for the home country. Though there is some concern about the effects of technology exports induced by all kinds of FDI, most recent attention has been directed to the labour-intensive, offshore activities of

Transfer of Technology and Home Countries

Table 8.3 *Breakdown of Foreign Direct Investments in Developing Regions by Broad Type 1970*

Region	Type of investment (%)			All investments	
	Raw material oriented	Local market oriented	Labour oriented	(%)	(US$m)
Southern Europe	19	62	19	6.3	2.6
Africa	60	34	6	19.4	7.9
Latin America	33	62	5	51.1	20.8
Middle East	91	9	—	8.8	3.6
Asia	30	36	34	14.4	5.8
Total (US$m)	17.0	19.6	4.0	—	40.7
Overall distribution (%)	42	48	10	100	100

Source: Sabolo and Trajtenberg (1976).

MNEs. It seems to be accepted that, as far as foreign investment designed to serve local markets is concerned, it is not often a real substitute for exports. Import control, non-tariff barriers, availability of local materials, transport costs, the need to be near customers, and the behaviour of competitors often combine to make the transfer of technology, through direct investment, a *necessary* condition for supplying the local market. Moreover, since the type of technology required for this may be available from other MNEs, the cost of *not* supplying the market may be to lose it to a rival.

With investment in labour-intensive processes or products designed to supply markets outside the host country, and particularly those presently supplied by the home country, the attitude towards outward investment is less accommodating. Here it is asserted that, in the absence of this investment, the competition to the investing country would not (or need not) have been so great, for two reasons: first, the technology required to mount the investment in the host country is unlikely to be as standardized as in the import-substituting case; second, because the home country can always protect its own industries from foreign competition generated by another country's MNEs. But what role have MNEs played in these industries?

In 1974, Nayyar (1978) estimated that MNEs accounted for 15 per cent of the manufacturing exports of developing countries. Data set out in Dunning and Cantwell (1987) suggest that by the late 1970s and early 1980s, this percentage had increased to between 30 and 35 per cent. In 1983, eleven countries accounted for nearly four fifths of developed country imports of manufactured goods from developing countries. Five of these countries – Malaysia, Singapore, South Korea, Brazil and Mexico – are among the NICs whose share of the exports of manufactures going to OECD countries increased from 25.8 per cent in 1963 to 65 per cent in 1985. The NICs have also recorded a faster than average rate of growth in industrial production; by 1985 they were responsible for

Table 8.4 *US Related-Party Imports as a Percentage of Total Imports of Selected Manufactured Products from Selected Newly Industrializing Countries 1977*

	Textiles 65[a]	Non-electric machinery 71[a]	Electric machinery 72[a]	Clothing 84[a]	Footwear 85[a]	Scientific instruments 86[a]	Total manufacturing
Israel	18.9	32.8	62.9	14.0	0.0	13.0	18.2
Portugal	2.8	24.7	78.4	0.4	0.2	82.5	12.5
Greece	3.7	52.2	99.1	5.0	0.8	2.2	7.8
Ireland	36.3	78.5	77.8	8.3	42.2	91.7	59.0
Spain	1.5	36.3	32.6	3.7	10.1	7.8	24.1
Yugoslavia	0.1	14.0	2.0	2.3	2.2	3.6	4.9
Argentina	0.5	39.1	76.1	2.9	0.8	10.0	9.2
Brazil	9.2	59.9	95.3	18.0	0.5	38.4	38.4
Colombia	1.5	16.8	3.9	15.7	81.2	87.8	14.1
Mexico	9.6	87.8	95.6	68.0	60.9	93.6	71.0
Taiwan	13.1	19.3	58.1	1.2	3.1	67.1	20.5
Hong Kong	4.9	68.5	43.4	3.4	3.6	30.4	18.1
India	6.1	30.5	58.7	15.8	6.1	16.7	10.1
South Korea	5.5	64.2	67.3	7.1	1.8	12.1	19.7
Malaysia	0.2	83.2	97.0	1.9	0.0	91.9	87.9
Philippines	28.9	69.7	31.7	53.4	0.0	27.0	47.5
Singapore	4.3	90.5	97.0	0.5	0.0	85.3	83.3
Haiti	2.9	33.7	36.5	24.8	77.2	97.9	28.4
Total all developing countries	7.8	63.5	75.2	11.5	4.4	51.2	37.0

[a]SITC category.
Source: Helleiner (1981).

Transfer of Technology and Home Countries 159

about 11 per cent of the world's production, excluding that of Eastern Europe and the Democratic Republic of Korea, compared with 9 per cent in 1965 (World Bank, 1987).

Nevertheless, of the fifty top exports of manufactured products in 1980, which accounted for about 80 per cent of the exports of these countries, MNEs were actively involved in only about one-quarter. These included those more competitive to those produced in OECD countries, for example, textiles, clothing and leather goods.[26] The one sector in which MNE affiliates do tend to dominate is in industrial and consumer electronics, the exports of which have risen very substantially over the past two decades.[27] Even so, this does not mean that MNEs have had no influence in the extent and direction of exports – far from it; MNE subcontracting and buying groups, particularly those of Japanese origin, have played a decisive role[28] even though the production is in the hands of indigenous firms. Moreover, a high proportion of exports of MNEs from NICs tend to be internalized. Data compiled by Helleiner (1981) from the US Department of Commerce data set out in Table 8.4 suggest that in the newer industries, in which NICs are beginning to gain an important stake in world trade, US related-party imports – mainly from US affiliates to their parent companies – account for the major proportion of all imports.

IMPLICATIONS FOR INDUSTRIALIZED COUNTRIES

The previous paragraphs have made four main points:

(1) The greater part of the direct investment by MNEs in developing countries has been directed towards import substitution and resource-based activities, with the exception of Southern Europe and East Asia, where it has also been directed to production of labour-intensive products and/or labour-intensive processes or high or medium technology-intensive products.

(2) Much of this investment has been prompted by a shift in the locational advantages of production from the developed to the developing countries, such that if MNEs of developed countries had (individually) responded by not investing they would have lost all or most of these markets.

(3) Until the mid–1970s, most of the growth of manufacturing exports from NICs was in industries in which MNEs did not generally play a major role. Moreover, the revealed comparative advantage (RCA) of developing countries has improved most significantly in sectors in which the degree of MNE penetration is low.[29] Exceptions include electronics and electrical equipment and photographic supplies. In other words, a substantial part of the increasing import competition from these countries has little or nothing to do with technology transfer by MNEs.[30]

(4) There is some suggestion that, in the 1980s, because of the impact of

160 *Multinationals, Technology and Competitiveness*

MNEs in restructuring the trade flows of developing countries in the newer industrial sectors, the role of MNEs will become more important. At the same time, due to the reduced labour content of some manufactured goods, and the introduction of computer-aided design and manufacturing processes, there is less incentive by MNEs to locate their activities in low-wage cost economies.

We now turn to some of the implications of these facts for the DMEs. First, from the viewpoint of international resource allocation, the transfer of technology by MNEs has had mixed effects. Where it has been prompted by import controls imposed by host countries, apart from those justified by the optimum tariff and infant industry arguments, it is likely to have had less beneficial effects than the exports. Where this has been coupled with MNEs acting as oligopolists and undertaking investment to advance product differentiation or to protect market shares, the result has almost certainly been a misuse of resource allocation. We have already referred to Professor Kojima's argument (Kojima, 1978) that much of US foreign investment in technology-intensive industries has been of an anti-trade kind, and operates to the disadvantage of both host and home countries. In the present context, we feel that the Kojima criticism would be better directed to the activities of MNEs *within* the DMEs, as a much smaller percentage of such activities in the developing countries is undertaken for defensive oligopolistic reasons. On the other hand, investment by MNEs to take advantage of resource or labour cost differentials has probably benefited the allocation of resources as it has freed the flow of technology which might otherwise not have taken place, or not have taken place to the same extent. Professor Kojima regards the technology exported by MNEs to promote this kind of activity as trade promoting and in accord with the principle of comparative advantage.

From the viewpoint of individual home countries, the crucial questions are:

(1) What would have happened had not the technology been exported?
(2) What effects can be attributed to it?
(3) What is the reaction of investing firms and home countries to these effects?

Let us now briefly look at the three types of activities by MNEs in turn.

Investment to Supply the Local Market

Elsewhere in this book, we have suggested that for firms of one nationality to supply foreign markets they must have, or be able to acquire, some competitive or O-specific advantage over local or other foreign firms. If they choose to supply that market from a local production base rather than by exports, then it is assumed this is because L advantages favour the host rather than the home country. The product cycle theory of investment suggests there is a natural progression from

Transfer of Technology and Home Countries

exports to foreign production. Thomas Horst (1974) has estimated that in the early stages of foreign production by US firms, US exports increase along with the production; eventually, however, as production becomes established, exports decline. But his calculations make no assumption as to what would have happened had the production not taken place. Other research suggests that, in those cases where it is realistic to assume the foreign investment substitutes for domestic (or other foreign) investment in the host country, it may permit exports to be higher than they otherwise would have been (Reddaway *et al.*, 1968; Hufbauer and Adler, 1968; Stopford and Turner, 1985).

Earlier we described some of the ways in which exports of the home country might be directly increased or reduced as a result of an internalized transfer of technology. There are other less obvious, but no less important, effects on the home country. For example, an expansion of the market for a firm's products may bring with it economies of increased size and scope, and the spreading of organization and administrative overheads and R & D expenditure. Where there are pressures on the firm's domestic operations, production abroad may release capacity for more productive use at home. There may be technological feedback from the affiliate to the parent company, especially where investment is made in a more advanced industrial country, or where the affiliate undertakes R & D on behalf of the MNE of which it is part. Firms may be better able to take advantage of the geographical diversification of activities in their purchasing arrangements, fund raising and management recruitment. By having their assets spread over many countries and denominated in different currencies, they can better cover their risks, take advantage of leads and lags, protect themselves against exchange rate changes, engage in transfer price manipulation, and so on. As a consequence of the transfer (or sharing) of the technology of production, the investing enterprise almost always strengthens its technology of information and choice and, in some cases, its technological capacity as well. Companies such as Philips of Eindhoven provide an excellent example of how domestic capacity released as a result of investment in developing countries may be used to produce new or upgraded lines and/or be given over to technologically more advanced or complex production processes.

Resource-Based Investment

The purpose of this investment is usually to supply the home firm or country and other countries with resources. The technology required for exploration, extraction and processing, together with the large amount of capital needs required, gives MNEs O advantages over domestic competitors in a number of industries. Here there is no substitution between foreign and domestic investment; the transfer is of technology to increase or protect the existing supply of minerals or materials, it is to be hoped on improved terms. Moreover, it may also strengthen the technological capacity of home companies in engineering, chemical design and consultancy and maintenance work.

162 *Multinationals, Technology and Competitiveness*

In some cases, technology transfer to promote secondary processing activities may be at the expense of secondary processing in domestic markets. Again, it may be that the firm has little choice but to locate or relocate the processing operations in host countries in response to the policies pursued by their governments. But the basic equation is the relationship between social and private opportunity costs. The amount or kind of technology transferred may be too high because FDI confers lower net benefits from a social rather than a private viewpoint.

Export Platform Investment

We have suggested that it is the transfer of technology associated with this kind of investment which is likely to have the most effect on domestic employment as it is concentratred in labour-intensive activities. Unlike import-substituting investment, where if an MNE wishes to supply a foreign market it must produce in that market, firms do have options on the location of their export platform investments.

There are two forms of this kind of investment. The one is to produce complete goods and/or services which require substantial inputs of labour. Here the advantages of specialization and division of labour would seem to dictate that MNEs should concentrate their production of labour or (natural) resource-intensive goods in labour and resource-rich countries; and capital or technology-intensive goods in countries that are rich in capital and technology.

The second kind of export platform investment is in labour-intensive parts of a production process for sale in world markets, the capital or technology-intensive part of the production being produced in the capital or technology-rich countries. Again, this conforms to the principle of the international division of labour, except in so far as the action is prompted by distorted markets or government policies.

Perhaps the reason why this kind of investment is strongly criticized is that the critics believe that, without it, the adverse effects on domestic employment can more easily be arrested. The fact that if the home country's MNEs did not invest other firms would do so, and compete the home firms out of the markets, cuts no ice, because it is also argued that this can be prevented by import controls. The fact that consumers may have to pay a higher price for their products and that domestic firms will earn lower profits is regarded as an acceptable price to pay for minimizing unemployment. But, to repeat an earlier point, it is not the transfer of technology by MNEs *per se* which is the root of the concern, but the general dissemination of technology from both developed and socialist countries to developing countries, coupled with the consequences of free trade.

Industrial Restructuring in the USA and Europe

One of the main conclusions of an earlier section of this chapter was that in the manufacturing sectors which are most likely to generate adverse

Transfer of Technology and Home Countries   163

effects on the DMEs from the transfer of technology to developing countries, and particularly the NICs, the role of MNEs (*qua* MNEs) was not generally a significant one. Such advantages as they did possess were mainly in the marketing of goods in the industrialized countries; hence the presence of multinational buying groups, trading companies and joint ventures with local firms. The major exception seemed to be where the technology was ownership-specific and where it could only be advantageously exploited within the same firm, rather than, for example, by licensing or subcontracting. In such cases, the MNEs remained the chief vehicle for transfer of technology and the main cause of concern for the home economies.

Yet, even in the industries which are the most highly penetrated by MNEs, their role is a decreasing one in the more rapidly developing NICs in East Asia. Moreover, unlike the dominance of US MNEs in Latin America and UK MNEs in many of the Commonwealth developing countries, the geographical parentage of FDI in East Asia is more widely diffused. This means that not only is the impact of any one home country's MNEs likely to be less significant, but the opportunity cost of any one country not investing in these areas is correspondingly greater.

It is not only through equity investments that MNEs may transfer technology, however. Following the example of Japan, many East Asian NICs are using a variety of non-equity routes to attract foreign technology. These include not only straightforward licensing agreements and management contracts, but a whole variety of other forms, involving various institutions, for example, local firms, host governments, international agencies, consortia of MNEs, etc. (Oman, 1984). As a consequence, not only are an increasing number of manufacturing MNEs setting up international project, consultancy and advisory divisions to deal with external technology sales, especially to the NICs, Middle East and Eastern European countries, but consultancy firms in project design and evaluation, industrial and chemical engineering and managerial systems, are mushrooming. Indeed, it seems likely that the growth of some NICs, notably South Korea and Taiwan, will rest more on their ability to induce externalized technology flows and technological capacity than to attract FDI. To the DMEs, the relative benefits of consultancy contracts are less clear-cut. While a firm like Firestone argues that had its projects division not sold know-how kits on tyre factory design, construction and operation to NICs and Eastern European countries, other tyre companies would have done so, it admits that, in the long run, the DMEs may not benefit as much as had their MNEs been directly involved.

In the case of the transfer of petrochemicals know-how, the possible clash of interests is more serious. The specialist contractors are primarily concerned with selling knowledge of how to construct and operate a chemical plant and market its end products. Their interests are served by an increasing output of petrochemicals, and they will do what they can to assist potential buyers to obtain the necessary finance from sources such as the World Bank. The petrochemical producers, on the other hand,

164   *Multinationals, Technology and Competitiveness*

will only invest in developing countries if they believe they can make a reasonable profit from selling the output they produce, and they will only normally wish to transfer knowledge of plant construction and operation if they believe that their own ability to sell petrochemicals in third markets is not adversely affected. Many petrochemical producers consider that whenever there is a surplus of petrochemical capacity in developing countries, it is this, aided and abetted by the transfer of technology and capital from developed countries, that is forcing down the price of petrochemical products to uncompetitive prices. The situation is further aggravated wherever host governments subsidize production and/or dump petrochemicals on the world market.

The problem just described is not confined to the petrochemicals industry; it has shown itself in the mining industry, and several other branches of manufacturing industry. It results in a genuine conflict of interests between the suppliers and the *existing* producers of end products using that technology, and is often exacerbated by the policies of host governments wishing to develop their own industries and break into the international market. It is the export of technology through specialized consultants which home governments need to be more perturbed about, rather than the transfer of technology through their own manufacturing MNEs, whose interests, at least in this instance, coincide with those of their governments. On the other hand, this is not something which an individual DME can curb without risking even greater loss to itself. It involves some kind of international stabilization agreement to prevent excessive technology flows from causing unacceptable fluctuations in the output and prices of essential commodities.

We have said that, at a micro-level, any adverse effects which a transfer of technology may have on the investing firm's capacity may provoke various responses, ranging from a cut-back in domestic capacity to a restructuring of production into new product and process lines. Where the latter is successfully achieved, then, in effect, the firm has borne its own adjustment costs. Where it is not able to do this unemployment results. We have suggested this is most likely to be the case in labour-intensive declining industries; although even in expanding industries restructuring is likely to take place towards more technology or capital-intensive products or processes. Here it is worth observing that most of the sectors in which MNEs have been prominent in the NICs, particularly of the export platform kind, are those in which technological change has been the most rapid and the effects on production processes, products and labour requirements have been the most pronounced.[31] This has been most obvious in the computer and consumer electronics sectors. Take a company like Philips of Eindhoven. Employment in the complex of plants located at Eindhoven fell by 10 per cent between 1965 and 1985, yet real output doubled. Over the same period, Philips' employment in the developing countries increased by 120 per cent. The company claims that technical development in the field of audio and video equipment, and particularly the technology of micro-electronics and computerization, has caused a major restructuring of its worldwide

Transfer of Technology and Home Countries 165

operations from which both the company and the Netherlands have benefited. Be that as it may, it is certainly true that today's leaders in the consumer electronics industries are also those that have been active in their foreign activities. The incapacity or reluctance of UK companies to engage in such investment may well have weakened rather than strengthened the position of the UK electronics industry in world markets.

The most obvious problems of technology exports occur in industries whose domestic markets are static or declining, where there is little product or process innovation, where output is specialized and where production methods are labour-intensive. The textile and clothing industry is the one most typically cited. In Western Europe it was estimated in 1980 that 40,000 people, or one-sixth of the labour force, had lost their jobs because of import competition from Asian and North African factories, where wages ranged from one-half to one-tenth of those in Germany or Belgium.[32] Between 1970 and 1976, exports from the NICs rose sixfold, and it has only been as a result of the multi-fibre agreement that imports since 1977 have slowed down. At the same time, the anti-protectionist lobby argues that the developed countries have more to lose from protectionism than developing countries because the rate of growth of exports from the developed to the developing countries is greater than that from the developing to the developed countries.

Very often, the problem of these declining industries – like those of the traditional industries, for example, coal, textiles, and shipbuilding, in the UK after the First World War – is highlighted by the fact that they tend to be located in the less prosperous regions of the home economies and use the type of labour which cannot easily find alternative employment or be retrained. The new jobs being created require different skills to those which they replace. In such cases structural unemployment persists. Most of these have been in the labour-intensive sectors, notably textiles and clothing, consumer electronics and light engineering. The EEC Commission has estimated that more than two million jobs in Europe have been lost as a result of import competition from developing countries.

That this is an age-old problem, and is the inevitable result of the emergence of newly industrializing economies, is of little comfort to those adversely affected. Neither is the fact that MNEs are not always actively involved in the industries. The fear is that import competition from a comparatively few industries today will spread to many others tomorrow. As NICs climb up the industrial ladder, will they not attract more markets away from the developed countries? And if they do, will not the MNEs become increasingly involved? In this respect, the participation of MNEs in audio and video equipment, in synthetic fibres, in pharmaceuticals, auto components and telecommunications equipment in some countries in Asia and Latin America is cited as a foretaste of the pattern of the future. But here the experience of Japan is salutary. Japan increased her share of world exports in manufactured goods from 6.9 per cent in 1960 to 15.7 per cent in 1985, with the minimum contribution from foreign MNEs. Yet to achieve this resurgence to

166 *Multinationals, Technology and Competitiveness*

industrial strength she imported a very substantial amount of technology, while building up an indigenous strength in the ability to absorb, alter and adapt that technology. For example, between 1950 and 1983, the Japanese government approved 2,212 contracts made by Japanese concerns involving purchases of technology from Western enterprises.[33]

It is a moot point whether Europe and the USA would have been better off without the Japanese economic miracle, but the point at issue is that it would have been difficult, if not impossible, for these countries to have used normal commercial channels to have arrested the miracle. At the same time, it is at least arguable that the USA and Europe would have been better off had they been allowed a stake in this miracle. The contrast to Japan is Brazil and Mexico, whose rate of growth of industrial production since the late 1960s has paralleled that of Japan, but in whose prosperity foreign-based (particularly US) MNEs have fully participated.

The exports of manufactured goods from the developing countries identified in Table 8.2 on p. 154 rose by 9 times (in value terms) between 1965 and 1976, and then slowed down to 3.5 times in the following nine years. Partly this deceleration reflected the very low export base of several developing countries in 1965; partly the reduced rate of world economic growth in the late 1970s and early 1980s; and partly technological advances in some industrialized countries, which resulted in a shifting back of some manufacturing activities which earlier might have been located in developing countries. Moreover, the fastest rate of growth of manufacturing exports between 1976 and 1985 has not been from the NICs but from other East Asian countries and some Southern European developing countries, for example, Turkey.

At the same time, the exports of manufactured goods, particularly intermediate products and capital goods, from DMEs to developing countries has sharply increased, as has the proportion of those shipped between MNEs and their foreign affiliates (US Department of Commerce, 1985). It would seem that while MNEs have played an important role in fashioning the restructuring of international economic activity, government industrial trade and FDI policy – particularly with respect to structural adjustment – may determine the success of both DMEs and developing countries in adapting to the changing international division of labour, brought about by economic development and technological advances. The evidence suggests, however, that the type of technology required by developing countries for upgrading their manufacturing activities is fairly readily obtainable in the open market, and that, far from reducing their domestic technological capacity, the additional markets created by MNEs from their FDI in developing countries help sustain that technological capacity. Indeed, the alternative proposition that developing countries are not attracting MNEs to transfer high value-added activities seems to us to warrant more consideration. In this connection, it is clearly important to distinguish between the short-term *employment* consequences for DMEs of a transfer of technology to developing countries and the long-term effects of such a transfer for the

Transfer of Technology and Home Countries 167

technological capabilities. Our conclusion is that the former effect is likely to give greater cause for concern among DMEs; the latter is more relevant to transfers of technology *between* DMEs – and especially between the triad of USA, Europe and Japan (Ohmae, 1985).

CONCLUSIONS: SOME POLICY IMPLICATIONS

It should be clear from the preceding paragraphs that the impact of transfer of technology carried out by MNEs on the economies of the home countries is but a tip of the iceberg of the adjustment problems now facing, and likely to face, the DMEs in the foreseeable future. The fact is that, although MNEs continue to account for the bulk of the commercial R & D carried out in the Western world, only a small amount of this is directly or immediately relevant to the *present* industrialization programme of the developing countries. Most of the product, process, materials, production, marketing, managerial marketing and organizational know-how currently required for much of this industrialization is not proprietary to individual firms but is generally available in the marketplace.

However, in the next decade, the picture may change quite dramatically as the NICs become more sophisticated in their product structure and production techniques. The first question to which DMEs have to address themselves – provided they are allowed to – is how far they wish to be involved in this industrialization programme. This chapter has no more than hinted that the net social benefits of being involved through technology transfer by their own MNEs may be higher than any alternative action they may pursue.

In response to increasing and more pervasive competition from the NICs there are basically three policies open to governments of DMEs. First, they can resort to some form of protectionism; second, they can enter into agreements with their newly industrialized competitors to control their increase in manufacturing exports or to insist that they should import from the DMEs as much as they export to them (the assurance of fair trading comes into this category); and third, they can seek to identify their future comparative advantage in resource allocation and introduce policies to encourage the necessary adaptation and restructuring. In the long run, assuming the last is judged the first best solution, to be successful it would need more decisive and far-reaching strategies to stimulate productivity, encourage innovation and promote the development of technology and information-intensive activities than have been introduced by most OECD countries up to now. In the interim, however, the problem is how to minimize the adjustment costs of market disruptions to maximize the smoothness of the adaptation and restructuring, and, where appropriate, to encourage firms affected by competition from NICs to be more efficient. To solve these problems, which because of market failure or rigidities may well mean controlling the character and pace of the restructuring process, some form of import control should not be ruled out.[34]

168 *Multinationals, Technology and Competitiveness*

It is, however, difficult to understand how controlling the activities of manufacturing MNEs in NICs can advance these goals, any more than the controls exerted by the UK on the export of technology in the nineteenth century helped its objective (Rosenberg, 1981).[35] If any attention is needed in this direction, it should be towards removing any distorting influences which may encourage MNEs to transfer different amounts or types of technology than they might otherwise have done, or which may interfere with their returning the maximum benefits to the home country. Again, action may involve changes to international patent, monetary or tax systems, etc., some of which at least would operate against the interests of the technology-receiving countries.

The area where home governments need to pay most attention, apart from that of defence and national security (Hawkins and Gladwin, 1981), is where their own firms, acting in a mainly consultative capacity, are transferring technology which cannot be obtained from other sources. Here the social opportunity costs of transfer may be considerably greater than the private opportunity costs, and ways may need to be found of redressing this difference.

We have argued that DMEs are likely to be differently affected by the industrialization of the developing world.[36] The role of their own MNEs in this process and the attitudes of their governments (compare the US and Japanese cases) also differ. We have also asserted that one reason why a particular firm or country may be reluctant to control technology exports is that its competitors may *not* do so. This suggests that the main area of international competition will continue to be *between* countries of the developed world. Only if DMEs adopted a common policy towards the actions of their MNEs would it be possible to control the outflow of technology specific to MNEs without any one DME feeling it was worse off as a result. While such a strategy, at least on economic grounds, seems very unlikely, the efforts of the developing countries, including the NICs, to strengthen their bargaining power vis-à-vis MNEs from the developed world may eventually provoke a countervailing reaction on the part of NICs to redress the balance which they believe to be against their own interests (Bergsten, 1974). A less controversial route to follow might be the search for harmonized policies between North and South designed to smooth the adjustment process, which might be of benefit to both older and newer industrialized countries.

One final observation. This chapter began with the expression of concern of developed countries about the possible adverse effects of exporting technology to developing countries through their own MNEs. It ends by asking the question: Can developed countries *not* afford to export technology to developing countries through their own MNEs? For if the activities of MNEs are seen not as a threat to domestic investment, jobs and technological capacity, but as a means of (1) exploiting international markets, (2) ensuring a stake in the prosperity of developing countries, (3) financing technological capacity, and (4) protecting or advancing the *international* competitive position of one DME relative to another, the question of whether North/South technology transfer is a

Transfer of Technology and Home Countries 169

'good' or a 'bad' thing takes on a completely new meaning. The case presented is not that this latter proposition is in any way proven, but that it deserves at least as much attention as the alternative thesis which is currently more in vogue and being more vigorously researched.

NOTES

1 For excellent summaries of the main issues involved see Helleiner (1975); Sagafi-Negad, Moxon and Perlmutter (1981).
2 Technology is defined as a flow of all kinds of commercial applicable knowledge; technological capacity is defined as a stock of assets, both physical and human, capable of generating technology flows.
3 In 1985 about three-quarters of all receipts of foreign royalties and fees received by the USA and the UK originated from the foreign affiliates of their own firms.
4 This is the nomenclature used by the UN; it essentially embraces the member countries of OECD.
5 These countries' share of world manufacturing exports fell from 36.5 per cent in 1967 to 23.0 per cent in 1985. Of the other industrialized nations, Japan has increased her share from 9.8 per cent to 15.7 per cent while France and Germany have maintained theirs at around 8 per cent and 15 per cent, respectively.
6 Quoted in Meyer (1978). See also National Science Foundation (1974).
7 As has happened in the UK pharmaceutical industry, where the share of output of indigenous firms has risen in the 1970s.
8 That is to say, a firm must expect to earn at least the opportunity cost of the capital invested in technological-creating activities.
9 For a discussion of the conditions under which an enterprise may prefer to externalize technology transfers, see Telessio (1979), Robinson (1978) and Teece (1981b).
10 For a review of the literature on the overseas R & D by MNEs, see Pearce (1987).
11 See especially Reddaway *et al.* (1968), Hufbauer and Adler (1968) and Stopford and Turner (1985).
12 A study by Kawaguchi (1978) suggested that Japanese joint ventures and subsidiaries in South East Asia buy between 30 per cent and 100 per cent of their inputs (in value terms) from Japan (see especially his Table V3, p.31). In our own study of Japanese manufacturing affiliates in British industry, it was found that 50 per cent of equipment and machinery purchased by the affiliates in 1982 was imported from Japan (Dunning, 1986).
13 In the macro sense, it is difficult to conceive of unrelated goods as all technology may, indirectly, affect the international competitive position of the recipient country.
14 In 1982, US MNEs accounted for over 4/5 per cent of all the R & D undertaken in US manufacturing industry.
15 Member countries of the Development Assistance Committee of the OECD.
16 In the period 1960–7, the world stock of outward direct investment rose by 8.1 per cent per annum; the corresponding percentage for 1968–72 was 11.1 per cent, for 1973–80 13.6 per cent and for 1981–4 3.8 per cent.
17 France, West Germany, Italy, Japan, the Netherlands, the UK and the USA.

170 *Multinationals, Technology and Competitiveness*

18 There has been rather less movement towards a symmetrical flow of technology. Though, generally, receipts from the export of technology by European countries and Japan have grown faster than those by the USA, in 1984 the USA still received from foreigners 16.3 times the royalties and fees it paid to foreigners.

19 The coverage of NICs varies according to source. The OECD and UNCTAD list Greece, Portugal, Spain, Turkey, Yugoslavia, Hong Kong, Singapore, South Korea, Taiwan, Brazil and Mexico as NICs. However, the UK Foreign and Commonwealth Office, in a report issued in 1979, also included India, Malaysia, Pakistan, Philippines, Thailand, Argentina, Israel, Malta, Poland, Rumania and Hungary. Countries included in the seven mentioned in the text are Brazil, Mexico, India, Malaysia, Argentina, Singapore, Hong Kong, South Korea and the Philippines.

20 Three-quarters of the inward capital stake of these eleven countries was in manufacturing industry.

21 However, as a percentage of GDP some Asian countries, e.g. Singapore and Hong Kong, spend more on other forms of technology imports than do Latin American countries (OECD, 1981).

22 Dunning and Cantwell (1987) estimate that over one-half of FDI in Africa in 1982 was in the primary product sectors compared to about 20 per cent in the case of non-African developing countries. For a comprehensive examination of the role of FDI in Africa see Cantwell (1987a).

23 However, the ratio between the stock of investment by MNEs in the manufacturing sector and manufacturing exports of developing countries is positively correlated to the share of total manufacturing exports allowed for by MNEs.

24 For further details see Pearce (1987).

25 Examples include the tropical drugs programme of the WHO, some tyre development (in India and the Philippines), and some product adaptation in toiletries, food products and agricultural and industrial machinery. A survey of R & D performed abroad by MNEs showed there were some applied R & D activities in several developing countries including Argentina, Brazil, Mexico, India, Hong Kong and Singapore (Behrman and Fischer, 1980).

26 For example, Keesing (1978) estimated that MNE manufacturing affiliates account for only 5 per cent of the exports of textiles and clothing from developing countries, and that the percentage is even lower for leather goods. Again, the proportions vary between MNEs of different nationalities with the Japanese being the most actively involved in these sectors.

27 It should be noted that the contribution of MNE affiliates varies considerably between NICs. In Singapore such affiliates provided work for 90 per cent of the work force engaged in the engineering and motor vehicles industries and 92 per cent in the textiles and clothing industries. The corresponding proportions for Taiwan in 1981 were 48 per cent and 13 per cent and for Brazil in 1977, 71 per cent and 26 per cent. On the other hand, in Yugoslavia, which is one of the leading exporters of domestic electrical appliances and electric power machinery, the role of MNEs is very limited indeed.

28 One estimate of the Netherlands Research Institute (in 1977) is that 70 per cent of all Hong Kong's exports of clothing passes through Western retail traders and import merchants.

29 Donges and Riedel (1977). Of the thirty-six product groups in which the RCA of developing countries in 1972–3 was greater than 1, in only six was

Transfer of Technology and Home Countries   171

the degree of MNE penetration a high one. Of the fifty-five groups in which the RCA of developing countries was less than 1, the corresponding figure was sixteen.

30 Excepting the technology of marketing or market areas, as made available by MNE buying and subcontracting groups.

31 For example, it has been estimated that over the period 1962–75, fifty times more jobs were lost through growth of labour productivity as were estimated through growth of imports from developing countries (Keesing, 1978).

32 The corresponding figure for the USA is 225,000.

33 For further details of the role of Japan as a technology importer and exporter see Ozawa (1985).

34 Harry Johnson (1975) makes the point that both adjustment assistance and adjustment safeguards should be considered in the *general* context of economic change rather than in the context of change mediated through changes due to international technology transfer.

35 The sluggishness of the UK to adapt to the structural changes required of her industrial economy in the late nineteenth century is an object lesson to DMEs faced with the competition from the NICs.

36 See also the OECD (1981) and studies quoted therein (e.g. in Chapters 3 and 4).

Chapter 9

Multinational Enterprises, Industrial Restructuring and Competitiveness: A UK Perspective

INTRODUCTION

Since 1970, the world has experienced a series of events which have had, and are having, a most profound effect on the allocation of economic activity, both between and within countries. Among those of greatest long-term significance are the rising economic stature of some NICs, particularly those from the Far East, and a series of technological breakthroughs, especially in the areas of information and telecommunications, and biotechnology. Of more immediate and pervasive impact has been a deceleration in world economic growth, coupled with a swing to neo-liberal policies of most governments and a more realistic appreciation of the costs and gains of economic interdependence.

These events have affected countries differently, according, for example, to their stage of development and economic structure, and to the way in which central authorities have adjusted to them. Most advanced industrial societies have found the repercussions both painful and destabilizing. While we should not minimize the impact of inflation and cyclical unemployment and the supply-oriented managerial policies to combat these, a more powerful impetus to industrial restructuring has been the dramatic cuts in price-cost margins. These, together with new technologies and growing international competition, have caused sweeping reappraisals of product, process and marketing strategies, and the location of production facilities. This has resulted in a good deal of structural unemployment, and has severely tested governments in their adjustment policies. Indeed, it is the combination of the pattern, pace and extent of these developments which has created so many of the problems of recent years.

This chapter examines the role of MNEs as engines of structural change and transmitters of change across national boundaries, and also as influences on the way in which the international community adapts to change. We shall consider these issues from a UK perspective and

Industrial Restructuring and Competitiveness 173

concern ourselves with the impact of the overseas operations of UK MNEs and of the UK affiliates of foreign-based MNEs on the allocation of economic activity, both between the UK and the rest of the world and within the UK.

In particular, we shall bear in mind two commonly held, but very different views; first that MNEs, by their favoured access to human and financial resources and their ability to move them across national boundaries and between industrial sectors, play a positive role in the structural modernization and the transformation of the UK economy; and second that MNEs' decisions regarding resource allocation, taken from a global perspective, may be detrimental to the long-term interests of the UK economy by locking it into an unacceptable international division of labour, by weakening its economic sovereignty and by frustrating its efforts to revitalize its industrial base and develop new technological initiatives.

HISTORICAL BACKGROUND

There can be no doubt that Britain's close involvement in trade and foreign investment has caused it to be particularly vulnerable to fluctuations in world economic events. Only at the time of the first Industrial Revolution can it be said that Britain was in control of its economic destiny; since then, partly because the country already had an industrial heritage, and partly because of the erosion of its technological supremacy, Britain has adjusted to, rather than been the prime mover in, structural change; that is, it has been dominated by exogenous rather than endogenous forces.

For example, in the years before the First World War, the second generation of technological advances based upon the internal combustion engine and electrical power were first commercialized in the USA, even though they often originated from Europe. Initially suited to the American economy and best exploited by large firms, they were transmitted back to the UK by the first wave of American multinational entrepreneurs. During the inter-war years, the new industries they generated, for example, motor vehicles, electrical engineering, etc., helped to compensate for the loss of some traditional markets, for example, textiles, shipbuilding, to the then industrializing countries, for instance, India and Japan. In this way, inward investment performed a useful restructuring role, while outward investment was mainly directed to resource-exploitative ventures in the Commonwealth.

The process of US technical hegemony was accelerated in the Second World War, reaching its peak shortly afterwards, and in the 1950s much of Europe's recovery was aided by US direct investment. At this point in time, the maturing MNEs were the main private repositories of technological innovation; they were also the main organizational route by which such innovations were transferred across boundaries, often aided by barriers to trade and lack of suitable licensees in host countries. In the early post-war years, there was some foreign investment by UK firms in industries in which the UK has lost, or was losing, her comparative advantage, but, by and large, this continued to be directed to resource-based activities or to service markets which were difficult or costly to supply from the UK.

Studies in the 1950s and 1960s on inward and outward investment found that it had a favourable impact on the post-war restructuring of the UK economy.[1] The evidence presented at the time strongly suggested that the UK's economic structure had been tilted more towards high technology and growth manufacturing sectors as a result of inward investment, while the foreign activities of UK MNEs were mainly directed to the primary and more traditional secondary sectors. In 1964, for example, some 71 per cent of the net foreign assets owned by the leading UK manufacturing MNEs were in the less technology-intensive sectors of food, drink and tobacco, household products, paper, metal products, building materials and textiles, and 29 per cent in the more technology-intensive sectors of chemicals, engineering, electronics, and vehicles (Reddaway, Potter and Taylor, 1968). By contrast, in 1965, 67 per cent of the net assets of foreign – mainly US – firms in UK manufacturing were in the more technology-intensive sectors and only 33 per cent in the former industries in less technology-intensive sectors. The data set out in Table 9.1 clearly show that while the foreign activities of UK MNEs in the 1960s were more oriented towards the traditional sectors than those of UK industry in general, the activities of foreign subsidiaries in the UK were more oriented to the high technology sectors.

To some extent, the pattern of activity by MNEs in the 1960s reflected their geographical destination or origin. Britain's past imperialistic ties steered investment towards those sectors in which it had a comparative trading advantage. In 1960, 61 per cent of the net foreign assets owned by UK MNEs outside oil, banking, and insurance was invested in Common-wealth countries. Over the last twenty years, the growing importance of the involvement by UK MNEs in Europe has shifted the sectoral distribution towards more high technology sectors. At the same time, these investments, like those of foreign MNEs in the UK, reflect the changing locational attractions of countries. Some foreign governments, for example, by nationalization or other deterrents, have virtually outlawed some kinds of MNE activity; much of the vertical disinvestment by UK firms since 1960 can be explained in these terms. Changing locational advantages also explain a lot of import-substituting investment in the inter-war years. Tariff barriers and other import controls induced US firms to set up factories in the UK, as did the shortage of US dollars after the Second World War. In the 1980s, European and US protectionism against Japanese imports is prompting Japanese MNEs to follow a similar strategy. Natural or artificially induced shifts in the locational pull of countries both affect, and may be affected by, the extent and balance of international direct investment; in other words, the structure of foreign direct investment – and hence its impact on the economy – is

Table 9.1 *The Industrial Structure of UK Inward and Outward Direct Investment in the 1960s*

	Inward (capital stake end 1965)		All UK firms (net output 1963)		Outward (capital stake end 1964)	
	£m	%	£m	%	£m	%
Food, drink and tobacco	207.9	12.7	1,292.0	12.5	537.6	39.3
Chemicals and allied industries	211.9	13.0	949.9	9.2	194.5	14.2
Metal manufacturing	134.4	8.2	1,500.2	14.5	132.2	9.7
Mechanical engineering	336.7	20.7	1,435.8	13.9	19.9	1.5
Electrical engineering	185.1	11.4	954.0	9.2	67.5	4.9
Motor vehicles	303.5	18.6	1,184.4	11.5	51.8	3.8
Textiles, clothing and footwear	34.9	2.1	1,234.1	12.0	94.1	6.9
Paper and allied products	46.2	2.8	845.6	8.2	118.8	8.6
Rubber products	58.4	3.6	167.7	1.6	74.3	5.4
Other manufacturing industries	110.4	6.8	755.3	7.3	76.2	5.6
All manufacturing	1,629.4	100.0	10,319.0	100.0	1,366.7	100.0

Source: Inward capital stake, *Board of Trade Journal*, 26-1-1968; all UK firms net output, *Census of Production*, 1963; outward capital stake, Reddaway, Potter and Taylor (1968).

176 *Multinationals, Technology and Competitiveness*

influenced by the disposition of immobile resource endowments, including government policy, as well as that of more mobile resource endowments.

Finally, the organizational mode of exploiting the O advantages of firms must be considered. It is, at least, possible that differences in the structure of UK outward and inward direct investment in the 1960s might reflect the differences in the relative costs of (international) intermediate product markets and those of hierarchies in the sectors, or between the investing and recipient countries in question. Most outward investment, for example, involved the transfer of mature and codifiable technologies, where proprietary rights could be protected, and quality control assured. By contrast, a higher proportion of inward investment involved idiosyncratic or non-codifiable technologies for which there were no or highly imperfect cross-border markets; in consequence, to appropriate fully their economic rent, the owning firm perceived it had to internalize their transfer. Moreover, the economies of size, scope and organizational synergy tended to be pronounced in sectors in which foreign subsidiaries were well represented, relative to those in which UK MNEs tend to be concentrated.[2]

A NEW INTERNATIONAL DIVISION OF LABOUR

During the 1960s, although there was some concern about the effects of outward investment on the balance of payments and of inward investment on competition, market structure and technological capability,[3] there was not much anxiety about the MNEs as vehicles for relocating domestic economic activity or for determining the pattern of employment and output across countries. Partly this reflected the macroeconomic climate of the day and partly the fact that few MNEs yet operated globally integrated product or sourcing strategies.

The slowing down of economic growth and increase in unemployment in Europe, the opening up of the Far Eastern economies, the move towards closer economic integration in Europe – and to a lesser extent in Latin America and Asia – the increasing ease with which organizations could be managed at a distance, and the spread of multinationalization *per se*, have quite dramatically affected the MNE's role in structural change. While the MNE's strength as a producer of technology, particularly of advanced technology, continues undiminished, it has attracted most recent attention as an agent in determining what kinds of technology are transferred to which countries to produce what products to be sold in which markets. As a result of the increased geographical diversification of activity under common ownership, and the closer relationships between firms at different stages of production processes, countries have become related to each other in a new international division of labour, which, if not actively engineered by MNEs, has been largely orchestrated and utilized by them.

In such a division of labour, the structure of international production is

Industrial Restructuring and Competitiveness 177

determined by MNE hierarchies competing among themselves, rather than by independent buyers and sellers at arm's length prices. Efficiency and success are judged from a corporate standpoint rather than from that of the countries in which the corporations produce. In such conditions, industrial restructuring by MNEs may link one economy with another in ways unacceptable to either or both. In such cases, the role of international hierarchies is less that of resource transferors, or tutors in resource usage, and more as allocators of economic activity to meet their global goals. Moreover, the process of adjustment may bring its own problems and require a modification in government economic strategies.

THE IMPACT OF NEW TECHNOLOGY

The arrival of the new technologies of the last decade is likely to have no less a far reaching effect. Over the years, technological change has become less activity- or customer-specific. Nowhere is this better seen than in the fields of telematics and biotechnology, in which tremendous strides are now being made. The micro-chip, the latest generation of computers, robotics, laser technology and optic fibres have multitudinous applications. Yet because equipment systems and techniques can be used jointly by firms engaged in related activities, there are good reasons for such firms to be linked to each other in the production chain. This is leading to hierarchical galaxies, with a pivotal group of firms (which control the key technologies) being surrounded by satellite suppliers and customers. In the case of information technology, the core firms are sometimes the computing and sometimes the telecommunications giants; in biotechnology, the battle for supremacy is divided between the food processing, chemical and pharmaceutical enterprises, but its uses extend from pollution control and mineral extraction to health care and agriculture.

Because most technological developments are transmittable across national boundaries, and different stages of the value-added chain have different locational configurations, the globally integrated MNE is in a strong position to capitalize on them. This may show itself in a regional or global marketing policy (that is, the development of a world product mandate) or in the international sourcing of components and raw materials. It certainly adds to the need for flexible production systems, low inventories, the integration between computer-aided design and manufacturing processes. All these developments are highly capital- and/or technology-intensive and only pay off if international markets can be captured. As a consequence, if countries (particularly smaller countries) wish to be in the van of progress, they need to generate their own MNEs and/or encourage the formation of national or international corporate alliances. This suggests that the MNEs of the 1990s will pose new challenges and opportunities to national governments and require a conscious re-examination of the technological and industrial policies.

THE STRUCTURAL IMPACT OF MNEs IN THE 1960s AND 1970s: SOME THEORETICAL CONSIDERATIONS

Multinational enterprises may affect the economic structure of the countries in which they operate in a number of ways. First, by the resources they transfer, and the control exerted over these and the local resources they acquire, they can directly affect the strategy, performance, and conduct of their foreign affiliates, while indirectly they may affect other firms, for instance, by linkages, example and competitive stimulus. Second, by their choice of activity they may influence the way resources are allocated. Third, by their internalization of product and factor markets they may impinge on both domestic and international market structures. Fourth, over time, the way they respond to changes in supply or demand conditions may influence the adaptive capabilities of the economies in which they operate. Fifth, by their mode of entry (takeover of green-field investment) and their global strategies, they may modify both market structure and the nationality of ownership of firms.

How far is it possible to identify an optimum economic structure for a country? This is exceedingly difficult, as the goals of government are multiple and extend well beyond the quest for economic efficiency. Many countries exercise some control over inward and outward direct investment for social or political reasons. A short run improvement in industrial composition may not necessarily be beneficial in the long run; neither does it follow that all groups in the community will gain, or gain to the same extent. In practice, there are trade-offs in goals and priorities which can be resolved only by political judgement and action. What happens if an improved structure leads to more unemployment? Is less national autonomy in decision taking an acceptable price to pay for more efficiency, and so on?

All first-year students reading economics are taught the conditions under which trade is beneficial. The well-known principle of comparative advantage holds good only under very restrictive conditions, for example, the existence of perfect competition, full employment, and immobility of factor services, and is concerned only with efficiency goals. The principle also assumes that the economic structures of the trading countries are different from each other, and ignores the role of technology, learning by doing and improvements in human capital in restructuring resource availability and usage. Few of these conditions apply in the modern world economy, though some are more relevant in (or between) some countries and/or sectors than in others. In particular, all sorts of obstacles and rigidities inhibit the speedy and efficient reallocation of resources required, while internal markets established by hierarchies may create entry barriers to countries seeking to cultivate new areas of comparative advantage. Governments, too, may play positive, as well as negative, roles in the creation and use of resources.

Since MNEs themselves engage in trade, and especially of intermediate products such as technology, it seems reasonable to suppose that their role in restructuring might be explained and evaluated using trade

Industrial Restructuring and Competitiveness

type analyses. Certainly they control or have access to resources which may not be easily available to uninational firms. Since they usually operate in several nation-states, and produce many products and processes, they are in a favoured position to respond to economic and technical change or take advantage of it; indeed, in many respects their affiliates are like countries trading with each other.

A Normative Proposition

Let us next turn to consider the UK's situation by making a proposition drawn from our understanding of trade theory. The proposition is that foreign MNEs producing in the UK should be encouraged to steer resources to, or help better to utilize resources in, sectors in which the UK is perceived to have, or is likely to develop, a comparative advantage. By contrast, UK MNEs should help steer activities away from the UK which require immobile resources in which the home country's comparative advantage is declining, but which can be put to good use by other countries, using the entrepreneurship, management, technology and organizational skills of firms of the home country. Here, one would expect foreign and domestic MNEs to operate in different industrial sectors; in such cases, foreign capital would substitute for domestic capital but the net result would be an improvement in national productivity. Quite a bit of MNE activity in and out of the UK fits in well with this kind of proposition – particularly that of a North–South orientation.

Increasingly, however, MNEs are also engaging in activities which cannot be evaluated in this way. Like trade, international production often takes place in different countries in similar sectors. Indeed three-quarters of all foreign direct investment is undertaken by advanced-country MNEs in other advanced countries, and most of this is in sectors in which there is a substantial amount of intra-industry specialization. Such specialization is usually undertaken to take advantage of economies of scale and scope and, because of the advantages of common governance, is usually conducted within MNEs.

The sectors in which MNEs operate are often capital-, technology- or information-intensive. They are also those which produce a wide range of processes or products springing from a common or generic technological or marketing base. Their market structure is characterized by oligopoly and usually international oligopoly. Over the years, their degree of multinationalization has dramatically increased and their strategy has become increasingly global. Already vertically and horizontally integrated cross national boundaries, the latest technological developments are causing them to become centres of new galaxies. It is the presence of the subsidiaries of these firms which might seem to offer host countries access to advanced technology, but some fear that this could turn out to be Trojan horse. At the same time, to keep up with their competitors in world markets, these same countries may need to generate their own MNEs. This inevitably results in the inter-penetration of markets and a growth in intra-industry trade. According to Kenichi

180 *Multinationals, Technology and Competitiveness*

Ohmae (1985), the scale of research and development necessary to maintain a leading competitive position in the knowledge-intensive manufacturing and service sectors requires firms in those sectors to have a marketing or production presence in each of the main industrial markets – the so-called 'triad' of the USA, Western Europe and Japan. From time to time, the country-specific characteristics of firms come to the fore, but, for the most part, competition is based on firm-specific product, production and marketing strategies.

Policy recommendations are more difficult, especially for small industrial countries, the wealth of which rests on their human capital and skills. Often specialization within sectors or close collaboration with foreign firms is the only alternative to opting out of the technological race altogether. Most larger countries have a wider range of choices, as they can opt for a policy of self-sufficiency; Japan is an obvious exception. For medium-sized countries like the UK, we believe the situation calls for a broader based strategy which encompasses both the courtship of inward investment as an example and a stimulus, and the encouragement of domestic MNEs to penetrate foreign markets and ensure the innovatory bases on which their future competitive prowess rests. Equally important, the government has a role in providing the infrastructure and the incentives to promote the kind of foreign investment which is most suitable to the long-term development of its indigenous resources, especially human capital, and in combating unfair competition from abroad. In the short term, some help in revitalizing and restructuring indigenous firms or sectors may be called for – especially where the prospects for the UK are favourable, but because of market failure, for example, in the capital market UK-owned firms are unable to catch up with foreign competition without external assistance. We shall return to these issues later in this chapter.

MEASURING THE IMPACT OF MNEs ON UK INDUSTRIAL STRUCTURE

Before considering the data we have regarding the impact of MNE activity on the industrial structure of the UK, let us briefly summarize the methodology followed. There have been two main approaches to evaluating the impact of MNEs on national economies. The first is the *alternative position* or *counterfactual* approach which tries to measure the effect of FDI on foreign production as the difference between the actual impact and that which it is hypothesized would have occurred in its absence. Such an approach was used by Reddaway in the 1960s to evaluate the effects of outward direct investment on the GNP of the UK (Reddaway, Potter and Taylor, 1968). The second, which in many ways involves similar reasoning to the first, is the *comparative factual* approach: this seeks to compare the activities of MNEs with those of their non-MNE competitors, arguing that the difference between the two

Industrial Restructuring and Competitiveness 181

may be attributable to the multinationality of the former. This methodology was used by Cohen (1975) in a study of the export performance of US and indigenous firms in South Asia. The advantages are obvious: actual data are available and a comparison of, or changes in, performance can be made. But the pitfalls are many, not least that of isolating the 'multinational' effect from other differences between the two groups of firms. Moreover, to draw any policy conclusions, for example with respect to encouraging or discouraging inward or outward investment, implicitly assumes that the marginal and average impact is the same, and that the real opportunity cost lies in the ownership of activity rather than in its direction. Finally this approach assumes just one 'alternative position'.

Nevertheless, we shall adopt this second approach. First, we shall review the main structural characteristics of inward and outward production financed by investment in 1971 and 1979, compared with that of UK-owned companies in the UK, and (where data permit) changes in these between these two years. Second, we shall examine the statistical relationship between a number of structural variables and the sectoral distribution with manufacturing industry of three types of production[4] (1) production of foreign-owned firms in the UK; (2) the foreign production of UK MNEs; and (3) the production of UK firms (including the UK-based MNEs) in the UK. Ideally we would have liked to have separated the UK production of UK MNEs from that of UK uninational firms, but the data do not allow us to do this. The purpose of this exercise is to compare the significance of the three groups of firms on economic structure. By itself, of course, any statistical association does not tell us anything about the direction of causation; we also accept that the level of significance of each variable may be influenced by other variables not included in the equation, and that there may be some multicollinearity between the independent variables.

We tackle the causation problem in the following way. First it could be argued that if, for example, foreign MNEs *respond* to a change in, say, trade competitiveness (RCA) in a more positive and significant way than domestic firms, this will have an impact on future RCA. It is possible to test the impact of whether the activities of the MNEs lead or lag structural change by examining the relationship between the relative change in production between 1971 and 1979 and the value of structural parameters at the beginning and the end of the period. This a later section of the chapter seeks to do.

The sources of the statistics used are set out in the Appendix to this chapter (see p.201). Suffice it at this point to say that they embrace all UK-owned forms and foreign affiliates engaged in manufacturing production from official statistics, and a selection of 188 of the largest UK MNEs covering an estimated 95 per cent of the value of overseas manufacturing investment. Data specially provided by the Department of Trade and compiled from company accounts enable us to classify the first two groups of firms by forty-four minimum list headings; from an examination of the company accounts of UK MNEs, we have classified these latter firms by twenty-nine headings.

182 Multinationals, Technology and Competitiveness

Table 9.2 *Comparisons Between Industrial Distribution of Sales of UK and MNE-Related Companies and Selected Structural Characteristics 1979 and 1971–79*

			UK firms in UK (UK)	Foreign affiliates in UK (FMNE $_{UK}$)	UK MNEs abroad (UK MNE$_f$)
Allocative efficiency (1979)					
(1) Trade competitiveness		BA	44.2	34.9	26.0
(RCA)		AA	49.2	59.4	61.7
(2) Labour productivity		BA	54.0	37.7	25.5
(LP)		AA	45.5	62.2	73.9
(3) Capital labour ratio		BA	69.1	42.7	38.7
(K/L)		AA	30.4	57.2	61.7
(4) Skill intensive ratio		BA	72.8	70.6	75.8
(NO/OWB)		AA	26.7	29.3	24.4
(5) Advertising ratio		BA	81.3	81.0	87.0
(A/S)		AA	16.1	14.2	12.8
(6) Concentration ratio		BA	48.0	31.6	19.4
(C)		AA	51.5	68.5	80.9
(7) Economies of scale		BA	72.5	76.4	64.2
(SP)		AA	27.0	23.5	36.1
Sectoral efficiency (1979)					
(8) Relative labour productivity		BA	58.8	48.7	39.0
		AA	34.1	49.1	57.3
(9) Relative total factor productivity		BA	55.1	47.0	37.4
		AA	37.5	48.9	48.0
(10) Relative skill intensity		BA	55.1	66.9	38.1
		AA	44.0	32.6	47.1
Adaptive efficiency (1971–79)					
(11) Growth in sales		BA	62.4	51.4	42.9
		AA	37.1	48.5	57.4
(12) Change in trade competitiveness		BA	50.5	50.0	30.9
		AA	45.4	46.0	57.6
(13) Change in labour productivity		BA	89.7	58.1	67.4
		AA	9.8	41.8	32.9
Other ratios					
(14) Intra-industry trade (1979)		BA	23.8	19.0	10.8
		AA	35.1	51.8	48.8
(15) Intra-firm trade (1977)		BA	49.5	20.3	37.3
		AA	26.1	56.4	48.2

Notes: BA and AA = % of manufacturing sales of firms in sectors with a performance ratio below or above the unweighted arithmetic mean.
For definitions of variables see the Appendix.

Table 9.2 sets out some of the structural characteristics of the three groups of firms under consideration. For each characteristic we wished to establish the proportion of the total output of the three groups which was in sectors with below or above the average valûe of the characteristic. For example, while 44.2 per cent of the sales of indigenous firms was in sectors in which the RCA trade competitiveness of the UK was below average, the corresponding proportion for foreign affiliates and the

Industrial Restructuring and Competitiveness 183

foreign activities of UK MNEs were 37.9 per cent and 26.0 per cent respectively. The conclusions of Table 9.2 are self-evident. They suggest, *a priori*, that there are important differences in the structural characteristics of the groups, and hence that there is likely to be a distinctive impact on these characteristics arising from the nationality of ownership of UK-based companies and/or geographical involvement of UK-owned firms.

THE STATISTICAL TESTING

Let us now list some specific propositions about the interaction between MNEs and economic structure.

Allocative Impact

We have suggested this may vary according to the type of MNE activity, the existing technical and allocative efficiency of UK-owned firms and the extent to which extra or imperfect market forces affect resource allocation. But first let us take a neo-classical type proposition.

Proposition 1. Relative to UK-owned firms producing in the UK, foreign-owned MNEs will produce in those UK sectors which are the most internationally competitive, while the production of UK firms abroad will favour those sectors in which the UK is the least internationally competitive.[5]

This proposition is intended to test the extent to which inward and outward direct investment, relative to the UK production of indigenous firms, is concentrated in sectors in which the UK economy is comparatively advantaged.

$$RCA = 1.03 - 0.0305 \; UK_i + 0.0221 \; FMNE_{UK} - 0.116 \; UKMNE_f$$
$$\qquad\quad (1.46) \qquad\quad (1.18) \qquad\qquad\quad (0.77) \qquad (1) \quad (n = 28)$$

$$RCA = 0.951 - 0.0245 \; UK_i + 0.161 \; FMNE_{UK}$$
$$\qquad\quad (1.06) \qquad\quad (1.14) \qquad\qquad\qquad\qquad (1a) \quad (n = 44)$$

The relationship set out in equations (1) and (1a)[6] lends some support to this proposition. In 1979, compared with a negative though insignificant, association between the ability of manufacturing sectors to compete in foreign markets, and the distribution of domestically produced output of UK-owned firms (UK_i), there was a positive, though insignificant association between RCA and the sectoral distribution of foreign affiliates ($FMNE_{UK}$). Indeed, in that year, 63 per cent of the output of such affiliates was in sectors in which the RCA was greater than 1, compared with 44 per cent of UK firms. In other words, relative to

184 *Multinationals, Technology and Competitiveness*

their indigenous competitors, foreign MNEs *are* more inclined to invest in sectors in which UK international competitiveness is above average.

The absence of any significant position relationship between RCA and $FMNE_{UK}$, in either of the two variants of the equation[7] set out, is explained by some major exceptions. In the office machinery and computer sectors, for example, the RCA ratio was 0.92, while the foreign participation ratio was 3.1; by contrast, the corresponding figures for bricks, pottery and glass were 1.21 and 0.33. While in some cases such discrepancies reflect the level of disaggregation,[8] in others, even in narrowly delineated sectors, they occur for more substantive reasons. Two of these deserve special mention. The first is that the RCA ratio is based on sales rather than value-added data and does not distinguish between cases in which imports and exports compete with each other and those in which they complement each other. In resource-based sectors such as non-ferrous metals, timber and food-processing, the latter is the more likely as imported semi-processed goods are necessary ingredients of the final output of a product. While RCA measures based on gross exports overcome this difficulty, they tend to overstate competitiveness in that they take no account of imports of similar products. The second is that in some sectors – noticeably those in which there is international oligopolistic rivalry – the prevalence of inward FDI cannot be separated from that of outward FDI. In such cases, firm-specific ownership characteristics rather than locational forces dominate the cross-hauling of international production which is as likely to be complementary as substitutable between countries.

The first equation also shows that, as far as outward direct investment is concerned, there is no suggestion that this is more concentrated (relative to the domestic activities of UK firms) in sectors in which the UK is comparatively *disadvantaged*. However, omitting oil refining and timber and furniture, the rank correlation coefficient between RCA and the industrial distribution of $UKMNE_f$ is -0.37, and significant at a 10 per cent level. Other research (Dunning and Walker, 1982) has demonstrated that outward direct investment is significantly correlated with *domestic* competitiveness, that is, it tends to be concentrated in those sectors which record above average productivity and profitability. That the relationship between the foreign activities of UK MNEs and lack of international competitiveness is not closer may again reflect the fact that, in some sectors, exports and outward direct investment complement, rather than substitute for, each other. Some MNEs find it profitable to exploit their O advantages to some countries via exports and others via foreign production, while, *ceteris paribus*, products at later stages of the product cycle are more likely to be produced abroad than those at earlier stages of the cycle. This is particularly likely to be so in the case of vertical *inter-* or horizontal *intra*-industry trade. We shall return to this point later.

The second proposition relates to the extent to which MNEs are, in some sense, better allocators of resources between sectors than uni-national firms. Here, much depends on in which sectors the MNEs

Industrial Restructuring and Competitiveness

perceive they have an advantage over their foreign competitors and whether the productivity advantages originate from the possession or use of mobile or immobile resource endowments. If the former, then both outward and inward investment may be concentrated in similar sectors; if the latter, for example, in resource-based sectors, the structure of the two may be different. The proposition set out seeks to test the latter view. We take two measures of allocative efficiency: productivity and profitability.

Proposition 2. Relative to UK-owned firms producing in the UK, foreign-owned MNEs will produce in those UK sectors which are of above average productivity or profitability, while the production of UK firms abroad will favour sectors which are of below average productivity or profitability in the UK.

The only index of productivity which is readily available is the gross value-added per head ratio, though ideally one would like to have used a total productivity index.[9] Equations (2) and (2a) suggest that this proposition is upheld for inward direct investment but not for the foreign activities of UK MNEs. Indeed $UKMNE_f$ is significantly more concentrated in above average productivity sectors than is $FMNE_{UK}$; by contrast, domestic investment by UK firms is significantly concentrated in below average productivity sectors. Both regressions suggest that MNEs prefer to invest in high-productivity sectors; this may also reflect the fact that, in the case of the UK, there is a lot of investment cross-hauling leading to intra-industry production. Finally, it would appear that exports and FDI are most likely to complement each other in above average labour productivity sectors.

$$LP = 8253 - 3195\ UK_i + 1158\ FMNE_{UK} + 3159\ UKMNE_f$$
$$\ (424)^{**}\ \ \ \ \ \ (1.8)\ \ \ \ \ \ \ \ \ \ \ (6.4)^{**}\ \ \ \ \ \ \ \ \ \ \ (2)\ \ \ (n = 29)$$

$$LP' = 8773 - 2946\ UK_i + 4229\ FMNE_{UK}$$
$$\ (3.32)^{**}\ \ \ + (7.78)^{**}\ \ \ \ \ \ \ \ \ \ \ \ \ \ \ \ \ (2a)\ \ \ (n = 44)$$

(Associations which are significant at a 10 per cent level are denoted by an asterisk * and those significant at a 5 per cent level by two asterisks ** in the above and subsequent equations.)

The equations on the relationship between profitability and resource allocation portray a similar picture. Defining π as the profit/gross sales ratio, both $FMNE_{UK}$ and $UKMNE_f$ are seen to be positively, though not significantly, associated with profitability, while UK_i is negatively associated with π.

$$\pi = 18.4 - 0.796\ UK_i + 0.280\ FMNE_{UK} + 0.054\ UKMNE_f$$
$$\ (1.64)\ \ \ \ \ \ (0.68)\ \ \ \ \ \ \ \ \ \ (0.17)\ \ \ \ \ \ \ \ \ (2b)\ \ \ (n = 29)$$

$$\pi' = 16.9 - 0.637 + 0.388$$
$$\ (1.60)\ \ \ (1.59)\ (2c)\ \ \ (n = 44)$$

186   *Multinationals, Technology and Competitiveness*

Allied to the second proposition are two others to do with the direction of MNE activity towards capital- or technology-intensive sectors or those in which product quality, consistency and reliability are important competitive advantages. These latter industries, mainly supplying branded consumer goods (or inputs to same), may be expected to generate above average by advertising to sales expenditure. In this case, one is identifying O-type advantages which apply irrespective of whether they are being exploited by trade or production. One might then expect one and/or other of the advantages to be positively related to both $FMNE_{UK}$ and $UKMNE_f$.

Proposition 3. Relative to UK-owned firms producing in the UK, foreign-owned MNEs will produce in UK sectors which record an above average (1) net capital expenditure per employee (K/L), (2) non-operative/operative wage bill NO/OWB, and/or (3) advertising/sales ratio (A/S); UK firms abroad will also produce in these sectors, although the sub-sectors of their particular strengths will probably differ.

Equations (3) and (3a) show that, unlike UK firms producing in the UK, both foreign affiliates of foreign MNEs and UK MNEs abroad concentrate in capital-intensive sectors, and in both cases significantly so. There is a positive but insignificant association between inward MNE activity and the skill-intensity ratio, (see equations (4) and (4a)), but the reverse relationship applies to UK firms producing both in the UK and abroad. There was a very weak negative association between A/S and inward and outward MNE activity, (see equations (5) and (5a)), but relative to the domestic production of UK firms, such activity is geared more to sectors supplying branded consumer goods in which quality control is perceived to be especially important.

$$K/L = 852 - 242\ UK_i + 121\ FMNE_{UK} + 269\ UKMNE_f$$
$$(3.59)^{**}\quad (2.1)^* \qquad\qquad (6.05) \qquad\qquad (3)\quad (n = 29)$$

$$K/L' = 829 - 207\ UK_i + 383\ FMNE_{UK}$$
$$(2.67)^{**}\quad (8.05)^{**} \qquad\qquad\qquad (3a)\quad (n = 44)$$

$$NO/OWB = 77.3 - 5.09\ UK_i + 1.97\ FMNE_{UK} - 1.24\ UKMNE_f$$
$$(1.64)\qquad (0.74)\qquad\quad (0.6)\qquad (4)\quad (n = 29)$$

$$NO/OWB' = 68.3 - 3.87\ UK_i + 0.97\ FMNE_{UK}$$
$$(1.44)\qquad (0.59) \qquad\qquad (4a)\quad (n = 44)$$

$$A/S = 3.27 - 0.346\ UK_i - 0.003\ FMNE_{UK} - 0.024\ UKMNE_f$$
$$(1.44)\qquad (0.01)\qquad\qquad (0.14)\qquad (5)\quad (n = 29)$$

$$A/S' = 3.03 - 0.339\ UK_i - 0.011\ FMNE_{UK}$$
$$(1.53)\qquad (0.08) \qquad\qquad (5a)\quad (n = 39)$$

Industrial Restructuring and Competitiveness 187

The final proposition in this section concerns the impact of market structure. Here the suggestion is that one of the main advantages of MNEs *qua* MNEs is the ability to exploit the advantages of international division of labour and the economies of synergy of multiple operations; that is, to capture economies internal to the MNE, but external to the individual affiliates of MNEs. If this is so, MNEs are likely to be attracted to sectors which have economies of firm size or those in which the concentration ratio is above average.

Proposition 4. Relative to UK-owned firms producing in the UK, both foreign affiliates in the UK and UK MNEs abroad will concentrate in sectors in which the competition is oligopolistic, as reflected by an above average concentration ratio (C) and/or where size of enterprise confers some productivity advantage (Sp).

Equations (6) and (6a) show that the first part of this proposition is generally supported, but that the association between $FMNE_{UK}$ and $UKMNE_f$ and C is statistically insignificant. Equations (7) and (7a) reveal that while UK firms at home and abroad tend to concentrate in sectors in which the largest firms record above average labour productivity, this is not so with $FMNE_{UK}$; indeed, if anything, the reverse seems to be the case. Excluding the oil-refining sector, the positive association between Sp and $UKMNE_f$ becomes significant at a 1 per cent level, but the association between Sp and UK_i becomes negative, at near 5 per cent level.

$$C = 56.4 - 1.93\ UK_i + 0.15\ FMNE_{UK} + 1.00\ UKMNE_f$$
$$(1.14) \qquad (0.1) \qquad\qquad (0.9) \qquad\qquad\qquad (6) \quad (n = 29)$$

$$C' = 50.0 - 1.14\ UK_i + 1.52\ FMNE_{UK}$$
$$(0.78) \qquad (1.69) \qquad\qquad\qquad\qquad (6a) \quad (n = 44)$$

$$Sp + 1.13 + 0.0130\ UK_i - 0.0362\ FMNE_{UK} + 0.0246$$
$$(0.38) \qquad\quad (1.23) \qquad\qquad (1.09) \qquad\quad (7) \quad (n = 29)$$

$$Sp' = 1.15 + 0.081\ UK_i - 0.0095\ FMNE_{UK}$$
$$(0.30) \qquad (0.57) \qquad\qquad\qquad (7a) \quad (n = 44)$$

The conclusion of the above statistical exercises is that the interaction between a number of indices of UK economic structure and the distribution of UK manufacturing activity by the affiliates of foreign MNEs and that of UK MNEs abroad is generally different from that of UK-owned firms in the UK, and that the direction of the difference is such as to suggest that the UK's involvement in international production has made a positive contribution to domestic allocative efficiency.

Technical Impact

We now turn to examine some propositions concerning the extent to which activities of MNEs are related to the technical or sectoral efficiency of UK production. The literature strongly suggests that, locational considerations apart, MNEs will invest in those sectors in which they perceive they have the most technological and other advantages over their indigenous competitors. It may therefore be reasonable to hypothesize that these advantages may result in higher productivity ratios – particularly labour productivity ratios – as many of the advantages are capital- or technology-intensive and labour-saving.

Proposition 5. Relative to that of UK firms in the UK, production by foreign MNEs in the UK is likely to be concentrated in industries in which the productivity of the foreign affiliate is highest relative to the domestic firms, while the foreign production of UK firms is likely to be concentrated in sectors where domestic firms have a productivity advantage over their foreign competitors.

Acknowledging the usual caveats of any measure of the performance of firms – and particularly that between MNEs, or parts of MNEs, and the total activities of uninational firms – we consider two such indices. The first is the relative net output per man year in the UK (RLP) of foreign affiliates;[10] and the second an index of relative total factor productivity of foreign affiliates (RTP).[11] Equations (8) and (9) show that there is some evidence to support proposition 5, but that the association is more pronounced using the RLP than the RTP measure.[12]

$$RLP = 1.30 - 0.0396 \ UK_i + 0.0081 \ FMNE_{UK} + 0.0476 \ UKMNE_f$$
$$(1.65) \qquad (0.39) \qquad (2.99)^{**} \quad (8) \quad (n = 27)$$

$$RLP' = 1.34 - 0.491 + 0.0571$$
$$(1.55) \quad (2.93)^{**} \qquad (8a) \quad (n = 41)$$

$$RTP = 1.07 + 0.0019 \ UK_i - 0.0071 \ FMNE_{UK} + 0.0235 \ UKMNE_f$$
$$(0.11) \qquad (0.45) \qquad (1.85) \qquad (9) \quad (n = 27)$$

$$RTP' = 1.09 - 0.0001 \ UK_i + 0.0139 \ FMNE_{UK}$$
$$(0.00) \qquad (1.27) \qquad (9a) \quad (n = 42)$$

The detailed statistics reveal that in 34 out of 41 sectors, foreign affiliates record a higher labour productivity than UK-owned firms, and in 30 out of 41 sectors a higher total productivity. Moreover, equation (8a) clearly shows that, relative to UK_i, $FMNE_{UK}$ favour sectors in which their O advantages are the most pronounced.[13] However, of greater interest, and contrary to expectations, is the highly significant *positive* association between outward direct investment and RLP. One possible explanation suggested by earlier equations is that there is some complementarity

Industrial Restructuring and Competitiveness 189

between different forms of foreign involvement, and that *firm-* rather than *country*-specific *O* advantages explain the presence of MNEs in certain sectors. It would also seem that UK firms are relatively more profitable overseas in industries in which the UK is most internationally competitive.[14] For example, in 1979, 62 per cent of the foreign sales of UK companies was in sectors in which the normalized RCA ratio was above average for manufacturing industry. Data on other structural variables for each of the three categories are not available to make other comparisons of technical efficiency. However, earlier published information on the comparative export propensity between all UK firms and US subsidiaries in 1973/74 (Dunning, 1976) suggests that, while in 22 of the 36 manufacturing sectors for which data are available, the export/sales of US subsidiaries exceeds that of all UK firms, there is significant correlation between the normalized share of the sales of US subsidiaries and differences in export propensity.

Adjustment Impact

There are various ways in which the efficiency at which resources are reallocated might be evaluated. We deal first with changes in market growth.

Adaptation to Market Needs
To what extent do foreign MNEs invest in growth sectors or in those in which the UK is becoming more internationally competitive? How do the affiliates of UK MNEs adjust to market changes relative to UK firms in the UK? The hypothesis to be tested is that the *O* advantages of MNEs enable them to be better choosers of growth sectors or to create growth, and/or allow them to redirect their attention to those sectors which are becoming more productive and/or internationally competitive.

Proposition 6. Relative to UK firms, foreign MNEs are more concentrated in growth sectors, while they adjust to changes in market demand better than UK firms. Depending on their position in the product cycle and the relative significance of O and L advantages, UK firms overseas will invest in sectors in which the UK's international competitive position is deteriorating.

We present four pairs of equations. The first pair – (10) and (11) – relate the sectoral shares of gross sales of the three groups of firms in 1979 to two measures of market growth, that is, growth of UK *output* (GUK) and growth of UK *demand* plus exports (GUKX); the second pair – (12) and (13) – the share of the *change* (Δ) in production between 1971 and 1979 of UK-based firms divided by the share of the production in 1971 of these sectors (UK_i and $FMNE_{UK}$)[15] to these same measures.

$$GUK = 319 - 12.1\ UK_i + 913\ FMNE_{UK} + 7.53\ UKMNE_f$$
$$(1.6) \qquad (1.41) \qquad (1.5) \qquad\qquad (10)\quad (n = 29)$$

$$GUK' = 327 - 12.0 \ UK_i + 16.0 \ FMNE_{UK}$$
$$(2.02)^* \quad (4.4)^{**} \qquad\qquad (10a) \quad (n = 44)$$

$$GUKX = 349 - 11.7 \ UK_i + 7.90 \ FMNE_{UK} + 8.13 \ UKMNE_f$$
$$(1.80) \qquad (1.28) \qquad\qquad (1.64) \qquad (11) \quad (n = 27)$$

$$GUKX' = 354 - 13.3 \ UK_i + 16.1 \ FMNE_{UK}$$
$$(2.62)^* \quad (5.33)^{**} \qquad\qquad (11a) \quad (n = 42)$$

$$GUK = 95 + 112 \ \Delta \ UK_i + 107 \ \Delta \ FMNE_{UK} + 23.7 \ \Delta \ UKMNE_f$$
$$(349)^{**} \qquad (0.87) \qquad\qquad (0.72) \qquad (12) \quad (n = 17)$$

$$GUK' = 109 + 23.8 \ \Delta \ UK_i + 195 \ \Delta \ FMNE_{UK}$$
$$(1.79) \qquad (4.28) \qquad\qquad (12a) \quad (n = 37)$$

$$GUKX = 233 + 89.5 \ \Delta \ UK_i + 26 \ \Delta \ FMNE_{UK} + 27.1 \ \Delta \ UKMNE_f$$
$$(2.32)^* \qquad (0.17) \qquad\qquad (0.70) \quad (13) \quad (n = 17)$$

$$GUKX' = 219 + 16.1 \ \Delta \ UK_i + 122 \ \Delta \ FMNE_{UK}$$
$$(1.18) \qquad (2.59)^* \qquad\qquad (13a) \quad (n = 36)$$

The equations suggest that foreign firms in the UK and UK firms abroad are distinctly more inclined to invest in growth sectors than UK firms in the UK, and that is is particularly noticeable when growth includes exports from the UK (GUKX). In equations (10a) and (11a) the $FMNE_{UK}$ coefficient seems to be positively significant at the 1 per cent level, but foreign production by UK MNEs is positively, but not significantly, related to growth. However, the bivariate correlation coefficients between the $FMNE_{UK}$ and $UKMNE_{UK}$ and the growth of the UK market plus exports work out at $+0.567$ and $+0.653$, and both are significant at a 1 per cent level. While 67 per cent of UK production by foreign affiliates in 1979 was in sectors which recorded above average rates of growth between 1971 and 1979, the corresponding proportion for indigenous firms was 32 per cent.

Between 1971 and 1979, foreign affiliates in the UK increased the value of their output at more than twice the rate of indigenous firms in the UK.[16] Moreover, as equations (12) and (13) show, there was also a tendency for foreign affiliates (relative to the UK competitors) to increase their market share in sectors which were growing fastest; indeed, the correlation coefficient between GUK' and $FMNE_{UK}$ in equation (12a) was $+0.631$ and significant at a 1 per cent level.

Over a slightly shorter period (1972/3–1979) the output of UK firms abroad grew relative to that of the domestic production by UK firms in 14 of 17 sectors. There was some tendency for domestic and foreign growth by UK MNEs to be complementary to each other and rank correlation between the two variables was $+0.29$, but excluding drink and tobacco $+0.45$.

Industrial Restructuring and Competitiveness 191

Adaptation to Structural Change
The next set of propositions examines the extent to which MNEs and other firms adapt their output to changes in economic structure. We shall take indices of such change for the period 1971-9:

(1) changes in RCA;
(2) changes in labour productivity;
(3) changes in non-operative/operative wage bill;
(4) changes in the labour productivity gap between foreign affiliates and indigenous firms;

and follow the methodology adopted in testing Proposition 7.

Proposition 7. Relative to UK firms producing in the UK, foreign affiliates of MNEs will produce in sectors in which (1) the RCA ratio has most improved, (2) productivity has most increased, (3) the human capital content has most increased, and (4) the productivity gap between affiliates and indigenous firms has (relatively) increased.

In the case of the foreign production of UK MNEs one might predict a positive relationship between its sectoral distribution and (2) and (3) and a negative relationship between that distribution and (1) and (4).
  And a dynamic version of Proposition 7:

Proposition 8. Relative to UK firms producing in the UK, foreign affiliates of MNEs may be expected to increase their share of production in sectors in which (1) the RCA ratio has most improved, (2) productivity has most increased, (3) the human capital content has most increased, and (4) the productivity gap between affiliates and indigenous firms has (relatively) increased.

The predictions for the activities of UK MNEs abroad follow those set out in Proposition 8.
  The set of equations (14)–(16) and (17)–(21)[17] set out below suggest a mixed interaction between MNE involvement and structural change.

$$\Delta RCA = -0119 + 0.060 \ UK_i - 0.438 \ FMNE_{UK} + 0.0398 \ UKMNE_f$$
$$ (0.37) \qquad (3.02)^{**} \qquad\qquad (3.41)^{**}$$
$$ (14) \quad (n = 28)$$

$$\Delta LP = 3.76 - 0.273 \ UK_i + 0.150 \ FMNE_{UK} + 0.183 \ UKMNE_f$$
$$ (3.04)^{**} \quad (1.96)^* \qquad\quad (3.1)^{**} \qquad (15) \quad (n = 29)$$

$$\Delta LP' = 3.88 - 0.282 \ UK_i + 0.330 \ FMNE_{UK}$$
$$ (3,37)^{**} \quad (6.45)^{**} \qquad\qquad (15a) \quad (n = 44)$$

$$\Delta NO/OWB = 1.11 - 0.006 \ UK_i + 0.012 \ FMNE_{UK} - 0.013 \ UKMNE_f$$
$$ (0.58) \qquad (1.3) \qquad\qquad (1.84)$$
$$ (16) \quad (n = 29)$$

$$\Delta RLP = 1.13 - 0.0300 \ UK_k + 0.0759 \ FMNE_{UK} - 0.0505 \ UKMNE_f$$
$$(0.86) \qquad (2.39)^* \qquad (2.0)^*$$
$$\qquad\qquad\qquad\qquad\qquad\qquad (17) \quad (n = 26)$$

$$\Delta RCA = -0.396 + 0.186 \ \Delta UK_i + 0.117 \ \Delta FMNE_{UK}$$
$$(2.85) \qquad (0.64)$$
$$- 0.004 \ \Delta UKMNE_f$$
$$(0.08) \qquad\qquad\qquad\qquad (18) \quad (n = 13)$$

$$\Delta RCA' = -0.553 + 0.0439 \ \Delta UK_i + 0.363 \ \Delta FMNE_{UK}$$
$$(1.25) \quad (3.0)^{**} \qquad\qquad (18a) \quad (n = 36)$$

$$\Delta LP = 2.41 + 2.73 \ \Delta UK_i - 1.49 \ \Delta FMNE_{UK} + 0.297 \ \Delta UKMNE_f$$
$$(3.6)^{**} \qquad (0.51) \qquad\qquad (0.38)$$
$$\qquad\qquad\qquad\qquad\qquad\qquad (19) \quad (n = 13)$$

$$\Delta NO/OWB = 1.24 - 0.048 \ \Delta UK_i - 0.26 \ \Delta FMNE_{UK}$$
$$(0.86) \qquad\quad (0.12)$$
$$+ 0.071 \ \Delta UKMNE_f$$
$$(1.23) \qquad\qquad\qquad\qquad (20) \quad (n = 13)$$

$$\Delta RLP = 1.21 + 0.068 \ \Delta UK_i - 0.291 \ \Delta FMNE_{UK} + 0.12 \ \Delta UKMNE_f$$
$$(0.66) \qquad (0.74) \qquad\qquad (0.12) \quad (21) \quad (n = 13)$$

$$\Delta RLP' = 1.61 + 0.123 \ \Delta UK_i - 0.700 \ \Delta FMNE_{UK}$$
$$(1.98)^* \qquad (3.27)^{**} \qquad\qquad (21a) \quad (n = 37)$$

For example, UK MNEs appear to be increasing their foreign activities in areas where the UK's RCA is increasing, while the reverse is the case for foreign affiliates in the UK (see equation (14)). On the other hand, both UK firms and foreign affiliates in the UK seem to be redirecting their output to sectors in which RCA is improving (see equations (18) and (18a)). Whereas UK MNEs tend to favour sectors in which labour productivity has risen the most, the opposite is the case for UK firms in the UK (see equations (15) and (15a)). However, this latter group of firms appears to be redirecting its output towards sectors with rising productivity (see equation (19)). No relations of any significance emerge between changes in the skill-intensity ratio and the distribution of output of MNEs vis à vis UK firms in the UK. Changes in the productivity gap (favouring $FMNE_{UK}$) seem to be positively and significantly associated with the distribution of output of foreign affiliates, but negatively associated with that of UK firms abroad (see equation (17)). On the other hand, UK firms producing in the UK have adjusted their output towards industries in which RLP is rising, while the opposite has occured in the case of foreign affiliates in the UK (see equations (21) and (21a)).[18]

Industrial Restructuring and Competitiveness 193

MNEs and the Organization of Transactions

There is one other structural aspect of MNEs which requires consideration. This concerns the role of MNEs as co-ordinators of separate economic activities across national boundaries, and the effect this has on domestic, that is UK, economic structure. While it is an inherent feature of MNEs that they internalize international intermediate product markets, they may also impinge on such markets *within* a country and on final goods traded between countries. This market-replacing effect is inadequately captured in the statistics but may have far-reaching implications both on the type of economic activity carried out and on its determinants. Received theory would suggest that relative to non-MNEs, MNEs will tend to concentrate in sectors in which there are the most opportunities for minimizing transaction costs. Data on such market-replacing activities are extremely limited. However, it might be reasonably argued that the greater the degree of product or process diversification within MNEs, and the more they practise product or process specialization between countries, the more likely the structural impact of MNEs will be of concern to those countries that do not wish to identify themselves with the resulting international division of labour. We illustrate from just two aspects of internalization: (1) vertical integration in the UK, and (2) international product or process specialization between different parts of the same MNE in different countries.

Proposition 9. To minimize transaction costs or capitalize on market failure, UK affiliates of foreign MNEs and/or UK MNEs abroad, relative to UK firms producing in the UK, will tend to concentrate in sectors which are vertically integrated (VAR), or are increasing their integration (ΔVAR), and/or, within an international context, offer opportunities for intra-industry (IIT) and/or intra-firm trade (IFT).

$$\text{VAR} = 37.8 - 0.203 \text{ UK}_i - 0.391 \text{ FMNE}_{\text{UK}}$$
$$\phantom{\text{VAR} = 37.8 -} (0.29) \phantom{\text{ UK}_i -} (0.9) (22) \quad (n = 44)$$

$$\Delta\text{VAR} = 1.95 - 0.542 \text{ UK}_i + 0.403 \text{ FMNE}_{\text{UK}}$$
$$\phantom{\Delta\text{VAR} = 1.95 -} (5.03)^{**} \phantom{\text{ UK}_i} (6.1) (23) \quad (n = 44)$$

$$\text{ITT} = 0.838 = 0.0279 \text{ UK}_i + 0.0126 \text{ FMNE}_{\text{UK}} - 0.0016 \text{ UKMNE}_f$$
$$\phantom{\text{ITT} = 0.838 =} (1.4) \phantom{\text{ UK}_i +} (0.96) \phantom{\text{ FMNE}_{\text{UK}}} (0.15) \quad (24) \quad (n = 22)$$

$$\text{IFT} = 39.2 - 2.51 \text{ UK}_i + 5.20 \text{ FMNE}_{\text{UK}} - 2.74 \text{ UKMNE}_f$$
$$\phantom{\text{IFT} = 39.2 -} (3.45)^{**} \phantom{\text{ UK}_i +} (2.34)^{**} \phantom{\text{ FMNE}} (25) \quad (n = 22)$$

These propositions are tested in equations (22) to (25).[19] We consider the results of each form of internalization separately.

Vertical Integration

There is no evidence that the affiliates of foreign-based MNEs are more vertically integrated in their UK activities than are indigenous firms (see equation (22)). In 1979, foreign affiliates in the UK recorded a higher net/gross output ratio than their UK competitiors in 17 out of 40 sectors and a lower ratio in 22 sectors. Neither is there any suggestion that the foreign participation ratio is highest in sectors with the highest value-added ratios. However, within industries, broadly interpreted, it would appear that foreign affiliates do concentrate in sectors with above average ratios (the main exception is oil). The degree of vertical integration in both foreign and domestic firms has changed little in the 1970s, but equation (23) suggests quite strongly that, in sectors in which foreign affiliates are most markedly represented, vertical integration has *fallen* either absolutely or relatively to indigenous firms. One reason for this may be that there is increasing specialization within sectors of products supplied by MNEs across national boundaries. The intra-industry trade equation (22) suggests there is a positive but insignificant association between ITT and the foreign participation ratio; excluding the $UKMNE_f$ variable increases the observations to 37, and the significance of the $FMNE_{UK}$ variable to 1.68. On the other hand, equation (25) shows there is a significant positive association between the propensity of foreign affiliates to engage in intra-firm trade and the sectoral distribution of their output. The association goes in the opposite direction for UK MNEs, but all the data suggest that UK-related MNE activity is likely to have had as much, if not a greater, effect on market-replacing activities between the UK and the rest of the world, than within the UK.

International Product Specialization
Regrettably, intra-industry data are rarely presented in sufficient detail to allow us to separate *vertical* from *horizontal* transactions. But again casual empiricism suggests that both UK and foreign-based MNEs are increasingly viewing Europe as a single market, and engaging in intra-plant product specialization. *Inter alia*, this is confirmed by the propensity of MNEs to concentrate in sectors in which the trade intensity of the UK is increasing. Between 1971 and 1979, the value of imports plus exports to total manufactured goods produced in the UK of all firms rose from 36 per cent to 50 per cent. However, in sectors in which foreign-based MNEs had a participation ratio of 1 or more, the average rise was from 44 per cent to 74 per cent. A rank correlation between the $FMNE_{UK}$ ratio in 1979 and change in trade intensity between 1971 and 1979 was + 0.424. Data on changes in intra-industry trade ratios and the distribution of MNE activity tell the same story. Both foreign affiliates and UK MNEs abroad are strongly concentrated in sectors in which the intra-industry trade ratio rose the sharpest between 1971 and 1979; this is not the case with domestic production of UK firms. That these latter sectors happen to be those in which MNEs are more likely to adopt a global strategy, and maintain a 100 per cent equity interest, suggests growing internalization of economic activity across national boundaries vis à vis that within national boundaries. This is an important conclusion which has far reaching policy implications; these are taken up in the final section of this chapter.

Industrial Restructuring and Competitiveness 195

Product Diversification
Data on industrial diversification are extremely limited but what there are[20] do not support the proposition that MNEs, either absolutely or relative to non-MNEs, tend to concentrate in sectors which are themselves diversified; indeed, compared with an average diversification index[21] for the leading MNEs in 1981 of 24.3, petroleum, automobiles, and office equipment – three of the most international of sectors – recorded ratios of 12.6, 16.9, and 20.5 respectively. And while it might be expected that enterprises, in a particular industry, which are the most multinational will be more diversified than non-MNEs, partly because they are larger and partly because they operate in different economic environments, in any one country, the range of output of their affiliates may well be less than that of indigenous firms. But the very fact that an affiliate is linked with an enterprise which is more diversified than its indigenous competitors may give it a competitive edge. Certainly there are several examples leading the diversification of many sectors, such as drink, tobacco, and chemicals in the last five years; unfortunately as far as the UK is concerned, there are no recent data on diversification trends to enable us to go beyond this casual empiricism.[22]

POLICY IMPLICATIONS

The previous sections have demonstrated that, in a variety of ways, MNEs have had an impact on UK economic structure different from that of UK indigenous firms producing in the UK (including the UK output of UK MNEs). This is a reflection both of the differences in the configuration of the *OLI* advantages facing MNEs and the way in which they have translated these into conduct and performance. Despite the imperfections of data, there are strong suggestions that the *O* advantages of MNEs have assisted the UK's economic restructuring in the 1970s towards higher allocative and technical efficiency; and that MNEs have adjusted to changing *L* advantages of UK resource endowments rather more positively than uninational indigenous firms. However, one cost of the greater internationalization of the UK economy may have been the loss of some structural autonomy on the part of the UK, as MNEs may encourage more corporate internalization between different parts of their operations and less sectoral or cross-sectoral integration within the UK. This may have the effect of reshaping both market and economic structure and, in so far as the common ownership of separate production affiliates matters, is relevant to the pattern of resource allocation. There is insufficient evidence to suggest whether or not this kind of impact on structure has worked to the long-term advantage of the UK economy; much depends on the international market structure in which MNEs compete and the signals given to them by various governments. There can, however, be little doubt that, by promoting structural interdependence between national markets, MNEs have made the

196   *Multinationals, Technology and Competitiveness*

UK economy more vulnerable to changes in international demand and supply conditions.

What should UK government policy be towards MNE activity? What modifications of existing policies are needed? Clearly, much depends on how far it is considered that foreign ownership and/or control of domestic resource allocation matters, and on one's judgement of the possible risk of being dependent on external economic and political forces. In practice, too, much will rest on the domestic macroeconomic policies pursued and particularly those relevant to structural change. What also seems to be increasingly likely is that, at least as far as investment within the OECD is concerned, internationalization of some industries by some form of cross-border alliances will continue. The important question is to ensure that, where it is thought appropriate, one's own firms can survive and compete with foreign firms. This inevitably requires governments to re-examine their role in producing the right economic environment and their means of achieving that goal. For it is a fact that as MNEs have become more footloose in their choice of markets to exploit and/or sites from which to produce, the influence of government-related locational variables has become more important. These range from import controls to encourage import-substituting investment, to providing the right educational, technological, and telecommunications infrastructure, and to aiding firms in newer sectors in the restructuring process.

The fact that the kind of impact we have attributed to MNEs has been associated with their increasing involvement in the UK economy suggests that the market may itself be the main adjustment mechanism. Why then should any government intervention be required, other than to ensure the market works properly? The answer lies in the divergence between private and social economic welfare and the very specific impact which MNEs have on this divergence. It is well accepted that in conditions where governments seek only economic goals, and in the absence of externalities or structural market imperfections, a *laissez faire* policy might be appropriate. In a modern industrialized economy, however, particularly one subject to rapid technological change and faced with all kinds of institutional rigidities and structural disequilibria, this is an extremely unlikely situation, as indeed is the belief that the only role of governments is a negative one. Indeed, in the long run, this could be worsened by foreign firms, which might be equipped to overcome the market failure, gaining a monopoly position and creating an even more unacceptable market position. Governments have the responsibility for positive interventionism whenever there are costs and benefits which it is not reasonable to expect individual firms to bear. In the past this included the provision of roads and public utilities. Today the modern equivalents include air transport and international data transmitting facilities.

To what extent is the growing internationalization of the UK economy arising from MNE activity in the long-term interests of the UK? The data set out in this chapter present a mixed picture. On the one hand they suggest that MNEs have aided the restructuring of UK industry in a way consistent with both its revealed comparative advantage and its

Industrial Restructuring and Competitiveness 197

domestic efficiency; on the other, MNEs appear to inject an additional element of economic vulnerability, in the sense that they increase the interdependence of the UK with the rest of the world. In particular, let us examine the proposition that such internationalization may reduce the freedom of action on the part of the UK to restructure the economy as it thinks fit. The argument takes as its starting point the tendency of MNEs, particularly in advanced economies, to encourage more corporate internalization between different parts of their operations in different countries, but to reduce sectoral integration within these countries. This may have a variety of·consequences, arising out of the conflict of interests between the global objectives of international hierarchies and the more domestically oriented goals of the UK government.

This is clearly demonstrated in the area of technology creation and dissemination, where not only may the innovatory activities on the part of MNEs be centralized in the home country, but the control which they exercise over the purchasing requirements of their affiliates throughout the world may have far reaching effects on the technological capabilities of suppliers in different countries. Thus, for example, while the presence of Japanese firms in the UK has undoubtedly raised the productivity of the assembly of colour television sets, any monopolization by them of this gain would be more than outweighed if (1) their greater efficiency forced UK competitors out of the industry, (2) they chose to import most of their high value electronic components from Japan and (3) the Japanese market was closed to UK component suppliers. In the latter case, there could be considerable spin-off effects on the UK economy as the fall in the demand for electronic components might weaken the ability of the industry to supply other purchasers with this product. Here the UK government has a positive role to play, in keeping a watching brief on the strategy of inward investors, in ensuring (where it considers appropriate) effective domestic competition, and in trying to persuade the Japanese government to open its markets to British products.

A further concern is the effect which MNE activity may have on the de-industrialization of the UK economy. This arises from the fact that the increasing international mobility of capital management and technology is resulting in *absolute* locational advantage replacing *comparative* locational advantage as a paradigm influencing the location of economic activity. Where this new disposition is decided by private capital in promotion of its own goals, it does not follow that the resulting distribution of output will be consistent with that which the countries in which MNEs operate are seeking. This new international division of labour is certainly accelerating the relocation of some industrial sectors from older to newer industrialized countries, although the current generation of computer-related technological advances is causing the return of some of these activities, so as to be closer to upstream or downstream production.

Within the industrialized world, while there is no *a priori* reason to suppose that the UK should be more adversely affected than any other country the fact remains that within Europe, at least, the deployment of

198   *Multinationals, Technology and Competitiveness*

MNE-related activity in the UK has expanded *least* in recent years. This is mainly due to the poor rates of return on corporate capital in the UK, itself partly attributed to the strength of organized labour. Multinationals have the flexibility to counteract such frictions by transferring output or increases in output across national boundaries; and, as Chapter 11 shows, over the past two decades, UK investment, especially in labour-intensive sectors, has increasingly preferred a Contintental European to a UK location.

There seems little doubt that the growth of corporate integration in Europe and the UK's accession to the EEC have reduced the freedom of the UK government to control the activities of both UK MNEs and foreign affiliates in the UK. While affiliates may be regarded as hostages, in the last resort, they have the power to withdraw their investment, or switch new investment away from the UK. This reduces the power of the government to introduce policies specifically adverse to MNEs; on the other hand, by more general policies it can affect the structure of outward and inward investment to make it better serve its long-term goals.

For many years now, successive UK governments have adopted a broadly non-discriminatory and liberal policy towards inflows and out-flows of direct investment. The main exception is the *ad hoc* negotiating stance on large new inward investments, particularly with respect to local sourcing requirements, as illustrated in the Nissan case. But there is little evidence that UK governments have consciously taken the growth of international corporate integration into account in the framing of their industrial trade or technological strategies. The implication of a no-action or *laissez faire* approach is that the allocation of economic activity, both within the UK and between the UK and the rest of the world, by UK and foreign MNEs, is consistent with the objectives of national aspirations.

In spite of the beneficial effects of MNE activity set out in this chapter, we question whether this is the case. We believe there are signs of MNEs linking the UK economy with the economies of other industrialized countries in ways which require some changes in (or changes in emphasis of) UK policy. We are not fully persuaded, for example, that, in the absence of positive action on the part of the UK authorities, MNEs will site their activities in the UK in a way consistent with the UK's long-term interests. To encourage this it is not only necessary for the private sector to offer the right kind of economic climate but that the technological, social and educational infrastructure should be at least as attractive as that offered by other countries. This is not primarily a question of special tax or other inducements to foreign investors. Numerous surveys have shown that investors, domestic and foreign alike, regard other supply side factors as much more important in influencing locational choice. These include availability of the right kinds of manpower at competitive wages; supportive (including university) research facilities; a well-motivated and co-operative labour force; first-rate telecommunication and transport provisions; a good network of suppliers; a consistent, well

Industrial Restructuring and Competitiveness 199

articulated and publicized industrial strategy; and a sympathetic climate for growth and innovation. In addition, UK MNEs, in their attempt to be competitive in world markets, look for government encouragement and strength in negotiating with foreign governments over unfair or ill-considered trading practices. These points are further taken up in Chapter 11.

However self-evident the above points may seem, it is clear that, in the view of both foreign and UK MNEs, the UK is not offering the locational attractions that it might. Let us take the wave of Japanese investment in the UK as an example. Most recent investment by Japanese firms has been to supply the European market with products previously exported from Japan. The UK has been preferred as a location to other countries of Europe, not primarily because of fiscal or other incentives but because of the quality and costs of labour, excellence of infrastructure and for cultural and language reasons. Similarly, firms which – particularly in the high technology sectors – have chosen Germany or the Low Countries have done so because of the perceived higher quality and better motivated labour (particularly electronic engineers), the excellence of the telecommunication facilities and the economic and industrial strategy of the governments. Much of what has been written applies to UK outward investment as well. The recent fortunes of the UK motor industry have been such that not only do foreign MNEs prefer the Continental to a UK location but UK component supplies have followed in their wake – at the expense of employment in the Midlands. Government support to British Leyland has helped, but an economic environment stimulating the application of modern computer controlled manufacturing and design techniques in the UK would do much more.

On the other hand, governments need to be aware of some of the challenges of inward investment. Japanese MNEs are participating in Europe as part of a long-term world wide strategy. Their aim is to dominate such sectors as electronics and motor vehicle manufacturing. However much the UK may gain in the short term through more employment in Japanese subsidiaries, if they act as a Trojan horse, not only by driving out competition but also through their design policies, and their insistence that purchases should be made from Japanese component suppliers (or their affiliates in the UK), a lot of high value-added activity will be lost to the UK. This is possibly the most serious structural challenge, which is being exacerbated by the problems faced by UK firms penetrating the Japanese market (either by export or local production). Again, the UK government has a catalytic and positive role to play, both by assisting its own firms to combat the competition and through its negotiating tactics with the Japanese.

CONCLUSIONS

Space precludes our giving further examples. The main message of this chapter is a simple yet important one. The growing internationalization

200 *Multinationals, Technology and Competitiveness*

of business, and the interpenetration of technologically advanced industries among industrialized countries, is making new demands on individual governments – and particularly those in integrated markets such as the EEC. Because of the footloose nature of MNE activity, and the increasing role played by mobile factors of production in the production process, the location of industrial activity is increasingly obeying the dictates of absolute, rather than comparative, advantage. At the same time, the role of governments is crucial in influencing the attractions of a particular location by the provision of infrastructure and appropriate macroeconomic policies. In the nineteenth century such intervention mainly took the form of the provision of public utilities, the foundation for the prosperity of industry which was largely locked into its existing location. In the late twentieth century their equivalents are airports, motorways, telecommunications, technical colleges and universities and an efficient economic system, which have to be at least as attractive as those offered by other governments to retain and attract an increasingly mobile population of firms.

Naturally, not all societies can attract all kinds of investment, which is why most countries, particularly smaller ones, need a selective technological, industrial and trade policy. Japan is the classic example of a case in which government and industry can work together to promote a positive and yet well-articulated policy towards both inward and outward MNE activity. The UK policy-makers could well learn from this experience, if they wish to use MNEs as servants rather than masters in their bid for efficient and harmonious restructuring.

NOTES

1 See e.g. Dunning (1958); Reddaway, Potter and Taylor (1968); Steuer *et al.* (1973).
2 It is interesting to observe, for example, that joint ventures and non-equity agreements between UK and overseas firms were considerably more competent relative to 100 per cent owned equity investments than between US and overseas firms.
3 This latter concern was most forcibly articulated by Jean-Jacques Servan Schreiber, and led to deliberate and sustained efforts by the EEC in the 1970s to build up a strong European counter-presence to US firms in high technology sectors.
4 We would be the first to accept that changes in the distribution of activity *between* manufacturing and the service sector in the UK have been at least as significant as those *within* manufacturing industry. Unfortunately, data on MNE activity in the service sector are extremely limited.
5 Competitiveness is measured by revealed comparative advantage (RCA). RCA is defined as $1 + (Xi - Mi)/(Xi + Mi) \div 1 + (Xt - Mt)/(Xt + Mt)$ where X = exports, M = imports, i a particular sector, t = all sectors.
6 In this, and in later relationships, we test the association of inward MNE activity together with outward MNE activity and separately from it. This is because we have forty-four observations for the former and only twenty-nine for the latter.

Industrial Restructuring and Competitiveness 201

7 Defined as the proportion of the total sales of foreign affiliates accounted for by a particular sector divided by the corresponding share of all UK enterprises of that sector.

8 As the extent of foreign participation may not be evenly distributed *within* the sectors.

9 Similar to the one used in testing Proposition 7. See also the Appendix to this chapter, below.

10 RLP = net output per head of foreign affiliates divided by net output per head of indigenous firms.

11 See the Appendix for definition.

12 This suggests that the relatively higher labour productivity of $FMNE_{UK}$ is at least partially offset by a lower capital productivity.

13 One major exception being other clothing where RTP of foreign affiliates in the UK was 188 while their participation ratio was 0.10.

14 For example, in terms of price cost margins, the rank correlation between the industrial distribution of the outward capital stake (1) and (2) net output per head and (3) profitability of the outward capital stake in 1971, 1974 and 1978 varied from $+60$ to $+0.94$ and in every case it was significant at a 5 per cent level (Dunning and Walker, 1982).

15 For example, taking a sector j

$$UK_{ij} = \frac{UK_{ij}\ 1979 - UK_{ij}\ 1971}{UK_{it}\ 1979 - UK_{it}\ 1979} \div \frac{UK_{ij}\ 1971}{UK_{it}1971} \ .$$

16 The growth of output of foreign affiliates was 446.5 per cent compared to that of indigenous firms (in the UK) of 195.0 per cent. Between 1972/3 and 1979, the output of UK firms abroad rose by an estimated 275.1 per cent.

17 We have set out the two (independent) variable equations only when the statistical significance of one or more of the variables is improved.

18 This is further evidence of narrowing of the spillover effect of inward investment in the UK and the productivity gap between foreign affiliates and UK firms.

19 A dynamic version of proposition 9 was also tested. This supported the findings of proposition 9 but revealed no new relationships.

20 As reviewed in Stopford and Dunning (1983); Dunning and Pearce (1985).

21 The percentage of sales in other than the industry to which firms are classified.

22 For a more thorough examination of the interaction between the geographical and industrial diversification of MNEs see Pearce (1983).

APPENDIX: SOURCES OF DATA

The Independent Variables

Data on the sectoral distribution of output (gross sales) of indigenous firms in the UK (UK_i) were obtained from the *Censuses of Production 1971 and 1979*. The gross sales of indigenous firms are equal to gross sales of UK enterprises less those of the subsidiaries of foreign-owned firms. Data on the sales of foreign affiliates ($FMNE_{UK}$) were obtained from the same censuses, supplemented by additional data

202 *Multinationals, Technology and Competitiveness*

provided by the Business Statistics Office. Data on UK firms abroad (UKMNE_f) for 1979 were calculated by the author directly from the accounts of 188 of the largest UK MNEs accounting for between 90 per cent and 95 per cent of all UK-foreign direct investment. The data were then checked for consistency with those on UK assets owned abroad published triennially by the Department of Trade (in *Business Monitor* M4). Data for UK MNEs for 1972/3 were derived from Houston and Dunning (1976).

The Dependent Variables

Much of the data on production-related variables was obtained from the *Census Production 1971 and 1979*. This includes: (1) labour productivity (LP) (net output ÷ total employment); (2) profitability (π) (gross output − gross value-added ÷ gross output); (3) skill ratio (NO/OWB) (non-operative wage bill ÷ operative wage bill); (4) concentration ratio (C) (percentage of gross output accounted for by five largest enterprises); (5) size effect (Sp) (average productivity of the largest two groups of enterprises in any sector ÷ by the average productivity of the rest of the sector); (6) output growth (GUK) (growth of gross output in UK 1971/1979); (7) the value-added ratio (VAR) (gross value-added ÷ gross output). The advertising ratio (AS) (advertising/sales) was obtained from data published in the *Census of Production, 1968*. The relative total productivity index (RTP) which attempts to measure the efficiency of FMNE_{UK} relative to that of UK_i is obtained by calculating (for 1979) the formula:

$$\frac{WL + \pi S}{W^*L + \pi^*S} \text{ for FMNE}_{UK}$$

where W = wage bill, L numbers employed, π the profit/sales margin, S = sales of FMNE_{UK} and $W^* + \pi^*$ the wage bill and profit/sales margin for UK_i. Separate calculations were made for non-operative and operative wages. The formula essentially relates to the actual value-added of FMNE_{UK} to the opportunity cost of the resources used; as a proxy for this opportunity cost the payments to the same quantity of comparable factor services by indigenous firms is used. For further details, see Dunning (1971).

For the main trade-related variable (RCA) as defined on p. 201, data were provided by the Department of Trade Statistics Division and are similar to those used to produce import and export ratios published by *Economic Trends*. The variable GUKX estimates the total demand for goods (UK-produced goods and imports) plus exports, and is derived from the same source, as were data for the ratio intra-industry trade (IIT). The intra-firm trade ratio (IFT) was derived from data published by the UK Department of Commerce (1981). As a proxy for this latter variable we took the imports from a proportion of total US imports in 1977 accounted for related parties (e.g. US affiliates abroad) as published in Helleiner (1981).

Chapter Ten

The UK's International Direct Investment Position in the Mid–1980s

INTRODUCTION

The underlying thesis of this chapter is that changes in the international direct investment position of a country are a reflection of changes in the international competitiveness of that country's firms, and the locational attractions of that country as a production base both for its own and foreign-based MNEs. An increase in outward direct investment may occur either because domestic MNEs have bettered their competitive position, vis-à-vis firms of other nationalities, or because the locational attractions of producing abroad relative to those in the home country have improved. On the other hand, an increase in inward investment by foreign MNEs could mean that they were penetrating a country's domestic markets at the expense of indigenous competitors, or that the domestic economic environment for production has become more attractive relative to that offered by other countries. We accept, straight away, that international investment flows are not the same thing as foreign capital expenditure on the part of MNEs, which, in the context of this chapter, is our primary interest. Net asset growth by MNEs may be financed from domestic or foreign sources; by the same token, a rise in outward or inward investment might be at the expense of domestic financing and this need not affect international capital formation.

SOME THEORETICAL ISSUES

In line with the terminology used in previous chapters, we distinguish between two possible reasons for international investment flows by referring to the O advantages of firms and the L advantages of countries. O advantages include all those producing and transacting strengths which a firm of one nationality may have over that of another nationality, when both are producing in the same location. These strengths may vary over time, but, at any given moment, they are unique to particular firms; however, within an enterprise many are transferable across national

204 *Multinationals, Technology and Competitiveness*

boundaries, that is to say, they do not have to be used where they originate. *L* advantages refer to the facilities which a particular country may offer firms to engage in value-added activities there, relative to those available in another country. While these facilities are specific to a particular location and immobile across national boundaries, they are available to firms of all nationalities. They include not only all natural resources and most kinds of labour but the institutional framework of the country, its political and economic system, and the attitude of its people to wealth creation, work, income distribution and foreigners. It is these latter components of a country's *L* advantages or disadvantages which can be engineered or fashioned by governments and influenced (by lobbying and other ways) by special interest groups.

The international competitive position of the UK depends upon the extent to which it possesses these two sets of advantages. The ability of the firms located in the UK to export reflects the *O* advantages of such firms and the extent to which it is profitable to exploit these from production outlets in the UK. By the same token, imported goods suggest that foreign firms have such advantages over UK firms which are best used with other resources in a foreign location. Where, however, UK firms have a competitive edge over foreign firms, which they find profitable to exploit from a foreign rather than a domestic location, then outward direct investment will occur. Similarly, the penetration of UK markets by the affiliates of foreign firms suggests that these firms possess advantages over UK firms, but that the UK is preferred as a production base to other countries.

This chapter first describes the trends in the UK's international direct investment position between the 1960s and mid-1980s. Second, it suggests the extent to which these changes reflect an improvement (or deterioration) in the *O* advantages of UK firms or an improvement (or deterioration) in the *L* advantages of the UK. Third, it examines some of the implications of these trends for the UK's economic welfare and for economic policy towards inward and outward direct investment.

FOREIGN DIRECT INVESTMENT AND ECONOMIC WELFARE

First, does it matter whether a country's enterprises engage in foreign production and if it is a net outward or inward direct investor? A country's economic prosperity rests mainly on the extent and quality of its resources and any other resources it can acquire, and its ability to transform these resources into end-products and market them. The output produced by these resources – the GNP – is equal to the output derived from all the resources used in the country, *less* any payments made to foreigners for resources imported, *plus* the income earned on resources exported, which are used in conjunction with the resources of other countries. In the national accounts this is equal to GNP plus or minus net investment income earned overseas. To the extent that inward

The UK International Investment Position

and outward direct investment (and/or capital formation by MNEs) affect both the level of resources available to the country and the extent to which indigenous resources are used (and the efficiency of their use), it is relevant to examine whether the investment is at its optimum level and properly directed.

It is admitted that *a priori* it may be very difficult to identify the optimum level or balance of international investment and/or capital formation. This will vary *inter alia* according to a country's level of economic development, its structure of resources, its social objectives, and so on. Indeed, as shown elsewhere (Dunning 1981, 1988), there is some evidence of a correlation between a country's stage of development and its propensity to be a net outward investor. Historically, too, those countries which are most well endowed in human capital and technology – the main O advantages of most industrial MNEs – have been those which have been the leading foreign investors; examples include the UK in the nineteenth century and the USA for much of the twentieth century.

Basically, of course, the same is true of trade. Although it may be difficult to generalize about an optimum level of trade, one.can identify the conditions under which trade is desirable, and one should be able to do the same for direct investment, which in many cases is a substitute for trade. The principle of comparative (trading) advantage asserts that countries should export those goods which require resources in which they are comparatively well-endowed and imports goods which require resources in which they are comparatively poorly endowed. Similarly, one might suggest that a country's firms should be encouraged to invest overseas to produce products which require resources in which they have a comparative O advantage but the investing country has a comparative L disadvantage, while inward investment should be directed to producing goods which require resources in which the recipient country has a comparative L advantage but in which its own firms have a comparative O disadvantage.

In the real world, of course, there are a host of distortions to the free movement of goods and resources caused by both imperfect markets and government intervention. Moreover, a good deal of trade between industrialized countries cannot be explained by neo-classical trade theory; and trade and investment, far from being substitutes for each other, often go hand in hand. Finally, the political economy of international investment is different from that of trade. In trade, the final decision of what is produced and where it is produced is taken within the exporting or importing country; in international investment, decisions may be taken outside the country in which they are implemented and their effect chiefly felt. This introduces questions of sovereignty and control which, while we acknowledge their importance, will not be considered in this chapter.

206 *Multinationals, Technology and Competitiveness*

UK INWARD AND OUTWARD INVESTMENT: THE STATISTICAL PICTURE

Central Statistical Office Data

At the end of 1985 the book value of the net assets owned by UK companies abroad (K_o) was £76,708 million, almost double the £40,550 million of the net assets in the UK owned by foreign companies (K_i). Along with the USA, the UK continues to be the leading net creditor in the world on long-term capital account; indeed, apart from the period around the Second World War, the UK has remained a net foreign creditor since the mid-nineteenth century.

Table 10.1 shows that, between 1974 and 1985, UK firms invested £61,353 million abroad, while foreign companies invested £30,237 million in the UK. For the first part of this period, the growth of the outward capital stake lagged behind that of the inward capital stake; taking 1974 as 100, the index of growth of the former by 1980 was 210.4 and that of the latter 256.2. Between 1980 and 1985, however, the growth of outward investment consistently outpaced that of inward investment, the respective growth indices (1980) = 100 being 230.0 and 153.1. As a result, the ratio between the outward and inward capital stake rose from 1.49 in 1974 to 1.89 in 1985, before having peaked at 2.17 in 1984.

Table 10.2 sets out some indicators of the significance of outward and inward direct investment to the UK economy. As a proportion of the UK's GNP, the combined inward and outward capital stake ($K_o + K_i$) increased from 31.7 per cent in 1974 to 38.4 per cent in 1985. Most of this increase is accounted for by a sharp rise in the outward capital stake; the inward capital stake, while increasing marginally until 1983, dropped back to its 1980 level in 1985.

An examination of investment (that is, change in capital stake, ΔK or I data) reveals fairly sizeable annual fluctuations, which is not surprising as the data include the value of acquisitions, or partial acquisitions, and are net of divestments. Because of this, too much should not be read into the data set out in Rows 3 and 4 of Table 10.2, except that they do underline the growing amounts invested overseas by UK companies and by foreign MNEs in the UK, relative to net capital expenditure in the UK. The earnings and profit data are more meaningful; they show that the share of earnings in outward investment to gross trading profits of UK companies rose in the late 1970s and early 1980s but since then slipped back to their 1975 level. The share of these same profits accounted for by foreign MNEs rose sharply to 1980 and has remained about the same since then.

The final rows in Table 10.2 relate inward investment to imports (M) (as these may be alternatives to servicing the UK market by foreign firms) and outward investment to exports (X) (as these may be alternative ways for UK firms and foreign affiliates in the UK to service foreign markets). They show that, until 1980, inward investment and imports have more or less kept pace with each other; since 1980 imports

Table 10.1 *The UK's Direct Investment Stake Position (1974–85) £ million*

	1974	1975	1976	1977	1978	1979	1980	1981	1982	1983	1984	1985
Investment overseas by UK residents (UK assets)												
Investment by												
UK banks	830	907	1,048	1,153	1,298	1,568	1,610	1,747	1,961	1,973	1,046	3,029
Other financial institutions	1,189	1,967	2,605	2,752	3,165	3,241	3,200	4,387	5,135	5,901	7,512	7,102
Industrial and commercial companies (including oil)	13,177	15,517	19,559	20,165	23,292	26,175	28,165	38,515	45,674	51,998	72,467	66,116
Public corporations	159	183	262	297	360	370	340	511	499	454	508	461
Total assets	15,355	18,574	23,474	24,367	28,115	31,354	33,315	45,160	53,269	60,326	81,533	76,708
Investment in the UK by overseas residents (UK liabilities)												
Investment in												
UK banks	457	535	669	801	933	1,083	1,261	1,453	1,880	2,232	2,906	3,483
UK insurance companies	99	101	108	137	186	227	259	310	431	611	410	200
Industrial and commercial companies (including oil)	9,617	11,300	12,700	14,450	16,348	20,077	24,034	27,262	28,328	32,101	33,320	35,370
Other (property)	140	167	219	328	416	624	867	987	1,133	1,347	1,407	1,497
Total liabilities	10,313	12,103	13,696	15,716	17,883	22,011	26,421	30,012	31,772	36,291	38,043	40,550
(3)/(8)	1.37	1.37	1.54	1.39	1.42	1.30	1.17	1.41	1.61	1.62	2.17	1.87
(5)/(10)	1.49	1.53	1.71	1.55	1.57	1.42	1.26	1.50	1.68	1.66	2.14	1.89

Source: Central Statistical Office *United Kingdom Balance of Payments (1986 edition)* Table 9.2A.

Table 10.2   *The Significance of Outward and Inward Investment for the UK Economy: Selected Indicators 1975/85*

	1975	1976	1977	1978	1979	1980	1981	1982	1983	1984	1985
Outward direct investment assets as a % of GNP[1]	19.2	20.4	18.8	18.8	18.1	16.7	20.6	22.5	23.1	29.1	25.1
Inward direct investment assets as a % of GNP[1]	12.5	11.9	12.1	11.9	12.7	13.3	13.7	13.4	13.9	13.6	13.3
Annual outward direct investment as a % of net domestic fixed capital formation[2]	29.2	45.4	43.3	50.0	73.1	61.7	104.1	72.9	112.0	73.4	78.7
Annual inward direct investment as a % of net domestic fixed capital formation[2]	33.5	31.0	46.0	27.9	37.6	54.5	50.1	50.0	72.6	5.2	36.3
Earnings on outward direct investment as a % of gross trading profits of UK companies[3]	13.0	14.8	11.3	11.5	16.6	14.5	14.6	11.4	12.4	13.7	13.3
Earnings on inward direct investment as a % of gross trading profits of UK companies[3]	4.0	5.0	8.0	8.0	11.4	13.7	12.6	11.3	10.8	11.4	12.7
Annual outward direct investment as a % of UK exports[4]	4.9	6.9	5.5	7.4	10.7	7.8	9.0	5.9	6.6	6.5	7.1
Annual inward direct investment as a % of UK exports[4]	5.2	4.5	6.0	4.3	5.5	7.5	4.8	4.4	4.4	0.5	3.4

Notes:

[1]Outward (inward) direct investment assets (from Table 10.1) as a % of GNP (at factor cost and current prices). From Table 10.1 and *National Income Blue Book* (1986 edition) Table 1.2.B.

[2]Annual outward (inward) direct investment as a % of net domestic fixed capital formation of industrial and commercial companies, plus financial companies and institutions, plus public corporations. From *National Income Blue Book* (1986 edition) Table 11.6 and *United Kingdom Balance of Payments* (1986 edition) Table 8.2A.

[3]Earnings as outward (inward) direct investment as a % of gross trading profits of UK industrial and commercial companies, plus financial companies and institutions, plus public corporations. From *National Income Blue Book* (1986 edition) Table 1.14 and *United Kingdom Balance of Payments* (1986 edition) Table 5.2A.

[4]Annual outward (inward) direct investment as a % of exports (imports) of goods and services. From Table 6.1.2 and *National Income Blue Book* (1986 edition) Table 1.10 and *United Kingdom Balance of Payments* (1986 edition) Table 8.2A.

The UK International Investment Position 209

have risen faster than inward investment. After a doubling in the importance of outward investment relative to exports in the later 1970s, the share has stepped back to the 6–7 per cent level in the mid–1980s.

The Department of Trade and Industry Data

Until 1984, the Department of Trade and Industry excluded oil investments from their annual estimates of outward investment flows, and oil and insurance investments from their estimates of inward investment flows. In their triennial surveys of the book values of the foreign capital stake owned by UK companies and the net assets owned by UK firms in the UK, oil, banking and insurance assets are excluded for all surveys up to, and including, that of 1981. The data for 1984 and previous years presented in Tables 10.3 and 10.4 are, therefore, not comparable.

However, the main thrust of the data set out in Tables 10.3 and 10.4 is clear enough. Over the past two decades, there has been a substantial redirection of the foreign activities of UK MNEs towards Western Europe (until around 1978), and then to North America (and particularly the USA), away from other developed and developing countries. On the other hand, the relative significance of the North American (and most noticeably US) direct investment stake in the UK has fallen quite dramatically – from 75.9 per cent in 1962 to 61.6 per cent in 1981 and 53.8 per cent in 1984. By contrast, over the same period, the share of Western European direct investment has risen from 20.8 per cent to 26.7 per cent to 37.4 per cent, although much of the rise since 1981 is accounted for by the inclusion of the oil investments of the Netherlands. Tables 10.3 and 10.4 also show that other developed and developing countries have increased their share of the inward direct investment stake. Since 1978, in particular, both Japanese investment in the UK and UK investment in Japan have grown very rapidly. By the end of 1984, in fact, Japan was the seventh largest investor in the UK.

The next step is to classify investments by their broad types which, up to a point, is quite easy to do. To the data on oil investments, which are separately published by the Bank of England, we may add investments in mining and agriculture, arguing that these investments are all of the resource-based kind. Beyond this point, it becomes more difficult. Obviously, some manufacturing investments, particularly those in the chemical, metal and food processing sectors, may also be influenced by the presence of the local raw materials, foodstuffs or minerals which they use. Because of the classification adopted by the Department of Trade and Industry, there is no means of identifying how much. In the developing countries in particular, however, this is likely to account for quite a substantial proportion of UK activities in the food, drink and tobacco sectors.

Most kinds of manufacturing investment can be classified as import-substituting or export oriented. Again, there is no way the data enable the two to be separated. We do know, however, the main industries and countries or regions in which the latter type of investment is most

Table 10.3 *Distribution of UK Outward and Inward Direct Capital Stake by Broad Geographical Area 1962–84*

		Western Europe		North America		Other developed countries		Rest of the world			Total
		£m	%	£m	%	£m	%	£m	%	£m	%
Outward capital stake[1]	1962	455	13.4	785	23.0	923	27.1	1,242	36.5	3,405	100.0
	1965	648	15.4	919	21.8	1,259	29.9	1,384	32.9	4,210	100.0
	1968	985	17.6	1,287	23.0	1,723	30.9	1,590	28.5	5,585	100.0
	1971	1,461	21.9	1,466	22.0	1,985	30.0	1,755	26.3	6,667	100.0
	1974	2,867	27.5	2,271	21.8	3,138	30.1	2,160	20.7	10,436	100.0
	1978	5,957	31.2	4,815	25.2	4,442	23.2	3,894	20.4	19,108	100.0
	1981	6,612	23.2	9,884	34.6	5,824	20.4	6,225	21.8	28,545	100.0
	1984	18,684	24.7	31,476	41.6	11,650	15.4	13,905	18.4	75,715	100.0
Inward capital stake[1]	1962	298	20.8	1,086	75.9	33	2.3	13	0.9	1,430	100.0
	1965	397	19.9	1,547	77.4	20	1.0	36	1.8	2,000	100.0
	1968	594	21.8	2,055	75.3	49	1.8	30	1.1	2,728	100.0
	1971	892	23.4	2,719	71.2	157	4.1	50	1.3	3,817	100.0
	1974	1,882	28.7	4,070	62.0	303	4.6	312	4.8	6,567	100.0
	1978	3,259	29.4	7,106	64.0	501	4.5	233	2.1	11,098	100.0
	1981	4,528	26.7	10,451	61.6	1,152	6.8	831	4.9	16,962	100.0
	1984	14,389	37.4	20,703	53.8	1,438	3.7	1,947	5.1	38,476	100.0

Notes: [1]Figures up to and including 1981 exclude oil, banking and insurance companies.
Source: *British Business* 22 May 1987.

Table 10.4 *Geographical Distribution of Outward and Inward Direct Capital Stake 1974/1984*

	Outward capital stake[1] (K_o)				*Inward capital stake[1] (K_i)*				K_o/K_i			
	1974	1978	1981	1984	1974	1978	1981	1984	1974	1978	1981	1984
Western Europe	2,867	5,957	6,612	18,684	1,882	3,259	4,528	14,389	1.52	1.83	1.46	1.30
EEC	2,494	4,926	5,910	15,949	1,120	2,037	2,607	11,436	2.23	2.42	2.27	1.39
Belgium and Luxembourg	325	681	529	1,234	210	371	343	677	1.55	1.84	1.54	1.82
France	461	823	1,064	1,896	186	493	575	1,782	2.48	1.67	1.85	1.06
Germany	669	1,465	1,510	2,872	168	262	627	939	3.98	5.59	2.41	3.06
Italy	199	282	384	566	114	129	72	136	1.75	2.19	5.33	4.16
Netherlands	245	583	1,098	7,240	337	615	738	7,392	0.73	0.95	1.49	0.98
EFTA	325	961	596	2,601	760	1,222	1,922	2,942	0.43	0.79	0.31	0.88
Sweden	94	169	157	462	166	299	471	604	0.57	0.57	0.33	0.76
Switzerland	113	607	287	1,334	502	789	1,255	1,833	0.23	0.77	0.23	0.73
North America	2,272	4,815	9,884	31,476	4,070	7,106	10.451	20,703	0.56	0.68	0.95	1.52
Canada	941	1,256	1,905	5,150	404	638	892	1,012	2.33	1.97	2.14	5.09
USA	1,331	3,559	7,979	26,326	3,666	6,468	9,559	19,691	0.36	0.55	0.83	1.34
Other developed countries	3,138	4,442	5,824	11,650	303	501	1,152	1,438	10.36	8.87	5.06	8.10
Australia	1,917	2,613	3,535	7,629	60	173	330	377	32.00	15.10	10.71	20.24
Japan	40	112	187	629	− 18	− 24	324	659	NC	NC	0.58	0.95
Rest of the World	2,159	3,894	6,226	13,905	312	233	831	1,947	6.92	16.71	7.49	7.14
Asia	932	1,601	2,617	5,734	203	149	523	812	4.59	10.74	5.00	7.06
Caribbean, Central and South America	477	957	1,711	5,772	108	126	207	869	4.42	7.60	8.27	6.64
Other countries including Africa	751	1,336	1,897	2,398	1	− 42	101	266	751.00	NC	18.78	9.02
World	10,436	19,108	28,545	75,715	6,567	11,098	16,962	38,476	1.59	1.72	1.68	1.97

Notes:
[1] Figures up to and including 1981 exclude oil, banking and insurance companies.
NC = not computable
Source: *British Business* 22 May 1987.

212 *Multinationals, Technology and Competitiveness*

prominent.[1] As a rough approximation (and because there is so little UK efficiency seeking investment this is all that is needed), we can, arbitrarily, take one-half of the investment in the electrical and mechanical engineering sectors and all the investment in textiles, clothing and footwear in Hong Kong, Singapore, Mexico, the Far East countries (other than the Indian sub-continent, Malaysia and Thailand) and Southern Europe. The balance is assumed to consist of import-substituting investments.

Of the tertiary investments it may be assumed that investments in distributive trades are export-promoting, while those in transport, communications, shipping, finance and insurance are primarily, though not exclusively, ancillary to other foreign investments. The rest consists of a 'rag-bag' of activities which include building and construction, a genuine direct investment, and property owning and managing, which may be a direct investment (for example, hotel management) or a portfolio investment – and various other activities.

It is generally accepted that the motives for, and effects of, the activities of MNEs may differ according to their country of origin and the location of their involvement. From the viewpoint of the home country, FDI might be substitutable for, or complementary to, domestic investment; most North/South FDI is of the former kind and is usually only one way. Most North/North investment is of the latter kind and leads to two-way intra-industry production. To this extent, although FDI tends to substitute for home investment, it is often complemented by inward investment in similar sectors. In this chapter, we shall concentrate our attention on investment flows of one main type (import-substituting manufacturing) and between the UK and one main region (Western Europe), as it is here that the greatest complementarity between inward and outward capital flows reveals itself, and where the data are most revealing in our understanding of Britain's international competitive situation.

Table 10.5 sets out data on the UK outward and inward direct capital stake for selected years between 1965 and 1984, classified by main type of investment. The following points may be highlighted:

(1)   The proportion of the K_o stake accounted for by manufacturing and service industries increased from 84.9 per cent in 1965 to 91.4 per cent in 1981. Over the same period, the share of resource-based activities fell from 15.1 per cent to 8.6 per cent. Due primarily to expropriation or the voluntary withdrawal of assets by UK firms, the most dramatic fall occurred in non-oil primary investment in developing countries, where its share of all investment fell from 18.2 per cent in 1974 to 13.8 per cent in 1981; on the other hand, new mining ventures in North America and Australia enabled the developed world to maintain its share of such investments at between 7 and 8 per cent.

(2)   The industrial distribution of inward investment has become considerably more diversified over the years, chiefly because of the

Table 10.5 *Distribution of Outward and Inward Direct Capital Stake by Economic Sector 1965/1984*

| | 1965 | | 1971 | | 1978 | | 1981 | | 1984 | |
	£m	%	£m	%	£m	%	£m	%	£m	%
Outward capital stake										
Primary products	636.1	15.1	1,001.1	15.0	1,180.4	6.1	2,463.7	8.6	25.226[2]	33.3
Manufacturing	2,103.4	50.0	3,934.3	59.0	12,147.9	63.2	16.166.9	56.6	24,112	31.8
Distributive trades	671.1	15.9	876.4	13.1	3,168.4	16.5	3,833.2	13.4	10,326	13.6
Other non-manufacturing	799.4	19.0	855.1	12.8	2,718.1	14.1	6,081.5	21.3	16,051	21.2
Total	4,210.0	100.0	6,666.9	100.0	19,214.8	100.0	28,545.1	100.0	75,715	100.0
Inward capital stake										
Primary products	N.S.A.	N.S.A.	N.S.A.	N.S.A.	N.S.A.	N.S.A.	N.S.A.	N.S.A.	13,227[2]	34.4
Manufacturing	1,629.4	81.5	3,180.2	83.3	8,118.7	74.1	12,188.3	71.9	15,694	40.8
Distributive trades	242.8	12.1	392.6	10.3	1,436.3	13.1	2,567.1	15.1	3,177	8.3
Other non-manufacturing	107.8	5.4	244.2	6.4	1,394.4	12.7	2,206.6	13.0	6,378	16.6
Total	1,999.9	100.0	3,817.0	100.0	10,949.2	100.0	16,962.0	100.0	38,476	100.0

Notes:
[1]Figures up to and including 1981 exclude the capital stake of oil, banking and insurance companies. In 1984 such companies are included.
[2]Agriculture and energy.
  Source: Business Statistics Office *Business Monitor M4* (various editions), *British Business* 22 May 1987.

Table 10.6 Distribution of Annual Outward and Inward Investment by Geographical Area and Sector of Economic Activity, 1960–1983

	All areas (£m)			Western Europe (£m)			North America (£m)		
	Outward (I_o)	Inward (I_i)	I_o/I_i	Outward (I_o)	Inward (I_i)	I_o/I_i	Outward (I_o)	Inward (I_i)	I_o/I_i
Investment in all activities (annual average)									
1960–1962	228.3	167.0	1.37	38.5	23.2	1.66	34.3	136.3	0.21
1963–1965	269.0	173.0	1.55	52.5	29.6	1.77	32.3	144.6	0.22
1966–1968	322.3	213.0	1.51	66.9	48.1	1.39	86.7	152.3	0.57
1969–1971	590.2	372.6	1.58	196.6	63.9	3.08	143.2	254.1	0.56
1972–1974	1,311.0	656.0	2.00	458.7	151.6	3.03	384.8	375.8	1.02
1975–1977	1,733.6	913.4	1.90	491.4	301.6	1.63	508.4	492.9	1.03
1978–1980	3,045.0	1,847.3	1.65	519.8	351.7	1.48	1,597.7	1,296.3	1.23
1981–1983	3,459.9	1,389.4	2.49	63.9	437.1	0.15	1,998.5	554.9	3.60
Manufacturing investment									
1960–1962	119.2	132.7	0.89	24.9	13.8	1.81	16.3	116.5	0.14
1963–1965	130.5	135.1	0.97	20.4	21.5	0.95	15.2	111.9	0.14
1966–1968	169.4	166.4	1.02	33.1	36.5	0.91	37.0	129.1	0.29
1969–1971	328.8	274.7	1.20	126.9	42.7	2.97	78.1	216.9	0.36
1972–1974	670.7	382.4	1.75	222.7	68.6	3.26	213.1	298.7	0.71
1975–1977	995.5	606.8	1.64	280.3	153.1	1.83	328.8	439.5	0.75
1978–1980	1,447.9	1,148.2	1.26	223.7	134.1	1.67	815.2	957.5	0.85
1981–1983	1,887.1	467.9	4.03	331.1	172.5	1.92	982.9	237.7	4.14
Distributive trades									
1960–1962	37.0	15.7	2.35	6.4	2.8	4.48	3.8	13.2	0.29
1963–1965	55.9	23.3	2.40	22.1	4.4	4.64	11.5	15.4	0.75
1966–1968	55.8	20.5	2.72	25.2	6.3	4.00	10.6	9.9	1.07
1969–1971	106.7	39.3	2.71	38.2	11.2	3.41	13.1	6.6	1.98
1972–1974	205.3	77.9	2.64	113.0	31.4	3.60	26.3	26.8	0.98
1975–1977	331.8	70.6	4.70	138.4	60.1	2.30	60.3	0.7	86.14
1978–1980	432.7	192.8	2.24	134.0	82.5	1.62	175.2	69.9	2.51
1981–1983	550.7	176.0	3.13	98.0	45.7	2.14	326.3	1.6	203.9
Other activities									
1960–1962	56.9	18.6	3.06	6.7	6.5	1.04	14.1	5.5	2.56
1963–1965	57.3	14.4	3.98	9.7	3.8	2.55	5.5	17.2	0.32
1966–1968	61.3	26.4	2.32	13.7	3.3	4.15	39.1	13.3	2.94
1969–1971	117.7	57.3	2.05	23.5	10.6	2.22	50.7	26.4	1.92
1972–1974	353.5	195.8	1.81	104.7	56.6	1.85	124.5	50.3	2.48
1975–1977	406.4	236.0	1.72	72.7	88.4	0.82	119.2	52.8	2.26
1978–1980	1,164.4	506.3	2.30	162.1	135.1	1.20	607.3	269.0	2.26
1981–1983	1,022.0	745.4	1.37	−365.2	219.0	NC	689.3	315.8	2.18

Note: NC = Not computable

Source: Business Statistics Office *Business Monitor M4* (various editions).

The UK International Investment Position

substantial capital inflow into North Sea Oil. North American (mainly US) firms have tended to dominate this sector, as they have continued to do so within manufacturing industry. In the service industries in the 1970s, however, there was a sizeable investment in the UK by some developing countries, especially in property management and development, distribution and financial activities.

(3) The ratio between the outward and inward capital stake (the K_o/K_i ratio) in manufacturing industry has risen from 1.23 in 1965 to 1.54 in 1984. In the oil sector, the ratio fell between 1965 and 1981, since when it has risen. In trade and distribution, the ratio moved sharply upwards in the early 1960s, fell back in the following decade, and then rose substantially. By contrast, some of the most remarkable falls in the K_o/K_i ratio have occurred in the other service industries.

Some of these trends are more dramatically highlighted by changes in the ratio between outward and inward investment (the I_o/I_i ratio). Because annual figures are considerably influenced by the acquisitions of share capital in a particular year, which often involve large sums of money and tend to be erratic, three yearly averages have been taken over the period 1960–83. Table 10.6 presents some relevant statistics. Here, one sees most clearly the faster rate of manufacturing investment by British firms abroad than by foreign firms in the UK, the acceleration being particularly marked in the early 1980s. In 1975, for the first time since 1960, there was more UK manufacturing investment in North America than there was North American manufacturing investment in the UK, and in the period 1981–83 there was four times as much. By contrast, whereas in the early 1970s British firms were investing in Western Europe at three times the rate of Western Europeans investing in the UK, since 1975, the rate of Western European investment in the UK has exceeded that of UK investment in Western Europe.

In the service sector there have been no less dramatic changes, with huge increases in both outward and inward direct investment in the non-distributive trades in the period 1978–83. United Kingdom investment in North American distributive trades has been especially buoyant since the mid–1970s, in contrast to only small amounts of new investments by North American firms in the UK. By contrast, the ratio between the outward and inward investment flows to and from Western Europe in the distributive trades has halved over the period.

The Picture Within Manufacturing Industry

Until 1971, there were no detailed data on the industrial composition of outward manufacturing investment. Table 10.7 sets out the distribution of manufacturing net assets owned by UK firms abroad and foreign firms in the UK at that date and in 1981. It also classifies sectors, according to

Table 10.7 *Distribution Within Manufacturing Industry of UK Net Assets Abroad and Foreign Net Assets in the UK, 1971 and 1981*

| | Outward assets | | | | Inward assets | | | |
| | £m | | % Share | | | £m | | % Share | |
	1971	1981	1971	1981	1971	1981	1971	1981
More technology-intensive sectors	1,672.8	8,254.8	42.5	51.1	2,191.1	7,968.3	68.9	65.4
Chemicals and allied manufactures	683.9	4,532.8	17.4	28.0	460.4	2,401.7	14.5	19.7
Mechanical and instrument engineering	263.4	1,014.2	6.7	6.3	684.4	2,168.5	21.5	17.8
Electrical engineering	498.0	1,621.8	12.7	10.0	466.4	1,753.5	14.7	14.4
Motor vehicles	93.4	532.5	2.4	3.3	385.3	1,293.4	12.1	10.6
Rubber	134.1	553.5	3.4	3.4	194.6	351.2	6.1	2.9
Less technology-intensive sectors	2,261.6	7,912.1	57.5	48.9	989.1	4,219.9	31.1	34.6
Food, drink and tobacco	1,104.2	4,384.4	28.1	27.1	391.9	2,009.4	12.3	16.5
Metal manufacture	142.7	320.8	3.6	2.0	258.6	654.6	8.1	5.4
Textiles, leather, clothing and footwear	298.6	691.8	7.6	4.3	30.9	119.9	1.0	1.0
Paper, printing and publishing	261.5	883.7	6.7	5.5	2.5	663.6	2.9	5.4
Other manufacturing	454.6	1,631.4	11.6	10.1	215.2	772.4	6.8	6.3
Total manufacturing industry	3,934.4	16,166.9	100.0	100.0	3,180.2	12,188.3	100.0	100.0

Source: Business Statistics Office *Business Monitor M4* (various editions).
 Data for 1984, which were published after this table was compiled, suggest a broadly similar structure of the outward capital stake (with the more technology-intensive sector accounting for 49.8% of all manufacturing assets). As far as the inward capital stake is concerned, the share attracted to the more technology-intensive sectors continued to fall in the early 1980s, reaching 62.6% of all manufacturing assets in 1984.

Table 10.8 *Ratio Between Net Assets Owned by UK Firms Abroad (K_o) and Foreign Firms in UK (K_i) 1971 and 1981*

	Western Europe		North America		All areas	
	K_o/K_i 1971	K_o/K_i 1981	K_o/K_i 1971	K_o/K_i 1981	K_o/K_i 1971	K_o/K_i 1981
More technology-intensive sectors	0.75	0.99[2]	0.22	0.53[2]	0.76	1.04
Chemicals and allied manufactures	1.25	1.93	0.67	1.01	1.49	1.89
Mechanical and instrument engineering	1.25	0.66	0.05	0.23	0.38	0.47
Electrical engineering	0.41	0.44	0.38	0.52	1.07	0.92
Motor vehicles	1.94	4.47	0.03	0.10	0.24	0.41
Rubber	0.20	N.A.	0.65	N.A.	0.69	1.58
Less technology-intensive sectors	2.08	1.91[2]	0.83	1.09[2]	2.29	1.87
Food, drink and tobacco	2.29	2.55	1.19	1.22	2.82	2.18
Metal manufacture	0.81	0.26	[1]	0.42	0.55	0.49
Textiles, leather, clothing and footwear	3.11	14.53	[1]	3.02	9.66	5.77
Paper, printing and publishing	1.48	1.06	2.10	1.22	2.83	1.33
Other manufacturing	2.44	3.17[2]	0.36	0.77[2]	2.11	2.11
Total manufacturing industry	1.07	1.33	0.42	0.71	1.24	1.33

Notes:
[1]Including other manufacturing. [2]Including partial estimate.
Source: Business Statistics Office *Business Monitor M.4* (various editions).
Later data for 1984 reveal a K_o/K_i ratio for the more technology-intensive sectors of 1.06 for Western Europe, 0.84 for North America and 1.22 for all areas. The respective ratios for the less technology-intensive sectors are 1.47, 1.30 and 2.06.

218 *Multinationals, Technology and Competitiveness*

whether they may be broadly described as more technology-intensive (MTI) or less technology-intensive (LTI).[2]

The following conclusions may be drawn from this table:

(1) Although the proportion of inward direct investment directed to the MTI industries was considerably greater in 1984 than that of outward direct investment to these industries (62.6 per cent compared with 49.8 per cent), the previous decade saw a change in the structure of both sets of investment flows. Table 10.7 shows a very large increase in the share of outward investment directed to the chemicals sector; indeed, between 1971 and 1984 that sector alone accounted for 30.3 per cent of the total increase in the outward capital stake. By contrast, and with the exception again of chemicals, foreign investors invested proportionately less in the MTI sectors and proportionately more in the LTI sectors, in particular in food, drink and tobacco, paper, printing, and publishing. In the two engineering sectors, both the share of inward and outward capital stake fell; indeed, their combined share fell from 55.6 per cent to 49.9 per cent. This contrasted markedly with the chemical sector, where over the same period the corresponding share of the inward plus outward capital stake rose from 31.9 per cent to 51.1 per cent.

(2) The above observations are confirmed by an examination of the K_o/K_i ratios for 1971, 1981 and 1984. Table 10.8 shows that in the intervening decade, the K_o/K_i ratio for the MTI sectors generally rose, while that for the LTI sectors fell. This is an extremely interesting change in the perception of domestic- and foreign-based MNEs to the UK's L advantages. It indicates that, relative to inward investment, outward investment has become more directed towards the MTI sectors, and, relative to outward investment, inward investment has become more concentrated in the LTI sectors. The trend towards the former has been more pronounced for Anglo-American capital flows, and that of the latter more pronounced for Anglo-European capital flows.

AN EXPLANATION OF THE DATA

How far can one explain the data just described, using the model of international production earlier put forward? Put another way: To what extent can one account for differences in the K_o/K_i or I_o/I_i ratios

(1) between the UK and different countries;
(2) between different industries; and
(3) between years in the same country and/or industry, in terms of differences or changes in
  (a) the O advantages of UK firms (compared to those of non-UK firms), and

The UK International Investment Position 219

(b) the L advantages of the UK (compared to those of other countries)?

It must be admitted that, *a priori*, there is no way of assessing whether a rise in the K_o/K_i or I_o/I_i ratios, such as that revealed in the data presented, reflects an improvement in the competitiveness of UK firms or a deterioration of the locational attractiveness of the UK as a production base, or some combination of the two. Yet clearly, from a policy-framing viewpoint, this is a matter of some importance. Is capital leaving the UK because British entrepreneurs, managers, and the technological capabilities of UK firms are perceived to be better (or becoming better) than their Continental European, US, Japanese, etc., counterparts? Or is it because UK firms perceive that the UK economic environment is becoming less congenial compared to that offered by other countries? Is the rate of increase in foreign capital entering the UK falling because foreign affiliates are less able to compete effectively with UK firms? Or is it because the foreign firms believe they can make a higher profit by producing outside rather than in the UK?

The rest of this chapter offers some hints about the likely role played by these two variables in influencing changes in the UK's manufacturing I_o/I_i ratio over the last ten years or so. In doing so it takes as an index of the change in the O advantage of UK firms that of the profitability of such firms relative to that of non-UK firms producing in the same country or group of countries; and, as indices of change in the UK's L advantage, two measures, that is, (1) the change in the profitability of UK and US-owned firms producing in the UK, relative to that of the same firms producing in other countries, and (2) the change in the UK export/import of manufactured goods (X/M) ratio.[3]

More specifically, and putting the two sets of indices together, we examine the following proposition.

Differences (or changes) in the K_o/K_i or I_o/I_i ratios reflect differences (or changes) in the profitability of UK firms relative to that of non-UK firms, and differences (or changes) in the profitability of UK (or other) firms producing in the UK, relative to the profitability of the same firms in other countries, or differences in the UK export/import of goods ratio.

This proposition will now be tested by an examination of (1) changes in the UK's manufacturing I_o/I_i ratio between 1960 and 1984 and (2) differences in the K_o/K_i ratios between particular industries and/or regions in 1971–73 and 1979–81.

Table 10.9 relates changes in the I_o/I_i ratio for all manufacturing industry between the UK and the rest of the world and the UK and Western Europe for selected years for the period 1960 to 1984 to changes in the indices of O and L advantages just set out.

A cursory examination of Table 10.9 suggests a positive association between the growth of I_o/I_i ratio, an improvement in the competitiveness

Table 10.9 UK–Foreign Investment Ratios in Manufacturing Industry, Ownership and Location-Specific Advantages 1961–84

	All countries						Western Europe					
	I_o/I_i	O_A	O_B	L_A	L_B	X/M	I_o/I_i	O_A	O_B	L_A	L_B	X/M
1961–62	0.93	0.73	1.11	1.21	0.86	2.09	1.84	0.67	N.A.	1.13	0.81	1.55
1963–64	1.01	0.79	0.91	1.10	1.05	1.90	0.94	0.55	N.A.	1.65	1.03	1.52
1965–66	0.97	0.82	0.82	0.91	1.05	1.80	1.49	0.67	1.27	1.25	1.13	1.39
1967–68	1.10	0.92	0.78	0.86	0.99	1.49	0.77	0.92	1.18	1.00	1.09	1.19
1969–70	1.26	0.82	0.76	0.73	0.74	1.49	2.32	0.84	1.21	0.61	0.68	1.30
1971–72	1.34	0.78	0.93	0.93	0.80	1.45	3.76	0.73	1.25	0.88	0.74	1.15
1973–74	1.80	0.82	0.87	0.64	0.66	1.04	3.62	0.74	1.53	0.67	0.61	0.93
1975–78	1.64	0.86	1.05	1.02	0.68	0.98	1.94	0.66	1.61	1.18	0.58	0.84
1979–81	1.12	0.87	0.61	0.64	1.26	1.01	1.28	0.60	5.23	0.98	1.45	0.95
1982–84	2.58	2.05	0.94	0.84	0.31	0.80	1.01	1.34	1.41	0.98	0.29	0.67

N.A. not available.

Sources: *Business Monitor M3* (various editions), *Business Monitor M4* (various editions), US Department of Commerce *Survey of Current Business* (various editions) and *UK Balance of Payments* (1986 edition). *British Business* May 22 1987.

Key to notations:

I_o = outward investment.

I_i = inward investment.

O_A = All countries – Rate of return on total UK overseas direct investment (excluding North America) in manufacturing divided by rate of return on US overseas direct investment (excluding Canada and UK) in manufacturing.

O_A = Western Europe – Rate of return on UK direct investment in Western Europe in manufacturing divided by rate of return on US investment in Western Europe (excluding UK) in manufacturing.

O_B = All countries – Rate of return on domestic manufacturing investment in UK divided by rate of return on all foreign direct investment in UK manufacturing.

O_B = West Europe – Rate of return on domestic manufacturing investment in UK divided by rate of return on Western European investment in UK manufacturing.

L_A = All countries – Rate of return on domestic manufacturing investment in UK divided by rate of return on total UK overseas direct investment in manufacturing.

L_A = Western Europe – Rate of return on domestic manufacturing investment in UK divided by rate of return on UK manufacturing investment in Western Europe.

L_B = All countries – Rate of return on US direct investment in manufacturing in UK divided by rate of return on US direct investment in manufacturing in the rest of the world excluding Canada.

L_B = Western Europe – Rate of return on US direct investment in manufacturing in UK divided by rate of return on US direct investment in manufacturing in the rest of Western Europe.

X/M = All countries – Total UK manufacturing exports divided by total UK manufacturing imports.

X/M = Western Europe – UK manufacturing exports to Western Europe divided by UK manufacturing imports from Western Europe.

For further definition of rates of return see footnotes to Table 10.12, p. 227.

The UK International Investment Position

of UK firms and a weakening of the competitive advantage of the UK as a production base. A rise in UK outward investment relative to inward investment has generally coincided with declining location profitability ratios (L_A and L_B) and X/M ratios and an increase in UK ownership profitability ratios (O_A and O_B). *Inter alia* the data show that, while in the years between 1961–62 and 1975–8, the I_o/I_i ratio for all countries doubled, and the profitability of UK relative to US direct investment in foreign countries has risen by two-thirds, both location profitability measures fell by two-thirds and the X/M ratio halved.

For Western Europe, a similar though less decisive pattern holds. The I_o/I_i ratio increased between the early 1960s and early 1970s. This coincided with a fall in the X(WE)/M(WE) ratio of 30 per cent, a halving of the location profitability ratio and a substantial improvement in the performance of UK firms relative to that of their competitors. Since 1975, the I_o/I_i ratio has fallen; and so has the O_A (but not the O_B) ratio. The location ratios have moved upwards.

Table 10.9 offers rather different explanations for the changes in the I_o/I_i ratio in the 1960s and 1970s. In the 1960s, the fall in the ratio (for all countries) by about one-half coincided with a halving of the location profitability ratios and a substantial fall in the X/M ratio. The competitive advantage of UK firms improved by a lesser extent, that is, about 18 per cent. In the first half of the 1970s, while there continued to be a decline in the attractiveness of a UK location, the main explanation for the rise in the I_o/I_i ratio appeared to be the improvement in the O advantages of UK firms. In the latter 1970s, a fall in the I_o/I_i ratio coincided with a rise in the O advantages – at least until the early 1980s – and a fall in the location ratios. The position again changed in the 1980s.

The data for Western Europe are less conclusive. In the first half of the 1960s, the I_o/I_i ratio fell; this was consistent with a rise in the location profitability ratios and a fall in the ownership profitability ratios. From 1965 to 1974, the I_o/I_i ratio rose markedly; however, this appeared to be mainly a reflection of a decline in the location profitability ratios rather than any improvement in the performance of UK firms. This is a significant finding as one suspects that investment by UK firms in Western Europe is the most likely to be substitutable for investment in the UK. Since 1975, the declining I_o/I_i ratios appear to be more associated with improvements in the location ratios than decline in the value of the ownership ratios.

Other evidence also tends to corroborate these findings. For example, since 1965, the increase in the value of manufacturing imports into the UK has consistently exceeded the increase in the foreign capital stake in UK manufacturing industry. In 1965 Western European firms exported to the UK 3.5 times the value of their capital stake in the UK; by 1984 this ratio had risen to 10.0. Similarly, up to the early 1970s, UK manufacturing exports to industrial countries lagged behind the growth of the UK capital stake in foreign manufacturing industry. Since 1973 there has been a reversal of this trend but, even so, the ratio of UK manufacturing exports to Western Europe to the UK capital stake in Western Europe

222   *Multinationals, Technology and Competitiveness*

in 1984 was the same as it was in 1965, viz. 5.3. This suggests that over the last decade or so UK firms have tended to exploit the European market both by the setting up or expansion of production units and by exports. By contrast, European firms have preferred to exploit the UK market by more exports than by the setting up or expansion of production units in the UK.

SOME STRUCTURAL CONSIDERATIONS

Data on the ratios just discussed for the main manufacturing sectors in 1971–73 and 1979–81 are set out in Table 10.10. It can be seen that they broadly support the explanations for the UK international investment position offered earlier. In particular, the industries with the lowest K_o/K_i ratio in both years, that is, mechanical engineering and motor vehicles, had among the lowest ownership profitability ratios and the highest location profitability ratios, that is to say, UK-owned firms perform comparatively badly relative to foreign-owned firms, but profits in UK industry compared relatively favourably to those earned in other countries. On the other hand, British firms generally did much better in the more traditional sectors, notably food, drinks and tobacco, textiles, and paper and publishing, where the overall UK competitive environment appears to be less congenial. In the case of chemicals, the ownership advantage ratios would suggest a rather lower K_o/K_i ratio than that actually revealed, while in electrical engineering the location advantage ratios favour production in the UK; in both cases, however, there are factors working in the opposite direction.[4]

Since 1971, the MTI sectors have shown the greatest rate of increase in their I_o/I_i ratios; with the exception of chemicals, these sectors have also shown the most pronounced fall in their E/M ratios.[5] The experience with changes in the profitability of UK firms at home and abroad has been mixed, while such data that are available on changes in the performance of UK firms relative to US firms suggest that the most substantial improvements of the latter have taken place in the MTI sectors.

Other data, published in *Business Monitor*[6] suggest that throughout the 1970s there was an increase in both the UK export/sales[7] ratio and the import penetration ratio.[8] This has been especially pronounced in the case of products in industries where intra-industry trade is above average, which are also those in which MNEs tend to be most concentrated (Panic, 1980). *Inter alia*, this reflects the growth of rationalized investment by US MNEs in Western Europe, and the entry of Japan as a powerful international competitor. For it is in those sectors where US investment in Europe relative to that in the UK, together with the Japanese impact, have made themselves most noticeably felt that the E/M ratio has fallen the most in the 1970s.

To summarize, then, the data set out in Tables 10.9 and 10.10 seem to point to one important generalization about the UK's international

Table 10.10   *Some Determinants of Foreign Capital Ratios Classified by Industry 1971–3 and 1979–81*

	1971–73				1979–81			
	K_o/K_i 1971	O_A	L_A	X/M 1971	K_o/K_i 1978–81	O_A	L_A	X/M 1978
More technology-intensive sectors								
Chemicals and allied manufactures	1.49	0.64	0.77	1.26	2.02	0.68	0.94	1.52
Mechanical and instrument engineering	0.38	0.56	0.71	1.99	0.44	0.78	1.01	1.46
Electrical engineering	1.07	0.79	0.75	1.68	0.97	0.80	1.54	1.17
Motor vehicles	0.24	0.82	0.71	3.63	0.35	N.S.A.	[1]	1.09
Rubber	0.69	N.S.A.	N.S.A.	3.18	1.24	N.S.A.	N.S.A.	1.58
Less technology-intensive sectors								
Food, drink and tobacco	2.82	0.64	0.56	0.75	2.45	0.82	N.S.A.	0.47
Metal manufacture	0.55	3.13	0.60	1.34	0.84	0.80	0.54	1.09
Textiles, leather, clothing and footwear	9.66	4.29	1.09	1.08	6.19	N.S.A.	0.37	0.79
Paper, printing and publishing	2.83	0.93	1.00	0.61	1.61	N.S.A.	0.27	0.37
Other manufacturing	2.11	1.33	0.97	2.21	2.15	1.14[2]	N.S.A.	1.03
Total manufacturing industry	1.24	0.84	0.80	1.56	1.35	0.90	0.57	1.02

Notes:
[1] Both figures negative.
[2] Includes rubber, textiles and paper.
   N.S.A. = not separately available.
   Source: *Business Monitor M.3* (various editions), *Business Monitor M.4* (various editions), US Department of Commerce *Survey of Current Business* (various editions) and *UK Balance of Payments* (1986 edition). Also, *British Business* May 22 1987.

224 *Multinationals, Technology and Competitiveness*

competitive situation. Since, in the last two decades, UK firms have been improving their performance relative to firms of other nationalities in world markets, the greater part of the explanation for movements in the UK's international investment position must be laid at the door of the competitiveness of the UK economy relative to that of other countries. This conclusion supports the contention of those writers who argue that the British 'disease' or 'predicament' is primarily due to factors specific to the UK economic environment, rather than any lack of technological capability, managerial expertise or entrepreneurial drive on the part of British firms.[9] It also corroborates the findings of two studies of US industry in the UK published in the mid–1970s (Dunning, 1976; Lincoln, 1975). In explaining the falling share of new US investment in Western Europe directed to the UK, both authors stressed that, in spite of the liberal attitude of the UK government towards inward direct investment, the availability of suitably trained labour, attractive investment incentives and a congenial working and living environment, the concern of prospective investors over inflation, the perceived lack of long-range government policy on taxes and nationalization, industrial unrest, the restrictive practices of trade unions, a social security system which produced a disincentive to work, and the better growth prospects of most other European countries, all militated against the UK as a production base. Since these reports were published, the depreciation of the pound, a lower rate of inflation, an improved balance-of-payments situation, a clearer indication from the government about its long-term industrial strategy and a considerable improvement in industrial relations have done much to revive the confidence of both foreign and domestic investors.

INTERNATIONAL DIRECT INVESTMENT AND THE EFFICIENCY OF RESOURCE ALLOCATION

The final issue to be touched upon concerns the effect of outward and inward investment flows on the structure of resource allocation within the UK and by UK firms. We shall confine ourselves entirely to two questions: Do outward and inward investment flows raise or lower the UK's GNP? What effect do these flows have on the structure of economic activity in the UK?

In the previous chapter it was suggested that the economic benefits of international investment should parallel those of trade which occur as a result of the specialization of a country's economic activities in those areas which require the use of (immobile) resources in which it is comparatively well-endowed. However, in as much as international investment involves the use of at least some resources which are mobile across national boundaries, assessment of its optimum level or structure from the perspective of a particular country has to consider the relative attractions of deploying its own enterprises' mobile resources, in a domestic or foreign location, and those of foreign companies within its national boundaries.

The UK International Investment Position 225

Table 10.11 *Profitability of UK and Foreign Firms in UK Manufacturing Industry and of UK Firms in Foreign Manufacturing Industry 1962–84[1]*

UK domestic firms		UK firms abroad			Foreign firms in UK		
(1)	*(2)*	*(3)* Western Europe	*(4)* North America	*(5)* All areas	*(6)* Western Europe	*(7)* North America	*(8)* All areas
1962–65	9.3	6.0	8.5	8.7	N.S.A.	N.S.A.	10.4
1966–68	7.5	8.6	9.5	9.2	6.7	10.7	9.9
1969–71	7.5	11.3	8.4	10.0	6.3	10.7	9.6
1972–74	9.0	13.3	12.7	13.0	8.4	12.0	10.8
1975–78	12.3	10.4	11.3	12.0	7.6	13.2	11.7
1979–81	7.2	7.3	11.0	11.2	1.4	15.4	11.7
1982–84	8.7[2]	8.8	7.8	10.4	6.1	10.3	9.2

Notes: N.S.A. = not separately available.
[1]Profits are defined net of tax and depreciation as a percentage of net assets.
[2]Provisional figures.
Source: *Business Monitor M4* (various editions); *Business Monitor M3* (various editions).

As a general principle, a country which is seeking to maximize its GNP or rate of economic growth should invest abroad in those sectors in which its own enterprises have a comparative O advantage but which need to be used with immobile resources in which it is comparatively disadvantaged. By contrast, it should encourage inward investment in those sectors in which foreign firms have a comparative O advantage but supply products which require the use of its immobile resources in which it is comparatively advantaged.[10]

This proposition may be examining the profitability and structure of UK outward, inward and domestic investment in manufacturing industry. It is assumed that each of these forms of investment is a substitute for the other, but that at all times the UK economy is operating at a full employment level.[11] It is also assumed that there are no feedback effects on the domestic profitability on UK firms as a result of their foreign investments, and none on the parent companies of foreign affiliates as a result of their investment in the UK.

Table 10.11 sets out details of the profitability of UK outward and inward investment in manufacturing industry and that of investment of all firms in UK manufacturing industry for the period 1962–81, while Table 10.12 presents average performance data for selected industries for the periods 1972–74, 1975–78 and 1979–81. Table 10.11 confirms very clearly the main findings of the previous section, namely, that the profitability of UK firms abroad has been rising relative to that of UK firms in the UK, while that of foreign affiliates in the UK has continued to outpace that of their indigenous competitors.

Suppose, now, that there was no direct international investment in these years, but that the resulting loss in investment would have been made up by additional investment by domestic companies. Suppose, too,

Table 10.12 *Profitability of UK Overseas Direct Investment; Foreign Investment in UK, and UK Domestic Firms 1972–81*

		UK outward investment[1]					Foreign investment[1] in the UK[1]			UK domestic firms[1]	
		Western Europe	North America	Other developed countries	Rest of the world	Total	Western Europe	North America	Total	Unadjusted[3]	Adjusted[3]
More technology-intensive sectors	1972–74	15.1	12.4	11.0	13.2	12.8	8.0	13.3	12.2	10.2	9.4
	1975–78	12.1[1]	9.5[1]	12.7[4]	15.4[4]	11.6	7.3	14.5	13.0	12.5[4]	12.7[4]
	1979–81	3.9	6.2[1]	12.3	8.5[4]	7.9	−4.4[4]	15.2	11.8	7.7	7.6
Chemicals and allied products	1972–74	12.4	14.5	16.0	16.1	14.4	7.5	12.4	10.7	11.5	10.5
	1975–78	10.7	7.7	15.6	17.4	11.9	7.3	10.1	9.5	11.4	11.2
	1979–81	5.8	5.4	13.6	11.2	8.2	0.8	11.3	9.0	7.9	7.7
Mechanical engineering	1972–74	18.8	11.0	9.4	14.6	13.5	9.3	17.5	16.5	9.4	8.2
	1975–78	15.1	18.3	16.0	17.9	16.4	12.6	16.8	16.1	13.7	13.2
	1979–81	4.3	9.9	12.4	11.8	9.6	6.7	13.1	12.0	9.8	9.8
Electrical engineering	1972–74	15.7	9.3	10.9	7.4	10.9	8.2	15.6	13.2	10.5	10.4
	1975–78	8.0	9.9	9.1	12.2	7.7	4.3	16.4	12.9	12.3	13.4
	1979–81	2.8	6.5	11.5	14.2	8.5	5.0[4]	25.1	18.2	12.2	13.1
Motors	1972–74	22.4	7.4	−6.2	18.5	6.7	2.9	3.8	3.8	5.0	4.7
	1975–78	2.7[4]	3.4[4]	2.8[4]	3.4[4]	12.6	1.9	12.9	12.4	14.4[4]	14.5[4]
	1979–81	−6.9[4]	4.0[4]	1.6	5.3[4]	−0.5	−155.0[4]	14.1	7.7	−4.4	−4.5
Less technology-intensive sectors	1972–74	12.5	13.0	13.0	15.5	13.3	6.1	9.9	9.1	9.8	8.2
	1975–78	9.4[4]	11.9[4]	11.3[4]	15.6	11.9	6.8	11.1[4]	10.1	12.0	12.1
	1979–81	9.9	14.6[4]	13.9[4]	16.9[4]	13.7	1.7[4]	16.2	11.7	8.4	6.8
Food, drink and tobacco	1972–74	15.3	17.0	14.0	15.5	15.5	6.0	15.3	13.5	9.3[5]	N.S.A.
	1975–78	12.0	10.3	14.8	16.4	14.6	8.7	12.7	11.4	12.2[5]	N.S.A.
	1979–81	8.9	16.1	15.9	16.9	14.1	7.8	18.8	15.6	11.4[5]	N.S.A.
Metal manufacture	1972–74	1.8	10.0	14.0	26.0	12.5	10.2	3.7	5.2	8.4	7.3
	1975–78	−4.2	5.4	8.9	12.0	6.4	5.1	8.5	6.1	9.0	9.4
	1979–81	6.0	6.6	9.2[4]	13.8[4]	8.1	−1.4[4]	10.4	4.4	4.8	4.4
Textiles, leather, clothing and footwear	1972–74	13.1	9.3	15.1	11.8	12.1	3.4	0.8	2.5	11.8	11.8
	1975–78	8.7	8.4	12.0	14.2	10.4	−5.2	3.4[4]	1.3	8.1	7.5
	1979–81	7.7	7.5	16.4	15.6	11.1	−63.8[4]	24.0	2.3	6.6	4.1

Table 10.12 *continued*

Paper, printing and publishing	1972–74	11.7	11.5	11.5	16.8	12.1	11.7	9.3	10.7	9.6	9.0
	1975–78	11.3	7.6	4.8	17.7	9.8	15.3	12.9	13.6	10.9	11.2
	1979–81	22.3	17.5	5.8	11.8	16.0	1.1	18.9	15.9	8.9	4.3
Other manufacturing	1972–74	8.7	7.2	10.9	15.6	10.8	4.4	9.4	7.4	9.7[6]	N.S.A.
	1975–78	5.9[4]	11.1[4]	9.0[4]	14.6	10.3	9.5	9.8[4]	9.8	13.7[6]	N.S.A.
	1979–81	8.8	13.6[4]	14.7	18.6	13.9	2.2	11.4	8.3	6.9[6]	N.S.A.
Total manufacturing	1972–74	13.6	12.8	12.0	14.8	13.0	7.1	12.1	10.8	10.0	9.0
	1975–78	10.4	10.9	12.2	15.5	12.0	7.7	13.5	11.7	12.2	12.3
	1979–81	7.3	10.8	13.1	14.8	11.2	1.4	15.5	11.7	8.1	7.2
All industry	1972–74	14.3	14.9	14.5	17.8	15.3	8.0	13.5	11.9	N.S.A.	N.S.A.
	1975–78	11.7	13.3	13.9	21.6	14.7	10.3	14.9	13.2	N.S.A.	N.S.A.
	1979–81	9.0	11.4	14.6	18.7	13.0	6.6	17.3	14.1	9.1	7.8

Notes:

N.S.A. = not separately available.

[1]For outward and inward investment, rate of return is calculated from *Business Monitor M4* data and is defined as profits divided by net assets, where profits include unremitted profits as well as those remitted to the parent, and are measured after deducting provisions made for depreciation of fixed assets and after provision for overseas tax on outward earnings and UK tax on inward earnings.

[2]For UK domestic firms, rate of return is calculated from *Business Monitor M3* data and is defined as net income less total tax divided by net assets, where net income is gross trading profit (net of short-term interest) plus investment and other revenue income and prior year adjustments other than tax, less hire of plant and machinery and depreciation provisions.

[3]Figures for UK domestic firms are based on the *Business Monitor M3* coverage of listed UK companies. These companies are predominantly UK-controlled. Thus in 1975, 94.3 per cent of listed companies in manufacturing plus distribution (manufacturing only figures were not available) were UK-controlled. The figures, however, while excluding UK 'companies operating mainly overseas' included the overseas operations of other UK companies. This overseas component, judging by the proportion of the companies' total tax paid overseas, is significant. In the first column no attempt is made to adjust for this overseas component. However, in the second column, from the *Business Monitor M3* data on assets and profits (i.e. including the domestic UK and overseas operations of the companies) the *Business Monitor M4* data on UK companies overseas operations have been subtracted. Though there are a number of deficiencies to this process (which are most likely to operate in the direction of exaggerating actual differences in rate of return, rather than providing misleading results) it is a useful way of getting close to isolating the results of UK-controlled firms' domestic operations.

[4]Author's estimate.

[5]Food and drink only.

[6]Includes tobacco.

Sources: *Business Monitor M3* (various editions); *Business Monitor M4* (various editions); US Department of Commerce *Survey of Current Business* (various editions).

Table 10.13 *Estimated Gains and Losses to the UK as a Result of Outward and Inward Direct Investment in Manufacturing Industry*

| | UK domestic firms | | UK firms abroad | | | | Foreign firms in the UK | | Columns | |
| | π after tax | $\bar{K}_o$ | π after tax | £m gain or loss[1] | $\bar{K}_i$ | | π after tax | £m gain or loss[1] | (5) + (8) | 8 as % of |
(1)	(2)	(3)	(4)	(5)	(6)		(7)	(8)	(9)	(10)
1962–65	9.3	1,899.0	8.7	− 11.4	1,417.8		10.4	15.5	4.1	378.0
1966–68	7.5	2,523.9	9.2	42.9	1,957.2		9.9	47.0	89.9	52.3
1969–71	7.5	3,439.2	10.0	86.0	2,725.7		9.6	57.2	143.2	39.9
1972–74	9.0	5,022.6	13.0	200.9	3,971.6		10.8	71.5	272.4	26.2
1975–78	12.3	9,015.7	12.0	− 27.0	6,517.8		11.7	− 39.1	− 66.1	59.1
1979–81	7.2	14,043.7	11.2	561.7	10,230.4		11.7	460.4	1,022.1	45.0
1982–84	8.7	18,953.5	10.4	322.2	13,941.0		9.2	71.1	393.3	18.1

[1] For explanation, see text.

Source: Data derived from Table 10.12 on p. 227.

The UK International Investment Position 229

that the average and marginal rates of return on each kind of investment are the same. Then, as Table 10.13 sets out, by multiplying the net assets owned by UK firms abroad and those of foreign firms in the UK by the profitability of the UK investment by UK firms (Column 1), and deducting the result from the actual profits earned on inward and outward investment, it is possible to obtain a crude first-stage estimate of the net gain or loss to the UK's GNP. We can also calculate what part of the gain or loss is due to outward investment and what part to inward investment.[12]

The data in Table 10.13 suggest that, between the mid-1960s and the early 1980s, combining the effects of foreign investment to manufacturing activities by UK firms and investment in UK manufacturing by foreign firms, produced net gains ranging from £4.2 million in 1962–65 to £1,022 million in 1979–81. However, whereas in the 1960s the main gain to the UK economy arose from the higher profitability of inward investment, by the mid-1970s, it was outward investment which was responsible for the greater part of the benefits. By the late 1970s the gains from outward and inward investment were fairly evenly balanced; but in 1982–4 it was outward investment again which provided most of the benefits.

Turning again to Table 10.12 it can be seen that it is the MTI sectors which seem to gain most from inward investment while the LTI sectors gain most from outward investment. Exceptions include inward investment in food, drink and tobacco, and in paper, printing and publishing, and outward investment in chemicals and allied products. The table also reveals that in the non-manufacturing sector, the profitability of both outward and inward investment is considerably greater than that of UK firms in the UK.

To what extent do these gains suggest that international direct investment improves the efficiency of resource allocation in the UK? For this to be so, it is necessary to show that the profitability of outward investment is highest in activities where the ownership profitability surpasses that of foreign firms, but where the location profitability ratio least favours the UK. By contrast, inward investment should be concentrated in those industries in which the ownership profitability ratio favours foreign firms and the location profitability ratio favours the UK.

While this hypothesis has not been fully tested, the information set out earlier in Table 10.10 on p. 222 does tend to support rather than refute this. Industries which have an above-average ownership profitability ratio and below-average location profitability and/or export/import ratio also tend to be those which have an above average I_o/I_i ratio. Industries which have a below-average ownership profitability and above-average location profitability and/or export/import ratio tend to have a lower than average foreign investment ratio. Examples of the first group include textiles, paper, printing and publishing, and metal manufacturing; of the second group, chemicals, motor vehicles, mechanical and instrument engineering and electrical engineering. The main exceptions to the rule are the food, drink and tobacco industries, but this may reflect the very different product composition of UK outward and inward investment as much as anything else.

CONCLUSIONS

While this chapter has not attempted a comprehensive analysis of the causes and effects of UK inward and outward direct investment, it has pinpointed a number of features which policy-makers would do well to consider. Four of these stand out. First, although, for all main groups of economic activity, the UK outward/inward direct capital stake has fallen over the last two decades, for that on which the future of the UK's international competitive position so much depends, that is, the manufacturing sector, it has risen considerably. Second, the explanation for this trend is to be found partly in the improved international competitive position of UK-owned firms, and partly in the increasing tendency of such firms to supply overseas markets – and particularly those in Western Europe – from production outlets outside the UK. By the same token, foreign, and especially Western European, firms have tended to exploit their UK markets by exports rather than by foreign direct investment. Third, assuming that the capital invested by UK firms invested overseas would not have been invested at home, then the gains to GNP from outward and inward investment have increased over the period, apart from in the period 1975 to 1978. Fourth, the evidence strongly suggests that international investment flows have improved the structure of resource allocation in the UK economy. Foreign firms in the UK tend to be concentrated in the more dynamic and technologically advanced sectors of the UK economy, while UK firms have exploited their advantages in the less technology-intensive industries by investing overseas. Since the late 1970s, however, there is some evidence to suggest that the pattern of UK inward and outward direct investment has begun to converge (Ammin and Smith, 1986).

All these conclusions support a basically liberal policy towards outward and inward direct investment, but a recognition that, by a wide range of policies, the UK government may affect both the O advantages of its own firms and the attractions of the UK as a production base for foreign affiliates. Indeed, it may be there is less justification for the imposition of investment controls than at the time of the Reddaway and Steuer reports, partly because the UK location profitability ratio has fallen and partly because the balance-of-payments constraints are less pressing than they once were. On the other hand, as suggested at the beginning of this chapter, the concern that, by replacing domestic investment, the foreign activities of UK MNEs have had an adverse effect on UK jobs and economic growth has become more pronounced. Our answer to this argument is that, if the reasons for the rising outward investment ratio set out in this chapter are correct, the best way for the government to reverse this trend is to focus its attention on improving the locational attractions for both UK and foreign producers. What it should *not* do is anything that might damage the competitive advantages of UK firms. And this is precisely what controls on outward investment would do, as their main effect would be to lessen their presence in overseas markets of UK firms, erode the revenue base for their innovatory

The UK International Investment Position 231

activities and increase the market shares of their competitors. This point is taken up further in the following chapter.

A final comment concerns the relationship between O- and L-specific advantages. This chapter has treated them as if they were independent of each other. While, at a given moment of time, this may be so, over a period of time this is clearly not the case. The ability of firms to undertake research and development and the incentives for them to do so will be influenced by a country's science, technology and educational policy, while the ability of a firm to benefit from economies of size may rest on market size and structure. The O advantages of Japanese firms today cannot be separated from the economic and industrial strategies of the Japanese government in the 1950s and 1960s. UK foreign investment policy should then be part and parcel of an international competitive strategy that will seek to identify and stimulate the O advantages of UK firms and improve the locational attractions of the UK. If this is done, then international production, along with international trade, can play its proper role in improving resource allocation in the UK and the efficiency of its industries.

NOTES

1   See, for example, various essays on intra-industry and intra-firm trade in Giersch (1979).
2   MTI industries spent at least 2 per cent of their net output on research and development in 1982; LTI industries spent a lower percentage. It is accepted that, within these industries, there were wide variations in this proxy for technological intensity. See Dunning and Pearce (1985).
3   It being argued that an increase (decrease) in the ratio indicates the UK endowments are becoming more (less) attractive to those of competition countries.
4   In the early 1980s, a rise in the I_o/I ratio was accompanied by a rise in the O advantages of UK firms and a fall in the L advantage of the UK economy.
5   For example, Panic (1980) noted that during the period 1971–78, particularly in the latter half of this period, the E/X ratio declined most in goods produced by sectors in which foreign participation was higher than average for manufacturing industry.
6   Particularly M 10 'Overseas Trade Analysed in Terms of Industries' and MQ 12 'Import Penetration and Export Sales Ratios for Manufacturing Industry'.
7   The ratio of exports to manufacturers' total sales.
8   The ratio of imports to total home demand.
9   See, for example, the study by Hood and Young (1980) of US manufacturing affiliates in Scotland. The authors also cite the conservatism of management in corporate headquarters as a contributory factor to poor industrial relations. See, too, Allen (1976) and Phelps Brown (1977).
10 Note that this is talking in terms of comparative advantage. It is possible that UK firms and the UK may both have an absolute advantage over other firms and that the UK may both have an absolute advantage over other firms and countries in the production of one or more commodities. If there were only one commodity being produced, then there would be no outward or inward

232 *Multinationals, Technology and Competitiveness*

investment. Once two or more commodities are considered, then even if the mobile and immobile resources of the UK were superior to those of other countries, both trade and international investment are likely to be beneficial.

11 This is a crucial assumption. Clearly, very different results would be obtained from the contribution of international investment if it was assumed that without inward investment there would be unemployed resources in the UK or, in the absence of outward investment, there would be no effect on capital formation in the UK.

12 It should be emphasized that this is only the starting point to calculating the costs and benefits of international investment. But since we are primarily interested in the allocative effects of such investment, they are sufficient for our purposes.

APPENDIX STATISTICAL SOURCES ON UK INTERNATIONAL DIRECT INVESTMENT

The most carefully prepared time series of the UK outward and inward direct capital stake and international investment flows is contained in the Central Statistical Office's annual publication *UK Balance of Payments*. The most comprehensive industrial and geographical breakdown of the annual foreign direct investment by UK firms and foreign direct investment by foreign firms in the UK is contained in the annual publication of the Business Statistics Office, *Business Monitor (M4) Overseas Transactions*; the data here relate to the year 1985. The most recent periodic *Census of Overseas Assets of UK firms Abroad and of Foreign Firms in the UK* is for the year 1981 and was published in 1984, but provisional data for 1984 were published in *British Business* 22 May 1987. Previous censuses were taken for the years 1978, 1974, 1971, 1968 and 1965.

Preliminary estimates of the UK's international direct investment position for any particular year and revised estimates for previous years are published in *Business Monitor*.

Details of the UK's international portfolio investment position annually set out in the *UK Balance of Payments* and the *Bank of England Quarterly Bulletin* (usually the June edition).

Chapter Eleven

The Anglo-American Connection and Global Competition

INTRODUCTION

The first part of this chapter considers some implications of the emergence and growth of the globalization of markets and production on one of the longest and most enduring cross-border direct investment relationships: that between the USA and UK. It argues that the increasing tendency for large MNEs – particularly in technology-intensive producer industries and in consumer good sectors supplying branded products – to integrate their marketing and production activities on a worldwide basis, is having a far reaching effect on the bilateral trade and investment flows between countries. It is postulated that whatever special economic relationship the USA and UK may have had with each other in the past, this has been largely eroded by the harsh realities of the latter part of the twentieth century. Such realities include an intensification of international competition, particularly from Japan and the newly industrialized economies of the Pacific Rim; the emergence of new forms of protectionism; the emphasis on 'created' or 'engineered' comparative advantage; and, despite the movement towards liberalization and deregulation, the growing significance of government as a co-ordinator and controller of economic activity. In particular, as part of the EEC, the UK is in competition with other member states, not only for direct investment from the USA but for all forms of technological and organizational assistance; while at the same time the UK is increasingly looking to Europe and Japan for its markets and to set up co-operative alliances.

The second part of the chapter looks at some of the challenges being presented both to the UK and US economies as a result of global competition, and suggests that the governments of each needs to take a leaf out of the books of their own MNEs, and to pursue more positive and systematic strategies geared towards the provision of a favourable innovatory and industrial environment, both for their own firms and for inward direct investors. In particular, it is argued that, as the role of technology and human capital becomes more important in determining a country's comparative advantage, the task of government in marshalling

234 *Multinationals, Technology and Competitiveness*

1 *Pre–1914*   *Pax Britannica*. UK investment in the USA exceeds that of US investment in the UK.

2 *1914–1975*   *Pax Americana*. The USA becomes a substantial net direct investor in the UK.

3 *1975–85*   The balance is restored. UK investors increase their stake faster in the USA than US investors do in the UK. In 1985, UK direct investors own 30% more assets in the USA than US investors do in the UK.

Figure 11.1   *The Three Stages of the Anglo–American Business Partnership*

the resources and entrepreneurship of a nation to exploit that advantage becomes of crucial significance.

AN HISTORICAL PERSPECTIVE

The Anglo-American business partnership – by which we mean the two-way flow of capital, goods, technology and human skills and talents between Britain and the USA – has a long, colourful and generally harmonious history. At its best, it has set a shining example of the rich gains which can be harnessed from dynamic entrepreneurship and unfettered trade and investment, and the record shows that overwhelmingly over the last two centuries, the alliance has operated to the mutual benefit of the participating firms and nations.

As might be expected from any collaboration which has endured so long, the role of the two partners, and the contribution of each to the other's well-being, has varied. We can, perhaps, identify three stages of the Anglo American partnership as it has evolved. These are summarized in Figure 11.1. The first covers the period until 1914, during which time, for the most part, US industrial development was strongly reliant on immigrant labour, capital and technology from Europe, and many hundreds of subsidiaries of British firms were established.[1] New industries were founded by British entrepreneurs, and others (notably railroads) were substantially financed by UK capital. At the turn of the century, fears were being expressed by some Americans lest a large part of the US manufacturing industry should fall into foreign (mainly British) hands; as Table 11.1 shows, by 1914, the embryonic British multinationals of the day had twice the amount invested in the USA as American companies had invested in the UK, and British exports of technology and manufactured goods to the USA outpaced those of the USA to the UK.

But the economic hegemony of the UK was already on the wane and that of the USA was rising fast. If the UK had been the home of the first industrial revolution based on steam power and had introduced the modern factory system, the US was leading the world in the development

Globalization and Anglo–US Investment 235

Table 11.1   *The Anglo–American Direct Investment Stake 1914–85[1] ($ million)*

| | Total | | | Manufacturing | | |
	UK in USA	*USA in UK*	*Net UK in USA*	*UK in USA*	*USA in UK*	*Net UK in USA*
1914	700	350	+ 350	N.A.	75	N.A.
1936	873	473	+ 400	N.A.	271	N.A.
1950	1,168	847	− 321	337	542	− 205
1960	2,248	3,194	− 946	722	2,164	− 1,442
1970	2,852	5,123	− 2,271	1,391	4,909	− 3,518
1980	14,105	28,605	− 14,500	6,159	13,893	− 7,734
1985	43,766	33,963	+ 9,803	11,884	12,560	− 676

Notes: [1]Book values of net assets.
N.A. = Not available.
Source: US Department of Commerce *Survey of Current Business* (various issues).

of electrical power, the internal combustion engine, the telephone and telegraph and new managerial and production systems (Chandler, 1977). Although for most of the inter-war years, the UK recorded a net credit balance on direct investment account with the USA and there were more than 600 subsidiaries or associates of UK firms operating in the USA in 1939, this was chiefly due to the country's huge investments in services, especially insurance (Lewis, 1938). In manufactures, the USA was already accumulating a trade surplus, and her direct investment in Britain's newer industrial sectors of motor vehicles, electrical equipment and appliances, rubber products and fine chemicals paralleled in importance those of the mid- or late-nineteenth century by UK firms in US cotton and woollen textiles, carpets, steel, tin plate, pottery, cutlery, brewing and flour milling (Coram, 1967; Wilkins, 1988).

It was in the two decades after the Second World War, however, that *Pax Americana* finally replaced *Pax Britannica*, and when the US partner most dominated Anglo-American trade and investment flows. For most of this period, the Americans looked upon the UK as the bridgehead by which US goods and services could be sold to a war-ravaged and economically devastated Europe, and a Commonwealth (outside Canada) short of US dollars. In the 1950s and 1960s, US entrepreneurship, technology and new marketing and managerial methods helped spearhead many UK industries into the second half of the twentieth century, particularly the computer, micro-electronics and pharmaceutical industries which are in the forefront of many of today's technological advances. During this period, there was some recovery of the British direct capital stake in the UK (most of that which had existed in 1939 had been liquidated during the war), but even in the late 1950s, more than one-half of the capital stake was in trade-related, marketing, insurance and financial activities.

The benefits of this phase of the transatlantic business alliance were strikingly apparent and have been amply documented elsewhere

236 *Multinationals, Technology and Competitiveness*

(Dunning 1958, 1969, 1976). The British consumer had access to goods which he would otherwise not have had, UK industry was given a shot in the arm just when it needed it, and the result was a marked improvement in productivity and the UK's balance of payments. Gradually, America's ownership of UK manufacturing industry began to rise; from 3 per cent in the early 1950s to 8 per cent in 1963 to 14 per cent in 1978 and to around 16 per cent in 1985. In the past five years, during which there has been a sharp drop in new US investment in the UK, the attention of American firms has been increasingly directed to the service sectors, and particularly, to finance and banking, business services and information technology. For their part, American corporations have been generally well pleased with their UK investments; they have returned good profits, opened up new markets and provided access to a mine of advanced technology and skills.

ANGLO-AMERICAN INVESTMENT FLOWS SINCE 1970

The last ten to fifteen years have witnessed the third phase in the Anglo-American investment relationship. It has been noticeable for three events set out in Figure 11.2. The first is the economic and technological rebirth of Western Europe. This has had two major consequences. First, there has been a marked improvement in the international competitiveness of UK and Continental European companies, and with this an increased penetration of the US market. Indeed, in many industrial sectors, the technology and management gap identified by observers such as Jacques Servan-Schreiber in the late 1960s has been largely closed, and with it the dollar has depreciated relative to most European currencies. As Table 11.1 shows, the trickle of new UK investment in the USA up to the early 1970s became a torrent in the later 1970s and 1980s. However, unlike much of US investment in the UK twenty years earlier, British investors in the 1980s were acquiring existing US companies rather than undertaking green field investments; indeed, some observers believe that while US companies invested in the UK to *exploit* a particular competitive (or ownership) advantage, UK companies are investing to *acquire* competitive advantages, particularly to gain access to and monitor the latest developments in advanced technology.[2]

Whatever the reasons, by 1984, the value of British-owned assets in the USA had exceeded those of US companies in the UK, and today the UK is once again a large net foreign direct investor in the USA. Even in manufacturing, as Table 11.1 shows, UK companies now have almost as much invested in the USA as American companies have invested in the UK. And although in broad terms the economic significance of both the UK capital stake in the USA and the US capital stake in the UK is generally much greater for the UK than the USA,[3] who can doubt that the huge takeovers of US corporations by such companies as BAT, ICI, BP, Imperial Tobacco, Prudential Assurance, Grand Metropolitan, and

Globalization and Anglo–US Investment

1 The changing European scenario

(a) European recovery.
(b) The EEC.

2 The Japanese challenge

3 New technological discoveries

(a) The rising costs of R & D.
(b) Quicker rates of obsolescence.
(c) Advances in communications and information technology.
(d) The need to seek out global markets.

Figure 11.2 *1970–1985: Three Events Affecting the Anglo–American Business Partnership*

the US operations of such conglomerates as Hanson Trust, are not making as much of an impact on the US economic scene as those of their illustrious counterparts such as IBM, Ford, Esso, ITT and Goodyear and Kodak in the UK?

Britain's role in Europe, and particularly that over the past decade, has been interesting for the Anglo-American partnership for a second reason. In the first half of the post-Second World War period, the motives, interaction between, and the outcome of transatlantic capital flows were essentially bilateral, that is, between the USA and the UK. In each case, the goal of the investing firms was largely to supply domestic markets, and the interaction mainly took the form of a transfer of technology, capital and management expertise from parent companies to subsidiaries, in exchange for profits and/or fees and royalties. The outcome was usually an improved competitive performance of the recipient country and a satisfactory return on investments for the investing company.

At the same time, the extent of the Anglo-American partnership was limited in a number of ways. With a few noticeable exceptions, for example, IBM and some of the pharmaceutical companies, most of the innovating capacities of the investing firms remained in the home country. There was little specialization of value-adding activity between parents and subsidiaries, and most affiliates were viewed as truncated satellites by their parent companies and as self-contained profit centres. There was very little intra-firm trade between affiliates and their parent companies, or between US subsidiaries in Europe, or between these subsidiaries and other subsidiaries outside the USA. Because of import restrictions, the intention of some US firms of using the UK as a bridgehead to penetrate Continental European markets achieved only partial success. In the 1950s and 1960s, parallel US subsidiaries were set up in other European countries, each to supply its own national markets. In these years, the MNE as we know it today had not come of age – not, at least, as far as the Anglo-American partnership was concerned.

238   *Multinationals, Technology and Competitiveness*

Table 11.2

(a)   *US Direct Investment Stake in the UK as a Percentage of All US Investment in Europe 1950–1985*

	All industries	Petroleum	Manufacturing	Other
		%		
1950	48.9	28.9	58.2	48.7
1960	48.1	34.8	57.0	38.4
1970	31.7	31.3	35.5	23.4
1980	29.6	32.3	30.6	26.4
1985	31.8	42.4	27.8	30.4

(b)   *UK Direct Investment Stake in the USA as a Percentage of All European Investment in the USA*

	All industries	Petroleum	Manufacturing	Other
		%		
1950	52.4	27.2	50.4	60.8
1960	47.8	33.0	44.8	57.4
1970	43.2	43.9	34.0	56.5
1980	25.8	− 2.5	28.1	36.3
1985	36.2	48.1	25.5	40.1

Source: US Department of Commerce *Survey of Current Business* (various issues).

The formation of the EEC fundamentally changed this situation. It heralded in an era in which a loosely organized group of US subsidiaries in Europe began to be co-ordinated into a regional network of interrelated activities. The Treaty of Rome helped launch a single European market of 250 million people, which, while even in 1988 is neither as homogeneous nor as integrated as its US counterpart, has allowed product and process specialization and intra-firm trade in a way which has long since been common practice among US domestic multi-plant firms. The dramatic rationalization and realignment of the European investments of US companies such as Ford, GM, Honeywell and Caterpillar Tractor and ITT all testify to the fact that, from the mid-1960s onward, the exclusivity of the Anglo-American partnership was broken; economically Britain was now a region in Western Europe, and neither the UK nor the USA could escape this fact. Moreover, up until the mid-1970s, Continental Europe was attracting an increasing share of UK outward investment; indeed, as Table 11.2 reveals, by 1974 the capital stake by UK MNEs in Europe was more than twice that in the USA. Similarly, the UK share of the European capital stake in the USA fell from 52.4 per cent in 1950 to 25.8 per cent in 1980.

Over the past two decades, the economic integration of Europe has presented new challenges and opportunities to the Anglo-US partner-

Globalization and Anglo–US Investment 239

ship. The opportunity has been for US business operations in Europe to be more efficiently organized to take advantage of the economies of large-scale production and geographical scope. The opportunity for the UK has been the opening up of a market four times its own size; the challenge to the UK has been to offer at least as satisfactory economic inducements as other European nations to attract US and other FDI.

The evidence suggests that, initially at least, the UK did not fully rise to these challenges; in the 1960s and 1970s, the share new US investment directed to the UK fell steeply, as the attractions of a Continental European manufacturing base increased. Take just two examples. In 1950, the UK attracted 51 per cent of all European investment on the part of US automobile producers; by 1975 this proportion had fallen to 28 per cent. In machinery the corresponding proportions were 51 per cent and 27 per cent; in chemicals 72 per cent and 25 per cent.

Since the late 1970s, following a difficult period in UK industrial relations, rising labour costs and a somewhat schizophrenic attitude by the Labour Government towards inward direct investment, the political and economic climate in the UK has improved considerably; with it the Anglo-American partnership has gained a new lease of life. Table 11.2 shows that, outside manufacturing industry, the UK's share of new European investment by US firms has risen since 1980, with the improvement being particularly marked in the service sectors.[4]

THE JAPANESE CHALLENGE AND NEW TECHNOLOGICAL ADVANCES

To the specifically European scenario we have just described, two other events must be added. The first is the emergence and growth of the economic challenge from Far Eastern producers, and particularly from Japan.[5] Although so far confined to a comparatively few sectors, notably textiles and clothing, motor vehicles, consumer electronics and photographic and data reproducing equipment (and it is sometimes overlooked that there is considerably more American and UK direct investment in Japanese manufacturing industry than there is Japanese direct investment in the USA and the UK[6] (Ohmae, 1987)), this has sparked off a widespread and controversial debate about the appropriate industrial and trading strategies of both nations and, in particular, the role of the Central (or Federal) government in initiating and influencing these strategies.

Secondly, and even more far reaching, there has been a quantum leap in technological and organizational innovation over the past decade, which among other things has led to quite dramatic falls in the share of the value-added accounted for by 'natural' factor endowments, notably material and labour costs, while it has substantially increased that of 'created' factor endowments, for example, technology and capital equipment.[7] Between the mid-1970s and mid-1980s the labour content of traditional assembly operations, for instance, motor vehicle production,

240   *Multinationals, Technology and Competitiveness*

dropped from 25 per cent to between 5 and 10 per cent (Ohmae, 1985), while in 1984 Japanese industry consumed only 60 per cent of the raw materials to produce the same volume of production as it did in 1973 (Drucker, 1986).[8] By contrast, the costs of R & D in such industries as biotechnology, semi-conductors, computers and robotics are measured in $billion rather than $million. In the mid–1980s, 70 per cent of the manufacturing costs of micro-chips and 50 per cent of that of ethical drugs was accounted for by innovatory or product development activities (Drucker, 1986). No less important, the lead time of major technological innovations has been drastically reduced; that of the latest generation of computers and micro-chips, for example, is measured in months, whereas only five years ago it would have been measured in years.

Two consequences follow from the advances in technology and the Japanese challenge just described. The first is that because of the high and rising costs of R & D and the accelerating pace of diffusion, firms have had increasingly to seek ways and means of capturing the largest possible market for their products as quickly as possible. Even countries with large domestic markets such as the USA have increasingly had to look abroad for their sales. Today, in most modern technological sectors, exporting, licensing and FDI are not luxuries; rather they are necessities for survival. Moreover, because the major competition is often between MNEs of different nationalities, increasingly, each has to be present in the other's major markets. In his fascinating book, *Triad Power*, Kenichi Ohmae (1985) argues that, to remain internationally competitive, the leading MNEs in the technologically advanced industries need both to sell to, and produce in the three main wealth-producing areas of the world, that is, the USA, Japan and Western Europe.[9] However, the openness of each of these markets to other members of the Triad varies a great deal; as does the degree of freedom of trade and homogeneity of consumer preferences within each market. Thus, the USA is the most open market, followed by Europe and Japan, while the European market is the least homogeneous of the three, and Japan is the smallest.

The second consequence, which we shall examine in more detail later in this chapter, are the implications of technological advances and Japanese competitive strategy for the organization of international economic activity and the concept of comparative advantage, and the role of governments as shapers and influences of both.

SOME EFFECTS OF GLOBALIZATION

Let us now consider a few of the implications of the globalization of markets and production for the Anglo-American business connection. We begin by tackling the question from a UK standpoint (although incidentally much of what is written could 'apply to other European nations such as France, Germany or the Netherlands).

Since the domestic market of the UK is smaller than that of the USA, (or, indeed, that of Japan) it follows that, to compete with the giant US

Globalization and Anglo–US Investment

Table 11.3 *Total UK and European Direct Investment Assets in the USA by Manufacturing Industry 1974–85*

| | | £million | | | UK share of investment from | |
		(1) UK	(2) Europe	(3) All countries	All Europe (1)/(2) %	All countries (1)/(3) %
Total manufacturing	1985	11,884	46,515	60,798	25.5	19.5
	1979	3,547	13,952	20,876	25.4	17.0
	1974	1,792	6,109	10,387	29.3	17.3
Food	1985	2,613	10,439	11,172	25.0	23.4
	1979	397	1,647	2,611	24.1	15.2
	1974	196	717	1,524	27.3	12.9
Chemicals	1985	4,035	17,150	19,502	23.5	20.7
	1979	1,216	5,321	7,212	22.9	16.9
	1974	601	2,489	3,385	24.1	17.8
Primary and fabricated metals	1985	869	2,783	7,462	31.2	11.6
	1979	666	1,577	3,020	42.2	22.1
	1974	256	584	1,332	43.8	19.2
Machinery	1985	1,942	6,509	9,447	29.8	20.6
	1979	456	2,325	3,600	19.6	12.7
	1974	253	1,239	2,031	20.4	12.5
Other manufacturing	1985	2,424	9,634	13,215	25.2	18.3
	1979	814	3,083	4,434	26.4	18.4
	1974	485	1,079	2,116	44.9	22.9

Source: US Department of Commerce *Survey of Current Business*, August 1986; US Department of Commerce – Bureau of Economic Analysis *Selected Data on Foreign Direct Investment in the US, 1950–79*.

corporations, the need for UK firms for foreign markets is that much greater. The difficulty of exporting to America without some assistance (for example, in establishing a distributing network) encourages some UK companies to buy out or form alliances with American companies to gain a presence in that part of the Triad which still offers the largest and most prosperous (albeit one of the toughest) markets. In addition, companies like ICI, Plessey and Rolls Royce are investing heavily in the USA to strengthen their technological capacities and to be in close proximity to some of the latest innovatory advances in their sectors.

Other MNEs, such as BP, BAT and Grand Metropolitan, are doing the same to gain entry into new sectors, while still others are concluding strategic partnerships with US companies in research and development. New petroleum investment has soared, while, as Table 11.2 on p. 238 shows, the UK capital stake in manufacturing industry has doubled over the past five years, mainly through acquisition or takeovers. The number of UK electronics and biotechnology companies setting up subsidiaries in Silicon Valley in California or along Route 1 in New Jersey near

Table 11.4 *UK and European Direct Investment Assets in the USA by Industry 1985*

	(1) UK		(2) Europe		(3) All countries		UK share of	
	$ million	%	$ million	%	$ million	%	European investment (1)/(2) %	All countries investment (1)/(3) %
Mining	291	0.7	1,435	1.2	4,070	2.2	20.3	7.1
Petroleum	12,246	28.0	25,437	21.0	28,123	15.4	48.1	43.5
Total manufacturing	11,884	27.2	46,515	38.5	60,798	33.2	25.5	19.5
Food and kindred products	2,613	6.0	10,439	8.6	11,172	6.1	25.0	23.4
Chemicals and allied products	4,035	9.2	17,150	14.2	19,502	10.7	23.5	20.7
Primary and fabricated metals	869	2.0	2,783	2.3	7,462	4.1	31.2	11.6
Machinery	1,942	4.4	6,509	5.4	9,447	5.2	29.8	20.6
Other manufacturing	2,424	5.5	9,634	8.0	13,215	7.2	25.2	18.3
Wholesale trade	3,858	8.8	12,533	10.4	27,514	15.0	30.8	14.0
Retail trade	2,989	6.8	5,018	4.2	6,698	3.7	58.9	44.6
Banking	2,539	5.8	5,963	4.9	11,503	6.3	42.6	22.1
Finance (except banking)	262	0.6	2,387	2.0	4,708	2.6	11.0	5.6
Insurance	3,727	8.5	8,921	7.4	11,069	6.1	41.8	33.7
Real estate	4,623	10.6	8,821	7.3	18,557	10.1	52.4	24.9
Other industries	1,347	3.1	3,816	3.2	9,912	5.4	35.3	13.6
All industries	43,766	100.0	120,906	100.0	182,951	100.0	36.2	23.9

Source: US Department of Commerce *Survey of Current Business*, August 1986.

Globalization and Anglo–US Investment 243

Princeton is increasing rapidly. They need to be there, and their partners need to welcome them, as each can benefit from the other's presence and be better able to compete in world markets. Outside manufacturing industry, UK direct investors have markedly increased their stake in the distribution, real estate and banking sectors.

Of course, other European companies are also moving in the USA. Indeed, in the most technology-intensive sectors, German, Dutch and French companies are relatively more active than the British; although there has been a sharp increase since 1979 of UK investment in the US machinery sector. Details are set out in Tables 11.3 and 11.4. Outside manufacturing, UK companies have a relatively large share of the European capital stake in the petroleum and most service sectors, but surprisingly not finance.

In part, of course, the failure of UK manufacturing MNEs to capture a larger share of the US market reflects their lack of motivation, entrepreneurship or international competitiveness. Furthermore, partly because of the potential synergy of interests and partly to maintain a presence in mainland Europe, American corporations are 'increasingly choosing Continental rather than UK partners when forming strategic alliances.[10] Similarly, when they look for a research or production base in Europe, while they might prefer a British location, if the economic prospects offered by other European countries are thought to be better, they will go there. And, as we have already seen, over the years the share of US investment in Europe directed to the UK has fallen, as, indeed, has that of the UK share of European investment in the USA.

The message of the globalization of markets for the Anglo-American business partnership is clear. While the combination of UK business in the USA and US business in the UK is by far the most important foreign cross-border commercial relationship the UK has (and outside Canada the same is true for the USA) each nation is now viewing its association with the other, not primarily as in the past to gain new resources or markets or to earn an economic rent on the assets transferred, but more in the light of how the partnership might contribute towards its global marketing and production objectives. This suggests that American MNEs view the UK as a region within Europe, which may or may not offer the production facilities for them to advance these objectives. Indeed, this point may be generalized for all foreign MNEs seeking to establish or enlarge their European operations, and to UK MNEs contemplating new production facilities in Europe.

To this extent, the trends in the Anglo-American business partnership are illustrative of a worldwide movement towards collaborative partnerships or consortia among the world's large industrial corporations (Contractor and Lorange, 1988). To remain competitive in world markets, companies are finding it increasingly necessary to form strategic alliances with each other. Most of these alliances involve no equity participation and are usually concluded for very specific purposes – sometimes in research and development, sometimes in production and sometimes in marketing and distribution. There has been an explosion of

244 *Multinationals, Technology and Competitiveness*

such agreements in recent years. A data base compiled by Ghemawat, Porter and Rawlinson (1986) identified 1,144 international coalitions concluded between 1970 and 1982. Another, established by the INSEAD Business School in France (Hergert and Morris, 1987), contains 839 collaborative agreements concluded between 1975 and 1986.

The great majority of these latter alliances involved firms from more than one country. Most of them were contractual arrangements and were formed for very specific purposes. Some 38 per cent involved joint product development, 23 per cent production and 17 per cent product development and production.[11] No less than 63 per cent of the agreements concluded were in the aerospace, electronics, telecommunications and computer sectors, and another 24 per cent in motor vehicles.[12] To compete in today's world, co-operation is the name of the game and often that co-operation is among firms who, in all other respects, are fierce competitors.

Successful companies, such as General Electric, Philips, Siemens, Coca Cola, Boeing, ICI, SKF, Toyota, Matsushita Electric, Canon, Fujitsu, and Dentsu, are all actively pursuing this kind of strategy, and in almost every case the ventures allow the participating firms a better or more assured access to technology, manpower or markets in each of the main areas of the Triad. Similarly – and this is perhaps a more controversial point – we would contend that *nations* also need to pursue both collaborative and competitive international industrial strategies. The economic strength of both the USA and UK rests not only on the exchange of information and co-ordination of macro-economic policies, but through providing the appropriate technological and economic infrastructure and incentives for domestic and inward investment, and for their own MNEs to pursue the global strategies necessary to promote and sustain their own competitiveness.

THE CONCEPT OF 'ENGINEERED' COMPARATIVE ADVANTAGE

Like some US observers (Zysman and Tyson, 1983; Scott and Lodge, 1985; and several authors in Teece, 1987), we believe that governments can, and often do, play a very positive role in furthering the interests of their international industries, and the rest of the chapter will address itself particularly to US and UK governments which, during the 1980s, have practised a 'hands-off' microeconomic strategy, but nevertheless have often entertained interventionist but unco-ordinated macroeconomic policies.

Let us identify some of the characteristics of modern global competition. These are summarized in Figure 11.3, but we shall concentrate on just three of these. It perhaps goes without saying that globally oriented companies, like all successful companies, need to identify the right products, to produce the best organizational structures and production methods to produce them, and the right markets in which to sell them. To

Globalization and Anglo–US Investment 245

1 Companies view production and marketing strategies from a world perspective and co-ordinate their multinational activities in a way to promote these global interests.

2 Companies compete with each other across national boundaries; they are as much interested in their competitive position in (some) foreign as in domestic markets.

3 Governments can vitally affect locational decisions of globally oriented companies.

4 Unrestricted trade and investment encourages specialization of economic activity; some of this activity is footloose – at least at the time the decision on 'where' to invest is taken.

5 As there is a convergence of 'natural' comparative advantage among industrialized countries, the importance of 'engineered' comparative advantage (and the role of governments) becomes more important.

6 Governments may play a *positive* role in supporting the private sector to engineer comparative advantage, via education, economic infrastructure, research and development and industrial and trade policies. The need is for a holistic microeconomic strategy, and one which is formulated with the co-operation and guidance of those who have to execute it.

Figure 11.3 *Some Characteristics and Implications of Global Competition*

do this, they must have the best access possible to the right type of factor inputs, the right climate for innovatory activities, the right spirit of entrepreneurship, the right degree of competitive pressure (Lawrence, 1987), the right incentives for investment, the active co-operation of their workers, the right exchange rate(s) and the freedom to market their products efficiently. Our first point is that these are not 'natural' attributes to any society. They have to be created and nurtured, and governments and the institutional framework within which they operate can vitally affect the extent and way in which this is done.

Secondly, and reflecting both advances in technology, including communications technology and the reduced barriers to trade in intermediate and final products,[13] both manufacturing and service firms are becoming more footloose in the choice of location of many of their value-added activities – at least within the Triad. Certainly, they are no longer captive in their own countries. The UK not only competes with the rest of Europe for investment from US and Japanese companies, but for investment from its own MNEs. Computer-aided technology is increasingly enabling firms to separate the place of production from that of marketing and sales, even though in some cases it is encouraging the geographical concentration of separate spatially dispersed value-adding activities.

Third, because of convergence of their economic structures, governments of advanced economies are playing a much more important role in influencing the location of value-adding activity than they used to. Like it

246 *Multinationals, Technology and Competitiveness*

or not, even an apparently neutral policy towards investment by one EEC country has to be set against a positive or negative policy by another. The fact is, however, that there is no such thing as a neutral investment policy. In considering the location for their new investment programmes, firms look at the package of incentives and disincentives which affect, or are likely to affect, the outcome of their investments (Guisinger, 1985). The ingredients of this package are not only the obvious ones of wage and raw material costs, taxes, tariff or non-tariff barriers and exchange and interest rates – all of which, incidentally, are influenced directly or indirectly by government policy – they also include the availability of skilled manpower, industrial relations legislation, facilities for R & D, the protection of property rights, competition policy, employment legislation, government procurement preferences and the institutional arrangements by which government and industry can keep each other informed about each other's plans and strategies. An inappropriate higher education policy, a squeezing of government support for R & D, or a failure to offer at least as good an educational and communications infrastructure as one's competitors, may cause a relocation of both US and UK innovatory activities in Europe. An unduly restrictive or inflexible stance towards mergers and collaborative agreements may cause US firms to realign their partnerships with firms from other countries, whereas energy, labour, communications, transport costs and taxes – all of which are government influenced – may crucially affect the siting of value-added activities. Moreover, as demonstrated by the Japanese and Korean examples, by appropriate incentives and penalties, for example, differential sales taxes, import quotas, etc., governments may influence levels and patterns of consumption, and hence supply capabilities.

The features of modern global competition just described suggest that it is no longer appropriate that governments should delegate sole responsibility to the private sector for the organization of resource allocation. Market failure and market distortions are facts of life. We live in a much more complex world than our parents or grandfathers. Most intermediate product markets are closely interwoven, externalities and economies of scale abound, and an increasing amount of economic activity involves the kind of oversight and co-ordination neither markets nor private hierarchies are suited to provide. The risks and uncertainties of modern society do not neatly fit in with text book paradigms of comparative statics or dynamics; capital markets do not always provide the resources for innovation and entrepreneurship which are socially desirable (Brander, 1987); and without some socialization of risks the private sector may not be prepared to respond to the challenges of economic and technological change in the way society may wish (Ozawa, 1987). A common governance and holistic approach is needed for dealing with such interrelated issues as education, taxation, the provision of economic infrastructure, industrial strategy, R & D, competition policy and trade and investment. For those who favour a 'let the market decide' philosophy, let them ask themselves where Japan, Korea and

Globalization and Anglo–US Investment   247

Taiwan would be today if those countries had adopted such a strategy twenty years ago; or where, for that matter, Germany, France and the USA would be if they had adopted such a stance in the last century.

We are not suggesting that, by themselves, governments can or should be responsible for dealing with these issues; much less that they should pursue interventionist policies of the kind associated with most socialist-inclined authorities. But we are suggesting that, in co-operation with firms and other sectoral interests and over time, governments of industrial societies whose ability to increase living standards rests in their technological heritage and the talents of their people, can and should do much to provide the institutional framework and engineer the appropriate economic policies to achieve this goal. Providing the right economic climate means a much more *positive* role for governments than those who subscribe to this philosophy seem to believe. It is difficult to imagine how any government of a modern industrial economy can perceive it can opt out of this responsibility, and it is certainly wishful thinking, or, as Behrman (1984) more colourfully puts it, 'ostrich-like', that other governments who act in this way will cease to do so. In the words of Ron Crompton and the Bow Group Industry Committee (1986) 'The real meaning of "industrial policy" is the sum total of all government actions which affect industry. Such an interpretation of "industrial policy" is central to the approach adopted by Japan, Germany and other successful industrial countries since the War.'[14]

The days of 'natural' comparative advantages dominating the pattern of international economic activity (at least between developed nations) are over; capital, knowledge, and (increasingly) people are mobile across national boundaries. Technology, information, attitudes, skills and entrepreneurship are not natural endowments – they have to be created, nurtured and sustained. Transaction costs are an increasing proportion of total costs and governments can play a vital role either in reducing them or to assist private firms and/or consumers to bear them. A good example is the high transactional costs associated with economic restructuring which governments may seek to reduce by appropriate retraining and relocation policies.[15] And because the costs and gains of engineered comparative advantage are not (or should not be) the property of any one firm or group of firms, governments on behalf of society have to take the responsibility for this.

SUMMARY AND CONCLUSIONS

The cultural and commercial affinity between the USA and the UK suggests that the business collaboration between UK and US MNEs may bring as much mutual benefit as the collaboration by US and UK governments on major world issues, even though in world markets, and in bids to attract investment, US and UK firms and the USA and UK nations may be in competition with each other. Indeed, the Anglo-American partnership has much to teach the world, even if it is in a state

248   *Multinationals, Technology and Competitiveness*

of flux. But to do so, such firms need to have the moral support and active co-operation of their governments. This support and co-operation vary, from providing the right kind of educational, communications and technological infrastructure to enhancing the efficiency of markets for highly trained personnel and encouraging the appropriate competitive structure (Ergas, 1987). Most of all it is concerned with governments creating the right ethos among its wealth-producing constituents and working with, rather than against, these constituents in the task of meeting the challenge of global competition.

If neither the USA nor the UK governments believe in the ability of their industries to meet the challenges of the late twentieth century, then both have much to fear from the internationalization of Japanese industry and that of the NICs; if the USA, but not the UK, provides the appropriate support for its industries, then the economic decline of the UK is certain; if the UK does so, but not the USA, then the UK will increasingly have its economic future tied to Europe. If, as may be hoped, both the USA and UK governments will realize their responsibilities to both engineering and restructuring the uses of their human and natural resources, not only is the future of the partnership likely to be assured but it promises to open up a new and more prosperous era.

In the last five years, both the US and UK governments have done much to help streamline the competitiveness of their industries. Deregulation and liberalization have helped industry rid itself of many of the shackles of unhelpful regulations and control. Yet, we doubt whether either government has fully appreciated the central overseeing and positive role it can play, both in encouraging its own firms to become competitive and in attracting investment in its own country by foreign firms. US and UK MNEs have to fight for their life in the international market place, against Japanese, German and French MNEs whose very *raison d'etre* appears to be better understood by their governments.

Such support does not *primarily* take the form of subsidies or protection (although these do occur); nor does it imply that governments should 'control, manage or coerce industry' to do things it considers uneconomic to do. But this does imply a recognition of the need on the part of governments (1) to work with their industrial leaders to carve out a particular share in world markets; (2) to recognize the role of inward and outward direct investment and technology transfers in the wealth creation process; (3) to adopt a holistic and integrated economic strategy; and (4) to 'effectively perform their direct responsibilities for education infrastructure, macro-economic and social policy to provide the right skills, facilities and climate for the new industries, the global industries and the entrepreneurial industries' (Crompton and the Bow Group Industry Committee, 1986).

While we believe the participating firms in the USA and UK see the continuation and strengthening of the Anglo-American partnership as contributing to their global competitive strategy, we are not fully persuaded their respective governments do. It is to be hoped that further study of the way in which their more successful competitors have

Globalization and Anglo–US Investment 249

managed their affairs in recent years will cause the governments to rethink their own role in co-operating with their firms to improve their international competitiveness, and for their economies to become more attractive for the location of value-adding activities which are best suited to the skills and talents, potential as well as actual, of their labour force.

NOTES

1 A comprehensive assessment of UK direct investment in the USA in the nineteenth and early twentieth centuries is contained in Wilkins (1988).

2 Hence the concentration of UK chemical, electronics and computer-related companies adjacent to Route 1 in New Jersey and Silicon valley in California. For an exposition of the location of high technology industry in the USA, see Hall, Breheny, McQuaid and Hart (1987).

3 For example, in 1985, as a proportion of the GDP of the UK, the US capital stake in the UK was 7.5 per cent and the UK stake in the USA was 9.6 per cent. As a proportion of the US gap the corresponding proportions were 0.9 per cent and 1.1 per cent.

4 And within the service sectors, in finance and banking, business services, telematics, hotels and trade and distribution.

5 Other Far Eastern producers, notably the Pacific Rim countries of South Korea, Taiwan, Singapore and Hong Kong, are also making inroads into traditional Western markets, but so far their own MNEs have not, in general, constituted any substantial threat to US and European companies in their export markets.

6 Ohmae (1987, pp. 26–8) reveals that in 1984, production and sales by the 300 largest US manufacturing subsidiaries in Japan, out of an estimated 3,000 in all, was $43.9 billion, compared with $12.8 billion of direct production by Japanese manufacturing affiliates in the USA.

7 For an extended discussion of the concept of 'natural' and 'created' factor endowments, see Zysman and Tyson, 1983; Scott and Lodge, 1985; Lipsey and Dobson, 1987.

8 Over a longer period, an unpublished study by the IMF (Sapsford, 1985) estimated that the amount of raw material required to produce a given unit of economic output has declined by 1.25 per cent a year (compounded) since 1900.

9 The GDP of these three countries or regions accounted for 76 per cent of the estimated world GDP in 1985.

10 This is particularly so in some high technology sectors such as computers, electronics and biotechnology. See Contractor and Lorange, 1988; Porter, 1986.

11 The classification of Ghemawat, Porter and Rawlinson (1986, pp. 357–8) is rather different. It reveals that in industry groups that involve missing technology, development (that is, exploration) is the primary motive for coalition formation, while in the tertiary sector, marketing, sales and service are the value-added activities most often addressed by coalitions. In manufacturing, the dominant reasons for alliances were described as 'operational and logistical'.

12 Outside manufacturing industry, Ghemawat, Porter and Rawlinson identified the energy, hard metals, agribusiness and financial services sectors as those which most frequently gave rise to coalitions.

13 Notwithstanding, a regulatory environment in some service sectors and the move towards protectionism with respect to some manufacturing products.
14 Though the Bow Group does not pretend to represent the views of either the Conservative Party or the government, it is generally sympathetic to Conservative philosophies and goals.
15 The hypothesis here is that where the social net costs of restructuring are less than the private net costs, the government should subsidize such restructuring. And it is worth pointing out that most of the costs of restructuring are transactional costs, over which the government often has a good deal of control or influence.

Chapter Twelve

Multinational Enterprises and the Organization of Economic Interdependence

INTRODUCTION: SOME TAXONOMIC ISSUES

The events of the last decade have sparked off a renewed interest in the economics and political economy of international economic interdependence. Such interdependence (IEI) may be loosely defined as mutual transborder transactions between economic agents located in different national states. It is implicit in IEI that the participants act in a dual capacity, that is, both as buyers and sellers of assets, goods, services or rights. Yet, except from a macro-balance-of-payments viewpoint, there is no reason why there should be a symmetrical relationship between either particular trading partners or forms of international involvement. Moreover, the effects of interdependency will depend on the relative negotiating and bargaining strengths of the participants, and on the nature of the transactions.

The need to engage in international commerce varies between countries. International interdependence may be classified in various ways. It may be bilateral, as between two parties, or multilateral, that is, involving more than two parties. It may be symmetrical or asymmetrical. Complete IEI occurs where there are zero barriers (or incentives) to the movements of goods and services, and each country is seeking to allocate its resources in a way which maximizes its comparative dynamic advantage. Partial interdependence suggests that there are certain constraints on the extent and form of international economic involvement dictated by the market. These limitations may be either endogenous or exogenous to individual countries and are less than would occur in conditions of full interdependence. Optimum interdependence is reached when, taking account of the objectives of the country in question and, given the exogenous factors, maximum net gains are achieved; *a priori*, this may be consistent with their complete or partial interdependence. Symmetrical IEI suggests that although each country may trade or invest with others, the benefits of co-operation, or the harm of non co-operation, may be different.[1]

By its nature, IEI involves a division of labour and specialization of

252   *Multinationals, Technology and Competitiveness*

economic activity between the participating countries. In particular, the literature distinguishes two main types of IEI: *vertical* and *horizontal* interdependence. Vertical interdependence occurs between nations which have a different structure of resource endowments: North-South transactions are of this kind. This results in inter-sectoral trade and (normally) a one-way exchange of goods, assets or rights. Horizontal interdependence involves transactions in similar or identical goods and is intended to capture the advantages of the economies of scale and plant specialization; this often results in intra-sectoral and cross-hauling of technology and capital, and North-North commerce is of this variety. The *raison d'etre* for these two types of IEI, and the countries involved, are often quite different, as are the consequences for the participants.

THE ORGANIZATION OF ECONOMIC INTER-DEPENDENCE

Most of the literature on IEI tends to focus on four main questions: (1) the extent of such interdependence; (2) its structure (for example, by whom, with whom and what kind); (3) its terms (usually viewed from the viewpoint of particular countries); and (4) its implications (positive or negative) on selected economic *et al.* variables (for instance, resource allocation, economic growth, sovereignty, development goals, income distribution etc.). Only *en passant* has attention been given either to the organization of IEI, or the ownership (as opposed to the location) of the resources involved. This is because the received theory of IEI has tended to be circumscribed by the assumptions of traditional trade and micro-economic theory. In particular, the allocation of economic activity is presumed to be determined by market forces, modified by government intervention, with transactions being organized in the spot market at arm's length prices by independent buyers and sellers. In fact, however, by far the larger percentage of international transactions are fashioned and undertaken by or within hierarchies; and particularly multinational hierarchies, or in pursuance of a contract, the terms of which allow one or other of the parties a right to control or influence the economic behaviour of the other. In such cases, IEI may respond less to market signals and more to the interest of institutions which have the most influence or control over the transactions. Where the hierarchies primarily undertake market-type functions, for example, arbitrage, the organizational mode of IEI may not matter a great deal, but there are many transactions where there are few organizational options and, in some cases, for example, those which involve goods or services which have to be jointly supplied, there may be only one viable transactional mode.

The extent and pattern of IEI comprises a large number of individual and usually quite disparate, cross-border transactions, undertaken by public and private institutions. The organization of these transactions is bounded by two extremes: the spot market and multinational hierarchies. In between, there are a host of intermediate forms of contractual or

MNEs and Economic Interdependence 253

co-operative arrangements, in which one of the parties is able (via the terms of the association contract) to control or influence resource allocation in the other (what we elsewhere have referred to as quasi internalization – Dunning and McQueen, 1981), through joint ventures to 100 per cent ownership but with little *de facto* control. Which route is chosen will depend first on the nature of the transaction, that is, what is being traded, and second the exogenous conditions affecting the choice of organizational mode for the exchange between the buyers in one country and the sellers in another.

THE NATURE OF TRANSACTIONS

Transactions may be variously classified. One common distinction is between intermediate and final products, a second is between goods and services, and a third is between assets and rights to assets. Neo-classical trade theory tends to downplay trade in assets or rights primarily because assets are assumed to be immobile across national boundaries. While this may be so for some assets it is not true for most kinds of capital and for many kinds of labour.

Perhaps a more serious weakness with the neo-classical theory is the way in which it deals with technology. Technology is assumed to be a free good and instantaneously transferred across national boundaries. Neither assumption is legitimate in the modern world. We prefer to treat technology as an intermediate product. It is both the output of an asset – technological capacity – and to this extent is on all fours with the output of other factors of production – and an input into downstream value-adding activities. Technology may be traded in its disembodied form as an intangible good or a right, or embodied in capital goods (machinery), parts, components and semi-finished goods (other intermediate products) or final goods. In principle, we see no real reason for treating transactions in technology any differently from those of any other good or service.

In the last resort, all classifications are ones of convenience; for our purposes we wish to group international transactions in a way which will best identify the determinants and consequences of their organizational form. The literature has a pretty clear answer: abstracting from government intervention, it depends on the net benefits or costs of using the market as a transactional mechanism compared with the next best alternative. In conditions of perfect competition, transactions are assumed to have no cost, no risk and to have no external effects; in such cases the market, as an exchange mechanism, cannot be bettered. At the other extreme, transactional costs may be infinite and/or the transaction be completely interdependent with another activity; in such cases, to be effective they have to be internalized within administrative hierarchies.

Does the way in which international transactions are organized matter? The answer in our present context is if the extent and pattern and implication of IEI is affected, then yes! This leads to the question, Is this

254   *Multinationals, Technology and Competitiveness*

likely to be the case and, if so, in what way and to whose benefit? It is to
these questions this chapter will address itself. We shall suggest that,
while in many cases there *are* genuine options as to the modality of
exchange of goods, assets and rights, in others, and particularly those in
which MNEs are involved, there are not. Moreover, the choice of the
preferred route (by both the transacting institutions and governments), is
partly dependent on what the assumed alternatives *are*. Some commentators, for example, tend to compare the international resource allocation of MNE hierarchies with some hypothetical first best market
situation. Or, where markets are imperfect, it is assumed governments
can more nearly create or simulate a first best situation than can private
firms. Other economists either take market conditions as they are, or
how they might reasonably be, and compare this situation with that
fashioned by MNEs. At the same time, however, governments might
wish to engage in interventionism for non-economic reasons. So
replacing the market by private or government fiat may have very
different effects on the international allocation or activity, and hence on
IEI.

What determines the form of IEI? Again one might usefully turn to the
markets v. hierarchy literature originally designed to explain the presence and growth of domestic firms. Among the motives discussed for
internalization are the economizing of transaction costs (Williamson,
1981; Teece, 1981a, 1986; Hennart, 1986), the maximizing of the gains
from the economies of common governance (Buckley and Casson, 1976,
1985) and the appropriability of economic rent (Magee, 1977). The
prevalence of these phenomena is discussed in the context of transaction
and transactor/transactee specific situations which may decisively influence which organizational form is likely to be favoured (Dunning, 1984).
But what of the effects of these different organizational forms of IEI?
Will they increase or reduce it? Will they make it more or less symmetrical? What impact will they have on the terms of IEI? The answer will
partly depend on the goals and aspirations of the parties to the transactions. At a macroeconomic level, for example, we need to talk in terms
of such variables as GNP, technological capacity, economic stability,
political autonomy, income distribution, growth rates, and so on. Hypotheses need to relate to the kinds of effects which each organizational
form might have on these goals *via* IEI, and the situations under which
they have most advanced these goals.

AN HISTORICAL REVIEW

Let us now be more specific. Even the most cursory look at the structure
of IEI today suggests that it is very different from its counterpart a
century ago. Measured in terms of the relationship between world trade
in goods, assets and rights and world product, IEI is probably greater.
However it is more constrained by market failure and government

MNEs and Economic Interdependence 255

intervention, and hence less optimal than it used to be. In some areas of the world, for example, within the advanced industrial countries, IEI is probably more symmetrical than it was; but between developed and developing countries it is almost certainly less symmetrical. Most important, while in 1870 almost all IEI was organized via the invisible hand of markets, today, about two-thirds of the value of all international transactions is undertaken by MNEs. What explains these differences, and, in so far as it is possible to identify an evolutionary pattern, what is it? First, we may note several features of the world of the 1870s.

1 Countries were clearly demarcated by differences in their resource capacities and structure, and no country, except at a very basic level and apart from the USA, was in a position to be economically self-sufficient.
2 Technology, including organizational and communications technology, was in a fairly rudimentary state; moreover it was largely non-proprietary, codifiable and comparatively easily transferred across national boundaries.
3 Markets for most kinds of traded goods and assets were generally well organized, and, apart from transport costs, there were relatively few exogenous restrictions on international commerce, except those imposed by some metropolitan powers on their colonies (Svedberg, 1981).
4 The costs of organizing and monitoring institutional hierarchies (particularly international hierarchies) were high; the optimum size of enterprises was generally small; firms were single- rather than multi-activity; there was little vertical or horizontal integration; and managerial capitalism was in an embryonic state.

Under the above conditions, and with the policies of metropolitan governments encouraging a particular kind of international division of labour between themselves and their colonies (Svedberg, 1981), IEI displayed the following characteristics:

(1) The ratio of external transactions to the GNP of countries was generally high.[2]
(2) Such interdependence was primarily vertical, and between colonies and mother countries (a form of intra-country trade!).[3]
(3) There were few MNEs or, indeed, cross-border contractual resource flows.

The result of these features was that although the IEI of the period appeared to conform to the principle of comparative advantage, government fiat played an important role both in influencing the pattern and terms of vertical trade and in assisting industrializing late-comers to engineer what they perceived to be their own comparative advantages.

256 *Multinationals, Technology and Competitiveness*

THE SITUATION PRIOR TO THE FIRST WORLD WAR

Several features combined to affect the organization of IEI in the forty years prior to the First World War.

1 The introduction of new technologies and the implication of these for organizing transactions (Chandler, 1977).
2 The growth of managerial capitalism and of interdependent activities within the same institution.
3 The increasing transaction costs (including risks) of marketing several primary goods, together with the growth in demand for new products (notably oil, which favoured vertical integration).
4 A reduction in communication and transportation costs (particularly at an international level).
5 The first stages of a trend towards the international homogenization of consumer tastes, encouraged by advertising and the growth of branded goods, and also towards a common technology of production – at least within the developed countries.
6 The growth of artificial barriers to trade imposed by governments (mostly by governments of developed countries).

Apart from the last, each of the above factors strengthened the movement towards IEI. By challenging the industrial hegemony of the UK they also reduced country-specific asymmetries – at least within the developed world, but, as technology became more idiosyncratic and less freely transferable between firms, new asymmetries arose. Moreover, with the terms of trade continuing to favour the industrial countries, uneven and vertical interdependence between industrial and developing countries increased. At the same time, new forms of transactions were evolved. Sometimes these made for more international commerce; sometimes they changed its organization.

The major organizational development of the late nineteenth century was the emergence of the MNE and the replacement of cross-border spot markets in intermediate and final products by contractual agreements and intra-firm transactions. A reading of the literature suggests that an extension of the Chandler/Williamson type hypothesis for the growth of large firms to embrace the differential risks of producing in different countries helps to explain this phenomenon. As far as internalization of vertical IEI is concerned, the absence of future markets and the failure of contracts to ensure a reliable supply of primary products at a stable price is the main explanation offered, whereas horizontal direct investment reflected the inability of contracts for property rights adequately to protect the interests of the owners against the actions (or possible actions) either of competitors or contractees (Vernon, 1983).

However, the key question for our purposes is to what extent and in what ways was the pattern of resource allocation initiated by MNEs different from that which the market might have decided? How far does the common ownership of resources across national boundaries affect

MNEs and Economic Interdependence   257

their disposition? Here we would make two points. First, most MNE activity in the period before the war was one-way and therefore created a dependent rather than an interdependent relationship between the participants. Second, the reason for internalization of markets by MNEs was better to appropriate economic rent on particular assets rather than to exploit the economies of co-ordinating interdependent activities. In particular, horizontal IEI was limited in this period, both between independent firms and those under common ownership; there was comparatively little inter- or intra-firm intra-industry trade. Most new forms of international involvement in the manufacturing and service sector were import-substituting, although they sometimes led to other forms of visible trade (as in parts, components and other finished goods). To the extent, then, that foreign direct investment substituted for trade in goods, it reduced IEI. Yet, via the control exerted by MNEs over the use of the intermediate products they transferred internally, IEI was increased. But it was a different kind of IEI, and because these products were themselves a necessary ingredient for growth, such control led to more dependence than interdependence between countries.

THE RETREAT INTO PROTECTIONISM

The main economic feature of the inter-war years was the retreat into protectionism by the industrialized world and the replacement of the gold standard by managed currencies. At the same time, there was a sweeping restructuring of the industrial framework of many developed economies; this, coupled with a world recession and deflationary monetary policies (especially in the 1920s), led to a good deal of rationalization of economic activity, and with it the growth of the large and diversified firm.

There were also many international mergers and cross-border agreements in this period, some of which partially replaced FDI as a form of IEI. In the 1920s and 1930s, organizational advances also favoured hierarchies.[4] Products invented before the First World War were now becoming standardized, while in response to import controls and as a part of a defensive oligopolistic strategy, the cross hauling of investments by MNEs led to more horizontal IEI.

On balance, the inter-war years were ones of retrenchment in IEI, with a marked change in its form from trade in final products to trade in assets, rights and intermediate products. International hierarchies continued to expand, particularly within industrialized countries, the economic structure of which continued to converge. But since horizontal FDI grew in response to trade barriers, it lessened rather than increased the efficiency of IEI, and led to more rather than less dependence on the part of recipient countries. The exception was in the case of some intra-industry direct investment which enabled international oligopolists to penetrate each other's markets, for example, in oil, motor vehicles, tyres, chemicals, etc. There was also some disinvestment by MNEs in the

258 *Multinationals, Technology and Competitiveness*

primary sector, as falling commodity prices reduced the impetus for internalization. Exceptions included some of the new hard minerals and oil, and also agricultural commodities – for example, bananas, coffee, pineapples – where technical and organizational advances, including those in international transport, favoured cross-border vertical integration (Casson, 1986).

The net results of the events of the inter-war years for IEI were threefold: first the growth of IEI as a whole was halted; second, an increasing proportion of trade took the form of intermediate products and assets; third, while enabling IEI to be higher than it otherwise would have been, because it was induced by government fiat and frequently as part of an oligopolistic strategy, it was asymmetrical, partial and less than optimal. Consequently, not only did the move towards economic self-sufficiency lead to a greater dependence on MNE hierarchies; due to 'beggar my neighbour' import substitution policies, these same hierarchies were inhibited from exploiting their arbitrage functions by engaging in the kind of intermediate and final product trade usually associated with symmetrical IEI.

THE MOVEMENT TOWARDS REGIONAL INTEGRATION

The first twenty-five years after the ending of the Second World War was a period of quite dramatic change and unparalleled expansion in all forms of IEI. Until 1971, although fixed exchange rates prevailed, the institutional framework for international commerce fashioned at Havana and Bretton Woods held firm. In the 1950s and early 1960s, foreign production was largely trade-replacing because of the shortage of US dollars, while for the rest of the period all forms of IEI grew rapidly. Between 1950 and 1970, international trade and the non-equity transfer of asset rights (for example, technology)[5] expanded at one-and-a-half times the rate of world output, and international production at twice the rate. For both political and economic reasons, the reduction of regional or global barriers to trade was favoured by many countries; hence the moves towards regional integration, for instance, the EEC and LAFTA. Such integration has generally favoured horizontal IEI and the promotion of intra-industry trade and production (Dunning, 1988). Elsewhere, the development of export processing or free trade zones has encouraged vertical MNE hierarchies and inter-firm trade. In both respects, the 1960s and early 1970s were years in which the different forms of international involvement complemented each other.

The first part of the post-war period was also noteworthy for the technological hegemony of the USA, the depletion of some non-renewable natural resources in some industrialized countries and the discovery of new minerals and man-made materials. Earlier, the Second World War had sparked off a new wave of technological breakthroughs, which a war-battered industrialized Europe and Japan and some of the larger

MNEs and Economic Interdependence 259

developing economies were anxious to exploit. Among these were major advances in air transport and communications and organizational technology, which facilitated trade in intangible assets. However, because an increasing proportion of these assets were ownership-specific, their international transfer tended to be internalized by the possessing firm. By the latter 1960s, the first wave of the post-war innovations had entered the mature stage of the product cycle, while the market for intangible assets had become less imperfect. As a result, the non-equity contract began to emerge as an important form of cross-border transaction in intermediate products.

The sectoral and geographical composition of IEI also changed in this period. While the enormous expansion in oil demand dramatically affected Middle Eastern development, no less did the commercialization in new, hard minerals have a marked impact on some African and Caribbean countries. However, in almost every case, right from the start, the markets for these primary products were internalized by MNEs and the exploration, mining, processing, transport and marketing activities were closely integrated. Post-war vertical trade became increasingly intra-firm, rather than between independent parties. Rationalization in other primary sectors, for example tea, coffee, sugar, cocoa, bananas and pineapples, had a similar result. Both the destination and terms of this trade were geared to the best interests of the investing companies, rather than that of the supplying countries. By contrast, in the case of some of the traditional primary products, future markets were set up which, by lowering transaction costs, made it less necessary for firms to engage in backward international integration.

The period ended with two opposing forces at work. While the thrust towards regional integration encouraged all forms of IEI, the spread of economic nationalism among various developing countries worked in the opposite direction. First, this reflected the imposition of import controls which reduced final product trade. Next, when foreign companies tried to circumvent these by setting up their own subsidiaries, attention was directed to ensuring that their activities and conduct were consistent with local developmental objectives, and the response of the MNEs was either to invest less or to try to offset the effects of that policy. This was then followed by governments expropriating the offending affiliates, or encouraging divestment. In any event, there was increasing pressure in the late 1960s and early 1970s for MNEs to disinternalize their cross-border resource flows. However, the non-equity and equity modalities were not as substitutable as many believed, and the net result was a further cutback in IEI. The combination of the dollar crises of 1971, the ITT affair in Chile two years later and the subsequent oil crisis heralded the end of two decades of international economic expansion and increasing IEI.

260 *Multinationals, Technology and Competitiveness*

THE SCHIZOPHRENIC NATURE OF INTERNATIONAL ECONOMIC RELATIONS

The last 15 years or so have confirmed the schizophrenic nature and impact of world events on IEI. On the one hand, the world economic recession, tougher international competition and the growing industrialization of some developing countries have encouraged more inward-looking economic strategies on the part of some of the older industrialized nations; European manufacturers, in particular, have reacted to import penetration from the Far East by adopting increasingly protectionist stances. Similarly, the larger energy consuming nations have attempted to devise means of reducing their dependence on imported oil. This confirms the proposition that IEI is likely to be threatened wherever one party perceives that it is not getting a fair deal from, or becoming too dependent on, the other, or, indeed, where the levels of international competitiveness differ markedly between participants (for example, compare the USA and Europe in the 1950s and 1960s with Japan and Europe in the 1980s), and where the adjustment costs necessitated by new competition and technological change are high. This is what has happened in the last ten years, during which time some of the benefits of IEI, earlier taken for granted, have been increasingly questioned.

On the other hand, as has been set out in Chapter 1, dramatic advantages in technology, including communications technology, have encouraged and, in some cases, forced many firms to adopt global production and marketing strategies (Ohmae, 1985). At the same time, the economic and political climate towards international production, after a difficult first half of the decade, has markedly improved. Partly this has reflected a shift of many governments to the right; partly the greater acceptance of Japan, the Eastern European bloc and China of the benefits of IEI; partly a better appreciation of the kind of contribution MNEs may make to economic development; partly the growth of a number of NICs, which by and large support IEI; and partly that the economic recession· has forced many host countries to adopt a more welcoming stance to FDI – particularly that of a job-creating kind.

The net results of these changes has been to reduce the significance of vertical trade in primary products but to increase that of vertical and horizontal trade in manufactured goods. However, the outcome has varied between particular countries and sectors. Up to the late 1970s, for example, most commerce between Japan and Europe took the form of trade in finished goods; there was very little international production. In the last half decade, Japanese manufacturing imports into Europe and the USA have been increasingly subject to quotas and other barriers, while Japanese direct investment has grown substantially. It seems likely that, in the later 1980s and 1990s, this pattern will continue.

Within Europe, however, and other free trade areas, and between some industrializing developing and developed countries, international hierarchies are likely to dominate the IEI scene. Because they produce in various locations, such hierarchies are able to exploit the economies of

MNEs and Economic Interdependence   261

international plant specialization and geographical co-ordination, and to fashion different patterns of IEI than would occur in their absence (Dunning and Robson, 1987). They can also gain from *extra* plant internalizing and *intra-group* trade economies which are not available to independent firms transacting at arm's length prices. In a contribution to an International Economic Association symposium, Behrman (1987) has analysed the conditions under which MNEs are likely to promote an acceptable pattern of industrial integration and he places a good deal of responsibility on the policies of the participating countries. Vaitsos in UNCTC (1982) takes a more critical view of the role of MNEs in affecting regional integration, and argues that the cross-border co-ordination of activities among international oligopolists may actually work to the detriment of the objectives of regional integration.[6] Jacquemin (1983) has distinguished between the monopoly power and the organizational efficiency of large firms. Paraphrasing his analysis, we might argue that where the gains of increased production and transactions efficiency by MNEs outweigh any losses arising from their (strategic) anti-competitive behaviour, the IEI promoted by them may be nearer the Pareto optimality solution than that of the next best practical alternative.

A priori, however, there is no way of generalizing about the likelihood of this occurring or, indeed, as to whether Pareto type goals are acceptable to individual nation-states. Suppose, for example, that MNEs operated a competitive international framework and government intervention was negligible, would they necessarily create a pattern of IEI consistent with each country's national well-being? The answer is no – except in the case where all countries were prepared to release some sovereignty over the disposition of their resources, and be concerned only with maximizing their GNPs in the short run. On the other hand, some countries might gain a great deal from such IEI, while all may gain whenever the next best alternative is a set of transactions conducted within highly imperfect markets. In other words, hierarchies may both aid and inhibit the competitive process.

Unfortunately little rigorous research has been undertaken to establish the net effect of international production on IEI.[7] That a substantial and increasing part of IEI is now controlled by MNEs is not open to question, neither is the increasing degree of multinationality of the world's largest companies (Stopford and Dunning, 1982), and with it the internalization of decision taking. But what is yet to be established is whether or not, compared to the next best practical alternative, the production and transaction efficiency gains of such enterprises outweigh any abuse of their power to engage in restrictive business practices or monopoly pricing. On the one hand, competition to, and between, MNEs as suppliers of assets, rights and goods and services, has been increasing over the last decade; on the other, the scope of at least some MNEs for internalizing transactions has also risen. The net effect on the extent, form and terms of IEI, although likely to be important, remains as uncertain as it has ever been.

262   *Multinationals, Technology and Competitiveness*

CONCLUSIONS

The organizational form of IEI has dramatically changed over the past century, from being largely determined by market forces to being determined by MNE hierarchies and governments. This has had important effects on the extent, character and terms of IEI. While the evidence supports the view that without international hierarchies IEI would be less than it is, it also suggests that such hierarchies have probably led to more asymmetrical vertical interdependence and have fashioned regional integration based on intra-firm transactions between international oligopolists. Moreover, while MNEs have helped aid economic structuring, particularly in some of the larger developed countries, their preference for centralizing their high value-added activities in their home countries may well have frustrated the efforts of some host countries to promote these activities for themselves. Owing to the increasing role of transaction economies in explaining the growth of large firms, however, and given the inherent imperfection of some markets, MNE activity has probably made for a more efficient structure and organization of IEI than would otherwise have occurred. Governments have played their roles, both in restricting IEI through import-substituting activities and in controlling the terms on which international production or technology transfers (aimed at replacing trade in goods) may be concluded. More generally, their anti-trust and competition policies have also affected the extent to which cross-border mergers and alliances have been permitted.

Over the past century, there have been swings both in the extent of IEI and in its character. IEI in trade in goods reached its zenith in the years before the First World War and after the Second World War. It plumbed to its nadir in the inter-war years, and there are fears that there will be another downswing in the 1980s. Non-trade forms of international involvement have continued to grow throughout the century, and in quantum terms and relative to trade in goods are more important today than they have ever been. Yet the extent to which such activities have been dominated by MNEs has shifted over the years,[8] as have their effects on IEI.

In the 1950s and 1960s, the hegemony of MNEs as suppliers of intangible assets and rights reached its peak. Since then, the source of these assets has widened, and the international market for many of them has improved. The international capital market is flourishing and many kinds of technology and management services are now widely available; for both economic and strategic reasons both vertical and horizontal alliances[9] have expanded rapidly. In some cases such transactions, and particularly those concluded among MNEs, have complemented FDI; in others, especially those concluded between developed and developing firms, they have replaced international production. The increasingly distinctive character of the large international firm is its ability to choose and organise the appropriate cross-border intra- or inter-firm transactions, and it is this capacity and the resulting effect on resource allocation which, for good or bad, has had – and for the foreseeable

MNEs and Economic Interdependence 263

future seems likely to have – the most far-reaching effect on both the location and ownership of international economic activity.

NOTES

1 For example, A may buy an essential raw material from B who is a monopolist, while selling a variety of goods to B under conditions of perfect competition.
2 An exception being those economies culturally or geographically isolated from the mainstream of economic activity, e.g. Japan and some developing countries.
3 That is, in a variety of ways home countries were able to restrict their colonies in what they produced and with whom they traded; this was a form of internalization in that home countries in attempting to advance their own interests controlled the impact of market forces on their colonies. For further details see, for example, Svedberg (1981).
4 Such as the financial control systems introduced by Dupont and General Motors, and the organizational innovations pioneered by the Bell system which helped free businesses from the dis-economies of scale inherent in the military form of organization (Quirin, 1980).
5 Measured in terms of the growth of royalty and fees of US firms.
6 As particularly experienced by some smaller members of the Latin American Free Trade Area, described in UNCTC (1982).
7 Exceptions include the work of Pelkmans (1984) and Robson (1987). See also, a special issue of the *Journal of Common Market Studies*, entitled 'Multinational corporations and European integration', edited by Peter Robson and John Dunning in December 1987.
8 As it has between countries and sectors.
9 For example, licensing and technical assistance agreements, collaborative arrangements, franchising, management contracts, etc.

References

Allen, G. C. (1976), *The British Disease* (London: Institute of Economic Affairs).

Ammin, A. and Smith, I. (1956), 'The internationalisation of production and its implications for the UK', in A. Ammin and J. Goddard (eds), *Technical Change, Industrial Restructuring and Regional Development* (London: Allen & Unwin).

Archer, H. (1986), 'An eclectic approach to the historical study of UK multinational enterprises', PhD thesis, University of Reading.

Baranson, J. (1976), 'A new generation of technology exports', *Foreign Policy*, 25, winter 1976–77.

Baranson, J. (1979), *Technology Transfer to Developing Countries* (New York: Praeger).

Behrman, J. N. (1984), *Industrial Policies: International Restructuring and Transnationals* (Lexington: D C Heath).

Behrman, J. N. (1987), 'Industrial integration and multinational enterprises' in J. H. Dunning and M. Usui (eds) *Structural Change, Economic Interdependence and World Development*, Vol. 4 (London and Basingstoke: Macmillan).

Behrman, J. N. and Fischer, W. A. (1980), *Overseas R and D Activities of Transnational Corporations* (Cambridge, Mass: Oelgeschlager Gunn and Hain).

Bergsten, C. F. (1974), 'Coming investment wars?' *Foreign Affairs*, 53, October, pp. 135–52.

Bergsten, C. F., Horst, T. and Moran, T. H. (1978), *American Multinationals and American Interests* (Washington, DC: The Brookings Institution).

Boarman, P. M. and Schollhammer, H. (eds) (1975), *Multinational Corporations and Governments* (New York: Praeger).

Brander, J. A. (1987), 'Shaping comparative advantage: trade policy, industrial policy and economic performance', in R. G. Lipsey and W. Dobson (eds), *Shaping Comparative Advantage* (Toronto: C. D. Howe Institute).

Brash, D. T. (1966), *American Investment in Australian Industry* (Canberra: Australian National University Press).

Brech, M. and Sharp, M. (1984), *Inward Investment: Policy Options for the United Kingdom* (London: Routledge & Kegan Paul).

Buckley, P. J. and Casson, M. C. (1976), *The Future of the Multinational Enterprise* (London: Macmillan).

Buckley, P. J. and Casson, M. C. (1985), *The Economic Theory of the Multinational Enterprise* (London: Macmillan).

Buckley, P. J. and Roberts, B. R. (1982), *European Direct Investment in the USA before World War I* (London: Macmillan).

Burstall, M. L. (1979), *The Transfer of Technology in the Pharmaceutical Sector* DSTI/SPR/79.25 (Paris: OECD).

Burstall, M., Dunning, J. H. and Lake, A. (1981), *Multinational Enterprises, Governments and Technology – The Pharmaceutical Industry* (Paris: OECD).

Burstall, M. and Senior, I. (1985), *The Pharmaceutical Industry of the European Community – Concentration, Competition and Competitive Strength* (Brussels: EEC).

References 265

Business International (1981), *Locating a West European Office* (Geneva: Business International).

Business Statistics Office (various dates), *Business Monitor*, M4, M10 and M12Q (London: HMSO).

Cantwell, J. A. (1985), *Technological Competition between European and US Companies in the Post-War Period*, Report submitted to the EEC, October.

Cantwell, J. A. (1987a), *The Role of Foreign Direct Investment in Development in Africa*, Report prepared for World Bank (mimeo).

Cantwell, J. A. (1987b), 'The reorganisation of European industries after integration: selected evidence on the role of multinational enterprise activities', *Journal of Common Market Studies*, xxvi, pp. 127–51.

Cantwell, J. A. (1988), *Technological Innovation and Multinational Companies*, Oxford: Basil Blackwell.

Cantwell, J. A. and Dunning, J. H. (1985), *The New Forms of Involvement of British Firms in the Third World*, Report submitted to the OECD, Paris.

Casson, M. C. and associates (1986), *Multinationals and World Trade* (London: Allen & Unwin).

Casson, M. C. (1987), *The Firm and the Market* (Oxford: Basil Blackwell).

Caves, R. E. (1980), 'Investment and location policies of multinational companies', *Zeitschrift fur Volkswirtschaft und Statistik*, 3, pp. 321–7.

Caves, R. E. (1982), *Multinational Enterprises and Economic Analysis* (Cambridge: Cambridge University Press).

Central Statistical Office (1978), *UK Balance of Payments 1967–77* (London: HMSO).

Chandler, A. D. Jr. (1976), 'The development of modern management structure in the U.S. and U.K.', in L. Hannah (ed.), *Management Strategy and Business Development* (London: Macmillan).

Chandler, A. D. Jr. (1977), *The Visible Hand: the Managerial Revolution in American Business* (Cambridge, Mass: Harvard University Press).

Chenery, H. (1977), 'Transitional growth and world industrialization', in B. Ohlin, P. O. Hesselborn and P. M. Wijkmar, *The International Allocation of Economic Activity* (London and Basingstoke: Macmillan).

Chenery, H. (1979), *Structural Change and Development Policy* (Oxford: Oxford University Press.

Chenery, H., Robinson, S., and Syrquin, M. (1986), *Industrialization and Growth* (Oxford: Oxford University Press).

Cohen, R. B. (1975), *Multinational Firms and Asian Exports* (New Haven: Yale University Press).

Contractor, F. J. (1980), 'The composition of licensing fees and arrangements as a function of economic development of technology recipient nations', *Journal of International Business*, *XI*, winter, pp. 47–62.

Contractor, F. J. and Lorange, P. (1988), *Cooperative Strategies in International Business* (Lexington, Mass: D.C. Heath).

Coram, T. C. (1967), *The Role of British Capital in the Development of the United States 1600–1914*, MSc. Economic thesis (Southampton: University of Southampton).

Crompton, R. and the Bow Group Industry Committee (1986), *Winning in Tomorrow's World: A Future Industrial Policy for the UK* (London: Bow Publications).

Davidson, W. D. and McFetridge, D. G. (1984), 'International technology transactions and the theory of the firm', *Journal of Industrial Economics*, *32*, pp. 253–64.

Deutsche Bundesbank (1965), *Monthly Report*, vol. 17, no. 12, December.

Deutsche Bundesbank (1980), *Monthly Report*, vol. 32, no. 4, April.

Donges, J. B. and Riedel, J. (1977), 'The expansion of manufactured exports in developing countries: an empirical assessment of supply and demand issues', *Weltwirtschaftliches Archiv, 113*, no. 1, pp. 58–87.

Dosi, G. (1983), 'Technological paradigm and technological trajectories', in C. Freeman (ed.) *Long Waves in the World Economy* (London: Butterworth).

Doz, Y. (1987), 'International industries: fragmentation versus globalization', in Guile, B. R. and Brooks, H. (eds), *Technology and Global Industry* (Washington: National Academy Press).

Drucker, P. F. (1986), 'The changed world economy', *Foreign Affairs, 64*, pp. 768–91.

Dunning, J. H. (1958), *American Investment in British Manufacturing Industry* (London: Allen & Unwin).

Dunning, J. H. (1970), 'Technology, United States investment, and European economic growth', in C. P. Kindleberger (ed.), *The International Corporation: a Symposium* (Cambridge, Mass: MIT Press).

Dunning, J. H. (1971a), 'United States foreign investment and the technological gap', in C. P. Kindleberger and A. Shonfield (eds), *North American and Western European Economic Policies* (London and Basingstoke: Macmillan).

Dunning, J. H. (1971b), *Studies in International Investment* (London: Allen & Unwin).

Dunning, J. H. (1972), *The Location of International Firms in an Enlarged EEC: An Exploratory Paper*, Manchester Statistical Society Occasional Paper.

Dunning, J. H. (ed.) (1974), *Economic Analysis and the Multinational Enterprise* (London: Allen & Unwin).

Dunning, J. H. (1976), *US Industry in Britain* (London: Wilton House Publications).

Dunning, J. H. (1977), 'Trade, location of economic activity and the multinational enterprise; a search for an eclectic approach', in B. Ohlin, P. O. Hesselborn and P. J. Wijkman (eds), *The International Allocation of Economic Activity* (London: Macmillan).

Dunning, J. H. (1979), 'Multinational mining companies and governments; a new detente?', *Multinational Business*, no. 1, pp. 12–18.

Dunning, J. H. (1981), *International Production and the Multinational Enterprise* (London: Allen & Unwin).

Dunning, J. H. (1983), 'Changes in the pattern of international production: the last 100 years', in M. C. Casson (ed.), *The Growth of International Business* (London: Allen & Unwin).

Dunning, J. H. (1984), 'Non-equity forms of foreign economic involvement and the theory of international production', in R. W. Moxon, T. W. Roehl and J. F. Truit (eds), *International Business Strategies in the Asia-Pacific Region* (Greenwich, Conn: JAI Press).

Dunning, J. H. (1986), *Japanese Participation in British Industry* (London: Croom Helm).

Dunning, J. H. (1988), *Explaining International Production* (London: Allen & Unwin).

Dunning, J. H. and Cantwell, J. A. (1983), 'American direct investment and European technological competitiveness', *L'Actualité Economique*, July–September, pp. 341–79.

Dunning, J. H. and Cantwell, J. A. (1987), *The IRM Directory for Statistics of International Investment and Production* (Basingstoke: Macmillan Reference Books).

References

Dunning, J. H. and Cantwell, J. A. (1988), 'The changing role of MNEs in the creation and diffusion of technology', in F. Arcangeli, P. A. David and G. Dosi (eds), *The Diffusion of New Technology* (Oxford: Oxford University Press).

Dunning, J. H. and McQueen, M. (1981), 'The eclectic theory of International Productions: a case study of the international hotel industry', *Managerial and Decision Economics*, 2, December, pp. 197–210.

Dunning, J. H. and Pearce, R. D. (1985), *The World's Largest Industrial Enterprises, 1962–1983* (Farnborough: Gower).

Dunning, J. H. and Robson, P. (1987), 'Multinational corporation integration and regional economic integration', *Journal of Common Market Studies*, XXVI, pp. 103–25.

Dunning, J. H. and Walker, P. (1982), *The Competitiveness and Allocative Efficiency of UK Manufacturing Industry and Foreign Direct Investment* (mimeo).

Dunning, J. H. and Webster, A. (eds) (1989), *Structural Change and the World Economy* (London: Routledge).

Eatwell, J. (1982), *Whatever Happened to Britain?* (London: Duckworth).

Economist (1987), 'Molecules and markets', *Economist* (Supplement p. 14), 7–13 February.

Ergas, H. (1987), 'Does technology policy matter?' in B. R. Guile and H. Brooks, *Technology and the World Economy* (Washington: National Academy Press).

Etemed, H. and Seguin Dulude, L. (1985), 'R & D and patenting patterns in 25 large MNEs', paper presented to the Association of Administrative Science of Canada Annual Congress, Montreal, May.

European Economy (1979), *Industrial Structure and Trade Specialisation*, no. 4, November, pp. 88–98.

Foreman-Peck, J. (1986), 'The motor industry', in M. C. Casson *et al.*, *Multinationals and World Trade: Vertical Integration and the Division of Labour in World Industries* (London: Allen & Unwin).

Franko, L. (1976), *The European Multinationals* (Stamford, Conn: Greyback).

Franko, L. (1985), *Global Corporate Competition: Who's Winning, Who's Losing and Why?* (mimeo).

Garies, H. (1971), 'Structure and functional aspects of a multinational pharmaceutical record organisation', *Lex et Scientia*, 8.

Ghemawat, P., Porter, M. E. and Rawlinson, R. A. (1986), 'Patterns of international coalition activity', in M. Porter (ed.), *Competition in Global Industries* (Harvard: Harvard Business School Press).

Ghoshal, S. and Bartlett, C. A. (1987), *Organizing for Innovations: Case of the Multinational Corporation*, Fontainebleau: INSEAD Working Papers, February.

Giersch, H. J. B. (ed.) (1979), *On the Economics of Intra-Industry Trade* (Tubingen: Mohr).

Gilpin, R. (1975), *US Power and the Multinational Corporation* (London: Macmillan).

Graham, E. M. (1981), *The Terms of Transfer on Technology to the Developing Nations: a Survey of the Major Issues. North-South Technology Transfer, the Adjustments Ahead* (Paris: OECD).

Graham, E. M. (1985), 'Intra-industry direct foreign investment, market struc-

268 *Multinationals, Technology and Competitiveness*

ture, firm rivalry and technological performance', in A. Erdilek (ed.), *Multinationals as Mutual Invaders* (London: Croom Helm).

Gruber, W., Mehta, D. and Vernon, R. (1967), 'The Rand D factor in international trade and internatonal investment of United States industries', *Journal of Political Economy*, February, pp. 20–37.

Guisinger, S. and associates (1985), *Investment Incentives and Performance Requirements* (New York: Praeger).

Hakanson, L. and Zander, U. (1986), *Managing International Research and Development* (Stockholm: Sverges Merkanforbund).

Hall, P., Breheny M., McQuaid D. and Hart D. (1987), *Western Sunrise* (London: Allen & Unwin).

Hawkins, R. G. and Gladwin, T. N. (1981), 'Conflicts in the international transfer of technology: a US home-country view', in T. Sagafi-Nejad, R. W. Moxon and H. V. Perlmutter (eds), *Technology Transfer Control Systems; Issues, Perspectives and Implications* (Elmsford, NY: Pergammon Press).

Helleiner, G. K. (1975), 'The role of multinational corporations in the less developed countries' trade in technology', *World Development*, *3*, no. 4, April, pp. 161–90.

Helleiner, G. K. (1981), *Intrafirm Trade and the Developing Countries* (London: Macmillan).

Hennart, J. F. (1986), *A Theory of Multinational Enterprise* (Ann Arbor: University of Michigan Press).

Hergert, M. and Morris, D. (1987), 'Trends in international collaborative agreements' in F. Contractor and P. Lorange (eds), *Cooperative Strategies in International Business* (New York: Praeger).

Hirsch, S. (1976), 'An international trade and investment theory of the firm', *Oxford Economic Papers*, *28*, pp. 258–70.

Hood, N. and Young, S. (1980), *European Development Strategies of US-Owned Manufacturing Companies Located in Scotland* (Edinburgh: HMSO).

Hood, N. and Young, S. (1981), 'British policy and inward direct investment', *Journal of World Trade Law*, *15*, no. 3, May–June, pp. 231–50.

Hood, N. and Young, S. (1982), 'U.S. multinational R & D: corporate strategies and policy implications for the U.K.', *Multinational Business*, no. 2, pp. 10–23.

Horst, T. (1974), American exports and foreign direct investment, Harvard Institute of Economic Research Discussion Paper no. 362, May.

Houston, T. and Dunning, J. H. (1976), 'U.K. industry abroad', *Financial Times*.

Hufbauer, G. C. (1970), 'The impact of national characteristics and technology on the commodity composition of trade in manufactured goods', in R. Vernon (ed.), *The Technology Factor in International Trade* (New York: Columbia University Press).

Hufbauer, G. C. and Adler, M. (1968), *US Manufacturing Investment and the Balance of Payments*, Tax Policy Research Study no. 1 (Washington, DC: US Treasury Department).

Hymer, S. (1970), 'The efficiency '(contradictions) of multinational corporations', *American Economic Review*, *60*, May, pp. 441–8.

Hymer, S. (1976), *The International Operations of National Firms: A Study of Direct Investment*, PhD Thesis (Cambridge, Mass: MIT Press).

Hymer, S. and Rowthorn, R. (1970), 'Multinational corporations and international oligopoly: the non-American challenge', in C. P. Kindleberger (ed.), *The International Corporation: A Symposium* (Cambridge, Mass: MIT Press).

References 269

Jacquemin, A. (1983), *Organisational and Industrial Actions for Efficiency and Market Power: An Integrated Approach* (mimeo).

Johnson, H. G. (1975), 'Technological change and comparative advantage: an advanced country's viewpoint', *Journal of World Trade Law*, 9, January–February, pp. 1–14.

Kaldor, N. (1985), *Economics Without Equilibrium* (Cardiff: University College Cardiff Press).

Katrak, H. (1981), 'Multinational firms' exports and host country commercial policy', *Economic Journal*, 91, pp. 454–65.

Kawaguchi, N. B. (1978), 'The role of Japanese firms in the manufactured exports of developing countries', unpublished manuscript, Washington, DC: World Bank, November.

Keesing, D. B. (1978), 'Developing countries' exports of textiles and clothing: perspectives and policy changes', unpublished manuscript, Washington, DC: World Bank, May

Khan, K. M. (ed.) (1987), *Multinationals of the South* (London: Francis Pinter).

Kindleberger, C. P. and Shonfield, A. (eds) (1971), *North American and Western European Economic Policies* (London and Basingstoke: Macmillan).

Knickerbocker, F. T. (1973), *Oligopolistic Reaction and the Multinational Enterprise* (Cambridge, Mass: MIT Press).

Kogut, B. (1985), 'Designing global strategies: profiting from operational flexibility', *Sloan Management Review*, 26, Fall, pp. 27–38.

Kojima, K. (1978), *Direct Foreign Investment* (London: Croom Helm).

Koopman, K. and Montias, J. M. (1971), 'On the description and comparison of economic systems, in A. Eckstein (ed.), *Comparison of Economic Systems* (California: University of California Press).

Krugman, P. (1981), 'Intra-industry specialisation and the gains from trade', *Journal of Political Economy*, 89, pp. 959–73.

Lake, A. (1976a), 'Transnational activity and market entry in the semiconductor industry. *National Bureau of Economic Research Working Paper*, 126, March.

Lake, A. (1976b), 'Foreign competition and the UK pharmaceutical industry', *National Bureau of Economic Research Working Paper*, 155, November.

Lake, A. W. (1979), 'Technology creation and technology transfer by multinational firms', in R. G. Hawkins (ed.), *The Economic Effects of Multinational Corporations* (Greenwich, Conn: JAI Press).

Lall, S. (1979), 'Developing countries as exporters of technology, a preliminary analysis', in H. Giersch (ed.), *International Development and Resource Transfer* (Tubingen: Mohr).

Lall, S. (1980), 'Monopolistic advantages and foreign involvement by US manufacturing industry', *Oxford Economic Papers*, 32, pp. 102–22.

Lall, S. (1983), *The New Multinationals* (Chichester and New York: John Wiley).

Lall, S. and Streeten, P. (1977), *Foreign Investment, Transnational and Developing Countries* (London and Basingstoke: Macmillan).

Landi, J. (1985), *Vertical Corporate Linkages and Technology Diffusion: The Case of Multinational Enterprises in the Nigerian Economy*, Ph.D Thesis, University of Reading.

Lawrence, P. R. (1987), 'Competition: a renewed focus for industrial policy', in D. J. Teece (ed.), *The Competitive Challenge* (Cambridge, Mass: Ballinger).

Lewis, C. (1938), *America's Stake in International Investment* (Washington, DC: Brookings Institution).

270 *Multinationals, Technology and Competitiveness*

Lim Lyc and Pang Eng Fong (1982) 'Vertical linkages and multinational enterprises in developing countries', *World Development*, *10*, pp.585–95.

Lincoln, R. A. (1975), *US Direct Investment in the UK*, London: Economist Intelligence Unit, QER Special no. 23.

Lipsey, R. and Kravis, I. B. (1985), 'The competitive position of US manufacturing firms', *Banca Nationale del Lavoro, Quarterly Review*, no. 153, pp. 127–54.

Lipsey, R. and Kravis, I. B. (1987), 'The competitiveness and comparative advantage of US multinationals 1957–1984', *Banca Nationale del Lavoro Quarterly Review*, no. 161, pp. 147–65.

Lodge, G. C. and Vogel, E. F. (eds) (1987), *Ideology and National Competitiveness* (Boston: Harvard Business School Press).

Magee, S. P. (1977a), 'Information and the multinational corporation. An appropriability theory of foreign direct investment', in J. N. Bhagwati (ed.), *The New International Economic Order* (Cambridge, Mass: MIT Press).

Magee, S. P. (1977b), 'Multinational corporations, the industry technology cycle and development', *Journal of World Trade Law*, *11*, July–August.

Magee, S. P. (1981), 'The appropriability theory of the multinational corporation, *Annals of the American Academy of Political and Social Science*, *458*, November.

Mansfield, E. (1974), 'MNEs and technology', in J. H. Dunning (ed.), *Economic Analysis and the Multinational Enterprise* (London: Allen & Unwin).

McGraw, T. K. (ed.) (1986), *America versus Japan* (Boston: Harvard Business School Press).

Meyer, H. E. (1978), 'Those worrisome technology exports', *Fortune*, *22*, May.

Morgan, A. (1978), 'Foreign manufacturing by UK firms', in F. Blackaby (ed.), *De-Industrialisation* (London: Heinemann).

National Science Foundation (1974), *The Effects of International Technology Transfers on US Economy* (Washington, DC: National Science Foundation).

Nayyar D. (1978), 'Transnational corporations and manufactured exports from poor countries', *Economic Journal*, *88*, March, pp. 59–84.

NEDO (1987a), *A New Focus on Pharmaceuticals* (London: HMSO).

NEDO (1987b), *Pharmaceuticals. Focus on R & D* (London: National Economic Development Office).

Nicholas, S. J. (1982), 'British multinational investment before 1939', *Journal of European Economic History*, *XI*, winter, pp. 605–30.

OECD (1977), Data concerning the balance of technological payments in certain OECD member countries: statistical data and methodological analysis, unpublished document DSTI/SPR 77.2, Paris, November.

OECD (1979a), *Trends in Industrial R & D in Selected OECD Member Countries, 1967–1975*, Paris, July.

OECD (1979b), *Impact of Multinational Enterprises on National Scientific and Technical Capacities: the Food Industry*, Paris, August.

OECD (1981), *North/South Technology Transfer. The Adjustments Ahead*, Paris.

Ohmae, K. (1985), *Triad Power* (New York: The Free Press).

Ohmae, K. (1987), *Beyond National Borders* (Homewood: Dow Jones–Irwin).

Oman, C. (1984), *Changing International Investment Strategies. The New Forms of Investment in Developing Countries*, OECD, Development Centre, Paris.

References 271

Ozawa, T. (1985), 'Macroeconomic factors affecting Japan's technology inflows and outflows, the post-war experience', in N. Rosenberg and C. Frischtak (eds), *International Technology Transfer: Concepts, Measures and Comparisons* (New York: Praeger).

Ozawa, T. (1987), 'Can the market alone manage structural upgrading? A challenge posed by economic interdependence' in J. H. Dunning and M. Usui (eds), *Structural Change, Economic Interdependence and World Development, Vol. 4, Economic Interdependence* (London and Basingstoke: Macmillan).

Panic, M. (1980), 'UK manufacturing industry: international integration and trade performance', *Bank of England Quarterly Bulletin*, March, pp. 42–55.

Parry, T. G. (1980), *The Multinational Enterprise, International Investment and Host-Country Imports* (Greenwich, Conn: JAI Press).

Pavitt, K. (1987), 'International patterns of technological accumulation', in N. Hood and J. E. Vahlner (eds), *Strategies in Global Competition* (Chichester and New York: John Wiley).

Pearce, R. D. (1983), 'Industrial diversification amongst the world's leading multinational enterprises', in M. C. Casson (ed.), *The Growth of International Business* (London: Allen & Unwin).

Pearce, R. D. (1987), 'The internationalisation of research and development by leading enterprises: an empirical study', University of Reading, Discussion Papers in International Investment and Business Studies, January.

Pelkmans, J. (1984), *Market Integration in the European Community* (The Hague: Martimus Nijhoff).

Perlmutter, H. (1969), 'The tortuous evolution of the multinational enterprise', *Columbia Journal of World Business*, pp. 9–18.

Phelps Brown, A. (1977), 'What is the British predicament?', *Three Banks Review*, December, pp. 3–29.

Porter, M. E. (ed.) (1986), *Competition in Global Industries* (Boston: Harvard Business School Press).

Poznanski, K. Z. (1981), Technology transfer from the West to Eastern Europe, paper read to Conference on MNEs in Latin America and Eastern Europe, Indiana University, March.

Quinn, J. B. (1987), 'The impact of technology in the service sector', in B. R. Guile and H.Brooks (eds), *Technology and Global Industry* (Washington: National Academy Press).

Reddaway, W. C., Potter, S. J. and Taylor, C. T. (1968), *The Effects of UK Direct Investment Overseas: Final Report* (Cambridge, Mass: Cambridge University Press).

Robinson, R. D. (1978), *International Business Management* (Hinsdale, Ill: The Dryden Press).

Robson, P. (1987), *The Economics of International Integration* (London: Allen & Unwin).

Ronstadt, R. C. (1977), *Perspectives and Development Abroad by US Multinationals* (New York: Praeger).

Root, F. R. and Ahmed, A. A. (1978), 'The influence of policy instruments on manufacturing direct investment in developing countries', *Journal of International Business Studies*, 9, winter, pp. 81–93.

Rosenberg, N. (1976), *Perspectives on Technology* (Cambridge: Cambridge University Press).

Rosenberg, N. (1981), 'The international transfer of industrial technology: past

272 *Multinationals, Technology and Competitiveness*

and present', in *OECD North/South Technology Transfer. The Adjustments Ahead* (Paris: OECD).

Rostow, W. W. (1959), *The Stages of Economic Growth* (Cambridge: Cambridge University Press).

Rugman, A. M. (1986), 'New theories of the multinational enterprise; an assessment of internalisation theory', *Bulletin of Economic Research*, 38, pp. 101–18..

Rugman, A. (1986), 'Canadian research and development', *Managing International Risk* (Cambridge: Cambridge University Press).

Safarian, A. E. (1966), *Foreign Ownership of Canadian Industry* (New York: McGraw-Hill).

Sagafi-Negad, T., Moxon, R. W. and Perlmutter, H. V. (eds) (1981), *Technology Transfer Control Systems; Issues, Perspectives and Implications* (Elmsford, NY: Pergamon Press).

Sanna Randaccio, F. (1980), European direct investments in US manufacturing, M.Litt. Thesis, University of Oxford.

Sapsford, D. (1985), *Real Primary Commodity Prices: An Analysis of Long-Run Movements*, IMF Internal Memorandum, 17 May (quoted by Drucker, 1987).

Scott, B. and Lodge, B. (1985), *US Competitiveness and the World Economy* (Boston: Harvard University Press).

Servan-Schreiber, J.-J. (1968), *The American Challenge* (London: Hamish Hamilton).

Soete, L. L. G. (1980), 'The impact of technological innovation on international trade patterns: the evidence reconsidered', paper presented at OECD Science and Technology Indicators Conference, Paris, September.

Spencer, B. J. and Brander, J. A. (1983), 'International R & D rivalry and industrial strategy', *Review of Economic Studies*, 50, pp. 707–20.

Steuer, M. D. *et al.* (1973), *The Impact of Foreign Direct Investment in the United Kingdom* (London: HMSO).

Stewart, F. (1981), 'Arguments for the generation of technology by less developed countries', *The Annals of the American Academy of Political and Social Science*, 458, November.

Stobaugh, R. and Wells, L. T. (1985), *Technology Crossing National Boundaries. The Choice, Transfer and Management of International Technology Flow* (Boston: Harvard Business School Press).

Stopford, J. M. (1974), 'The origins of British-based multinational manufacturing enterprises', *Business History Review*, 48, pp. 303–35.

Stopford, J. M. and Dunning, J. H. (1983), *Multinationals: Company Performance and Global Trends* (London: Macmillan).

Stopford, J. M. and Turner, L. (1985), *Britain and the Multinationals* (Chichester: John Wiley).

Streit, C. (1949), *Union Now: A Proposal for an Atlantic Federal Union of the Free* (New York: Harper).

Svedberg, P. (1981), 'Colonial enforcement of foreign direct investment', *Manchester School of Economic and Social Studies*, 50, pp. 21–38.

Svedberg, P. (1982), 'Colonialism and foreign direct investment profitability', in J. Black and J. H. Dunning (eds), *International Capital Movements* (London: Macmillan).

Teece, D. J. (1977), 'Technology transfer by multinational firms: the resource costs of transferring technological know-how', *Economic Journal*, 87, pp. 242–61.

References 273

Teece, D. J. (1981a), 'The multinational enterprise: market failure and market power considerations', *Sloan Management Review*, *22*, pp.3–17.

Teece, D. J. (1981b), 'The market for know-how and the efficient international transfer of technology', *Annals of the American Academy of Political Science*, *458*, November, pp. 81–96.

Teece, D. J. (1986), 'Transaction cost economics and the multinational enterprise', *Journal of Economic Behavior and Organisation*, *1*, pp. 21–45.

Teece, D. J. (1987), *The Competitive Challenge* (Cambridge, Mass: Cambridge University Press).

Telessio, P. (1979), *Technology Licensing and Multinational Enterprises* (New York: Praeger).

UN (1973), *Multinational Corporations in World Development*, Department of Economic and Social Affairs, E73 II A11 (New York: UN).

UN (1979), *Transnational Corporations and the Long Term Objectives of the Developing Countries* (New York: UN Centre on Transnational Corporations).

UNCTC (1978), *Transnational Corporations and World Development. A Re-examination*, New York, UNCTC E78, II, A 5.

UNCTC (1981), *Transnational Corporation Linkages in Developing Countries*, New York, UNCTC E81, II, A 4.

UNCTC (1982), *Regional Integration Cum/Versus Corporate Integration*, New York, UNCTC E82, II A 6.

UNCTC (1983), *Transnational Corporations and World Development: Third Survey*, New York, UNCTC E83, II, A 19.

UNCTC (1988), *Transnational Corporations and World Development: Fourth Survey*, New York, UNCTC (to be published).

US Tariff Commission (1973), *Implications of Multinational Firms for World Trade and Investment and for US Trade and Labour* (Washington, DC: US Government Printing Office).

US Department of Commerce (1981), *US Direct Investment Abroad 1977* (Washington DC: US Government Printing Office).

US Department of Commerce (1985), *US Direct Investment Abroad 1982* (Washington, DC: US Government Printing Office).

US Department of Commerce (1987), *Statistics of World Stock of Direct Investment Abroad*, 1960–84 (mimeo).

US Department of Commerce (various dates), *Survey of Current Business* (monthly publication).

Vaitsos, C. V. (1979), *The Visible Hand in World Production and Trade* (mimeo).

Vandenbroucke, F. (1985), 'Conflicts in international economic policy and the world recession: a theoretical analysis', *Cambridge Journal of Economics*, *9*, no. 1, pp. 15–42.

Vaupel, J. W. and Curhan, J. P. (1974), *The World's Multinational Enterprises* (Geneva: Centre for Education and International Management).

Vernon, R. (1966), 'International investment and international trade in the product cycle', *Quarterly Journal of Economics*, *80*, pp. 190–217.

Vernon, R. (1974), 'The location of economic activity', in J. H. Dunning (ed.), *Economic Analysis and the Multinational Enterprise* (London: Allen & Unwin).

Vernon, R. (1979), 'The product cycle hypothesis in the new international environment', *Oxford Bulletin of Economics and Statistics*, *41*, pp. 255–67.

274 *Multinationals, Technology and Competitiveness*

Vernon, R. (1983), 'Organisational and institutional responses to international risk', in R. J. Herring (ed.), *Managing International Risk* (Cambridge: Cambridge University Press).

Wells, L. T. (1983), *Third World Multinationals* (Cambridge, Mass: MIT Press).

Wilkins, M. (1970), *The Emergence of Multinational Enterprise: American Business Abroad from the Colonial Era to 1914* (Cambridge, Mass: Harvard University Press).

Wilkins, M. (1974a), 'The role of private business in the international diffusion of technology', *Journal of Economic History*, *34*, no. 1, pp. 166–88.

Wilkins, M. (1974b), 'Multinational enterprises', in H. Daems and H. Van der Wee (eds), *The Rise of Managerial Capitalism* (Louvain: Louvain University Press).

Wilkins, M. (1988), *Foreign Investment in the United States* (Harvard: Harvard University Press).

Williamson, O. E. (1981), 'The modern corporation: origins, evolution, attributes', *Journal of Economic Literature*, *XIX*, December, pp. 1537–68.

Wilson, C. (n.d.), 'The multinational in historical perspective' in K. Nakagawa (ed.) *Strategy and Structure of Big Business* (Tokyo: Tokyo University Press).

World Bank (1987), *World Development Report 1987* (Oxford: Oxford University Press).

Wyatt, S. M. E., Bertin, G. and Pavitt, K. (1985), 'Patents and multinational corporations: results from questionnaires', *World Patent Information*, 7, pp. 196–212.

Yuan, R. T. (1987), *Biotechnology in Western Europe* (Washington International Trade Administration: US Department of Commerce).

Zysman, J. and Tyson, L. (1983), *American Industry and International Competition* (Ithaca: Cornell University Press).

Index

absolute advantage, concept of 8
access, to markets 11
advantage
  asset-based 11, 104
  location-specific 6, 11, 15, 65–6
  ownership-specific 2, 6, 9, 10–11, 15, 24,
    65, 69, 95
  transaction cost-based 15, 105, 114
  see also comparative advantage
affiliate companies 41–2, 44
  impact on economies of developing
    countries 152, 153, 156–7
  revealed technological advantage
    110–11
  see also United States affiliate
    companies
Africa, foreign direct investment 152
Anglo-American business partnership
  effects of European economic
    development 236–9
  effects of global competition 244–7
  effects of Japanese challenge 239
  effects of technological innovations
    239–40
  evolution of 234–6
  implications of globalization of markets
    240–4, 248
  role of government 248
  stages of 234
asset advantage 11, 104
assets
  creation and usage 3
  power 29–30, 32, 38
  widening of sources 20

balance of payments *see* technological
  balance of payments
Belgium, foreign pharmaceuticals
  investment 132, 142
biotechnology, international collaborative
  agreements 127, 128

Canada 43
  inward direct investment 58
cartel arrangements 36
  and transfer of technology 37
chemicals industry, European improved
  technological capacity 93

closed econoy, measuring competitiveness
  59
Commission on Transnational
  Corporations 19
comparative advantage
  "created" 233, 244–7
  principle of 178, 205
competition
  among MNEs 41
  and decentralization of R & D 110–11
  between developed and developing
    countries 156–9, 167–8
  global 233, 244–7
  import 165
competitiveness 1, 47–50, 63
  and foreign direct investment 5, 115,
    203–4
  and strategic alliances 243–4
  effects of MNEs 2, 57–9
  European 69–73
  impact of international transfer of
    technology 52, 61–3
  measures of 1–2, 59–61
  of countries 2, 70
consultancy, as method of technology
  export 163, 164
contractual relationships 3, 244, 259
corporate integration 43, 55, 72, 114, 198
  vertical 193–4
cost-benefit analysis, of
    internationalization of
    pharmaceutial research 133–6
costs
  of technology transfer 112, 148, 168
  see also transaction costs
cumulative technological causation 115
  international trade patterns 116–18
  see also technology-induced circles

decentralization
  in pharmaceutical industry 123
  in pharmaceutical R & D activities 124,
    126, 128
developed market economies (DMEs)
  competition with developing countries
    156–9, 167–8
  implications of technology exports
    145–7, 151–2

276   *Multinationals, Technology and Competitiveness*

implications of technology transfer to
   developing countries 159–67
developing countries
   competition with developed countries
    156–9
   degree of MNE penetration and exports
    154, 166
   impact of technology transfer 151–6
   role of MNEs 22–3, 152
   technology transfer problems 39–40, 53
   types of foreign direct investment 157
   see also newly industrialized countries
    (NICs); OPEC countries
distribution of factor endowments theory 1
diversification strategies 41, 195
dollar
   devaluation 18
   shortage 16, 37–8

economic activities
   of governments 4, 24
   organization 3
   rationalization of 257
   value-adding 1, 2, 3
economic cooperation
   international trends 25
   role of governments 248
   see also Anglo-American business
    partnership; European Economic
    Community; OPEC
economic distance 13
economic growth and development 10
   decline 145
   models 21
economic interdependence 251–2
   early 254–5
   factors affecting 257–9
   nature of transactions 253–4
   organization of 252–3, 262–3
   pre-World War I 256–7
   regional 7, 19, 24
   types of 252
   see also regional economic integration
economic nationalism 259
economic organization theory 1
economic power 29–31
economic structure
   impact of MNEs 183–92, 195–9
   optimizing 178
economic systems 13–14
efficiency
   and resource allocation strategies 55–6,
    224–9
ESP paradigm 13–14, 52
Europe
   company growth 78–80
   effects of American inward direct
    investment on competitiveness
    69–73

impact of American subsidiary
   companies 80–90, 99
impact of transfer of technology on
   domestic competitiveness 61–3
influence on Anglo-American
   investments 236–8
investment in USA 90–1, 242–3
job losses and import competition 165
post-war penetration by American
   MNEs 38, 55
technological capacity 83, 85
trading position in relation to USA
   74–5, 99
European Economic Community 13
   as influence on Anglo-American
    partnership 238–9
   exports growth in relation to USA 74–8
expansion, through vertical integration 36
export growths
   European 75–8
   NICs 154, 166

firm
   competitiveness 1–2
   economic power of 29–31
   growth 78–80
   structural characteristics and output
    182–3
fiscal policies, effects of 4
food processing industry, OECD report
   on impact of MNEs 89
foreign direct investment (FDI) 5, 151
   as modality of technology transfer 51–2,
    54–5, 64, 147, 150–1
   by NICs 20
   early 34, 35
   implications of 17–18, 47
   influence of government intervention
    strategies 13, 19
   in developing countries 152
   in manufacturing industries 90–1
   intra-industry 57
   Japanese 115
   types of 115–6, 157
France
   company growth 79–80
   pharmaceutical industry 132, 141
    foreign research investment 132
    restrictions on foreign firms 129
    reduction of US investment 80

General Agreement on Trade and Tariffs
   (GATT) 27, 37
geographical distribution
   of UK outward and inward direct
    capital 209–11
Germany
   company growth 80
   foreign pharmaceutical research 132

Index

277

Germany *cont.*
impact of US technology 52
government intervention 5
and the ESP paradigm 13–14
as protectionism 27, 28, 37
in economic distance 13
governments
influence on competitiveness 4
influences on international business 13, 24
role and influence in MNE activities 7, 18–20, 21–4, 25–7, 44, 121, 129, 196, 198, 199, 200
role in supporting economic cooperation 248
Gross Domestic Product (GDP) 59, 60
gross national product (GNP) 204
and national competitiveness 2, 53, 60
benefits of MNE activity 6

hierarchies, international 177
high technology industries, MNE technology transfer 155, 156
host countries
gains from technology transfer 53, 150
interaction with MNEs 16–21, 35, 41
R & D invetment in 130–3, 135

income, generated from transfer of technology 150
industrialization programmes, implications for DMEs 167–9
industrial policies
implications of MNE activities 115–21
implications of technology transfer to developing countries 167–9
Industrial Revolution 31–3
second 33
information retrieval and dissemination systems
impact on organizational structures 23–4
international agreements 16, 127, 128, 258
international business climate, and economic development factors 21–7
international direct investment
and economic welfare 204–7
and efficiency of resource allocation 224–9
as indicator of competitiveness 203–4
development cycle 21–2
in pharmaceutical industry 123–8
in pharmaceutical R & D 128–30
relationships 233
see also foreign direct investment
international division of labour
structural adjustment to 66, 166, 176–7, 197
international economic relations 260–1
see also economic interdependence

international economy
and foreign direct investment 17
factors influencing instability 18
International Monetary Fund 37
international production paradigm 1, 21–2, 69–70, 103
international transfer of technology 5
and economic power 31–2, 34–7, 38–40, 43
and global investment strategies of MNEs 111–14, 160–2
costs 112
FDI as modality of 51–2, 54–5
impact on competitiveness 47–50, 52, 63–4
impact on developing countries 151–5
impact on European competitiveness 61–3
impact on host countries 53
impact on patterns of cumulative causation 115, 116–18
implications for source countries 144–7, 162–9
influence of industrial organizational structures 106–11
to developing countries 39–40
intra-firm transactions 23, 80, 156, 194
investment
export platform 162
factors 15
import-substituting 113, 150
non-equity forms 163
resource-based 113, 161–2
to supply the local market 160–1
UK inward and outward data 206–18
see also foreign direct investment; international direct investment; inward direct investment
inward direct investment 20, 40, 58, 113, 119
Italy, foreign pharmaceuticals investment 132, 142

Japan 24
government strategies for development 120
impact of US technology 52, 53
industrial renaissance 10, 165–6
influence on Anglo-American investment partnership 239
international agreements in biotechnology 128
investment in UK and US 115, 199
market strategies 27, 66, 199
pharmaceutical research 133, 142
technological advancement 40, 98, 106
joint stock company 10

Korea 24
industrial strategies 66

278 *Multinationals, Technology and Competitiveness*

labour, as investment resource 113
  see also international division of labour
labour displacement
  and technology transfer 149, 164, 165
Latin America, importance of foreign
    direct investment 152, 166
limited liability 10
location
  advantages 203–4
  factors influencing investment 199
  of innovative capacity 107
  variables 5, 11–12

manufacturing industries
  emergence 33–4
  export growths 166
  growth of integrated MNEs 44
  participation rates of MNE affiliates in
    developing countries 153
  patterns of European/American direct
    investment 90–1
  UK investment data 215–18, 225–9
market efficiency, and government
    intervention 5
market failure 3–4
market globalization 234–6, 260
  implications for Anglo-American
    investment partnership 240–4
market power 36
market relationships 7–8
market share, as measure of
    competitiveness 1–2
market trading
  factors influencing 260
  of technology and information 50–3
motor vehicles industry, UK decline 120,
    199
multinational enterprises (MNEs)
  characteristics of 15
  criticisms of 18
  developing roles of 25–7
  diversification 41
  early foreign production systems 34–5
  evolution 9–12, 32, 33, 40
  impact on UK economic structure
    183–92
  influence on national competitiveness
    57–9
  interaction with host countries 16–21
  investment strategies 160–2
  investment strategy and technology
    diffusion 111–14
  manufacturing subsidiaries expansion 38
  rationalized investment 22, 43
  relationship with governments 25–8
  research investment motivations 128–30
  role in economic strategies 115–17
  roles in international economic
    interdependence 261

structural impact of 178–80
technology transfer within 54–6, 112
UK 174–6
multi-plant domestic enterprise 9–12

natural resources
  early investment in 32, 35
new technology
  and conflicting interests 27
  impact of 177
  MNE market domination 23
  see also high technology industries
newly industrializing countries (NICs)
  as competitors 167–8
  foreign direct investment 152
  implications of technology transfer 6, 44
  industrialization 167
  manufacturing exports 157–9
  non-equity investment inducements 163
  within world economy 145

Okun's Law 117
Organization for Economic Cooperation
    and Development (OECD)
  study of MNEs impact on food
    processing industry 89
  study of MNEs impact on
    pharmaceutical industry 89
OECD countries
  manufactured products exports 159
  technology exports 151–2
OPEC countries, FDI and technology
    transfer 152
OPEC oil price rise, influence of 18
open economy
  and regional integration 58
  measuring competitiveness 59
organizational structure 36
  influence of technology transfer and
    diffusion 106–11
output
  increase, and technology transfer 149

patents 10, 95
  American decline 146
  as indicator of sectoral patterns of
    technological advantage 107–8,
    109–10
  growth in registrations 96–7
  Japanese 98, 106
petrochemicals industry 163–4
pharmaceutical industry
  cross-border collaborative agreements
    127–8
  decentralization strategies 123, 134–5
  impact of MNEs on technological
    capacity 89
  international direct investment in
    research 128–30

Index

pharmaceutical industry *cont.*
  post-war American MNEs European
    penetration 38
  UK 136–7
Pharmaceutical Price Regulatory Scheme
  138
pharmaceutical research and development
  decentralization 126, 128
  expenditure 125, 126
  internationalization of 129–30, 133–6,
    141–2
  investment 123
  location of facilities 124, 126, 130–3
  motives for MNE investment 128–30
  UK 120, 136–41
political influences,
  on international business 20–1
price-cost margins, impact of cuts 172
product cycle model of investment 71–2,
  160–1
profitability, of UK outward and inward
  investment in manufacturing
  industries 225–9
protectionism 27, 28, 233, 257–8, 260

regional economic integration 19, 24, 43,
  58, 258–9
research and development
  by subsidiaries 43
  decentralization and international
    technological competition 110–11
  donor nation position 135–6
  internalization by parent company 38–9
  USA relative decline 146
  see also pharmaceutical industry
    research and development
resource allocation 42
  and technology transfer 554–6
  strategies to maintain comparative
    advantage 167, 224–9
resources, efficient use of 2
  see also resource allocation
revealed technological advantage (RTA)
  109–11
royalties and fees, European growth 91–3,
  94

sales-export ratios 80–90
sales growth rates 78–80
semi-conductor industry 38, 89
service sectors, growth of integrated
  MNEs 44
subsidiary companies
  American contribution in Europe 80–90
  influence on competitive positions 74–8
  role in technology transference 43
Sweden 53
  company growth 80
  economic decline 145

Switzerland
  pharmaceutical industry 126
  foreign investment 141

technological advantage
  revealed technological advantage
    (RTA) of American firms 109–10
technological balance of payments 91, 99
  UK 137
technological capacity 103
  indicators 91–5
  European recovery 95, 98, 113
  MNE transfer 148, 156
  obstacles to 114
technological cumulation 6, 103
technological innovation 6, 23, 40–1, 173
  and competitiveness 49, 104
  and organizational structure 107
  and spatial diversity 12
  effect on Anglo-American investment
    partnership 239–40
  in United Kingdom 31
  nature of 103, 104–6
  reduction 107
technology
  as vehicle of economic development 10
  export through specialised consultants
    164
  factors affecting diffusion and
    dissemination 111–14
  importance in growth of MNEs 104, 105
  links between creation, transfer and
    diffusion 115–21
technology cycle 41
technology-induced circles
  vicious 6, 116, 119
  virtuous 6, 116, 119, 120, 137
technology transfer 6, 50, 65, 144–5
  accelerating 73
  adverse effects of 53, 162–7
  benefits of 148–51
  control of 6, 167–8
  costs 112, 148, 168
  gains from 147
  within MNEs 54–6, 112
  see also international transfer of
    technology
textile industry, impact of technology
  transfer 165
Third World countries 43
trade 12
  theories of 2, 15, 63
  theory of comparative advantage 178,
    179, 205
trade rules and regulations 27
trading enterprises 12–13
transaction costs 13
  economizing 11, 41, 193
  high 22, 34, 58

280 *Multinationals, Technology and Competitiveness*

reduced 41
transaction power 30–1, 34
transactions, international 253–4
transnational enterprises (TNEs) 152–3

unemployment problems 6
  and inward direct investment 20
  as cost of technology transfer 148–9,
    164, 165
United Kingdom
  company growth 80
  direct investment in US 238, 241–3
  drug research investment conditions 129
  early technological leadership 31
  economic and industrial decline 137, 145
  economic and industrial structure 173–6,
    180–3
    as disincentive to investment 224
    MNE adjustment impact 189–92
    MNE allocative impact 183–8
    MNE coordination of economic
      transactions 193–5
    MNE technical impact 188–9
  exports growth in relation to USA and
    Europe 77–8
  income from transfer of technology 150
  international competitive position 204,
    218–24
    government strategies for 230–1
  international direct investment 6, 151
    and resource allocation efficiency
      224–9
  internationalization of economy 196–7
  inward and outward investments 206–18
  Japanese investment in 199
  MNE activities 174–6, 195–6, 198–9
    and government policies 196, 198, 199
  motor vehicle industry 120, 199
  pharmaceutical industry 120, 136–7
    and government policies 140–1
    foreign investment in 132, 137–8

impact of research
  internationalization 138–40, 141
reduction of US investment 80, 83, 224,
  236
structural adjustment problems 6
see also Anglo-American business
  partnership
United States affiliate companies
  contribution to European exports 80–90
  influence on host countries 73
United States of America
  companies' growth rates 78–80
  competitiveness with Europe 74–8
  direct investment in Europe 6, 38, 55,
    62, 90–1
  direct investment in UK 224, 238
  economic problems 145
  European investment 90–1
  exports growth in relation to Europe
    74–8
  imports from NICs 158
  inward direct investment in Europe
    69–73
  MNE evolution 9–12
  outward direct investment 151
  pharmaceutical research 132,
    141
    foreign investment 132–3
  post-war technological hegemony 16,
    37, 40, 173
  relative decline in R & D 146
  second Industrial Revolution 33–4
  technological advances 41
  see also Anglo-American business
    partnership

world economy 18, 37, 145, 172
  and overseas investment 38–40
World War II
  post-war increase in international
    production 37

CPSIA information can be obtained
at www.ICGtesting.com
Printed in the USA
JSHW011319201219
3107JS00002B/34